The Trapped
Woman

SAGE SOURCEBOOKS FOR THE HUMAN SERVICES SERIES

Series Editors: **ARMAND LAUFFER** and **CHARLES GARVIN**

A source is a starting point, a place of origin, information, or payoff. The volumes in this series reflect these themes. For readers they will serve as starting points for new programs, as the place of origin of advanced skills, or as a source for information that can be used in the pursuit of professional and organizational goals.

Sage Sourcebooks are written to provide multiple benefits for both professionals and advanced students. Authors and contributors are recognized authorities in their fields or at the cutting edge of new knowledge and technique. Sourcebooks deal with new and emerging practice tools and current and anticipated policy issues, transforming knowledge from allied professions and the social sciences into information applicable to the human services.

1. **MANAGING THE HUMAN SERVICE ORGANIZATION**
   by RICHARD STEINER (out of print)

2. **MASS MEDIA AND HUMAN SERVICES**
   by EDWARD A. BRAWLEY

3. **DESIGNING INTERVENTIONS FOR THE HELPING PROFESSIONS**
   by EDWIN J. THOMAS

4. **THE TRAPPED WOMAN:** Catch-22 in Deviance and Control
   edited by JOSEFINA FIGUEIRA-McDONOUGH & ROSEMARY SARRI

5. **FAMILY THERAPY WITH ETHNIC MINORITIES**
   by MAN KEUNG HO

6. **WORKING IN SOCIAL WORK:** Growing and Thriving in Human Service Practice
   by ARMAND LAUFFER

The Trapped Woman

Catch-22 in Deviance and Control

Josefina Figueira-McDonough
& Rosemary Sarri, editors

SAGE SOURCEBOOKS FOR THE HUMAN SERVICES SERIES
VOLUME 4

SAGE PUBLICATIONS
The Publishers of Professional Social Science
Newbury Park   Beverly Hills   London   New Delhi

TABLE OF CONTENTS

Copyright © 1987 by Sage Publications, Inc.

The Trapped woman.
  (Sourcebooks for improving human services ; v. 4)
  1. Women's rights—United States.   2. Feminism—
United States.   I. Figueira-McDonough, Josefina.
II. Sarri, Rosemary C.   III. Series.
HQ1236.5.U6T73 1986   305.4'2'0973   86-27967
ISBN 0-8039-2614-6
ISBN 0-8039-2615-4 (pbk.)

For our daughters
Cathy, Graça, Julia and Kristen

PREFACE

In the past century women have joined together to form two powerful movements to bring about major social change. From the 1840s until 1920 women organized to achieve suffrage and equal rights in the voting place. Then, in the 1960s women joined together to achieve gender equality. The latter movement is still underway, and this book was written in the context of that continuing movement. The debate over women's rights is an important one, and one that has provoked much controversy. We hope that this book will inform the debate. The issues are contentious and challenge traditional values long held by many persons in positions of power.

Two particular concerns motivated us to organize this book. We both have had a long-standing interest in gender and deviance and felt that the literature in this area needed further clarification from the perspective of the rights of women. Through the centuries women have built their lives within the constraints of various economic, political, and social structures. Contemporary gendered societies, although costly for women, tend to have the legitimacy of an established order and a resilience born of fear of change. We have tried to alert the reader to the consequences of a gender-unequal order and to the mechanisms sustaining it.

We also wished to provide literature which would be of interest and benefit to policy makers and practitioners as well as to students and scholars. Such an effort is inevitably problematic— only the readers can tell us whether or not it has accomplished the dual objectives.

This book is the result of the collective effort of many people: the several authors who contributed their ideas and wealth of experience, the several editors and the publisher, the various readers and critics, and the many colleagues, students, and teachers from whom we have benefited over many years. Their comments and criticisms have all been helpful to us as we have attempted to clarify our thinking about gender, deviance, and social control. We are deeply grateful to the authors who contributed chapters to this book; each of them struggled with our suggestions as we sought to clarify the sociological conceptualization and achieve some integration among the various areas. However, as the two primary editors and authors, we bear the ultimate responsibility for its contents.

We hope that this book will sensitize the reader to the position of women and the United States in the 1980s and will encourage them to initiate and support policies and programs for change in the social structures that perpetuate the subordinate status of women and the many Catch-22 situations.

To Margaret Lourie, Mary Frank Fox, and William Barton we give our special thanks for their help in editing this volume. Most of all we are deeply grateful to Deborah Eddy who typed and retyped this manuscript with kindness, cooperation, and friendship that both of us truly value. Finally, we particularly acknowledge the support and encouragement of our spouses, Peter and Romilos, and of our daughters—Cathy, Graça, Julia, and Kristen. Without their patience and forbearance it would not have been possible.

Josefina Figueira-McDonough
Rosemary C. Sarri
Ann Arbor, Michigan
January 1987

CHAPTER 1
CATCH-22 STRATEGIES OF CONTROL
AND THE DEPRIVATION OF WOMEN'S RIGHTS

Josefina Figueira-McDonough
Rosemary C. Sarri

Although numerically the majority of the population, women are a minority group in terms of their power and influence in the United States. They are a minority group in the sociological sense because of the individual and collective discrimination that they experience and because of their inability to resist being either thought of or treated as inferior. Whenever power discrepancies between the dominant and the dominated group are great, even the majority of the population can be treated as a minority (e.g., blacks in South Africa or Catholics in Northern Ireland).

Ever since the midnineteenth century women's rights have been an important political issue. First, women fought for equal treatment for blacks as they fought for their own right to vote. But it took them until 1920 to achieve the latter, and equal rights for women are still not a reality in 1986, almost a century after the Fourteenth Amendment was passed.

This book addresses the present status of gender inequality and its relationship to being defined as deviant and subjected to social control in ways that will prevent the attainment of equality. In the various sectors of society that are examined, the dominant group maintains inequality through their control of the deviance-defining and social control institutions.

Our objective is to unveil gender differences that persist in a variety of social institutions. Some of the differences might at first appear minor or natural, but in fact they have snowballing effects on the status of the majority of women. For example, the widespread acceptance of the "nurturant" vocation of women comes to determine their assigned duties and obligations in a variety of social arenas and ultimately to limit their equal access to social rights.

While progress in gender equalization has been made (for example, in the number of women professionals), there are important gaps that have not been closed; often they are not even fully acknowledged. Gender equalization refers to both equality in numbers and in relative power of the statuses and roles of women in society. We view the persistence of those gaps as obstacles to the equalization process; they threaten the progress already made. Eleanor Holmes Norton (1985) contends that only continuing and diligent effort will ensure the pursuit of policies for affirmative action and comparable worth, both of which are necessary if women are to obtain equal justice.

In the Durkheimian tradition we contend that normative enforcement of gender-specific roles is a function of the strength of the definitions of deviance attached to them. Internal and external sanctions against deviant behavior reinforce normative behavior. There is a growing literature on the relationship between gender-role constraints, female subcultures, women's patterns of association, and attachment networks with women's deviant behavior (e.g., Cloward and Piven 1979; Harris 1977; Figueira-McDonough 1980; Hutter and Williams 1981). While this is relevant to the discussion in this book, our focus is on the use of deviance as a control mechanism. We argue that historically persistent restrictions on women's rights can be understood from this perspective because: (a) definitions of deviance impose restrictions on the rights of those labeled deviants; (b) women are often viewed as "all-purpose deviants"; and (c) extensive definitions of deviance trap women in no-win situations.

THE SOCIAL CONTROL PERSPECTIVE

Attribution, conflict and control theories of deviance are particularly useful for an interpretation of women's "inferior" status in society. Collectively these theories construe deviance as a social definition which results in negative personal and social status. Thus they provide the rationale for an analysis of social control as a strategy to bar powerless groups (in this case, women) from access to a variety of resources.

A quick examination of the tenets of these theories highlights their relevance to the thesis of this book. The basic postulate they share is that deviance is not a property inherent in certain forms of behavior but a property conferred upon persons by a social audience (Becker 1963; Erickson 1962). If definitions of deviance are socially created, the relevant questions become: by whom, for what, and how?

Study of the historical patterns and processes through which definitions of deviance emerge and become institutionalized indicates that they tend to be imposed on the powerless by the powerful (Rothman 1980; Thompson 1977; Foucault 1975). Radical and conflict sociologists further argue the self-serving nature of this phenomenon. The purpose of creating and controlling deviance is to protect the interests of the dominant classes and to prevent access to their resources by outsiders (Quinney 1977).

To be complete, this "domination model" of deviance must explain how it can be implemented. Historical evidence does not support sustained enforcement of deviance definitions; therefore, questions about acceptance by social groups and the deviants themselves have to be answered. Deviant definitions must be justified, reinforced by institutions and then accepted. The control perspective proposes at least two ways through which this may be accomplished. The process of justification depends on defining deviant groups as different and inferior in one or more dimensions (Page 1984; Schur 1983); and second, the institutionalization of differential treatment of these groups results in the internalization of the deviance label and adjustment of their behavior to this self-definition (Schur 1983; Kitsuse 1962; Lemert 1964). Given highly stratified societies with conflicting interests, deviance and the control apparatus are created to prevent the powerless from pursuing their interests, particularly if that pursuit involves gaining access to resources monopolized by the powerful. Outlawing strikes at the onset of the labor movement in this country and the failure to pass the ERA amendment stand as examples of this argument. Furthermore, to the extent that the agents of control belong to the dominating group, an overall system of devaluation of the powerless group can easily be implemented. Schur (1983) contends that male control of deviance labeling (in the criminal system, mental health system, schools, work) results in their continued dominance in most spheres of life.

In sum, within this perspective the justification for the use of control strategies that limit the rights of certain groups depends on their characterization as deviants (e.g., denial of full citizenship by the criteria of the period and place). Examples abound regarding control of labor, religious, political, and ethnic groups (e.g., the barring of landless or illiterate individuals from voting, women from ownership of property, Jews from political participation, communists from public office, unionized workers from jobs, "promiscuous" poor from welfare, etc.).

There is a heuristic utility to this perspective on the study of gender inequality in society because the deprivation of rights of women as a group has been historically justified by their definition as inferior human beings. At present, the evidence of little change in patterns of equity in such areas as work, family responsibilities, political access, and legal rights is well documented (Matthei 1982; Treiman and Hartman 1981; Powell and Jacobs 1984; Weitzman 1985; Anderson 1983; England 1984; Stallard et al. 1983). This stagnation has continued in spite of reported attitudinal support for gender equalization, affirmative action, feminist activism, and some favorable legislation (Cherlin and Walters 1981; Figueira-McDonough 1985; Herzog and Bachman 1982; Mason et al. 1976; Parelius 1975; Thornton and Freedman 1979; Thornton et al. 1983). If women have been and are as a group deprived of rights, it is important to investigate the definitions (deviant) and social arrangements (control) that perpetuate their position as social outsiders (Cohen and Scull 1983). Since definitions of deviance legitimate social controls, they are potentially efficient means to perpetuate women's second class citizenship and reduced access to resources.

In line with the theories of deviance reviewed here, a group's deprivation of rights can be interpreted as a reflection of their imputed inferiority or deviance. This in turn justifies the creation of controls barring that group from access to rights. The validity of this argument in explaining gender inequality depends on (1) the evidence supporting the attribution of social inferiority to the status of womanhood, (2) the uncovering of control mechanisms directly related to that definition of womanhood, and (3) the identification of the effect of such controls on the deprivation of rights.

NATURALLY DIFFERENT AND UNEQUAL

The constraints on women's rights can be interpreted as a function of the successful definition of women as different and inferior to men. As Simone de Beauvoir (1948) pointed out,

> This humanity is male and man defines woman not in herself, but as relative to him; she is not regarded as an autonomous being....She is defined and differentiated with reference to man and not he with reference to her; she is the incidental, the inessential as opposed to the essential. He is the Subject, he is the Absolute—she is the Other. (86)

Declaring Women Different. To understand the maintenance of women's status one needs to analyze the specific content of socially constructed relationships between the sexes. The complex set of shared images and conceptions that are stereotypically attributed to women are mediated and maintained in a variety of ways. Once the image of "normal woman" gains ascendance, it becomes part of the formation and implementation of social policy and shapes day-to-day relations among individuals. For example, opposition to state programs in child care has been based on the assumption that "normal" mothers are involved full time in the care of their children in spite of available evidence that nearly half of the women with children participate full time in the labor force.

Sex role norms clearly differentiate men from women. When these norms become internalized, they are accepted as facts and seldom questioned. Goffman (1977: 303) refers to gender ideals as the essential source for maintaining gender differences. These ideals, he argues, "provide...a source of accounts that can be drawn in a million ways to exercise, justify, explain, or disapprove the behavior of an individual or the arrangement under which he lives." When norms are not explicit or clearly articulated, or are undergoing change, problems emerge. For example, sex role norms are changing in the workplace as more and more men and women work together in similar positions. Women may be in supervisory positions over men with roles that require assertive and executive behavior which some men find difficult to accept or tolerate because of contrasting perspectives internalized earlier by men.

The assigning of inferior group status starts with the imputation of categorical difference, because awareness of similarities is conducive to empathy and therefore an obstacle to discrimination (Goodin 1985). Schur's (1983) analysis of womanhood as stigma is very important in this context. He argues that womanhood has the characteristics of a master status. In all types of interactions a master status leads to a categorization that precedes and dominates all others. He argues that females in any type of situation, as well as in roles and positions involving a variety of attributes and actions, are first and foremost categorized as women. This predominant classification then characterizes the processes of stigmatization (Page 1984). It is not unusual for media coverage of public women to pay greater attention to their physical appearance and family roles as compared to public men. The descriptor of "attractive looking" was frequently used when Geraldine Ferraro was first introduced to the nation, and the investigation of her husband's finances had no parallel in the history of American politics. Her gender made her, rather than

Walter Mondale, the target of the furor of the prolife movement despite the fact that she had a more qualified position on abortion than Mondale. The usual perceptual filters of femaleness (sexual and family roles) set her apart from other candidates.

According to Page (1984), stigma is harder to resist when the referent deviant characteristic is highly visible (color, sex) and when it serves to define a category of people (e.g., caste or tribal stigmatization). He further contends that in instances of tribal stigmatization the members become socialized into the disadvantageous situation even while they are learning and incorporating those standards against which they supposedly fall short.

There is little question that to a large extent women born into a gendered society have developed characteristics different from men. Awareness of this permeates the feminist literature. In Komarovsky's (1953) words, "to be born a woman means to inhabit, from early infancy to the last day of life, a psychological world which differs from the world of men." To this As (1980) adds her observation that "women live in such a different economic, cultural and social world from men that their reactions cannot be understood from a master model developed in male society" (149). Millet (1970), long a fighter for gender equality, elaborates the same point, "Because of our social circumstances, male and female are really two cultures and their life experiences are utterly different."

What is in question is not the existence of gender differences but the extent to which such differences justify restrictive role assignments to each gender. There is little disagreement regarding the cultural construction of gender, but there are conflicting views on the role biological factors play in such development. Some authors argue that beyond genitalia the objective sex differences are minimal. There is greater variance of other attributes within each sex than between the sexes (Maccoby and Jacklyn 1974; Fausto-Sterling 1986). Other scholars such as Rossi and associates (1983) contend that some biological differences are systematically prevalent between sexes but do not propose that gender roles are biologically determined.

Gender categorical differentiation is maintained when male-female similarities are played down and the within-group differences homogenized. This can be accomplished by assigning very limited normative roles to the stigmatized group. Women's roles will be more limited than those assigned to men. On the other hand, traits that women might share with men—intergroup similarity—will be interpreted as accidental or deviant. Thus female aptitude for nursing is taken for granted while business talent is still considered exceptional regardless of the actual distribution of these abilities in the female population. The elements of control and deviance are therefore contained in the process of differentiation of women as a major category.

Defining Women as Inferior. The narrow definition of women as breeders and caretakers defines, in principle, any other roles as deviant. This restricted range of normality led to Schur's (1983: 37) observation that definitions of female deviance are in fact so extensive that virtually every woman becomes a perceived offender of some kind. His view of women as "all purpose deviants" has still broader implications and is particularly important to the understanding of the devaluation of womanhood. It suggests that women function as a residual group. The categorical definition of women is essentially exclusionary—a definition by negation: women are non-men and therefore a deviant class. The evidence of the sociohistorical-cultural invisibility of women is consistent with this view. If men are the social norm, to be a woman is by definition to be lesser and deviant.

This conceptualization is consistent with theories of group solidarity and with the view that the role of deviance is to establish boundaries between in-groups and out-groups (Erickson 1962). To the extent that women may be defined as out-groups, their claims to full citizenship are restricted automatically. Notions of citizenship have historically been reinforced by definitions of outsiders as homogeneously deviant and threatening (see the description of communists in political rhetoric or the depiction of Japanese during the World War II). Reinforcement for this exclusionary and devalued imagery in relation to women can be found in Creationism—Eve as a part of Adam—or in Freudianism—women as incomplete human beings missing critical parts of their bodies (the penis) and obsessed by their incompleteness (penis envy).

Outsiders are not only nonmembers; their contributions are evaluated as of lesser value. There is growing awareness that when one speaks about the history, art, music, or literature of earlier centuries or about theories of behavior and moral development, it is men's literature, history, and social behavior that is taken as universal. Documentation of women's pervasive exclusion from what is defined as the significant human culture is overwhelming. For example, women's art in quilt-making, sculpture, needlepoint, and so forth is recognized, at best, as "craft culture" (Rowbotham 1976).

Justifying Women Stereotypes. The irrefutable evidence of pronounced gender inequality within social and economic systems, of negative cultural symbols and of women's special relation to deviance confirms the devaluation of womanhood (Schur 1983: 35). But for these definitions to be successfully applied—as they have been in the past and in the present (Kirp et al. 1986)—powerful and immutable rationalizations are necessary. The basis of female inferiority has to be presented as inalterable, not susceptible to intervention by men or women. In other words, it has to be presented as "natural" order. The translation of morally discriminating assumptions and expectations into natural laws confers on gender constructs a universal validity superseding cultural and historical variations. At the heart of this argument is the procreative capacity of women. Only women can become pregnant; and procreation, and by extension childrearing, is their major social function to the exclusion of any others that might imperil this central role.

The influence of this rationalization has been so overpowering that in spite of ambivalent scientific support (Maccoby and Jacklin 1974; Fausto-Sterling 1986; Burton 1985; Rossi, 1983), most feminist texts include a chapter on biological differences and trace the origins of gender inequality to procreation and childrearing. Although procreation still remains in our technological times the exclusive realm of women, the indissoluble connection between procreation and childrearing that comes to justify the master status or stereotype of women and their differential access to all resources—in fact, to personal, economic, social, and political rights—is a social construct. The perpetuation of such an argument at a time of bottle feeding, simplified housekeeping, and extensive female labor force participation can only be interpreted as an ideological commitment to prevent changes in the status of women rather than a response to biological determinism. It is this assumption nonetheless that is at the core of double standards of behavior for men and women.

In sum, gender comes to act as a normative system, a pervasive network of interrelated norms and sanctions through which female (and male) behavior is controlled. The process of devaluation of women's roles reinforced by their general social and economic subordination creates substantial blocks to women's autonomy. These circumstances have a powerful impact not only in social institutions but in the organization of interaction and individual self-definitions.

CATCH-22 CONTROLS AND EFFECTIVE BLOCKAGE OF RIGHTS

That women have been systematically deprived of rights in the past is not a matter of dispute. Less consensus exists, however, about their position in the present. For example, Kirp, Yudof, and Franks (1986) see in women's access to political suffrage, economic freedom, divorce, and more recently procedural equity, clear indications that to a large extent the battle for gender equality has been won. They argue that women may still suffer discrimination at the individual level, but such behaviors receive no institutional support and time will cure individual machismo.

On the other side, those who look at the evidence for the persistence of female subordination in specific institutions (family, education, labor) and the failure of the Equal Rights Amendment contend that progress is more cosmetic than real (e.g., Treiman and Hartman 1981; Gelb and Palley 1982; Broom, 1984). They argue that female devaluation is so pervasive that the legal strategies used to redress it are largely inadequate. Merely to legislate for the removal of overt control is insufficient to remove the invisible, interconnected controls pervading the various institutions (Hutter and Williams 1981). Equity laws intend to sustain passive rights and are therefore inadequate because inequality reproduces itself in social and political arrangements and gender constructions (cultural spillover) that need attention in their own right (Burton 1985: 20). Weitzman's (1985) examination of the consequences for women of the no-fault divorce is a case in point. Although the no-fault divorce reform would qualify as an equitable law (treatment of both marriage partners equally), because it disregards the economic inequities created during marriage, it has produced dramatically inequitable results mostly because of the family roles assigned to women. Weitzman's study reveals that one year after divorce women's standard of living had decreased by 73 percent while men's increased by 43 percent.

Nonetheless, progress is being made. The dramatic increase of women in the labor force, the activism of women's groups, and the penetration of new attitudes into the socialization of youth have had some effect in discrediting gender stratification (Lengerman and Wallace 1985). But there continues to be much evidence of persistence of gender inequality in major social institutions. Furthermore, the emergence of a reactionary movement intent on eroding gains made by affirmative action threatens the stability of the gains made. The development of a gender egalitarian society depends therefore on understanding the forces opposing it. This requires investigation of the roots of resistance to granting women full citizenship as well as of the mechanisms that serve such resistance.

Resistance to Change. In his seminal work on the evolution of citizen rights, Marshall (1965) proposed that modern states are pressed into granting civil rights as a necessary precondition to creating internal solidarity. He further demonstrated that in democratic/capitalist societies this creates an irreversible trend toward an expansion of citizen rights (political and social) and a centrifugal pull of marginal groups into full citizenship. By comparison to minority male groups (workers, blacks, immigrants), the progress of women toward the attainment of full citizenship in this country seems to have been slower and more erratic. It has been argued that the ineffectiveness of women's suffrage in producing full citizenship is directly tied to the narrowness of women's role and to their emotional ties to members of the dominant class. Because women have been bound to the private sphere, their chances of organization have been very low; personalistic ties between oppressed and oppressors also militate against class identification (Thompson 1965).

This explanation is, however, unsatisfactory given the now extensive participation of women in the public sphere and the increasing convergence in attitudes concerning equal gender rights. We propose, instead, that female inequality is essential to the maintenance of the extant male-dominated social system, and that granting women equal rights would be not only dysfunctional but highly disruptive and threatening to the social order. The defeat of the Equal Rights Amendment (ERA) by a male-dominated political system is the strongest evidence for this point, further corroborated by President Reagan's statement that equity legislation is more effective in improving the lot of women. The significance of the Equal Rights Amendment is that it grants full citizenship to all women, a powerful stroke against gender-role differences. Equity legislation, on the other hand, deals with discrete issues and on a case-by-case basis, assuring a slow and disconnected process that to a large extent leaves intact gender-role stratification. Current active resistance even to this type of legislation is evident in the 1985–86 proposals by the Reagan Administration to "take the teeth out of" equity legislation that actively promotes affirmative action.

The motivations of those in power who oppose equal rights for women are irrelevant to this analysis. They might truly believe in "natural" sex differences or they might simply show a familiar resistance to sharing power with any new group. It is also unimportant to predict how effective the ERA would be if passed. What is important is to understand the basis for the resistance; this can best be done by evaluating the consequences for the present social arrangements of "freeing women" from their traditional gender roles.

Any new group that becomes fully integrated into a society extracts a high price from the dominant classes, even in a non-zero sum situation (Offe 1984; Thompson 1963). The costs of integrating a group that is numerically the majority can easily be perceived by the dominant groups as catastrophic. Burton (1985) and Berk (1985) give some examples of the radical restructuring of the economy and the costs that a program to eliminate gender inequality would involve: the payment of women as unpaid house laborers, national programs for child care, equalization of pay scales, etc. Burton (1985) concludes that it is not childbearing, physical weakness, or any other presumed biologically determined differences that are the basis of women's subordination within industrial and postindustrial societies. Rather the obstacles lie within the system of production and its dependence on the gender division of labor. Conversely the vicious circle of the division of labor within the household and sex-segregated occupations is the major block of access to strategic resources (Berk 1985).

If women's primary responsibility is child care, their participation in the labor market is likely to be delayed and/or interrupted, in turn justifying both lower short- and long-term rewards. Recent data on women professionals indicate how the primary assignment of family responsibilities to women and the consequent need to respond to crises in this sphere have had negative consequences on the progress and rewards in their careers (Johnson 1985; Hewlett 1986). Furthermore, even when women are not encumbered by family duties, or when they make sure those duties do not disrupt their work, the perception that such disruption could occur legitimizes their treatment as less valued workers.

The conclusion that gender division of labor is at the heart of women's differential access to rights is hardly novel. Nor can the failure of the Equal Rights Amendment explain the resilience of such role assignments or why women respond to new demands put on them while still being held accountable for the old ones. There is no doubt that this state of affairs is highly functional for the present social order. Adding to the gratuitous work done in the private sphere, women are now cheap contributors to the public sphere; no system other than slavery could produce a higher surplus value. The question that needs to be answered is how women are "forced" to accept these conditions.

Women's Entrapment. The evidence of gender inequality and the maintenance of the subordination of women implies the existence of control mechanisms that limit their opportunities and perpetuate the existing stratification system. It also suggests the existence of an array of psychological and social processes by which the society reproduces a complex set of social arrangements that act as social controls.

The chapters in this book specifically examine the nature and permanence of these mechanisms in recurrent patterns of social interaction (institutions) and their role in blocking women's rights either deliberately or serendipitously. Such an analysis requires the investigation of cultural and symbolic systems by which women's subordinate position appears as somehow natural and therefore not requiring redress.

Since we posit that the present social system has a lot to lose by the emancipation of women, it stands to reason that the need to ensure conformity in the midst of social change would require especially effective control strategies. After all, efforts at defining deviance are typically grounded in the definer's perception that the group poses some kind of threat to their specific interests or social positions (Schur 1983: 7). We argue that the effectiveness of gender control in contemporary societies rests on a proliferation of deviant definitions that trap women in no-win situations (Schur 1983). The exhaustion and confusion resulting from these Catch-22 situations diffuse the potential resistance of women to the multiple demands put on them by a parasitical society.

Catch-22 deviant definitions for women can emerge in a variety of ways.

1. There might be contradictory demands within the "traditional" gender norms. For example, young girls simultaneously are required to be chaste and sexy (the Vanessa

Williams syndrome). Chastity promises respect and invisibility; sexiness, glamor and ostracism.

2. Tribal stigmatization and the equation of normalcy with maleness tend to produce double deviance for women. Page (1984) argues that in cases of group stigmatization the members become socialized into their disadvantageous position, but at the same time they incorporate the standards against which they supposedly fall short. Thus high school girls have been found to have simultaneously high achievement standards and limited occupational aspirations.

Interactive and institutional processes can reinforce this dualism. The role of mental health professionals in contributing to stratified gender definitions of "normalcy" was illustrated in the now classic study done by Broverman and associates (1981). They found that "normalcy" for women was defined at a "lower" level of mental health functioning than what was considered "normal" for men; women who ranked high in mental health measures became by definition "deviant." Therefore, if women had good mental health, something was wrong with their womanhood; if they were well adjusted to their gender role, they had poor mental health.

3. The emergence of new norms competing with the traditional ones sets up a situation in which following one rule means violating another (Erickson 1966). For example, even where traditional norms are still dominant, women may be asked to assume paid work responsibilities (e.g., workfare for mothers of preschool age children). By their own criteria they are defined as deviants. Or conversely, women supporting egalitarian norms might be reduced to traditional roles of caretaking when they are single parents or when domestic demands impose work disruption on one of the parents. In this latter instance it will almost always be the woman who adjusts since it is normally less costly to the family to lose the woman's lower income. To add insult to injury, women who accept such familial responsibility are classified by employers as unreliable workers.

Women, in their roles as caregivers and cheap labor, absorb much of the costs of the major social changes of modern times. For example, as divorce becomes normative, women increasingly have become the sole providers of children's material and social needs; as Americans live longer, women are called upon to be the caretakers of parents and parents-in-law; as society's demands for service expand, they become the low cost labor that supports the expansion. They find themselves, both normatively and behaviorally, in no-win situations as they extend themselves to meet standards that in conjunction are self-defeating. For example, while women are still seen predominantly as mothers, it is becoming increasingly evident that motherhood responsibilities, together with those of sole provider, throw many single mothers into poverty. Although women have been expected to stay home (not work) and care for their children, when they do work, the perception of them as mothers first and workers second allows employers to pay them at lower salaries than male "breadwinners."

4. In spite of actual gender-role convergence, differential standards persist in the definition of deviance. In fact, the very changes in women's roles are sometimes blamed for their mounting deviance. So poverty among women increases, either because women working out of the home come to neglect their families and eventually get divorced or because, dismissing the double standard in sexual behavior, they engage in premarital sex and become single mothers. Moreover, since they now encounter the strain of men's work, women's levels of stress are said to have increased along with their consumption of alcohol or other drugs (including those prescribed for them because of their stress behavior). Similarly, women's greater access to nontraditional occupations supposedly exposes them to more criminal opportunities, producing higher female crime rates.

The underlying nature of these arguments is camouflaged because the objections are not leveled against the changes promoting gender-equalization but against the negative side effects of the process. Nonetheless, by establishing the expectation of "deviance correlated with gender-role changes," this perspective encourages the development of control strategies that trap women in situations of diminished rights (Hutter and Williams 1981). The question is not whether everyone subscribes to these interpretations but rather whether they gain enough ascendancy to impact changes in social policy affecting women and men differentially, and thereby justify punishing responses to control behavior (Mead 1986). The current national debate in the United States over welfare dependency exemplifies this situation. Women become single parent heads of household because of a variety of events, certainly not alone of their making. They are expected to be the primary child-care givers and socializers, but in at least three ways society obstructs their performance of these roles. First, little or nothing is done to see that noncustodial fathers provide adequate child support, nor does the state do so when fathers cannot. Second, mothers are expected to care for their children and provide for them and themselves. Third, women, on the average, receive wages that are 60 percent of what men make, often in occupations where no health and unemployment benefits are provided (Powell and Jacobs 1984). When they cannot perform their roles satisfactorily because of inability to earn sufficient income, they may attempt to secure supplementary income support through AFDC grants, Medicaid insurance, or Food Stamps; but then they are defined as deviant and dependent personalities—as exemplified in the writing of both liberal and conservative authors such as Anderson (1978), Gilder (1981), Goodwin (1983), and Bernstein (1984).

In a more encompassing rationalization, the women's movement, by promoting role equalization, is said to "cause" deviance in two ways: (1) through disruption of role-learning, which leads to confusion or normlessness (e.g., mental illness, family breakdown, drug abuse); (2) by unrealistically increasing expectations that lead to frustration and rebellion (e.g., stress, crime).

Within almost any institutional setting (family, welfare, work, health, education, and politics) contradictory norms offer almost limitless opportunities to define women as deviant and justify restriction on rights. Apparently unrelated women's issues such as child care and mental health, or wife battering and work equity, can be interpreted within this framework. The convergence of these control mechanisms is clearly functional for the existing social order and thus dysfunctional for the achievement of a new gender integrated order. Therefore, progress toward gender equality requires the identification and neutralization of these complex processes of control.

HOW THE BOOK IS ORGANIZED

The following chapters explore how multiple definitions of deviance bar women from access to rights. The book is organized around specific rights areas to permit a closer examination of the argument that women do not enjoy full citizenship. It starts with assessments of personal rights and moves to economic and social rights, and ultimately to political and legal rights.

Personal Rights: Reproduction. Personal rights guaranteed by the Bill of Rights are both for this nation as for most Western societies the basis of democracy and stand in Marshall's

(1965) evolutionary scheme as prior to any other rights. Since the ability to biologically reproduce is the ultimate sex difference and at the "core" of all discussions concerning "natural" gender differences, personal rights for women are foremost represented in reproduction rights. Chapter 2 by Chilman, Chapter 3 by Figueira-McDonough, and Chapter 4 by Rowland address issues related to those rights.

Chilman reviews the history of reproduction norms in the United States. She posits that the push toward more liberal norms of reproduction originated from demographic changes and economic incentives rather than concern with women's personal rights. Her firsthand account of the tentativeness and ambiguity in the formulation of federal policies to implement the new norms reflects the ambivalence surrounding gender role changes.

Figueira-McDonough focuses on contemporary opinions about abortion. She finds that there is a reasonable fit between normative and legal support for personal rights in reproduction in spite of moderate resistance. Examination of that resistance reveals that it is related to the fear of change in women's roles and that it tends to be reinforced by institutions with a clear stake in a patriarchal order.

Rowland looks at the implications of new reproductive technologies for the personal and social rights of women. She examines the belief that these technologies will liberate women from what is assumed to be the basis for their subordinated status. She contends that in a gender-stratified society loss of control over reproduction might reduce women to total powerlessness. Paradoxically, women are contributing to the emergence of this "misogynic brave new world" through their attempts to conform with the "motherhood norm."

Personal Rights: Role Choice. Personal rights include the freedom to pursue one's happiness and choice of occupation. The assumed "natural" link between reproduction and child care is at the roots of a gender organization that made women on the one hand economic outcasts and on the other all-purpose nurturants. The contribution of industrialization and its functional counterparts, liberal individualism and the nuclear family, to the Catch-22 aspects of contemporary division of labor merit close scrutiny. First, as role specialization grew, so did the impermeability of the boundaries between the family and other social groups. In a market society the confinement of women to the private sphere by definition negates their social adulthood and economic citizenship. Since men were assigned the role of family providers, women became automatically economically dependent, their economic status a function of their marital relationship (Gil 1974). The principle of individual autonomy and the division of labor in the nuclear family are therefore antithetical. Second, the false identification of private with personal and public with impersonal transforms woman's work in the private sphere into nonwork. Since work in the private sphere is defined as the expression of love, it can and should not be remunerated nor can it be in any other way measured or compared with utilitarian work efforts. Reactions to proposals for mother's wages clearly reflect the strength of these definitions (Gil 1974). These two principles, basic to gender organization, set the stage for the limitless demands put on women as caregivers and their entrapment in situations of victimization. Chapter 5 by Fox and Allen, Chapter 6 by Hooyman and Ryan, and Chapter 7 by Carlson examine the limits and strains imposed on women by the traditional division of labor.

Fox and Allen examine the enormous gap between the need and the availability of child care in the United States. They explore the mythical assumptions grounded in the "vanishing" nuclear family and superiority of the "nonexisting" full-time mother care, behind this national policy of child-carelessness, and the price that both mothers and children pay for it. They also highlight the low status and lack of support for programs and persons providing organized child care in this society. With three out of four women with minor children in the labor force, their observations and recommendations are highly relevant today.

Hooyman and Ryan examine the consequences of the demographic explosion of elderly dependents for women. Lifelong caregiving duties are the natural outcome of the dominant and foremost definition of women as self-sustaining nurturants.

Carlson writes on the relation between the normative asymmetry of marital relations and the entrapment of women in abusive situations. She examines how the reinterpretations by both control and help organizations of the solutions chosen by these women converge in "blaming the victim."

Economic Rights: Work and Welfare. The persistence of the nuclear family standard (with its strict division of labor) in face of the overwhelming evidence of its disappearance is a crucial element in the obstruction of both personal and economic rights. The massive move of women into the labor market held the promise of individual autonomy. However, as Mary Fox demonstrates in Chapter 8, unequal opportunities and rewards produced limited economic rights. The division of labor institutionalized by the nuclear family is reproduced in gender segregated labor markets. This in turn permits the perpetuation of the devaluation of women's work. The secondary economic status imposed on women rests on the normative priority attributed to their family obligations. This justification is doubly profitable for the economic system in place since it creates a pool of cheap labor without incurring responsibilities for child care.

The circumstances of multiple and contradictory demands set on women is particularly dramatic for single poor mothers. In Chapter 9 Zinn describes how welfare mothers are expected to fulfill the roles of competent nurturants and self-sufficient providers under very punitive conditions. She further documents how stigmatizing language paradigms (Thomas 1986) have influenced and continue to affect political decisions, and how policy formulation effectively perpetuates the deprivation of the personal, economic, and social rights of these women. Minority women are particularly heavily impacted by these policies and are nearly wholly denied access to legitimate roles and opportunities.

Social Rights: Health and Education. Health and education are among the social rights to which Marshall (1965) argues citizens should be equally entitled. Contrary to most postindustrialized societies, universal access to these rights is assured in the United States only in relation to primary and secondary education. The free market is assumed to be a better vehicle for access in relation to most health needs and higher education. It is axiomatic that since women have, as a group, lower access to economic rights, they will automatically also be deprived in the area of social rights (Gil 1974).

The evidence given by Bush in Chapter 10 and Blackburn and Holbert in Chapter 11 of how educational institutions reproduce economic inequality further specifies the interconnecting web of social controls on women.

Bush focuses on the ways gendered socialization operates as a social control mechanism at home and at school during adolescence. She reviews evidence indicating that not only content but also the processes of school socialization differ by gender. Secondary schools are found to contribute to the reproduction of the asymmetrical social organization of gender.

At the other extreme of the educational spectrum, Blackburn and Holbert evaluate the status of women in academia. The persistence of the use of invalid human capital explanations and fallacious self-selective justification for the low status of women in academia highlights how much unequal treatment of women depends on "retrospective interpretations." Kanter's (1977) propositions on the constraints befalling women who enter male-dominated work settings are supported in this analysis.

Fisher in Chapter 12 and Rothblum and Franks in Chapter 13 address health issues, bringing to the fore the crucial interrelation between the categorical definitions of gender and women's health status and care. Fisher analyzes how cultural definitions of womanhood are mirrored in the way women confronted with a hysterectomy negotiate their sense of self. The role of the medical profession in affecting such negotiations is traced to the mutually reinforcing power asymmetries of professional/recipient and male/female.

Rothblum and Franks examine the impact of gender roles on mental health. Their review shows the toll taken on women by the excessive demands of caregiving. Conversely, the relationship they find between good mental health and women's autonomy is in clear contradiction with the feminine role defined as socially desirable.

Political and Legal Rights. The argument that equal political rights have been granted to women through universal suffrage is at best naive. Voting is a necessary but by far not a sufficient condition for gender parity in politics. Two major obstacles stand in the way of such parity. First, given the close relationship between economic and political power, women as a group are at a disadvantage. Second, women as newcomers in overwhelmingly male institutions have to contend with issues of internal legitimacy and its demands of conformity (Ferree 1974). Palley in Chapter 14 and Sarri in Chapter 15 examine the political and legal reality of women. Palley's analysis of the political successes and failures of women's groups identifies the enormous obstacles to the viability of promoting gender role changes under these circumstances.

Sarri's discussion of legal rights and outcomes for women charged with crime, as well as those victimized by crime, shows how women are in jeopardy in the criminal justice system. Female crime is viewed as "truly" deviant because it is law breaking by persons expected to uphold the norms of society, and because women may socialize their children to crime. Minority women are particularly at risk in all stages of the criminal justice system, and they are afforded even less protection than are majority women. The popular belief that the male-dominated criminal justice system treats women with greater benevolence is at odds with present trends of longer and more frequent incarceration.

In the conclusion we consider the evidence and arguments presented in these chapters and examine them in relation to alternative policy and institutional responses. We argue for the necessity of compensatory policy to achieve gender justice. We further demonstrate that, to protect women's rights, it is imperative that the types of control imposed on them be regularly evaluated by legitimate criteria of deviance and responsibility.

References

Anderson, M., 1978. Welfare: The Political Economy of Welfare Reform in the US. Stanford, CA: Hoover Institute Press.

Anderson, M.L., 1983. Thinking About Women: Sociological and Feminist Perspectives. New York: Macmillan.

As, B., 1980. "On Female Culture: An Attempt to Formulate a Theory of Women's Solidarity and Action," Acta Sociologica 28: 142–61.

Beauvoir, S., 1948. The Second Sex. Trans. by H.M. Parshey. New York: Alfred Knopf (1983).

Becker, H., 1963. Outsiders. New York: The Free Press.

Berk, S.F., 1985. The Gender Factory: The Apportionment of Work in American Households. New York: Plenum.

Bernstein, B., 1984. "Welfare Dependency," pp. 125–52 in L. Bawden (ed.) The Social Contract Revisited. Washington, DC: Urban Institute.

Broom, D.H. (ed.), 1984. Unfinished Business. Sydney: George Allen and Unwin.

Broverman, I.K., D.K. Broverman, F. Clarkson, P. Rosenkrantz and S. Vogel, 1981. "Sex-Role Stereotypes and Clinical Judgements of Mental Health," pp. 86–97 in E. Howell and M. Bayes (eds.) Women and Mental Health. New York: Basic Books.

Burton, C., 1985. Subordination: Feminism and Social Theory. Sydney: George Allen and Unwin.

Cherlin, A. and P.B. Walters, 1981. "Trends in United States Men's and Women's Sex Role Attitudes: 1971–1978," American Sociological Review 46: 453–60.

Cloward, R. and F. Piven, 1979. "Hidden Protest: The Channeling of Female Innovation and Resistance," Signs 4, 4: 651–69.

Cohen, S. and A. Scull, 1983. A Political Economy of Deviance. New York: St. Martin's.

England, P., 1981. "Assessing Trends in Occupational Sex Segregation, 1900–1976," pp. 273–96 in I. Berg (ed.) Sociological Perspectives on Labor Markets. New York: Academic.

Erickson, K., 1962. "Notes on the Sociology of Deviance," Social Problems 9 (Spring): 307–14.

Erickson, K., 1966. Wayward Puritans. New York: Wiley.

Fausto-Sterling, A., 1986. Biological Theories About Women and Men. New York: Basic Books.

Ferree, M.M., 1974. "A Woman for President," Public Opinion Quarterly 38: 390–91.

Figueira-McDonough, J., 1980. "A Reformulation of the 'Equal Opportunity Explanation' of Female Delinquency," Crime and Delinquency 26, 3: 333–43.

Figueira-McDonough, J., 1985. "Gender, Race, and Class: Differences in Levels of Feminist Orientation," Journal of Applied Behavioral Science 21, 2 (March): 121–42.

Foucault, M., 1975. Discipline and Punish. Translated by A. Sheridan. Middlesex, England: Penguin.

Gelb, J. and M.L. Palley, 1982. Women and Public Policies, 2nd ed. Princeton, NJ: Princeton University Press.

Gil, D.C., 1973. Unravelling Social Policy: Theory, Analysis and Political Action Towards Social Equality. Cambridge, MA: Schenkman.

Gilder, G., 1981. Wealth and Poverty. New York: Basic Books.

Goffman, E., 1977. "The Arrangement Between the Sexes," Theory and Society 4: 301–31.

Goodin, R.E., 1985. Protecting the Vulnerable. Chicago, IL: The University of Chicago Press.

Goodwin, L., 1983. Causes and Cures of Welfare. Lexington, MA: Lexington.

Harris, A.R., 1977. "Sex Theories of Deviance: Toward a Functional Theory of Social Scripts," American Sociological Review 42 (February): 3–16.

Herzog, A.R. and J.G. Bachman, 1982. Sex Role Attitudes Among High School Seniors: Views About Work and Family Roles. Research Report Series. Ann Arbor: Survey Research Center, Institute for Social Research, The University of Michigan.

Hewlett, S.A., 1986. A Lesser Life: The Myth of Women's Liberation in America. New York: William Morrow.

Hutter, B. and G. Williams (eds.), 1981. Controlling Women: The Normal and the Deviant. London: Croom Helm.

Johnson, G., 1985. "Women's Labor Force Participation." Comments at the University of Michigan School of Law Conference on Comparable Worth, October.

Kanter, R.M., 1977. "Some Effects of Proportions On Group Life: Skewed Sex Ratios and Responses to Token Women," American Journal of Sociology 82: 965–90.

Kirp, D.L., M.G. Yudof and M.S. Franks, 1986. Gender Justice. Chicago, IL: The University of Chicago Press.

Kitsuse, J.I., 1962. "Societal Reactions to Deviant Behavior," Social Problems 9 (Winter): 247–56.

Komarovsky, M., 1953. Women in the Modern World. Boston, MA: Little Brown.

Lemert, E.M., 1964. Human Deviance, Social Problems and Social Control. Englewood Cliffs, NJ: Prentice Hall.

Lengerman, P.M. and R.A.W. Wallace, 1985. Gender in America: Social Control and Social Change. Englewood Cliffs, NJ: Prentice Hall.

Maccoby, E.D. and C.N. Jacklyn, 1974. The Psychology of Sex Differences. Stanford, CA: Stanford University Press.

Marshall, T.H., 1965. Class, Citizenship and Social Development. Garden City, NY: Doubleday.

Mason, K.O., J.L. Czaijka and S. Arber, 1976. "Change in U.S. Women's Sex Role Attitudes, 1964–1974," American Sociological Review 41: 573–96.

Matthei, J.A., 1982. An Economic History of Women in America: Women's Work, The Sexual Division of Labor and the Development of Capitalism. New York: Schocken Books.

Mead, L.M., 1986. Beyond Entitlement: The Social Obligations of Citizenship. New York: The Free Press.

Millett, K., 1970. Sexual Politics. New York: Doubleday.

Norton, E.H., 1985. "Ivory Tower Faces Challenge Inequality Battle." Speech delivered at the Equity and Excellence in Higher Education Conference at Michigan State University, East Lansing, April.

Offe, C., 1984. Contradictions of the Welfare State. Cambridge, MA: MIT Press.

Omnibus Budget Reconciliation Act of 1981, PL 97–208.

Page, R., 1984. Stigma. London: Routledge and Kegan Paul.

Parelius, A.P., 1975. "Emerging Sex-Role Attitudes, Expectations and Strains Among College Women," Journal of Marriage and the Family 37: 146–53.

Powell, B. and J.A. Jacobs, 1984. "The Prestige Gap: Differential Evaluations of Male and Female Workers," Work and Occupations 11, 3 (August): 283–308.

Quinney, R., 1977. Class, State and Crime: On the Theory and Practice of Criminal Justice. New York: David McKay.

Rossi, A., 1985. "Gender and Parenthood," pp. 161–92 in A. Rossi (ed.) Gender and the Life Course. New York: Aldine.

Rothman, D.J., 1980. Conscience and Convenience. Boston, MA: Little, Brown.

Rowbotham, S., 1976. Hidden From History: Rediscovering Women in History from the 17th Century to the Present. New York: Vintage Books.

Schur, E., 1983. Labeling Women Deviant: Gender Stigma and Social Control. Philadelphia, PA: Temple University Press.

Stallard, K., B. Ehrenreich and H. Sklar, 1983. Poverty in the American Dream: Women and Children First. New York: Institute for New Communications.

Thomas, K., 1986. "Politics as Language," New York Review of Books (February 27): 36–39.

Thompson, E.P., 1965. The Making of the English Working Class. New York: Random House.

Thompson, E.P., 1977. Customs in Common. New York: Pantheon Books.

Thornton, A. and D. Freedman, 1979. "Changes in the Sex Role Attitudes of Women, 1962–1977: Evidence From a Panel Study," American Sociological Review 44: 831–42.

Thornton, A., D. Alwin and D. Camburn, 1983. "Sex-Role Attitudes and Attitude Change," American Sociological Review 48: 211–27.

Treiman, D.J. and H. Hartman, 1981 (eds.). Women, Work and Wages: Equal Pay for Jobs of Equal Value. Washington, DC: National Academy Press.

Weitzman, L., 1985. The Divorce Revolution. New York: The Free Press.

PART I

PERSONAL RIGHTS: REPRODUCTION

CHAPTER 2

REPRODUCTION NORMS AND SOCIAL CONTROL OF WOMEN

Catherine S. Chilman

For the first time in history, women seem to be gaining relatively safe, inexpensive, socially approved legal control over their own reproductive lives, independent of men. This new control rests mainly on the fairly recent (1960) development of intercourse-independent contraceptives for women (primarily oral contraceptives and the newer contraceptive implants), government-subsidized family planning services (1966 and following years), legalized abortion (1973), and the proliferation during the 1970s and 1980s of female physicians and lawyers able to provide needed services.

If this female liberation and independent control continue, there will be a sharp break in the widespread historical patterns of male-female relationships outlined below. On the other hand, the ready availability of high-quality, inexpensive family planning and abortion services is currently being threatened by reactionary forces in the traditional sectors of society, including that of the Reagan administration. The issues are currently in the balance and are highly politicized by activists of both the conservative and liberal persuasions.

This chapter provides a brief overview of some of the major interacting biological, historical, social, psychological, demographic, economic, and political forces that underlie the current debate on women's reproductive roles. Its central focus is on the situation in the United States, with some attention to the larger social-historical forces that have affected and continue to affect reproductive norms.

DEMOGRAPHIC AND ECONOMIC FACTORS

During much of the period from early Christianity onward, high fertility norms were widespread throughout Western Europe in association with such threats to the population as wars, plagues, famines, and high infant and maternal mortality rates. Then, too, the numerous agrarian societies tended to favor large families as a cheap source of labor. Although techniques of birth control had been developed in the earlier Egyptian, Greek, and Roman civilizations, knowledge about them had largely been forgotten or suppressed by the anticontraceptive teachings of the Catholic Church (Tannahill 1980).

Beginning in the late eighteenth century in England and America, middle and upper class norms began to favor smaller family size. There is considerable evidence that birth control was practiced in these groups through delayed age at marriage, mutually agreed upon abstinence (initiated by wives), or "coitus interruptus." These practices continued in some sectors of society through the nineteenth and into the early twentieth centuries (Degler 1980).

Infanticide was widely practiced as a means of birth control from ancient times until the nineteenth century in Europe. It became particularly widespread when the discovery of immunizing techniques, such as smallpox vaccine, created far larger families than most parents, especially mothers, could handle. Infanticide became so common in some parts of England and France that it was accepted as virtually normative. Alternatively, unwanted babies, both legitimate and illegitimate, were placed in foundling homes or with "wet nurses," where infant death rates were extremely high (Schlossman 1976). Abortion was also common in the eighteenth- and nineteenth-century United States until it was prohibited by the late 1890s (David 1973).

In the late nineteenth and early twentieth centuries, the social norm of small family size continued to spread among the urban and industrial sectors of Western Europe and the United States. This trend can be partly explained by the decline in the usefulness of children as a cheap source of labor, particularly after child labor was prohibited by law. During the early twentieth century the norm of small family size grew increasingly popular among upper middle-class liberal and intellectual elites, gaining strength from the women's suffrage movement, as well as from the emerging fields of maternal and child health, contraception (largely by means of diaphragms or condoms), eugenics, and child development. These values frequently clashed, however, with more traditional ones that prescribed women's central role as homemaker and mother of large families, values held particularly by Catholics (especially recent immigrants) and fundamentalists, predominantly working-class Protestant groups.

During the 1930s traditional reproductive values were weakened by the exigencies of the Great Depression, and from 1940 to 1947 birth rates remained low because of World War II and the absence of men from home. Beginning in 1948, the birth rate rose sharply until 1958. Scholars fail to agree on the causes of this "baby boom," but it seems likely that the social pressures for high birth rates chiefly arose out of deferred parenthood during the Depression, the reunion of couples after World War II, and the idealization of high fertility associated with the country's predominantly agrarian past (Chilman 1968).[1] In the 1950s rapid increases in industrialization and geographic mobility heightened this nostalgia for the rural past. Americans tried to turn back the clock to what they thought had been an age of patriarchal control and family "togetherness" when men were unquestioned family heads and wage earners, and women were relegated to homemaking, childbearing, and childrearing.

After 1958 the birth rate began to decline and continued to dwindle through the mid-1970s. Since then it has remained low, at somewhat less than population replacement level (U.S. Department of Commerce 1985a). These recent downward trends can be explained in part by economic factors. Rising aspirations for the "good life" of material abundance, increased household technology that simplified homemaking but made it more expensive, expanded roles outside the home for women, and inflation have all combined to increase the lure of small family size and hence the possibility of extended female employment outside the home. In addition, the changed nature of jobs, which now depend primarily on interpersonal, technical, or professional skills rather than on brute strength, has made women at least as desirable employees as men.

During the 1960s and early 1970s, the small birth cohorts of 1930–48 and the exodus of young males to the war in Vietnam meant that relatively few people were available for the then expanding job market. Moreover, the social planners of the War against Poverty in the mid-1960s spread the word that large family size was linked to low per capita income and female unemployment, which drain the nation's social and economic resources. Some conservative groups that normally opposed birth control were persuaded that large families often meant poverty, which translated into "tax eaters instead of tax payers." The costs/benefits ratio of subsidizing family planning for the poor thus took on considerable appeal to eager tax savers (Chilman 1968).

By the late 1970s economic and demographic conditions had changed dramatically, and changed in a way that may eventually reverse the recent downward slope in birth rates. In the first place, baby boomers had grown up and were flooding the labor market. As the economy weakened due to deindustrialization and increased competition from abroad, unemployment rose in this country, hastened in the 1980s by the fiscal policies of the Reagan administration. Women became threatening competition to men in the tightening job market, especially as many women took further occupational training and proved themselves capable in fields formerly dominated by men (Bernard 1974). It seems likely that the present conservative drive to reduce birth control programs and oppose the Equal Rights Amendment stems partly from a desire to push women out of the labor market and back into their traditional roles.

Moreover, some demographers and other social scientists warn that unless the fertility rate increases, labor shortages and a variety of other problems will arise by the year 2000. For example, the cohort of people then in the labor force may be too small to provide adequate Social Security funds for the aging 1948–58 baby boomers. In addition, if demographic trends continue at less than population replacement level, some worry about our power balance with high birth rate nations, especially those of South America. Thus groups opposing public subsidy of family planning programs and legalized abortion may attract further support in the coming years, and attempts to reestablish the norm of plentiful motherhood may gain increased popularity.

SOCIAL-PSYCHOLOGICAL FACTORS

Because childbearing and childrearing are tasks that must be undertaken by a large number of women (it only takes one man to impregnate many females, and no man can breastfeed the young), social norms in most historical periods have strongly endorsed mothering as women's central role. These norms have celebrated the assumed rewards of maternity, partly to persuade women to assume the burdens of pregnancy, childbirth, and infant care.

So much has been made of these rewards that in the past women usually kept a guilty silence about any anger or exhaustion they may have felt as mothers. It wasn't until Betty Freidan broke the silence (1963) that numerous women were freed to say that they wanted larger roles in employment and community involvement outside the home. Ironically, many women today feel guilty when they do embrace motherhood wholeheartedly and stay home full-time to care for their young. Whatever the reproductive norms to which women have been socialized, the outcome seems to breed a sense of guilt and inferiority. The issue becomes more complex when the norms change part way through a woman's life and new beliefs and behaviors are called for. Such changes are also apt to induce mother-daughter conflicts and other struggles within the family system (Smith-Rosenburg 1985).

Historical factors help explain the sources of women's guilt over their reproductive functions and roles. Ancient social and religious teachings still affect today's attitudes, even though in recent years many have tried to free themselves from outworn reproductive and sexual codes.

Because the sex drive is so strong, and potentially harmful if totally uncontrolled, all societies develop norms that define the parameters of sexual behavior for both males and females (see, for example, Ford and Beach 1951). Punishments are prescribed for the violation of sexual codes. Some cultures are more severe and repressive than others in these respects. The Christian religious tradition has shaped one of the more repressive cultures, with strictures varying from sect to sect over the ages. Its prescriptions affect sexual norms and child socialization behaviors in Western Europe and the United States to this day.

Prominent in Christian doctrine, especially as developed by the Roman Catholic Church, is the teaching that reproduction and childrearing are woman's most central and "sacred" function. St. Augustine's writings on marriage and sexuality in the fourth century, more than those of any other Church father, have influenced attitudes on these topics down to the present day. He taught that male celibacy was preferable to marriage but that, if a man married, he must attempt to engage in intercourse without "lust" and must not use any form of birth control. In fact, procreation should be the main purpose of intercourse.

Augustine also stressed the doctrine of original sin. Through accepting the apple of knowledge offered by Eve, Adam implicated himself and all his descendants in sin and lust. Eve, like all women, was the fatal temptress who could lead men into sin and hence needed to be controlled (Clark 1985).

By the eleventh or twelfth century, the cult of the Virgin Mary had spread through Europe and had become especially prominent in England. This cult was infused with the medieval concept of courtly love, whereby a pure and spotless upper-class lady remains forever unobtainable by her chivalrous lover. In this tradition love was reserved for the high-born lady and sex for the lower-class woman. Marriage was essentially a business arrangement for acquiring property and producing legitimate heirs.

Apparent in the courtly love tradition is the double standard of sexual morality, including its social class aspects, that still has wide currency today. According to this view, nonmarital sex is acceptable for males, who are naturally sexual, but only occurs among females who are lower class, degraded, unmarriageable, and unworthy of mothering a "good man's" children (Skolnick 1983; Stephens 1963). Through fidelity in marriage and motherhood, women attempt to prove their sexual purity and preserve their class standing. They present their sexuality as exclusively in the service of procreation, accepting the burden of motherhood as payment for their Eve-like sexual sins. Men, feeling guilty for robbing their wives of their presumed purity, share the view that motherhood can help excuse women's sexual behavior.[2] Thus the cult of motherhood helps defend men as well as women from a guilty sense of sexual sin.

In the eighteenth century racist attitudes, as well as those of class discrimination inherited from prior centuries, began to inform the double standard of sexual morality. European explorers and traders in the Americas and Africa had sexual relations with many native American and black women. Influenced by prevalent European norms and their own associations of these women only with sexuality, they saw the resulting children as belonging to an inferior racial and social group, savage and immoral. This attitude and the concomitant exploitative behaviors spread with slavery in the following centuries and persist in white racist attitudes today.

The massive social and economic changes of the nineteenth century might have been expected to lead to changes in sexual norms and behaviors. Traditional family life was transformed in many parts of the United States as huge migrations to the cities and to the West created new economic centers and opportunities. These rents in the socioeconomic fabric stimulated nondominant groups, including women, to develop new aspirations and assume new roles. Extending their prescribed roles as "keepers of the home and Christian morality," middle- and upper-class women became leaders of social reform movements outside the home.

But these new public roles posed such a threat to the "orderly conduct" of male-dominated political, economic, and social life that men evolved the Cult of True Womanhood to keep women out of the public sphere. According to this code, woman belonged in the separate world of the home, where she provided a haven of purity, harmony, and peace and where she found her most noble and fulfilling role as the bearer and tender of children. Thus according to Smith-Rosenburg (1985), the severe social disruption of the nineteenth century was perceived metaphorically as biological disruption, and human sexuality was thus thought to be dangerously out of control. By harnessing the female body and female sexuality firmly to reproduction within the confines of marriage, men hoped to regain some control over the "body" politic.

Quite different explanations of the centrality of motherhood have been proposed by psychoanalysts. Only a few of the more prominent theories can be sketched here because of space constraints. Freud and some of his followers espoused the view that the mother is the first love-sex object for both boys and girls. This attraction creates a special problem for boys, who fear the fantasized jealous wrath of their fathers and resultant castration by them. The resolution of this impasse is to give up the mother as a primary love-sex object and identify with the father. If the so-called Oedipal conflict is thereby satisfactorily resolved, the boy eventually falls in love with a woman of his own age and directs his love-sex attractions toward her. However, earlier incestuous guilt often remains, so that relationships with the new love-sex object are perpetually tinged with anxiety, castration fears, and repressed memories of the early mother-son relationship. Impregnating the new love-sex object so that she can become a mother like the one he lost, can convert her, in his eyes, to the "pure" mother of his childhood, thus resolving some of his sexual guilt but further complicating the marital relationship (Freud 1953).

According to Freud, women also have a tendency to accept the motherhood role ambivalently as a result of their development in the family. Theoretically, the little girl "falls in love" with her father, thereby provoking the jealous rage of her mother. She must therefore identify rather than compete with her mother and give up her father for another male. As with the boy, the girl often fails to surrender this early "love affair" completely so that in later life she may feel guilt over her incestuous fantasies and anxiety over her love-sex relation with her mate. She may view other women as jealous, competitive mother objects with whom she is identified, thereby inducing self-fear and self-hatred in the mother role but, simultaneously, a compulsion to repeat this role (Freud 1953).

Some writers also argue that women have a particularly

difficult time establishing their own identity separate from their mothers because of the strong mother-daughter identification. For instance, Chodorow (1978) maintains that women tend to be tied to viewing their primary roles as reproductive because of their identification with their mothers and their concomitant socialization within the family and elsewhere.

Freud also claimed, albeit somewhat tentatively, that women were essentially breeders and bearers whose uteri forever mourned the fantasized loss of their male organs and male identity (Freud 1953). Indeed, all the most authoritative psychoanalysts have concurred that the "true" nature of women is to find fulfillment in the traditional role of wife and mother (Chesler 1972).

Melanie Klein (1957) suggests, perceptively, that male envy of the mother and her breast are central to male devaluation (and valuation) of females in their mothering roles, a view seconded by Otto Kernburg (1972). Horney (1932), reviewing myths and social norms through the ages, emphasizes that males are perpetually envious of the superior procreative powers of females. Women can clearly prove that they are givers of human life, but males can never be sure that they are fathers. The obvious importance of females to reproduction has been a pervasive source of anxiety and suspected self-inferiority among males over the ages and has generated an enduring masculine need to prove their superiority over women.

From a socioeconomic, as well as psychological, perspective, men have wanted to be sure that their children, especially their sons and heirs, were truly their own. To ensure that this was the case and to keep property within the family, they have strongly supported the norm that wives be proven virginal at marriage, that they have coitus only with their husbands, and that they prove their worth by becoming "the mothers of their husbands' sons."

BIOLOGICAL FACTORS

If men and women of the present and future choose to become parents, they will have to decide how to manage the reproductive process. They will have to consider whether to opt for "test-tube babies" or artificially inseminated mothers who make a profession out of reproduction. Viewed objectively, the traditional method of procreation through coitus, followed by nine months of pregnancy, followed by the pains and strains of childbirth, followed by breastfeeding seems excessively time-and-energy consuming, primitive in its do-it-yourself craft characteristics in an age when almost everything else is produced quickly in a standard format on a mechanized assembly line—a line increasingly run by robots.

These decisions about whether and how to handle the biological aspects of reproduction may depend to some extent on how deeply ingrained parenthood is in the human psyche. Some argue that from an evolutionary point of view, it makes sense that both males and females, but especially females, would have an instinctive drive toward parenthood. Others call this "sheer nonsense," maintaining that human beings are characterized far more by socialization through learned, rather than instinctive, behavior.

Those who argue against an instinctive drive toward motherhood cite the high rates of infanticide practiced by women in the past (Skolnick 1983). However, this behavior does not characterize all, or even the majority, of women. Such accounts need to be balanced by evidence of women's chiefly positive reaction to motherhood.

Most females and males (perhaps particularly males) apparently experience strong biological drives for sexual contact (Kinsey et al. 1948, 1953), including intercourse—the prelude to pregnancy. Moreover, there is evidence that females and, to a lesser extent, males tend to be biologically programmed through the effect of hormones on the central nervous system to respond positively to new borns and to bond with them given the appropriate opportunities for holding and relating to them (Money and Ehrhardt 1972; Bardwick 1971; Rossi 1985).

This is not to imply that all mothers (and to a certain extent, fathers) have positive, bonding reactions to their infants; a biological predisposition is not synonymous with actual feelings and behaviors, which are mediated by a host of other physical, social, psychological, and economic variables. Even so, we should not overlook the biological component of programming for parenthood.

POLITICAL FACTORS: CONTRACEPTION

As sketched earlier, recent demographic trends have made population control a must in this country and many others throughout the world. The Planned Parenthood Federation, formerly the National Birth Control League, with its many affiliates throughout the country, has been the nation's leading advocate for effective family planning since the 1920s. Before the development of today's contraceptives, Planned Parenthood clinics especially advocated the diaphragm and spermicidal jelly as the most efficient birth control method, partly because, unlike condoms or coitus interruptus, they were entirely controlled by the woman.

The Catholic Church, with leadership from its high-ranking male clergy, vigorously opposed the policies and programs of Planned Parenthood, effectively inhibiting the spread of family planning services.[3] In many communities the Church threatened to withdraw all of its support from the United Way (then the Community Chest) if Planned Parenthood affiliates were allowed any of its benefits. Especially in communities with a sizable Catholic population, these affiliates were forced to raise their own funding from voluntary donors and consequently remained small and poorly financed organizations.[4]

In these localities the Church also exercised controls over hospitals and their medical staffs, threatening to boycott them if they offered birth control services. Then, too, staff members in both public and private social agencies in many communities were forbidden by agency policies (influenced by the Catholic Church and other conservative groups) from discussing birth control with any of their clients. Similar prohibitions were frequently in place in public and private schools and universities. In short, strong barriers were erected by official Catholic doctrine and other like-minded philosophies against the spread of family planning information and services.

These barriers meant, among other things, that effective methods of birth control were beyond the reach of most poor women since the Planned Parenthood clinics were small and inadequately financed. More affluent women could obtain prescriptions for diaphragms and jelly from certain private physicians. However, the diaphragm and jelly were not only fairly expensive but required high degrees of motivation and skill to apply. Thus they failed to win a large number of enthusiastic users.

With the development of the intercourse-independent "orals" and IUDs (intrauterine devices) in the early 1960s, family planning "for the masses" became a much more realistic possibility. This development, along with the other economic, political, and social changes described above, forms the backdrop for the revolutionary pro-family planning federal policies of the 1960s and 1970s.

In 1966 publicly subsidized contraceptives began to be made available to low-income adults, through the mechanism set up in 1965 to administer Medicaid. Since 1973 this birth control program has been extended to adolescents, in accordance with a Supreme Court decision affirming the right of contraceptive choice to women and men without limitations on their age or marital status. In 1977 the Supreme Court upheld the right of adolescents, either married or single, to confidential family-planning assistance without parental involvement (Chilman 1983).

To implement the 1966 federal policy, each state, following federal guidelines, was to make its own health services plan, with most of the costs being met by the federal government. The pro-family-planning federal policy statement mandating that each state offer contraceptive services was carefully constructed through negotiations with numerous pronatalist as well as procontraceptive local, state, and national advocacy groups. Among these groups were religious organizations; health, education, and welfare agencies; and specific population planning groups, including Planned Parenthood, the Ford and Rockefeller foundations, and the Population Crisis Committee.

As the only woman and the only behavioral scientist on the otherwise all-male, all-physician federal planning task force set up to implement this policy, I quickly learned that my colleagues thought in terms of delivering contraceptive services to women in a narrow gynecological context. I tried to advance the concept that males as well as females had contraceptive responsibilities and that services should have a broad social-psychological-educational, as well as specifically biological, approach, but other members of the task force seemed unable to understand these recommendations, much less act on them.

Difficulties in launching family planning programs that effectively reach males remain a problem to this day, despite the fact that males are more sexually active than women, especially in adolescence and young adulthood. As a result, females have been left with the central contraceptive responsibility. Even though intercourse-independent contraceptives provide women far greater power and control over reproduction than they have had in the past, these contraceptives have a number of adverse physical and psychological side effects. Women are still paying a penalty for their reproductive functions and roles.

Despite these drawbacks the new contraceptives and the publicly financed family planning programs have been a boon to millions of women and, to a large extent, their mates. However, providing these services nationwide has not been simple. In many states no physicians had been trained in contraceptive technology. Further, many did not wish to undertake this training because of either personal opposition to artificial contraception or fear that many of their patients would criticize them for offering family planning services. Moreover, largely due to long suppression of contraceptive information and to the prevailing discomfort with discussing human sexuality, social service and education personnel also lacked the requisite knowledge and skills to provide family planning information, counseling, and referral.

Similarly, many federal and state human service administrators and their staff opposed the family-planning programs, thus delaying the development of services in many communities. This delay was supported by numerous local, state, or national conservative organizations, whose basic argument was (and still is) that the widespread availability of contraceptives would encourage uncontrolled sexual promiscuity and undermine the "moral sanctity of the home," especially if contraceptives were made available to adolescent and single women.

By contrast, the "new morality" advocated by many family planning organizations such as Planned Parenthood taught that "responsible sex" should be the norm. That is, contraceptives should be used whenever necessary to avoid giving birth to "unwanted" children who would both overburden families and cause further overpopulation problems. It was assumed that most human beings could not be successfully restrained from having intercourse and that, therefore, birth control was the only route to effective population control (an assumption bolstered by the findings of such researchers as Kinsey et al. 1948; Kinsey et al. 1953; Masters and Johnson 1966). Thus some family planning advocates proclaimed the slogan "Sex for recreation, not procreation."

The idea of socially desirable sexual responsibility through "contraceptive vigilance" was advocated partly to reduce the sense of sexual guilt many people had been socialized to feel. This was especially necessary if women were to admit their sexual desires and plan in advance for intercourse by taking contraceptive pills or having an IUD inserted. Other simultaneous social movements such as counterculture ideologies and feminism also attacked such outworn concepts as the double standard of sexual morality, the "sin" of contraception, and women's expiation of their amoral "lust" through their sacrifices as mothers (Chilman 1983; Yankelovich 1974). Questions were also raised about classic psychoanalytic theory, especially its applicability to contemporary American society and the validity of its theories of sexual guilt and the centrality of motherhood for women.

All in all, in order for realistic, scientifically sound birth control methods to succeed, the new "contraceptive culture" had to deal with all the vestiges of ancient guilty attitudes toward female sexuality as well as with the specifics of contraceptive technology. This necessity continues to create profound disturbances in the social-political fabric of our society and has stimulated resistance on the part of many conservatives.

Some of these conservatives advance racist and elitist rationales for opposing the government subsidy of family planning, arguing that such services are wasted on the poor. Ironically, other racist and elitist elements support public family planning, hoping that it will reduce the numbers of the poor. Liberals, on the other hand, maintain that poor people, like others, should have ready access to services that they want and need, including birth control services (see, for example, Chilman 1968, 1983).

In the face of the many political factions for and against federal support of family planning, it soon became apparent that local programs would fail to develop satisfactorily through the Medicaid mechanism alone—a mechanism that reimbursed physicians for service rendered. Thus various pieces of legislation, including Title X of the Public Health Services Act, were passed during the 1970s. This legislation provided the means for launching specific family planning clinics for low-income persons at the local level, with Planned Parenthood affiliates often taking the leadership role. By 1978 over 3,000 agencies provided Title X family-planning services in over 5,000 cities and virtually every county of the United States with programs being run variously by health departments, Planned Parenthood affiliates, hospitals, and health maintenance organizations.

The growth in the 1970s of publicly provided contraceptive services, including those for adolescent and single persons, was especially impressive in view of the formerly strenuous and powerful opposition of conservative religious and political organizations to any form of birth control. However, in the 1980s political pressures, supported by the Reagan administration, are reemerging to reduce the federal-state funding of family planning programs, including those for teenagers. Recent federal legislation to reduce adolescent pregnancy emphasizes projects that provide moral education and self-control rather than family planning services.

POLITICAL FACTORS: ABORTION

Because another chapter deals specifically with abortion, it is noted only briefly here as a central element in reproduction and social control. Historically, little official attention was paid to abortion in this country and Western Europe before the 1870s (David 1973). Common law had established the acceptability of early abortion before "quickening" (about the end of the first trimester of pregnancy) as a means, among other things, of regulating menstruation (Smith-Rosenburg 1985). In the late nineteenth century, however, as part of their drive to professionalize the practice of medicine, physicians began to argue that they should have the exclusive right to decide whether or not a woman should be allowed to have an abortion. The criterion that abortions should be permitted only when the mother's life was endangered gave doctors the expert control over abortion they wanted.

Religious leaders did not openly oppose abortion until 1869, when Pope Pius IX declared the Catholic Church would regard abortion at any stage as murder. Protestant clergy in the United States, often stimulated by physicians, also took an increasingly active stand against abortion as an immoral act. They joined with leading doctors and politicians to lobby for government restrictions (Smith-Rosenburg 1985; Mohr 1978; Huser 1942). By 1900, through legislation and the actions of various state courts, anti-abortion statutes existed in every state in the Union (Tannahill 1980). Thus for over 70 years abortion was unobtainable legally in most of the United States. Reportedly, wealthy women were able to get abortions through their own physicians or trips to other countries. Poor women suffered from self-induced or illegal, frequently dangerous abortions performed by "back alley" practitioners.

By the 1960s the abortion issue had become highly politicized, especially by feminist groups demanding the right to control their own bodies (Bernard 1974). Between 1965 and 1972 public opinion polls revealed a marked increase in favorable attitudes toward abortion, including abortion for such "soft" reasons as being single and not being able to afford a child. Those who favored abortion tended to be white and Protestant and to have higher income and education levels.

In the late 1960s and early 1970s a number of states passed legislation legalizing abortion, and in 1973 the Supreme Court declared unconstitutional all state laws that prohibited or restricted abortion during the first trimester of pregnancy—a period during which abortions are especially safe, medically speaking. In this decision the Court also limited state intervention in second trimester abortions to the "regulation" of medical practices involved insofar as they affect the woman's health. Decisions about third trimester abortions were left to the states. In 1974 a further blow for women's rights was struck when the Massachusetts Supreme Court ruled that a husband does not have the right to prevent his wife from having an abortion.

However, federal public subsidy of abortion, which made it affordable to poor women through Medicaid, lasted only a few years. By 1980 the Hyde Amendment had relieved the federal government of its obligation to provide funds for abortion costs. Although seventeen states continued to make their own Medicaid funds available for abortion and some others partially funded this service when a woman's life was endangered by a pregnancy, women in most states could no longer get financial help with abortion costs, regardless of their physical or financial plight.

As of autumn 1985 abortion, legalized nationwide, remains a bitter political issue, ardently contested by so-called "pro-life" groups, some of which are led by members of the "radical right." Many of these leaders favor a traditional patriarchal society that puts males back in control of home and community, assigns "respectable" females to traditional roles as full-time mothers and homemakers who "submit" only to marital sex and then only for procreation, and brings teenagers back to their parents for their moral and sexual education.

SUMMARY

Until recently, dominant social norms in the United States prescribed motherhood as the major role for women. Biological, demographic, psychological, economic, social, religious, and political factors all interacted to create and support this prescription. However, dramatic changes since the mid-60s have created new life options, such as no-child or few-child families, a wide range of lifestyles for both women and men, birth control, and employment for women (including mothers) outside the home. These transformations call for fundamental changes in many basic norms concerning female and male sexuality, masculine and feminine roles, and relationships between the sexes. To a large extent, what was formerly considered deviant (such as nonmarital intercourse) has now become virtually normative, and what was normative (such as full-time wife and mother roles for most women) has now become virtually deviant.

However, cultural prescriptions are still confused and confusing, with old pronatalist norms conflicting with newer pro-choice ones. Many women feel guilty if they follow traditional norms and remain in the home as full-time mothers or if they opt for the newer pattern of few or no children plus paid employment. Men also experience conflicts over changing norms, finding traditional women easier to control but modern women more attractive as equal partners.

Current societal changes, such as low fertility rates, continuing high unemployment, and conservative backlash, are creating conditions that may undermine women's recent emancipation from life-long, full-time commitment to motherhood. Evidences of this backlash include attempts by conservative groups to abolish state funding of abortion for poor women, to have abortion declared illegal, to prevent adolescents from obtaining contraceptives or abortion without parental involvement, to reduce government funding of family planning services, and to abolish sex education in the schools.

As of 1985, the battle lines are drawn on these and related issues, with confrontations occurring between liberal and conservative groups. Although the nature of today's society seems to call for expanded, diverse roles for both women and men, with reproduction being but one of these roles, centuries-old traditions may force at least a partial retreat from the advances of the past 20 years.

Notes

[1]A thorough examination of the especially American phenomenon of the prolonged "baby boom" during this decade is beyond the scope of this chapter. However, it was partly owing to the sharp increase in the fertility rate of black women during this period. Speculations by demographers as to the reason for this increase include the decline in black maternal and infant death rates and the decrease in sterility of black couples. These changes were

associated, in part, with urbanization and improvements in provisions for maternal and child health (Chilman 1968; Lunde 1965).

[2]Men seemed to evolve a new variation on the theme of trinity: three kinds of women—one despised and sexual; one forever pure and loved from afar; and one for procreative sex, childbearing, and homemaking. Thus there was no way for a woman to become integrated as a whole person: loved, sexual, and a wife, equal partner though not necessarily a mother. This traditional, trinitarian view of woman is currently being challenged, especially by feminists.

[3]Although the opposition of the Catholic Church to birth control programs during this period was particularly outspoken, a number of other groups, including Orthodox Jews and fundamentalist Protestant sects, were also opposed.

[4]While Catholics are a minority in this country, they have the largest organized church, which exercises unified authority over one-quarter of our population. This, together with the fact that they are predominantly urban, explains their strong influence on halting the development of family planning services at this time.

References

Bardwick, J., 1973. "Psychological Factors in the Use of Oral Contraceptives," in J. Fawcett (ed.) Psychological Aspects of Population. New York: Basic Books.

Bernard, J., 1974. Women, Wives, Mothers: Values and Options. Chicago: Aldine Publishing Co.

Bernard, J., 1975. The Future of Motherhood. New York: Dial Press.

Bettelheim, B., 1965. "The Commitment Required of a Woman Entering a Scientific Profession in Present-Day American Society," in J.A. Mattfield and C.G. Van Aken (eds.) Women and the Scientific Professions. Cambridge, MA: MIT Press.

Campbell, A., P. Converse and W. Rodgers, 1976. The Quality of American Life. New York: Russell Sage Foundation.

Chesler, P., 1973. Women and Madness. New York: Avon Books.

Chilman, C., 1968. "Fertility and Poverty in the United States: Some Implications for Family Planning Programs, Evaluation, and Research," Journal of Marriage and the Family 30, 2 (May): 207-28.

Chilman, C., 1979. "Parent Satisfactions-Dissatisfactions and their Correlates," Social Service Review (June): 195–213.

Chilman, C., 1980. "Areas of Parent Satisfaction and Dissatisfaction," Family Coordinator 29, 3 (July): 339–46.

Chilman, C., 1983. Adolescent Sexuality in a Changing American Society: Social and Psychological Perspectives for Professionals in the Human Services. New York: Wiley and Sons.

Chodorow, N., 1978. The Reproduction of Mothering. Berkeley, CA: University of California Press.

Clark, E., 1985. Personal communication. Professor, Department of Religion, Duke University, Durham, NC.

David, H., 1973. "Abortion in Psychological Perspective," in J. Fawcett (ed.) Psychological Aspects of Population. New York: Basic Books.

Degler, C.N., 1980. At Odds. New York: Oxford University Press.

Ford, S. and F. Beach, 1951. Patterns of Sexual Behavior. New York: Harper.

Freud, S., 1953. Three Essays on Sexuality. London: Hogarth.

Gelinas, D., 1981. "Identification and Treatment of Incest Victims," in E. Howell and M. Bayes (eds.) Women and Mental Health. New York: Basic Books.

Horney, K., 1932. "The Dread of Women." International Journal of Psychoanalysis 13: 348–86.

Huser, R., 1942. The Crime of Abortion in Common Law. Washington, DC: Catholic University of America Press.

Jung, C.C., 1928. Contributions to Analytic Psychology, II. Translated by G. Barnes and C. Baynes. London: Routledge and Kegan Paul.

Kernburg, O., 1972. "Barriers to Being in Love." Unpublished manuscript. Topeka, KN: Menninger Foundation.

Kinsey, A., W. Pomeroy and C. Martin, 1948. Sexual Behavior in the Human Male. Philadelphia, PA: W.B. Saunders.

Klein, M., 1957. Envy and Gratitude. New York: Basic Books.

Lamb, M., 1980. "The Development of Parent-Child Attachments in the First Two Years of Life," in F. Pedersen (ed.) The Father-Infant Relationship: Observational Studies. New York: Praeger.

Lunde, A., 1965. "White-Nonwhite Fertility Differentials in the United States," Health, Education and Welfare Indicators (September): 23–27.

Masters, W. and W. Johnson, 1966. Human Sexual Response. Boston: Little, Brown and Co.

Mohr, J., 1978. Abortion in America: The Origins and Evolution of National Policy. New York and Oxford: Oxford University Press.

Money, J. and A. Ehrhardt, 1972. Man and Woman, Boy and Girl. Baltimore, MD: Johns Hopkins University Press.

Parke, R., 1979. "Perspectives on Father-Infant Interaction," in J. Osofsky (ed.) Handbook of Infant Development. New York: Wiley.

Rossi, A., 1985. "Gender and Parenthood," in A. Rossi (ed.) Gender and the Life Course. New York: Aldine Publishing Co.

Schlossman, S., 1976. "Before Home Start: Notes Toward a History of Parent Education, 1897–1929," Harvard Educational Review 46, 3 (August): 436–67.

Skolnick, A., 1983. The Intimate Environment. Boston: Little Brown Co.

Smith-Rosenburg, C., 1985. Disorderly Conduct. New York: Alfred A. Knopf.

Stephens, W.N., 1963. The Family in Cross-Cultural Perspective. New York: Holt, Rinehart and Winston.

Tannahill, R., 1980. Sex in History. New York: Stein and Day.

U.S. Department of Commerce, Bureau of the Census, 1985a. "Marital Status and Living Arrangements in March 1984," Current Population Reports, Series P-20, No. 399. Washington, DC: U.S. Government Printing Office, July.

U.S. Department of Commerce, Bureau of the Census, 1985b. "Estimates of the Population of the United States," Current Population Reports, Series P-20, No. 396. Washington, DC: U.S. Government Printing Office, March.

Veroff, J., E. Douvan and R. Kulka, 1981. The Inner American. New York: Basic Books.

Yankelovich, D., 1974. The New Morality: Profile of American Youth in the 1970's. New York: McGraw-Hill.

Yankelovich, D., 1981. "A World Turned Upside Down," Psychology Today (April): 35–91.

CHAPTER 3

TO PROTECT OR TO CONTROL:
AN INQUIRY INTO
THE CORRELATES OF OPINIONS ON ABORTION

Josefina Figueira-McDonough

> Here is the truth, I tell you—see how right I am.
> The woman you call the mother of the child is not
> the parent, just a nurse to the seed, the new-sown
> seed that grows and swells inside her. The *man* is
> the source of life—the one who mounts. She, like a
> stranger for a stranger, keeps the shoot alive unless
> god hurts the roots.
>
> Aeschylus The Oresteia
> Translated by Robert Fagles (1966)

THE SYMBOLIC NATURE OF ABORTION

On November 8, 1985, Dr. John Wilke, the president of the National Right to Life Committee, appeared on the McNeil/Lehrer News Hour accusing ABC of presenting a biased view of abortion in a segment of its popular show "Cagney and Lacey." He argued that, while the pro-choice position was rationally argued, the pro-life position was reduced to religious commitment.

Against the historical background tracing the right-to-life movement to the Family Division of the National Conference of Catholic Bishops (Littlewood 1977), and more recent information identifying pro-life activists as 80 percent Catholics (Luker 1984), ABC can be presumed to have acted in good faith. Dr. Wilke insisted, however, that the essence of the movement he heads is not denominational belief but commitment to the human rights of the fetus. This distancing of the pro-life movement from its Catholic roots is an important political move (Weyrich 1979). On the one hand, a restricted religious identification is replaced by a "traditional American value" with a broader mass appeal. On the other hand, as religious belief is metamorphosed into the secular principle of individual rights, the insoluble issue of the fetus's personhood recedes into the background (Glover 1985).

Understanding this transformation is essential to a revision of the simplistic characterization of pro-life, pro-choice movements as adversaries in a battle of rights: children's rights versus women's rights. In fact, the abortion debate is based on judgments of quality and value, not scientific fact, and cannot therefore be rationally decided. Positions are derived from social norms that may have originated from religious principles, humanistic ethical systems, personal experiences, and perceptions of social order. Because ours is a pluralistic society, individuals develop different moral sensitivities based on a variety of cognitive, affective, and evaluative tools (Abernethy 1984). Even when a population subscribes to a common national ideology, a variety of different concrete implications are derived from it, as evidenced in public opinion surveys (Lamanna 1984).

Particular moral issues that acquire public notoriety have exigencies of their own as components of a world view, so that the connections between the specific stance and other public issues are brought forward. The abortion issue has triggered a search for value consistency, because it is closely linked to broader and more encompassing views and life commitments (Callahan and Callahan 1984a). The abortion debate can therefore be interpreted as a process through which individuals attempt to make abortion fit into some overarching scheme of values, combining personal convictions with more broadly held social values. Because abortion stands at the juncture of a number of value systems (relating to sex, reproduction, gender, family, economics, law, etc.) that are only loosely integrated and jousting with each other for dominance, it is hard to predict the position on abortion from any single set of values.

A review of the literature on the subject reveals a common concern with the processes through which abortion becomes integrated into varied organizing value structures. The purpose of this chapter is to identify the types of value resolutions proposed in the literature and investigate the associational validity of each. Aware that single resolutions might coalesce and/or interact, I will also examine their relative power in describing groups of individuals sharing the same position relative to abortion.

This study follows on the steps of the essentially qualitative research that preceded it. In the sequence of knowledge building, it moves from the use of purposive small samples to a national representative sample, and from Gestalt interpretations to more systematic measurement.

HYPOTHESIS ON THE VALUE CORRELATES OF OPINIONS ABOUT ABORTION
Religious Dogma

Religions have traditionally functioned as mechanisms for the integration of a variety of value systems. The more dogmatic the religion, the more effective it becomes in producing an integrated value system. It does so by providing an apocalyptic framework which, since it is beyond rational analysis, validates moral absolutism (Curran 1954). The importance of the Catholic Church in the pro-life movement is tied to the dogmatic nature of its magisterium (teaching). It should be remembered that at issue in the Protestant/Catholic schism was the free interpretation of the Bible. The Catholic hierarchy has, to a much greater extent than other Christian churches, retained control over the normative guidance of its church members. It actively constructs a value superstructure which carefully justifies links among value subsystems. It also, more than most other religions, provides its members with detailed maps of the practical implications of adherence to such a structure (Noonan 1966).

Since 1841 abortion and contraception have emerged in this country as a special concern of the Catholic Church. From that period up to the 1960s, encyclicals prepared by four popes defined unambiguously the position of the Church on these issues (Grisez 1970). At the core of the pro-life position of the Catholic Church is the belief in the personhood of the fetus. To share such a belief is to reject any form of abortion. The role of the National Conference of Catholic Bishops in the creation of the right-to-life movement was a necessary requirement of the belief—a mission to save lives. Hence the popular view that most pro-lifers are Catholics appears to be based on sound historical and dogmatic information (Huser 1942).

Humanitarian Commitment

More than in preceding national elections, the issue of abortion was defined in terms of humanitarianism in 1984. That the confrontation on the issue revolved mostly around a female candidate might have been of significance. In her historical review of the taboo on abortion in the United States, Luker (1984: 107) notes that it was only in the 1960s, with the emergence of the women's movement, that arguments about abortion come to be formulated in terms of competing life rights: the rights of the "emancipated" woman and of the unborn child.

The pervading humanitarian theme portrays the unborn baby as the most helpless of all citizens, and therefore most in need of protection (Mohr 1970; Degler 1980). The pro-life activists described by Luker (1984: 154) felt very strongly that a person's life should not be dependent upon his or her self worth. These feelings extended from the unborn baby, to disabled people, and to minorities. From this perspective abortion is opposed as an expression of a system that puts a social price tag on humans. It is seen as a dismissal or marginalization of the powerless to the benefit of the powerful.

The same theme emerges in the Callahans' work, expressed in principles such as respect for the individual's right to life, even if uncertain or borderline, and the need to protect the weak and powerless, so that they can develop to their potential unencumbered by the powerful (Callahan and Callahan 1984b). The Callahans (1984a), however, caution against acceptance of an association between humanitarianism and the pro-life position. All participants in their study, pro-life and pro-choice, showed high levels of humanitarianism but differed in their belief in the personhood of the fetus. Since their sample was almost completely female, one wonders if this lack of differentiation might reflect the relational moralism of women (as presented by Gilligan 1982 and Miller 1976) and therefore be quite independent of support or opposition to abortion. Along these lines, after examining the arguments between the two groups, Petchesky (1984: 372) concludes that the ethics of maternal responsibility (giving the unborn child the right to be born vs. giving each child born the right to be loved and the means to develop to its full potential) rather than woman's liberation, is dominant among women on each side of the argument.

Much less work has been done on men's opinions about abortion. However, if Gilligan's argument that men tend to develop a more abstract/rational morality is correct, then humanitarian commitment should distinguish more clearly the male supporters from the male opponents of abortion.

Control of Women

Attempts to define women's relationship to their fertility (when and whether to have sex and become pregnant, with whom and how) by institutions representing patriarchal authority (church, lay moralists, husbands, medical profession) have been a historical constant (Rich 1980; Daly 1978). As recently as the late 1970s, Nathanson and Becker (1977) found that physicians performing abortions in Maryland required the husband's or father's consent.

In view of this background the feminist interpretation of the anti-abortion movement as an extension of the tradition of control of women is amply justified. They argue that larger issues about women's sexuality—its boundaries, subjects, forms, and age limits— are expressed through the conflict over abortion (Eisenstein 1984). Further, in an all-encompassing way, since the 1970s abortion has come to symbolize the "emancipated woman." The right to women's sexual self-determination, together with increasing economic independence, forecasts the end of traditional gender and sexual relations and therefore of male dominance (Petchesky 1984: 209). Opposition to abortion from this perspective is expected to come predominantly from men (and women) who also oppose women's equal rights.

Normative Self-Justification

The traditional assumption that norms and attitudes cause behavior has been challenged by Bem (1970). He argues for a reversal in the causal order: behavior causes attitudes. His theory of self-perception proposes that the origins of an individual's self-knowledge is derived from observing his/her own behavior. Further, inspired by Festinger's theory of cognitive dissonance (1964), a more interactionist approach, whereby norms and attitudes are thought to adjust to behavior, has been developed.

This theoretical outlook is consistent with some of Luker's (1984) findings in her study of pro-life and pro-choice activists. She describes how these women's attitudes on abortion are explained in terms of investments they have made in their lives. Thus for women who have devoted most of their lives to mothering, either bringing up large families or coping with handicapped children, abortion was viewed as a devaluation of the meaning of their lives. Conversely, those who had committed themselves to careers saw in the pro-life movement a threat to their achievements and a latent labeling of their life choice as deviant and unwomanly.

In line with this theory, pro-life supporters as a group are expected to have more children and to be more often housewives (or in the case of men to have spouses who are housewives) than respondents that either tolerate or support abortion.

Fear of Change and the New Right

Petchesky (1984: 241–285) argues that to the extent that abortion symbolizes change in the organization of gender, it provokes defensive reactions on the part of those who feel threatened by social changes. Resistance to change has been found to be typical of closed subcultures and among groups with precarious material security. The first factor contributes to a rigid world view, the second to fear that tinkering with institutions will disrupt a precarious balance and hence the survival of those groups (Vidich 1958: 101–105). Explanations of the resistance of the peasants to the French Revolution of 1789 and of the American working class to welfare reforms have included these considerations (Tilly 1964; Aronowitz 1973).

In light of this argument one could postulate that to the extent that abortion is associated with the debate surrounding modernism and traditionalism (Callahan and Callahan 1984: 285, 302), it will be resisted by those anxious to keep the "safe boundaries" of their world. Conversely, those who feel more in control of their lives (maybe as a function of education, income, and age) are more likely to perceive changes as advantageous or at least be confident that they can turn them in their favor. This latter group's approach to abortion is likely to be more pragmatic; that is, to favor individual choice.

Furthermore, the link between the pro-life movement and the New Right can also be understood in this context. In a highly politicized environment traditional private values tend to be manipulated by interest groups in search of new members, supporters, or temporary allies (Freemand and Gamson 1979). Petchesky (1984: 243–45), in her brilliant analysis of the connection between abortion politics and the politics of the New Right, shows how abortion was transformed into a symbol of sexual promiscuity, family disintegration, economic ruin, and communism.

Playing on the fear of changes, interpreted as a threat to the safe boundaries within which most people organize their lives, a wall of opposition is erected against demands for equalization of participation of the poor, the young, minorities, and women (Weyrich 1979). The moralistic fervor of the anti-abortion campaign is thereby extended to political goals that seem unrelated to sex, religion, and the family but are the traditional fare of the New Right (racial segregation, welfare cutbacks, and militarism).

The fear of change argument permits the prediction of two

types of associations with opinions on abortion: (1) stance on abortion will vary significantly by certain demographic characteristics such as urbanism, income, and education, and (2) conservative attitudes in relation to a variety of social issues will be associated with opposition to abortion.

EMPIRICAL INVESTIGATION
Opinions on Abortion

The second part of this chapter will be devoted to the investigation of the validity of the explanations outlined in the previous section. The goal is to test, with a representative national sample and systematic measurement, the explanations predominantly induced from qualitative research with restrictive samples.

Data from the 1984 National Election Study of the Institute for Social Research, at the University of Michigan, are used in this investigation. Respondents were selected through a multistage random sample of all American adults. The size of the sample is 2,257 cases (for a description of the sample, see Miller 1985). Opinion on abortion was measured by a single categorical question. Respondents were asked to indicate which of the following alternatives was closer to their views:

1) By law abortion should never be permitted.
2) The law should permit abortion only in case of rape, incest, or when the woman's life is in danger.
3) The law should permit abortion by reasons other than rape, incest, or when the woman's life is in danger—but only when the need for abortion is well established.
4) By law a woman should always be able to obtain an abortion as a matter of personal choice.

Categories 1 and 4 define the pro-life and the pro-choice positions and were selected respectively by 13.3 percent and 36.4 percent of the respondents. Categories 2 and 3 represent conditional acceptance of abortion. The conditions described under 2 have come to be designated as "hard reasons"; this position had the support of 30.3 percent of the sample. "Soft reasons" characterized the conditional acceptance of abortion under item 3 and were chosen by 20 percent of the individuals surveyed. This distribution shows pro-lifers as a small minority and none of the other groups with a clear majority.

Other polls reviewed by Sachett (1985) are in agreement with ours in showing the middle position as dominant. In fact, the results of the 1985 CBS News/New York Times poll are almost identical to ours (13 percent in favor of outlawing abortion, 38 percent in favor of keeping present laws, 45 percent supporting conditional abortions).

To infer from this information how Americans would side in a confrontation between pro-life and pro-choice supporters depends on which assumptions can be made about the middle groups. Lamanna (1984) predicts that the middle will side with the pro-choice group. First, accepting abortion even under restricted conditions indicates a willingness to depart from the dogma of fetus personhood. Second, since the present controversy is defined in terms of repudiating or supporting the Roe decision, those who recognize the need for abortion in certain circumstances would have to support the Roe decision (Calabresi and Bobbit 1978). Lamanna argues that this will be reinforced by the recognition that legal implementation of conditional abortions is practically impossible.

Blake and del Pinal (1981) make the opposite argument. In their view the will to subordinate abortion to restrictions expresses moral resistance to abortion on demand. In keeping with the ordinal ranking of the choices it could also be argued that supporters of hard restrictions might side with pro-lifers, while supporters of soft restrictions would go with pro-choice groups. Even assuming that those accepting abortion only under "hard reasons" might join forces with the pro-life group, the pro-choice side would still hold a clear majority. Findings reported by Sachett (1985) that the majority of people think that abortion is wrong (53 percent), but only half of those think it should be illegal, and most believe that outlawing it would be dangerous (92 percent), gives substantive indirect support to Lamanna's position. In this case the influence of the pro-life movement is clearly more a function of the dedication of its activists than a reflection of the scope of its support.

Religion

To the extent that personhood is central to the pro-life position and for the reasons discussed previously, Catholics are expected to be overrepresented among those rejecting abortion.

This expectation is not supported. Catholics are only slightly more likely to reject abortion than Protestants (14 percent vs. 12 percent) and less likely than Fundamentalists (20 percent). Non-Christians lead the way in support for abortion (64 percent).[1] The only difference between Protestants and Catholics is that more of the latter support restricting abortion for hard reasons (33 percent vs. 28 percent). Also, the largest difference by gender in the religion-abortion opinion is among Catholics—a greater proportion of women than men support abortion on demand (38 percent vs. 31 percent).[2]

Since denomination may not be a good indicator of religiosity (e.g., attachment to the organized Church and its teachings), the association of church attendance[3] and religion with position on abortion is examined. As Table 1 shows, frequency of church attendance varies directly with pro-life support for all religions, but the previous ranking is confirmed. That is, within the same level of attendance there is little difference between Catholics and Protestants; Fundamentalists are always the least and non-Christians the most supportive of abortion. In fact, among frequent church goers Catholics' support of abortion by choice is higher than the Protestants' (21 percent vs. 16 percent) and second only to the non-Christians'.

From this we conclude that, at the present time, the magisterium of the Catholic Church on the subject of the personhood of the fetus and prohibition of abortion does not affect its members any more than the more diffuse guidelines of the other Christian religions.

This stands in contrast to the forceful and highly visible pro-life positions taken by some of the Catholic bishops in the United States. For example, Cardinal O'Connor's overt conflict with Geraldine Ferraro on this issue, and his recent drive against Medicaid abortion in New York, received widespread media coverage.[4] In the public mind these statements are taken as representative of the position of Catholics in general. However, the opinions of Catholics on abortion shown in this study do not correspond to such expectations; instead, the opinions parallel their use of artificial contraception in spite of Church prohibitions (Moore 1973). The discrepancy between the official policy of the Church and the pragmatic adaptations of the majority of its members indicates an erosion in the hierarchical control of the centralized Roman Church. Vatican II and its impulse toward secularization best explain this situation.

Table 1

Opinion on Abortion by Religion and Church Attendance

	Pro-Life 1	Conditional Abortion— Hard Reasons 2	Conditional Abortion— Soft Reasons 3	Pro-Choice 4	N
Protestants					
High Church Attendance	24%	39%	21%	16%	202
Medium	12	30	29	28	260
Low	7	22	22	49	470
Fundamentalists					
High Attendance	31%	52%	6%	11%	134
Medium	15	38	28	18	110
Low	14	34	22	30	157
Catholics					
High Attendance	25%	41%	13%	21%	182
Medium	15	32	22	31	156
Low	6	29	15	50	224
NonChristians					
High Attendance	12%	25%	25%	38%	8
Medium	—	12	41	47	17
Low	2	10	14	74	57
N	277	626	402	672	1977
	14%	32%	20%	34%	

Contingency Coef. = .39
X^2 = 211.82
Sig < .000

Humanitarianism

As noted by the Callahans (1984a, 1984b), part of the ideology of the pro-life position is the conviction that moral principles should be enacted into law to protect the rights of the less powerful. The implicit assumption is that leaving vital issues to be resolved at the private level leads to the exploitation of the weakest members of society. Therefore, what is at issue in differentiating pro-life and pro-choice attitudes is not private support of humanitarian values but support for public enforcement of humanitarian values. The question to be examined is the

Table 2

Analysis of Variance of Humanitarian, Women Control,
and Conservatism Indicators by Opinion on Abortion

		Life	Hard R.	Soft R.	Choice	Sig. L.	Range	N
Humanitarian Indicators								
Environment	M	1.8 Δ	1.7	1.6	1.6	.08	1−3	799
	F	1.8	1.8 Δ	1.7	1.6	.002		985
Soc. Sec	M	1.5 Δ	1.6	1.6	1.6	.07	1−3	803
	F	1.3 Δ	1.5	1.4	1.4	.02		1030
Black's Position	M	1.8	1.6 Δ	2.0	1.8	.09	1−3	404*
	F	1.6	1.9 Δ	1.9	1.4	.006		507
Civil Rights	M	1.5	1.5	1.5	1.6	NS	1−3	392*
	F	1.5	1.6	1.3 Δ	1.1	.003		498
Women's Position	M	3.8	3.9	4.0	3.8	NS	1−7	808
	F	3.8	3.9	3.9 Δ	3.6	.06		1025
Job and Income	M	3.6 Δ	4.2	4.5	4.3	.009	1−7	840
	F	3.8	3.9	4.0	4.1	NS		1025
Gender Control Indictors								
Men Better Imp. Roles	M	3.3	3.7	4.0	4.1	.0000	1−7	925
	F	3.5	3.7	4.0	4.4	.0000		1227
Woman's Place At Home	M	2.5	3.0	3.3	3.7	.0000	1−7	847
	F	2.2	2.5	3.2	3.8	.0000		1025
Men Better at Politics	M	2.7	3.0	3.2	3.6	.0000	1−7	916
	F	2.6	2.8	3.3	3.6	.0000		1221
Conservative Beliefs								
Work Ethic	M	3.5	3.4 Δ	3.2	3.1	.0001	1−5	909
	F	3.5	3.3	3.3	3.2	.016		1192
Opportunity	M	3.6 Δ	3.4	3.2	2.3	.004	1−5	910
	F	3.4	3.4	3.5	3.5	NS		1200
Non-Equal	M	2.7	3.0	2.9 Δ	3.2	.001	1−5	899
	F	2.8	2.9 Δ	3.1 Δ	3.4			1169
Military Strength	M	2.9	3.0	2.9	3.3	.0000	1−5	880
	F	3.2	3.2	3.3 Δ	3.5	.0004		990

Lower scores indicate highest support for the item.
Δ=intergroup differences with higher than overall sig. level.
*Questions asked only of the post-election subsample.

consistency between support for government's protective role in relation to the fetus and the same role in relation to other vulnerable citizens (e.g., children, the sick, the poor, women, and minorities).

The questions selected to test this proposition elicited opinions about the appropriate role of the government in the areas crucial to child development (education and health) as well as in supporting services designed to improve the quality of life (environment, social security, and right to a job) or to protect the weakest in society (the poor, the unemployed, blacks, and women).[5]

Of all eleven measures used nearly half (five) showed no significant association with opinions about abortion. Support for greater government commitment in the areas of health, education, nutrition, job creation, and services to the poor was the same across the four groups. In all instances women were slightly more supportive of government intervention than men.

Table 2 shows the group means on the measures found to be associated with position on how abortion should be regulated. For the most part, the association is in the inverse direction predicted by the humanitarian hypothesis. That is, both men and women who favor free abortion or abortion with "soft" constraints are significantly more supportive of increases in federal spending to protect the environment, social security, and blacks than the other two groups. Two other measures (promotion of civil rights and policies designed to help the socioeconomic plight of women) vary in the same direction, but for women alone. In all, only in relation to one variable (government guarantee of jobs and minimum income) was the association, for men, in the predicted direction. That is, pro-life men believe that the state should increase its role in this area.

These findings are consistent with those reported by Granberg (1978) who, using 1975 National Opinion Research Corporation (NORC) data, found no association between humanitarian values and a pro-life position. However, the evidence in this study points to an inverse relationship: that is, humanitarian positions are more likely to be found among pro-choice supporters (Wuthnow 1985). Since both groups use humanitarian arguments to justify their position (protection of the child before birth vs. protection of the child after birth), these findings indicate greater coherence on support for the protective role of government among the pro-choice proponents. Prolife humanitarianism appears to be more issue specific. Its demand for government intervention in

Table 3

Spouses Education Inconsistency
and Pro-Choice Support

Male Respondents				
		Husband Less	Same	Husband More
Education	1		20	30
Level	2	23	30	38
of Wife	3	26	40	38
	4	40	53	—

N = 611 Cont Coeff. = .34 X^2 = 78.297 Sign.L. = .0000

Female Respondents				
		Wife More	Same	Wife Less
Education	1	15	22	—
Level of	2	34	32	20
Husband	3	62	50	28
	4	—	51	40

N = 612 Cont. Coeff. = .30 X^2 = 61627 Sign.L. = .0002

protecting the fetus appears, therefore, to be less related to public enforcement of quality of life protections and more to the imposition of a particular moral value.

The gender-specific associations are also interesting. Pro-choice women appear to be more sensitive to the plight of women and also more concerned about civil rights in general. This suggests that their position on abortion might be directly tied to their concern for women's rights. On the other hand, the single concern of pro-life men with income and job supports might reflect a self-interest rather than humanitarian attitude if those men are found to occupy predominantly low income, vulnerable positions. This possibility will be explored later in the chapter.

Control of Women

The expectation raised by this interpretation of opposition to abortion is that conservative views on the subject will go hand in hand with traditional views of gender differences. Agreement/disagreement with the following three statements was used to assess attitudes on female/male roles: "men are just better cut out than women for important positions in society," "women's place is in the home," "most men are better suited emotionally for politics than are most women."

All items are significantly associated with opinion on abortion in the predicted direction. The more conservative the stance on abortion, the greater the support for the traditional private/public dichotomy of gender roles. Inspection of means and significance levels in Table 2 also indicates that the association is stronger for women than men. Prolife and pro-choice women respondents hold more consistent opinions about women's role than do men. This greater within-group agreement is to be expected; abortion is clearly an issue of greater immediate relevance for women than men. According to these data, the "control of women" proposition appears to be valid.

An extension of the control perspective proposes that status inconsistency in marriage favoring the wife exacerbates men's need for control of women (Hornung et al. 1981). In these situations one would predict that men would oppose abortion more strongly than in egalitarian marriages or marriages in which status inconsistency favors men. As shown in Table 3, within each educational level men are most conservative when less educated than their wives and most liberal when they have higher education. However, this associational pattern is true for female respondents as well. They are more conservative when their husbands are relatively more educated and less so when they themselves have a higher level of education. It appears, therefore, that for both genders, a position of status inferiority is associated with a pro-life stance and a position of relative superiority with pro-choice support.

This finding fits better a "fear of change" than a "control of women" explanation. An anti-abortion position seems to be related to a sense of lower control vis-à-vis one's marital partner regardless of sex. The arguments given by pro-life activists in Luker's (1984) study can also be interpreted from this point of view. They claim that abortion, rather than giving more power to women, fosters irresponsibility in men. This perspective makes sense for women who feel dependent on men and see children as a means of strengthening their ties to them through demands of sexual responsibility and support rights.

Normative Self-justification

In her analysis of the influence that the abortion issue had on women's lives, Luker (1984: 194–201) identified two major factors demanding different validating normative positions: number of children and commitment to work. The first was associated with a pro-life stance, the second with pro-choice.

We find that male pro-life supporters tend to have more children than other groups but that there is no significant difference in number of children among women with different opinions on abortion. As shown in Table 4, although housewives tend to support abortion by choice less than women in the labor market (25 percent vs. 40 percent), the same low levels of support were found for disabled and retired women (24 percent). Men whose spouses are housewives tend to be somewhat more liberal, although the distribution pattern of abortion opinions is similar. It appears, therefore, that being house-bound is the important circumstance rather than the housewife role proper. The extent to which the position on abortion is a result of adjustment to prior choices (of having a large family or going to work) appears to be uncertain from this evidence.

Fear of Change

This hypothesis has two components, both based on the assumption that abortion is perceived as a force of modernization and social change. First, certain demographic characteristics are assumed to be associated with' fear of change and therefore with opposition to abortion. Second, resistance to abortion is expected to be associated with resistance to a series of other social changes, as an expression of a desire for stability (conservatism).

Table 4 presents the associations between certain demographic variables (age, income, education, growing up locality) and position on abortion. All of these associations are significant and in the expected direction. Those opposing abortion tend to be older, less educated, poorer, and more often raised in a nonurban environment than those supporting abortion.

Four indices (constructed on the basis of the results of the factor analysis of 14 opinion items)[6] were used to test the traditionalist hypothesis. The factors on which the indices were built conveyed four belief dimensions: work ethic, opportunity, right to equality, and national military strength. Support for the work ethic, belief in the open opportunities of the American society, and commitment to national military superiority are interpreted as representative of traditional American values. Right to equality, on the other hand, is interpreted as antithetical to such values because of its socialist implications and is therefore taken as a negative indicator of conservatism.

The results shown in Table 2 are mixed. Egalitarianism and antimilitarism are, as expected, more common among pro-choice than pro-life groups. However, the same is true of the traditional values on work ethic and belief on social opportunity. Prolife supporters appear to believe less in the work ethic and in the availability of opportunities in this society than those more accepting of abortion. If the validity of the four indicators of American values is accepted, then we have to conclude that a pro-choice position cannot be labeled un-American. It is interesting to note that while pro-lifers are anti-egalitarian, they also believe less than any other group in the all-American values that work leads to success and theirs is the land of opportunity. Even when the traditional values have eroded (possibly due to experiences with economic failure), a new social order (favoring a more egalitarian economic distribution) is rejected. In conjunction, these attitudes express fear of change under vulnerable circumstances. Egalitarianism can be perceived as a threat to those with scarce resources since it implies the economic integration (and therefore competition) of previously excluded groups (the poor, women, blacks).

Summary

Only the demographic part of the "fear of change" and "the control of women" propositions are clearly validated by the bivariate analysis. Support for the normative self-justification and for the traditional ideology explanations is mixed. And no evidence is found that contemporary pro-life positions in America reflect predominantly Catholic beliefs, or that those opposing abortion tend to support a more humanitarian society than those defending it.

This exercise helps clarify the validity of characteristics

Table 4

Number of Children, Work Status, and
Demographics by Position on Abortion

	Pro-Life		Hard Reasons		Soft Reasons		Pro-Choice		Sign.L.		N	
	M	F	M	F	M	F	M	F	M	F	M	F
Self Justification												
Mean # of Children	1.9	1.9	1.9	1.7	1.7	1.8	1.5	1.7	.0000	NS	936	1235
Work Status %									.05	.0000	632	1234
Working	10*	10	31*	27	22*	22	32*	40				
Retired/												
Disabled	21	22	42	39	15	15	23	24				
Housewife	14	19	34	38	23	15	28	28				
Student	22	19	11	34	44	4	22	42				
Demographics												
Mean Age	46.9	47.9	45.6	47.6	42.6	43.9	41.7	40.5	.004	.0000	936	1224
Place Grew Up %									.0000	.0000	932	1226
Farm/Country	18	22	39	44	21	15	22	18				
Small City	11	12	27	33	25	23	37	32				
Md/Lg City	11	14	25	23	19	17	45	47				
Very Lg Cty	6	1	15	21	15	15	64	63				
Education									.0000	.0000	932	1232
< Hsch	23	23	37	43	16	13	24	21				
High Sch	11	14	33	34	22	21	34	32				
Some Post HS	7	7	23	25	27	20	42	44				
College+	7	7	19	20	20	20	54	53				
Income									.0000	.0000	858	1073
<6,999	27	22	27	39	11	17	35	21				
7,000–21,997	11	15	37	35	19	17	33	33				
22,000–49,999	10	9	26	27	25	23	39	42				
50,000+	6	4	22	19	23	14	49	62				

*These columns refer to the work status of the wives of male respondents.

attributed to supporters and opponents of abortion. It also permits a concrete operationalization of various perspectives and subsequent investigation of the relationship of each indicator with position on abortion. Conclusions therefore can be traced to their empirical referent.

Bivariate analysis, however, does not address the real possibility that the several independent variables might be associated with each other and, when taken together, might affect each other's association with the dependent variable.

The perspectives covered in the literature review, while emphasizing certain interpretations, contain for the most part multivariate arguments. For example, Luker's (1984) work suggests that various dimensions coalesce in the characterization of activists of neither side of the abortion issue. Demographic characteristics, religion, and normative self-justification are part of her analysis. On the other hand, in the summary of their study the Callahans (1984) emphasize the complex interactions that go into opting for or against abortion.

Reviewing our findings with this in mind, a series of new questions can be posed: Can religious affiliation and number of children demarcate pro-lifers from other groups? If we control for demographic characteristics, would the association between fundamentalism and position on abortion hold? Do the indicators of "control of women" vary inversely with education, and income with conservatism? If so, which dimension of each pair is more strongly associated with position on abortion?

In the pursuit of a more exact description of the groups holding different opinions on abortion, we turn to multivariate analysis.

INTERACTIVE ANALYSIS

THAID was chosen as the multivariate strategy congruent with the goal of identifying group characteristics. This program is designed for the sequential analysis of nominal scale dependent variables. Based on Delta as a criterion statistic, the data are sequentially partitioned into two groups determined by the independent variables. The criterion selects a hierarchy of split groups whose probability distribution on the dependent variable differ maximally from the original group and therefore from each other (Morgan and Messenger 1973). Figures 1 and 2 show sets of male and female subgroups, characterized by the terms of the independent variables, whose distributions of opinions on abortion are maximally different.[7]

For both males and females, church attendance (the first split criteria) is the most important variable. However, the maximum difference is found in the final groups which result from the interaction between church attendance, demographic characteristics (education, background, and/or income), and single indicators of control (gender equality), self-justification (number of children), and humanitarianism (job guarantee). The distribution of opinions on abortion for each final group is given at the bottom of Figures 1 and 2. Final groups are characterized by varying attributes (defined by the independent variables) and have opinions on abortion which are distinct from the general distribution. These distinctive opinions are boxed in and are the basis for the relative classification of the groups as pro-life, pro-choice, or conditional. This means that each final group shares a given set of characteristics and supports a given position on abortion significantly more than any other group.

Inspection of the results from the male subsample reveals that the greatest support for abortion is among groups who have low church attendance combined either with having been raised in an urban environment or belief in women's equality (G5 and G6). Traditional values towards women shown in Groups 14 and 15 decrease the support for free abortions especially among high-income respondents. Conversely, the groups closer to the pro-life position (G10 and G13) are frequentchurch goers, are disillusioned with the work ethic, and either have large families or are not very educated. High education and a small family (G12) or belief in the work ethic (G9) make for a more tolerant attitude. Church attendance appears, however, to be the crucial variable differentiating between pro-life and pro-choice supporters. So, in spite of sharing tradition prone characteristics (low income, traditional gender attitudes, and non-urban background), nonchurch goers in Group 14 are much less in favor of pro-life (5 percent) than the church participants in Group 10 (19 percent).

In this descriptive analysis elements of different propositions play a role in characterizing men holding different opinions about abortion: religiosity, fear of change (demographic background; urban/nonurban), normative self justification (number of children), and control (gender equality). The same ordered pattern is, however, not found in the female subsample. For example, the three groups most supportive of free abortion (11, 15, and 19) have different profiles. One group has rather libertarian characteristics, with low church attendance, medium to high education, and not much in support of job and income guarantees (G11). The other two groups are made up of rather well educated women with metropolitan background who, in spite of medium to high church attachment, are still overwhelmingly pro-choice (G15 and 17). A nonmetropolitan background (G16) makes women more willing to impose hard conditions on the right to abortion.

Female groups leaning to the pro-life position are also very diverse. Group 4 is not very involved with the church but feels quite strongly that job and income guarantees should exist. The other two show high church attendance and have either a rural background and are poor or have a metropolitan background and are uneducated (G12, 14). A high income appears to have the effect of moderating the pro-life position for women with a nonurban background (G13).

The findings are more clearcut for men than women. Male supporters of abortion can be described as nonreligious, urban, educated, and holding liberal opinions. Those more favorable to the pro-life position tend to have the opposite characteristics. At the same time, we find women at both extremes of the spectrum of the

Figure 1

THAID Tree--Male Sample
Dep. Var.=Opinion on Abortion

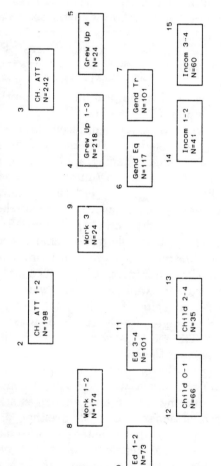

Final Group Characteristics

	Prolife 1	Hard Conditions 2	Soft Conditions 3	ProChoice 4	N
	9.1	29.3	23.9	37.7	440
	--	--	4.2	95.8	24
	5.1	17.9	22.2	54.7	117
	--	29.2	25.0	45.2	24
	19.2	47.9	15.1	17.8	73
	9.1	22.7	42.4	25.8	66
	17.1	48.6	20.0	14.3	35
	4.8	39.0	12.2	143.9	41
	10.0	30.0	35.0	25.0	60

Group 5 - Lo Church Att., Metropolitan
Group 6 - Loc Ch. Att., Nonmetrop., Gend. Eq.
Group 9 - Hi Ch. Att., Hi Wk Ethic
Group 10 - Hi Ch. Att., Lo Wk Ethic, Lo Ed.
Group 12 - Hi Ch. Att., Hi Wk Ethic, Hi Ed., Lo Child
Group 13 - Hi Ch. Att., Hi Wk Etic, Hi Ed., Hi Child
Group 14 - Lo Ch. Att., Nonmetr., Gend. Trad. Lo Inc.
Group 15 - Lo Ch. Att., Nonmertr., Gend. Trad., Hi Inc.

Cumulative Variance Expl. 13.4%

Figure 2

THAID Tree--Female Sample
Dep. Var.=Opinion on Abortion

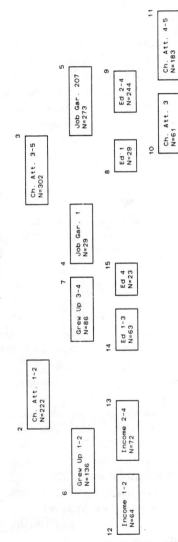

Final Group Characteristics

	Prolife 1	Hard Conditions 2	Soft Conditions 3	Prochoice 4	N
	9.5	25.9	20.8	43.7	524
	20.6	31.0	31.0	17.2	29
	3.4	41.4	10.3	44.8	29
	2.7	10.9	20.8	65.8	183
	20.3	51.6	9.4	18.7	64
	11.1	36.1	29.2	23.6	72
	19.0	33.3	14.3	33.3	63
	17.4	8.7	4.3	69.5	23
	--	26.3	50.0	23.6	38
	4.3	13.0	13.0	69.6	23

Group 4 - Lo Ch. Att., Hi Job Gar.
Group 8 - Lo Ch. Att., M-L Job Gar.
Group 11 - V. Lo Ch. Att., M-L Job Gar., M-H Ed.
Group 12 - Hi Ch. Att., Nonurban, Lo Inc
Group 13 - Hi Ch. Att., Nonurb., M-H Inc.
Group 14 - Hi Ch. Att., Urban, Lo Ed.
Group 15 - Hi Ch. Att., Urban, M-H Ed.
Group 16 - Med. Ch. Att., M-L Job G., M-H Ed., Nurb
Group 17 - Med. Ch. Att., M-L Job G., M-H Ed., Urb

Cumulative Variance Expl. = 17.4%

abortion issue who are religious and nonreligious, more and less educated, with humanitarian and traditional values.

CONCLUSION

It is tempting for a pro-choice sympathizer to conclude that pro-life proponents tend to be old, poor, noneducated, nonurban, prejudiced against women and minorities, and devout members of fundamentalist churches. The associations found between position on abortion and demographic, religious, humanitarian, and women control indicators are consistent with such an inference. Any contradictions of Luker's and the Callahans' reports can be attributed to sampling differences. While these authors studied the leaders and the intelligentsia of each movement, I examined the opinions of the general public. This study describes the characteristics of people to whom the messages of each movement might appeal, not of those, such as Dr. Wilke, responsible for the creation, justification, and interpretation of these messages.

Together, the demographic attributes of the pro-life group describe circumstances of limited opportunity. It could be argued that repudiation of social change (in terms of opening opportunities to other groups—women and minorities) and attachment to fundamentalist churches function as protective devices for people who feel rather powerless. The results of the multivariate analysis lend some support to this interpretation. It is of interest, however, to note that the most salient characteristic of male pro-lifers is their church involvement. Other "traditional" correlates, such as rural background, support for unequal gender roles, and poverty, do not produce nearly as high a level of opposition to abortion without church involvement. This suggests that the abortion issue does not automatically fit into a conservative world view unless it is redefined by moral entrepreneurs (Becker 1963). The churches, therefore, appear to play an important role in the symbolic transformation of abortion into a conservative moral issue.

The descriptive profiles of women holding various positions with respect to abortion call for a more complex interpretation. Of special interest are the deviant subgroups (by comparison to men) among pro-life and pro-choice supporters. Not only groups of women highly favorable to the pro-life position reported little or no religious activity, but also high church involvement did not inhibit other groups of supporting overwhelmingly abortion on demand. In sum, church attachment does not have the same pervading influence in defining the abortion issue for women as it has for men. Even among Catholics, significantly more women than men support abortion.

This evidence suggests (although it does not prove) that in the matter of abortion, women are less likely than men to submit to organizational definitions of morality. This might be interpreted as a reflection of the different gender process of moral development as expounded by Miller (1976) and Gilligan (1982). Certainly, the finding that some women committed to humanitarian values take a pro-life stance in spite of religious indifference is consistent with this explanation.

In addition, male/female differences might be specific to this issue. As Petchesky (1984: 354) points out, abortion is intrinsically a women's issue. Only women can get pregnant, therefore abortion has for them an existential meaning that cannot be shared by men, nor as easily defined (and regulated) by abstract principles.

Since the abortion debate is ultimately centered around the fetus's personhood—a question of judgment and value—I have argued that the position people take on this issue depends on how it fits into their dominant value structure. In general terms, anti-abortion positions have been identified with conservative/traditional world views in spite of the fact that for most of the American history abortion has been considered legitimate. The creation of abortion in the nineteenth century as a moral problem required the entrepreneurship of physicians, church leaders, and eugenic planners (Luker 1984: 11-39). The findings of the study suggest that in our time organized churches play an important role in perpetuating abortion as moral deviance and integrating this definition into a conservative ideology based on fear of change. In other words, churches act as moral entrepreneurs.

According to Becker (1963: 147-64) moral entrepreneurship can be identified by three characteristics: (1) leading crusaders who are fervent, righteous, and believe their mission to be holy; (2) groups that join the true believers because they see in the movement potential to promote their own interests; (3) imposition of morals by a dominant group on others less favorably placed in the social structure.

Listening to Cardinal O'Connor in St. Patrick's Cathedral denouncing abortion as the worst of sins or seeing the children's candle vigil organized in the archdiocese of Chicago to save the unborn child makes it easy to identify the first characteristic mentioned by Becker. On the other hand, examination of the messages of the moral majority linking abortion to family dissolution, economic disaster, and communist takeover (Brozan 1982) and information on their long-term political plans (Danzig 1982) give evidence of the second characteristic of moral enterprise. Finally, knowledge that the Church's hierarchy and the political leadership of the radical right are exclusively male and their organizations unambiguously supportive of the patriarchal order buttresses the interpretation that their goal is to impose a pro-life morality on women. The finding that males appear more accepting of that message as it is filtered through religious organizations is understandable from this perspective.

This scenario reflects more than the usual gender power differentials. Since abortion is intrinsically and intimately a women's issue—given their exclusive capacity for pregnancy—externally mandated prescriptions on the subject imply a dehumanization of women by interfering with their most immediate personal decisions (Harding 1984). Organized infringement of women's personal rights in this area is easily recognized when made for eugenic or "social engineering" purposes (e.g., sterilization and forced abortion of Jewish women under the Third Reich or in mainland China). However, more subtle control through creation of moral deviance with the intent of controlling reproduction through public policy has exactly the same meaning. In both instances it can lead to the worst form of alienation for women—self-alienation. The evidence reported in this study, that groups of women appear to resist organized pressures from either side, is a hopeful note for the cause of women's personhood.

Notes

[1]Religious affiliation was coded into four categories: Protestant (reformation era and pietistic); Catholics (Roman and Greek); Fundamentalist (Neo-Fundamentalist, Mormon, and Jehovah's Witnesses); Non-Christian (Jewish, Non-Judeo Christian).

[2]Fleming (1984) reports a similar distribution in a study based on National Opinion Research Corporation (NORC) data.

[3]Respondents were classified as having high attendance if they reported going to church more than once a month. Middle attendance included from monthly to more than annual frequency, and low attendance was annual or less.

[4]It is interesting to note that both of these campaigns had as targets members of the Catholic Church (Vice Presidential candidate Ferraro and Governor Cuomo) who publicly disagreed with the Church's position.

[5]The items used were the following: Government should provide fewer services in areas such as education and health (agreement/disagreement) scale 1–7; Government should see that every person has a job and a good job and a good standard of life (same scale); Government should make an effort to improve the social and economic position of women (same scale); If you had a say in making up the federal budget this year, which programs would you like to see increased (1), decreased (3), kept about the same (2)?—environment, public schools, Social Security, Food Stamps, Medicare, job creation, assistance to blacks. Do you think that civil rights leaders are trying to push too fast (1), are going too slow (3), or are moving about right (2)?

[6]The items included in each index were the following: Work Ethic—hard work does not guarantee success; people who do not do well work as hard as those who do; any person who is willing to work hard has a good chance of succeeding. Opportunity—a problem with this country is that we don't give everyone an equal chance; if people were treated more equally in this country we would have many fewer problems. Equality—we have gone too far pushing equal rights in this country; this country would be better off if we worried less about how equal people are; it is not really that big a problem if some people have more of a chance in life than others. Strength—do you think we should spend much less money on military defense or should it be greatly increased?; do you think we should try to cooperate more with Russia or we should be much tougher in our dealings with Russia?

[7]The program was set to stop when the next split would account for less than 1 percent of the variance. Independent variables not present in Figures 1 and 2 fall into this category.

References

Abernethy, V., 1984. "Children, Personhood and a Pluralistic Society," in S. Callahan and D. Callahan (eds.) Abortion: Understanding the Differences. New York: Plenum Press, pp. 117–36.

Aeschylus, 1966. The Oresteia. Translated by R. Fagles. New York: Viking Press.

Aronowitz, S., 1973. False Promises: The Shaping of American Working Class Consciousness. New York: McGraw-Hill.

Becker, H., 1963. Outsiders. New York: The Free Press.

Bem, D.J., 1970. Beliefs, Attitudes and Human Affairs. Belmont, CA: Brooks/Cole.

Blake, J. and J.H. Del Pinal, 1979. "Predicting Polar Attitudes toward Abortion in the United States," in J.T. Burtchaell, C.S.C. (ed.) Abortion Parley. Kansas City, MO: Andrews and McMeal, pp. 29–56.

Brozan, N., 1982. "Parley Asserts U.S. Undercuts Family," New York Times (July 28): A18.

Calabresi, G. and G.P. Bobbit, 1978. Tragic Choices. New York: Norton.

Callahan, S. and D. Callahan, 1984a. "Breaking Abortion Stereotypes," Commonweal (October 5): 520–23.

Callahan, S. and D. Callahan (eds.), 1984b. Abortion: Understanding Differences. New York: Plenum Press.

Curran, F.J., 1954. "Religious Implications," in H. Rosen (ed.) Therapeutic Abortion: Medical, Psychiatric, Legal, Anthropological and Religious Considerations. New York: Julian Press, pp. 153–65.

Daly, M., 1978. Gyn-Ecology: The Metaethics of Radical Feminism. Boston, MA: Beacon.

Danzig, D., 1982. "The Radical Right and the Rise of the Fundamentalist Minority," Commentary 33: 291–98.

Degler, C., 1980. At Odds: Women and Family in America From the Revolution to the Present. New York: Oxford, University Press.

Editorial, 1976. Commonweal 2 (January): 4.

Eisenstein, Z., 1984. Feminism and the State: Reagan Neoconservatism and Revisionist Feminism. New York: Monthly Review Press.

Festinger, L., 1964. Conflict Decision and Dissonance. Stanford, CA: Stanford University Press.

Figueira-McDonough, J., 1985. "Gender, Race and Class: Differences in Levels of Feminist Orientation," Journal of Applied Behavioral Science 21, 2: 121–42.

Freeman, B. and W.A. Gamson, 1979. "Utilitarian Logic in the Resources Mobilization Perspective," pp. 8–44 in M. Zald and J.D. McCarthy (eds.) The Dynamics of Social Movements. Cambridge, MA: Winthrop Publishers.

Friedman, L.M., 1977. Law and Society: An Introduction. Englewood Cliffs, NJ: Prentice Hall.

Gilligan, C., 1982. In a Different Voice: Psychological Theory and Women's Development. Cambridg, MA: Harvard University Press.

Glover, J., 1985. "Matters of Life and Death," The New York Review of Books (May 30): 19–23.

Granberg, D., 1978. "Pro Life or Reflection of Conservative Ideology," Sociology and Social Research 62, 3: 414–27.

Grisez, G., 1970. Abortion: The Myths, the Realities and the Arguments. New York: Corpus Books.

Harding, S., 1984. "Beneath the Surface of the Abortion Dispute: Are Women Fully Human?" in S. Callahan and D. Callahan (eds.) Abortion: Understanding the Differences. New York: Plenum Press.

Hornung, C.A., B.C. McCullough and T. Sugimoto, 1981. "Status Relationships in Marriage: Risk Factors in Spouse Abuse," Journal of Marriage and the Family 43: 675–92.

Huser, R., 1942. The Crime of Abortion in Canon Law. Washington, DC: Catholic University Press.

Kenrick, F., 1841. Theologiae Moralis. Philadelphia: Eugenium Commiskey, pp. 110–13.

Lamanna, M.A., 1984. "Social Science and Ethical Issues: The Policy Implications of Poll Data on Abortion," in S. Callahan and D. Callahan (eds.) Abortion: Understanding the Differences. New York: Plenum Press, pp. 1–23.

Littlewood, T.B., 1977. The Politics of Population Control. South Bend, IN: University of Notre Dame Press, pp. 148–49.

Luker, K., 1984. Abortion and the Politics of Motherhood. Berkeley, CA: University of California Press.

Miller, J.B., 1976. Toward a New Psychology of Women. Boston, MA: Beacon.

Miller, W.E. and the National Election Studies, 1985. American National Election Study, 1984: Pre- and Post-Election Survey File. Ann Arbor, MI: ICPSR, Institute for Social Research, The University of Michigan.

Mohr, J.C., 1978. Abortion in America: The Origins and Evolution of National Policy. New York: Oxford University Press, pp. 147–70.

Moore, M., 1973. Death of a Dogma? The American Catholic Clergy's View of Contraception. Chicago: Community and Family Study Center, University of Chicago.

Morgan, J.N. and R.C. Messenger, 1973. THAID, A Sequential Analysis Program for the Analysis of Nominal Scale

Dependent Variables. Ann Arbor, MI: Institute for Social
Research, The University of Michigan.

Muller, C., 1978. "Insurance Coverage of Abortion, Contraception
and Sterilization," Family Planning Perspectives 10 (March/
April): 71–77.

Nathanson, C.A. and M.H. Becker, 1977. "The Influence of
Physician's Attitudes on Abortion Performance, Patient
Management and Professional Fees," Family Planning
Perspectives 9 (July/August): 158–63.

Nix, C., 1986. "Catholics Open Drive Against Abortion," New York
Times (January 20): 15.

Noonan, J.T., 1966. Contraceptives: A History of its Treatment by
the Catholic Theologians and Canonists. Cambridge, MA:
Harvard University Press, pp. 86–90.

Penning, J.M., 1984. "Changing Partisanship and Issue Stands
Among American Catholics." Paper delivered at the Annual
Meeting of the American Political Science Association,
Washington, DC.

Petchesky, R.P., 1984. Abortion and Woman's Choice: The State,
Sexuality and Reproductive Freedom. Boston, MA:
Northeastern University Press.

Rich, A., 1980. "Compulsory Heterosexuality and Lesbian
Existence," Signs 5 (Summer): 69–71.

Sachett, V., 1985. "Between Pro-Life and Pro-Choice," Public
Opinion (April/May): 53–55.

Tilly, C., 1964. The Vendée. Cambridge, MA: Harvard University
Press, 1964.

Vidich, A.J., 1958. Small Town in Mass Society: Class, Power and
Religion. Garden City, NY: Doubleday.

Weyrich, P., 1979. "Building the Moral Majority," Conservative
Digest 5 (August): 18–19.

Wuthnow, R., 1985. "American Democracy and the
Democratization of American Religion." Paper presented at
the Annual Meetings of the American Sociological
Association, August, Washington, DC.

CHAPTER 4

WOMEN AS LIVING LABORATORIES: THE NEW REPRODUCTIVE TECHNOLOGIES

Robyn Rowland

> To possess the end and yet not be responsible for the means, to grasp the fruit while disavowing the tree, to escape being told the cost until someone else has paid it irrevocably: this is...the chief hypocrisy of our time.
>
> Cahn 1962: 368–72

Development of the new reproductive technologies in Australia has been moving at a rapid pace. Australia has now produced the first child from a frozen embryo and recently produced the first twin born a considerable amount of time after her sibling because she was kept in a frozen embryo bank (McIntosh 1985). These kinds of advances were at one time kept away from the public eye. But in May 1984 my resignation from the Chair of a Research Co-ordination Committee at the major hospital involved in reproductive technology in Australia triggered off a public debate which is still continuing (Horin 1984; Whitlock 1984; West 1984; Sydney Morning Herald 1984).

I resigned from the committee, which was to coordinate the social and psychological research on donor programs at the Queen Victoria Hospital where the Monash University team worked under the leadership of Professor Carl Wood, for a number of reasons. First, it had become clear that the welfare of the patients was not a primary concern of the medical team involved as there were no adequate counseling facilities and no consideration of the social implications of their work. Second, they were about to introduce a new technique, "flushing," which I will discuss later in the chapter, without informing the public of this new move, within a climate of growing community anxiety and scrutiny. And third, the manipulation of women and their bodies on these generally unsuccessful programs was alarming. The technique itself has specific dangers for women, but also means a change in the way that children are created. In addition, as I became more critical, the independence of my own research into artificial insemination came under threat. The public outcry in Australia over the rapid pace at which this work is moving has led each state government to establish a committee of investigation with respect to reproductive technologies, some of which have already reported. In addition, the Family Law Council of Australia set up a committee chaired by Justice Asche, of which I was a member, to look at the implications for creating children within these technological "advances." This report has now been tabled by the Attorney General in the Federal Parliament, and the Federal Government is moving on these issues. At the same time, however, the researchers, led particularly by the Monash University team, have forged ahead and commercialized their enterprise under a company called "IVF Australia."

In Australia generally there is active debate about the social implications of these new technologies. For the first time human beings are now able to create other human beings without sexual intercourse of any kind. In England the British government set up the Warnock Committee to investigate these issues. Apart from a bill banning commercial surrogacy, the British Parliament has yet to legislate. In the United States of America, however, there is no uniform approach to these issues. Some states have specific pieces of legislation, but in general commercial enterprises have taken up this technology and are making large amounts of money out of it. This is particularly so in the area of surrogate motherhood, which I will discuss later.

During this discussion about these new technologies it is important to remember a number of factors. First, it is impossible to withdraw the technologies once they are in place. People find it very difficult to deny access to the use of a technology once it has been established and a need created. And indeed, once commercial enterprises are involved, it is nearly impossible to take a product or a process off the market. Second, within this area there is a rationale for all the technologies which will be discussed. There are, for example, very interesting rationales for the development of the cloning of human beings. But a rationale does not necessarily mean that we should go ahead with technologies if they have major detrimental implications for human society. Third, it is important to stress that we are not talking about science fiction here. If, for example, a person had indicated to me a year ago that researchers would be putting a baboon heart into a three week old baby, I would have recoiled in horror and said that no ethics committee would allow such a thing to happen. Yet in North America the famous Baby Fae case has already gone ahead, with the child dying after the process. There are indications in this instance that more such experimentation will be carried out.

It is important also to understand that we are dealing here with a process of interlocking but separate technologies. We cannot take in vitro fertilization technology and look at it in isolation, as it has implications which lead us toward genetic engineering. Then again, each technology does have a different basis and also different implications. One thing that they do have in common is that they are leading us essentially to change the face of humanity. We are now involved in processes which create children outside of a sexual relationship. Though many may see this as a liberating force, a clear analysis of the power dimensions involved, particularly for women, indicates that it leads to a loss rather than a liberation. In addition, we have yet to assess the impact of knowledge of their conception on the children who are created through these processes. They do not remain children all their lives but become adults with very firm opinions about how they should have been conceived and what the responsibilities of our society were to ensure, for example, that they had access to information about their biological heritage. Finally, it cannot be stressed enough that we are <u>not</u> dealing with <u>medical issues</u>, but we are dealing here with <u>social issues</u>. It is not good enough for scientists to act as if they are above or beyond the strictures of a society in which they live and to whom they are accountable.

In particular, it is wise for women to look very carefully at these technologies and their implications for the future of women as a social group. Although many Western middle-class women now have a choice about child rearing, and in fact some of them chose not to have children, for many women the world over motherhood is a power base through which they ensure their existence. I have argued elsewhere that if we continue in this forward rush of reproductive technology, we may ensure that the fragility of women's power is worn to gossamer and finally fades (Rowland 1985a, 1985b, 1985c, 1986a). Much as we turn from consideration of a nuclear aftermath, we turn from seeing a future where children are neither borne nor born of woman, or where women are forced to bear only sons and to slaughter their fetal daughters. Chinese and Indian women are already trudging this path. It is essential to understand that we are not dealing with a technology restricted only to Western cultures but that women the world over will be affected by these technologies just as they have been affected by contraception and abortion. The future of women as a group may be at stake, and we need to ensure that we have thoroughly considered all possibilities before endorsing a technology which leaves male-dominated culture to control not only birth but the very conception and procreation process itself.

CONTEXT OF THE DEVELOPMENT OF REPRODUCTIVE TECHNOLOGY

I will not discuss the development of artificial insemination by donor, which is a simple process by which sperm is inserted into the vagina of a woman who hopefully then becomes pregnant. This process was the beginning of the intervention of medicine into the area of conception, but it does not involve the technological interference which newer technologies involve. In vitro fertilization was the first technology which broke the relationship between intercourse and procreation. I will discuss this in detail later in the chapter, but here I want to consider in general the forces behind the development of these new technologies. Gena Corea, in her book The Mother Machine (1985), has clearly demonstrated the relationship between animal experimentation and human experimentation in this area. As she indicates, the movement has been from mice to rats to sheep to cows and then to women. The lesson that this now holds for us is that if we wish to look at the developments which may lie ahead for humans, we should take a very clear and deep look at the research being undertaken in the animal area.

The scientific ethic has clearly been part of the push in this area. Many writers have considered the male face of science with its stress on domination and control (Easlea 1981, 1982). The scientific ethic involves pushing the boundaries in the great race to acquire knowledge first. Corea (1985) has pointed out that much of the work in reproductive technology is couched in the language of the race track. In fact, many of the terms used indicate a certain desire to control women's reproduction in the same way that science desires to control nature. Researchers talk, for example, of "harvesting" and "grading" the eggs which are collected from a woman. Just as science has attempted to control the ecology and nature in general, it now tightens its grip on women's reproductive processes.

Scientific researchers working in this area are also motivated by the aura of wonder which surrounds this work and the kudos which can be gained. One example of this was an article on

Professor Carl Wood who leads the Monash team in Australia, titled "The Lonely Lifestyle of a Test Tube Hero" (Woodfall 1984). In Britain, Steptoe and Edwards have been described as the "fathers" of the new reproductive technology, and one of them was named father of the year (Sydney Sun Herald 1985). There is then a great patriarchal control involved in this work, and many of the researchers discuss their work as if they themselves were the fathers of the children created.

But researchers constantly cry that their motivation is to "help the infertile" and that "women want it." In fact, their claim to be helping the infertile is a dubious one when we come to look at the results of their work, which we will do later in this chapter. In vitro fertilization technology for example, is singularly unsuccessful. In addition, in Australia the Monash team has now entered into a commercial enterprise called IVF Australia, which makes their claim to be purely helping the infertile seem laughable. The argument that "women want it" has been intended to stop the debate among women about the political and power implications of the use of this technology. Critics of the technology worry that when they discuss the social implications of these technologies or attack the pace at which this work is going, they are seen to be right-wing or harsh with respect to the infertile. And finally, the scientific ethic itself involves a narrow laboratory tunnel vision: researchers just deal with human tissue. Many scientists talk about this problem in terms of research: they become so involved in dealing with a small part of the world it is impossible for them to extend their horizons and consider the social implications of their work.

PRONATALISM AND THE EXPERIENCE OF INFERTILITY

To understand the impact of infertility, we need to understand that we live within a society which says that it is good to have children. That is, one which has pronatalist values. Government policies can influence when, where, and how many children women may have and often associate child-bearing only with a marriage relationship. Socialization toward having children is very strong, and evidence of this abounds. The little girl who is encouraged to play with dolls is being prepared for motherhood. The exclamations of wonder whenever we see something young, vulnerable, and cuddly such as a kitten are also reinforcing the desire for children.

We can ask the question here: Why do people have children? There are many reasons why people have children, and most of them give rise to quite heated debate. Some people argue that there is a natural parenting instinct and particularly that there is a maternal instinct. Feminists have argued quite strongly that the maternal instinct does not exist as such and that women can choose to have children or not to have children if they are fertile. But leaving aside the question of a biological cause, which in fact cannot be either proved or disproved, we can look at the social factors which reinforce the decision to have children. Parenting marks a change in status from being a child to being an adult: a parent is seen as a mature person. In terms of development, psychological theories such as those of Erikson indicate that a stage of "generativity" is part of the development of an adult person. "Generativity" is a stage of development in which the adult person looks for a way to establish and guide the next generation; to feel themselves part of a generational process. There are many ways of expressing this sense of generativity, but most people see children as their means of doing so.

For women, the pressure to have children is strong because motherhood is a primary characteristic of their traditional role. Studies of couples who choose not to have children indicate the stress and pressure exerted, not just by social forces but by their own families to parent. There is also pressure exerted by the fact that people of the same age group or cohort are having children (Rowland 1982; Veevers 1980).

Many people marry on the assumption that they will have children and create a family. Some people have children in order to solidify their relationship. Others also experience a sense of power through childbearing and childrearing, which many individuals find difficult to experience in any other way. And finally, many people have children because they like them!

It is in this context of pronatalism that infertility becomes problematical for some people. The knowledge of one's infertility is a dramatic shock to the individual because we all assume we are fertile and, in fact, protect ourselves against that fertility showing itself at unwanted times. The testing processes to detect whether an individual is infertile and what the cause of that infertility is can be extremely intrusive and exhausting. It can take from six months to six years for a person to be finally diagnosed as infertile. In many instances where the woman is in a heterosexual relationship, she is assumed to be the infertile partner, and many tests are carried out on her before the man is tested (Eck-Menning 1977; Mazor 1979: 101–12). This can lead to problems within the relationship when it is discovered, for example, that it is the male who is infertile. He may feel that there is something more unusual about a man's infertility than a woman's infertility, and the woman may feel resentment that the assumption was that she was "at fault" and tested first.

Mazor (1974) has outlined the testing processes for infertility for women and men. The tests are more extensive, difficult, and painful for a woman. Mazor (1979: 104) describes the processes as "assaultive" in nature, as people are required to "expose their bodies for tests and procedures" and to "expose the intimate details of their sexual lives and their motivations for pregnancy." The length of these testing procedures can also lead to an obsessive focusing of attention on the body and its "malfunctioning." They involve the individual or the couple in a cycle of raised hopes, despair, and frustration as they move from test to test in the hope that the infertility will be cured (Pfeffer and Woollett 1983).

The experience of infertility has been called a "life crisis." Part of that crisis comes from the knowledge that something over which the person thought they had control was in fact not within their control. Many women particularly feel frustrated and resentful if they have been using, for example, the pill or an IUD for seven years for no good reason. The lack of control that a person feels is very important because it affects the self-image and self-esteem. The infertile persons loss of personal control over their lives, which they now experience, can often create a negative self-image for them of being "barren" and a "wasteland" which will not regenerate. Their self-image and self-esteem are severely battered. Many people also experience feelings of punishment about having had many sexual relationships. Some women feel very guilty about having had an abortion and may feel that they are being punished for that act by infertility. Others can feel that it is a religious punishment given out by God. This expresses itself in a harsh community attitude that God meant infertile couples not to have children.

The reactions to the news of infertility have been likened to those of the grief experience after the death of a loved one. The death here is symbolic: it is the death of the child or the family the woman hoped to achieve. The grief experience involves a number of phases over a period of time: disbelief, anger, guilt, and one hopes resolution (Schultz 1978). Initial reactions to the news of infertility are usually disbelief followed by anger and even rage. Concomitant with anger is guilt. A husband may feel guilty because he cannot help his partner produce a child. The wife may feel guilty because she cannot reproduce. Or a wife who is infertile may feel guilty because she cannot produce the desired child (Mazor 1979; Avidan and Avidan 1976).

Because of this range of emotions and feelings, problems can develop within a relationship, and it is clear that many people need someone to talk with and to assist them to come to an acceptance of their infertility. It is for this reason that new legislation on infertility in the state of Victoria requires that counseling be available for infertile people. Couples who are participating in new reproductive technology programs, who are themselves infertile, point out that counseling is needed by people like them at the point when the person is told of their infertility and not after she or he has entered a reproductive technology program. Some of the issues which need to be resolved through counseling are: a reinforcement of the individual's sense of self, which is not based on their ability to have children; a need to accept that people are good and worthy even if they are not parents; and a new definition of sexuality which is not based on procreation. It is important for all people to understand that whichever path a person takes with regard to parenting, whether they have children or not, there will be periods of regret through their lives when they will consider the alternatives which were available but remained unexplored. We need a new definition of parenting which is not biologically based, as many children being born now are not the genetic offspring of their social parents. Parenting should then be defined as the caring for and rearing of children.

The pain of the experience of infertility then cannot be overestimated. I have worked with infertile couples for three years and know that it is a very lonely experience. Many people cannot discuss it openly with their friends or their families because they fear loss of face. Barbara Eck-Menning, who wrote A Guide for the Childless Couple and began a national support group for infertile people, quotes an infertile woman who talked about the experience of being isolated through infertility and who suddenly saw fertility everywhere in the world except within herself. This woman said:

> I remember going to the market one night and being assaulted by the fertile world. At the bubble gum machines a mother was helping her toddler put a penny in the slot. A bit

further down the aisle, I was passed by a woman balancing a quart of milk and four containers of yoghurt on her protruding belly. At the bakery one woman shouted across the buns to a young man, "was it a boy or a girl?" It is an unwritten law that what you want most seems to elude you, but not anyone else. The gnawing desire to become pregnant is accentuated by every young or expectant mother you see, and take my word for it—they are everywhere.... (Eck-Menning 1977: 107)

The Technological Fix

Into this context of the pain of infertility came the "technodocs." They came, not with the intention of educating people to prevent infertility, not with a solution to the problem of infertility itself, but with the promise of a technological fix. And the product of that technological fix was a baby: not a solution to infertility, but a baby.

And this technological fix was a false promise. The so-called "success" rates of IVF should really be called the "failure" rates. Of every hundred women who go onto an IVF program, at least 86 percent of them will fail to become pregnant. A recent article in the New England Journal of Medicine discussed a study of couples who were treated for infertility and couples who were not (Collins et al. 1983). Of the 589 couples treated for infertility, 41 percent became pregnant. Of the 548 untreated couples, 35 percent became pregnant. The authors conclude "that the potential for a spontaneous cure of infertility is high" (Collins et al. 1983: 1201).

Though the public is often presented with media pictures of the smiling couples and happy babies, statistics on these programs leave much to be desired in terms of "success." The figures from the Perinatal Statistics Unit in Sydney indicate that until December 31, 1984, 909 pregnancies were achieved in eleven centers throughout Australia and New Zealand. Only 45 percent resulted in live births. Five percent of pregnancies were ectopic, 19 percent resulted in spontaneous abortions, and there were 22 still births. Perinatal mortality was 4 times that of the normal population. The programs also have an unusually high caesarean rate of 43 percent. Doctors seem very keen to have these births delivered by the medical profession and kept tightly within their control. Thirty-four percent of the babies were born with low birth weight, which is four times that of the normal population. In addition, of those pregnant,

63 percent of the women had had previous pregnancies. This indicates that some of them had existing families and many of them had been sterilized and remarried. We can ask the question then: Does this change our attitude to in vitro fertilization? If a technology, supposedly designed to help an infertile couple have a child who would not otherwise ever have had one, is now used by couples as a way to avoid sterilization, does this put a different slant on our reasons for having IVF and for contributing such large amounts of money to the technology?

In an interesting survey recently published in the Medical Tribune, Corea and Ince (1985) give results which indicate that many IVF hospitals use misleading statistics to engage patients. Many clinics quote a 20 percent success rate using what they see as the worldwide average. Yet of the 54 clinics which responded to the questionnaire, half had never sent a patient home with a baby. "Those zero success clinics have been in business from one month to three years and have treated over six hundred women and collected, by conservative estimate, over $2.5 million in patient fees." Corea and Ince (1985) detail the way statistics are manipulated in these hospitals, explaining that some of the so-called pregnancies were in fact just chemical changes which may indicate an early sign of pregnancy. Many hospitals cite pregnancies as a success rate as opposed to live births, and many hospitals include their twins and triplets in the reported totals of live births.

This kind of manipulation of statistics and indeed the giving of false statistics, which lure patients to clinics to undergo extensive medical interventions with little possibility of a baby at the end of the process, has been severely criticized by Dr. Soules in an editorial of the journal Fertility and Sterility. He writes: "...the truth with regard to the expected pregnancy rate after IVF procedures has been widely abused (primarily by IVF practitioners)." He goes on to say that the "widespread practice of exaggerating the IVF pregnancy rate appears to be a marketing ploy," and that it is competition which is encouraging this as "many IVF programs in this country are struggling to treat a sufficient patient volume to maintain the program" (Soules 1985: 511–13). Medical researchers obviously do not look at the experience of IVF itself as a cause of dropping patient numbers. Could the process itself be turning people off?

In Vitro Fertilization (IVF). There are a number of variations within the IVF procedure now. The original procedure was one in which the egg was taken from a woman, the sperm from her husband or partner, and the two were put together within fluid in a Petri dish. This led to the term "test tube baby." The resulting embryo was then placed back inside the woman's uterus to enable implantation and, hopefully, pregnancy. It was originally designed to enable a woman who was infertile for reasons such as blocked or diseased fallopian tubes to have a child. A new technique is IVF with a surgical extraction of sperm. This involves the removal of sperm from the husband's testicle which is then used to fertilize the wife's egg (or the egg of another woman). It is intended to assist some types of male infertility.

A third procedure is IVF with donor sperm, where the sperm from a donor is used to fertilize the woman's egg. A fourth variation is IVF with donor ova. This procedure would use the sperm of a husband or a donor to fertilize an egg donated by a donor woman. The embryo created is then placed into the infertile woman's uterus with the hope of pregnancy. In this case the child is then the biological child of the husband, if it has been his sperm which is used, and is not the genetic child of the wife. There is, however, some debate about whether or not she is the mother. Is the woman who carries the child for nine months the mother of the child if the genetic material (that is, the egg) is not from her body? I would argue that she is.

And finally the last variation on IVF involves a donor embryo. This is where a donor sperm and donor egg are placed together creating an embryo and the embryo is implanted in a woman's uterus. So the man and woman become social parents, but not the genetic parents of the child. The woman, however, carries the child and should be termed the "biological mother."

Though these procedures are simply said, the practical experience of the IVF program is painful, costly, and emotionally exhausting. The process of determining the causes of infertility has already been briefly discussed. With in vitro fertilization there is again a series of tests which the woman must undergo. An IVF cycle lasts for at least two weeks. Mao and Wood (1984: 532) write:

> This involves about a week of outpatient monitoring by the daily estimation of plasma 17-beta-oestradiol levels, the daily scoring of cervical mucus, and one or two ovarian ultrasound examinations. This is followed by another week of inpatient care, involving frequent hormonal assays, the laparoscopic

collection of oocytes and, in the event of successful oocyte collection and fertilization, the embryo transfer.

A laparoscopy is carried out to collect "ripe" eggs for sterilization. It is an operation done under general anaesthetic with all the attendant risks. A fine suction needle and a guide are inserted into the uterus and led to the ovary where collection takes place. Most women on the program are superovulated. This means that they are given doses of hormones or fertility drugs to increase the number of eggs produced per cycle. A woman's body normally produces one egg per month, but medical researchers need to replace more than one embryo in order to have a chance of a successful pregnancy. They therefore superovulate the woman so that she produces more than one egg per cycle, usually five or six, but on occasion up to eleven (Wood 1984). Her body is then being asked to produce five or six times the normal amount of eggs for that month. There is a risk here of hyperstimulation of the woman's ovaries. There is also some risk that medical researchers may be tempted to superovulate a woman past the necessary number of eggs in order to have so-called "spare" embryos for the purposes of experimentation.

The drugs most commonly used are Clomiphene citrate and a gonadotropin with the brand name Pergonal. Using Pergonal doctors exclaim at the wonderful increase in the eggs to be "harvested." One study reported the collection of 87 eggs from eleven treatment cycles (Porter 1984).

The possible detrimental side effects of constant use of these hormones is yet to be investigated. There are, however, some dangers which have already been discussed in the literature. Hyperstimulation of the ovaries is one of them (Pfeffer and Woollett 1983). An article in The Medical Journal of Australia has indicated some potential problems: the body's defense mechanism against superovulation is overridden, and there may be maternal risks associated with ovarian hyperstimulation, such as "Meigs'-like" syndrome and thrombosis (Kovacs et al. 1984). One side effect is also that of multiple births. Other problems can include an unexpected low pregnancy rate and a higher incidence of ectopic pregnancies (Birkenfeld 1984). Henriet and associates (1984) warn that "superovulation is not a simple multiplication of a normal ovulation." The long-term effects of superovulating women in these ways are still unknown.

But what are the costs involved in in vitro fertilization: the financial costs and the costs to the couple and to the woman involved? The financial cost to the couple is considerable. In Australia it amounts to between $2,000 and $3,000 per cycle attempt. About two-thirds of this is refunded on medical benefits. In the United States the cost is $1,375 to $7,000 per IVF attempt (Corea and Ince 1985). But this is not the only cost for the couple, as many have to travel to the clinics and lose work time. In a study of 228 patients who withdrew from programs in Australia in 1983, Mao and Wood (1984) found that financial cost was the primary reason for withdrawing. The emotional costs were the second reason. The following were mentioned in order of importance: anxiety, depression, disruption of a normal life and of work-career patterns, and the strain on the marriage. This research indicates a high drop-out rate, but it is difficult to get exact estimates as hospitals neglect to keep the figures.

It is only recently that consumer views of women on IVF programs are being heard. Two recent studies have given an interesting insight into the experiences of these women. They show the lack of dignity involved in the process. As one woman wrote: "It affected my self-esteem. It made me depressed for at least twelve months. It affected our relationship. It affected my sexuality. I felt powerless" (Burton 1985). Many of the women commented on the lack of information given to them about the program and in particular about the lack of success on IVF programs. Just as the general public has been impressed by pictures of happy babies and happy couples, so too women on the programs have been influenced by this media presentation of IVF. Some complaints refer to the doctor-patient relationship. As one woman said, "I would like the doctors to participate more. They just pick up the eggs and put them back, the rest of the time you never see them, it's rush, rush, all the time. You don't like to ask questions. Even when they inform you, you don't take it all in. You don't like to phone them and make a nuisance" (Burton 1985).

The experience of "failing" is devastating for women who go through the program. After the experience of infertility itself, the testing for infertility and then the IVF procedure, there is a lot at stake for the women involved. As one woman who failed to become pregnant put it: "I just wanted to sit in a corner and die." Another said: "My husband went to pieces, I felt I was dying, I was really crook but I didn't let any emotion come out, I had to look after him"

(Burton 1985). The stress incurred by couples on these programs is enormous (Haseltine 1984).

In the 1985 Burton study women complained particularly about the lack of feedback and lack of support from the medical staff. One said, "You don't get any feedback. It would be nice to be given a reason, a follow-up phone call from the coordinator—it should be medical—you want to be told it is not your fault you bombed out. You just go home and feel a failure." A second woman said, "I would really like to have gone back and talked to [my gynecologist] after it didn't work out, but as [the IVF scientist] says, 'you're history, we're onto the next one, we haven't time for you now, we want to get on with it.'" The medical teams are ill prepared to cope with the stress of patients. The IVF scientist referred to in the above comment said: "One way the teams cope with failure is to avoid follow-up contact with failed patients."

Women themselves are more attuned to the side effects their bodies are experiencing and resent the fact that they are not listened to on this issue. One woman on the program who was a doctor herself said that the hormones had induced enormous emotional turmoil even though they were told there would be no side effects. Another woman said, "The professor tells us that according to the labels in his books, they don't have side effects. Once someone comes out of this experience brave enough to say, 'you get side effects,' other women say so too. I think that's what he's worried about—that side effects are catching." Many of these comments are resonant of descriptions of the historical relationship of women and medicine; their anxieties and their concerns are not given validity by the medical profession. One patient expressed the concern for the potential results of all of this superovulation in ten to fifteen years time. As she pointed out, "Our generation were guinea pigs for the Dalkon Shield, and now we're guinea pigs for the new form of modern technology" (Burton 1985).

Patients are unable to wield any power in the traditional doctor/patient relationship and are too involved often to consider the wider social implications of IVF. One patient wrote:

We as patients, are not in a position to comment objectively about many IVF issues. Always we are conscious of the fact that we are in the "compromising" position. For most couples our dearest wish is to have a child so we do not publicly complain about the endless experimental procedures, the dehumanized method of treatment, the pain, cost and emotional strain that is an integral part of IVF. I have known some to complain, but only to incur the wrath of the IVF team.[1]

The cost of IVF procedures for the community is difficult to estimate because figures on the financial details are unavailable. Recent figures in the report of the Family Law Council tabled in the Federal Parliament in Australia indicate that one such pregnancy can cost the community from $10,000 to $1,000,000, depending on the care required for the mother and the postnatal care of premature babies. Costs to society also include the use of hospital expertise, staff, research funding, and the hospital facilities. In addition, hospitals will now be required to provide counseling services.

So in vitro fertilization is basically a dangerous, expensive, and unsuccessful form of reproductive technology. But in today's terms, it is a simple procedure compared to some of the others being used or being developed. Let us consider some of these and their social implications.

Surrogate Embryo Transfer (SET) is also called "flushing" or "lavage," and is a technology being developed in North America. Recently the National Health and Medical Research Council in Australia accepted its ethics committee's recommendation not to develop this technology at the present stage in this country. It was the procedure which the Queen Victoria/Epworth Hospital/Monash University team was intending to introduce when I resigned from the Committee in 1984. The negative outcomes of this technology can be anticipated and permission for its use can be refused before it is implemented. In this technique a fertile donor woman is inseminated with the sperm of an infertile woman's partner. She conceives and the embryo is flushed from her body and placed into the infertile woman—if all goes well.

In North America this procedure has already been used (Bustillo and Buster 1984). Twenty-nine artificial inseminations of donor women using sperm from the husbands of the infertile women were implanted on a research program and resulted in twelve embryos. These twelve were transferred to the infertile women, yielding two successful pregnancies and an ectopic pregnancy, "which was surgically removed 30 days after the transfer" (Jones 1983: 2182). One donor woman, however, had a "retained pregnancy" that spontaneously aborted. The risks to the donor are considerable. She may experience pelvic infection and/or ectopic pregnancy, "either one of which could terminate her physiological reproductive career" (Walters 1983: 2183).

The analogy with animal work discussed earlier can lead us to investigate the potential of SET. In animals SET involves the superovulation of the donor through large hormone doses similar to those used with IVF patients, in order to produce more than one egg, and therefore more than one embryo. Once flushing is introduced, this would be the next logical step with donor women. After all, it has been done with animals and is cost effective, so why not? In fact, Walters, in the Journal of the American Medical Association, warns of the "potential risks of uterine lavage—and, in the future, of possible superovulation—to the embryo donor" (Bustillo and Buster 1984: 1173). Indeed, the researchers responsible for the application of this technique wrote that "donor fecundity needs to be improved" (Annas 1984).

One of the interesting things about this particular piece of research was that it introduced the commercial element into the reproductive technology area. The research was not funded by the National Institute of Health but was funded by the Fertility and Genetics Research Incorporated, a Chicago-based for-profit company. Researchers were primarily from the UCLA medical center, but three of the researchers were from the company, and all have now been offered shares in it. However, one researcher is reported to have resigned in disgust. The company has applied for a patent on both instruments used in the procedure and on the process itself. If granted, it will mean that this company owns and controls both the instruments and the process, thereby restricting evaluation by other researchers and empowering it to deny information and use of the technique (Holmes et al. 1981).

Sex Predetermination Techniques. These techniques are being developed and can be used at two phases of conception: during pregnancy or before conception itself (Kishwar 1985). During pregnancy amniocentesis can be used to assess the sex of the fetus. Amniocentesis is a procedure in which a needle is inserted into the cavity of the womb and amniotic fluid from around the fetus is withdrawn. It was developed to "help women" detect an abnormal fetus and terminate the pregnancy if that were deemed necessary. It also provides information on the sex of the fetus. With such knowledge it is possible to abort the fetus if it is undesirable (The Australian 1983). This is the current practice in India, where the abortion of female fetuses is rapidly increasing. Madhu Kishwar (1985) has recently indicated that the sex ratio balance in India has changed since 1901. In that year there were 972 women per 1000 men. In 1981 there were 925 women per 1000 men. The "deficit" in women was 9 million in 1901 and 22 million in 1981. Practices in China, where families are restricted to one child only, have led to an increase in the abortion of the female fetus. The sex of the fetus has also been detected successfully by ultrasound at fifteen to sixteen weeks.

A less traumatic way of determining sex is to do so before conception. A number of methods are currently being worked with in this area. Male-determining sperm are lighter (being less complex and the chromosome carrying less genetic material) and have a different electrical charge than that of the female-determining sperm. By means of centrifuge (spinning the sperm to divide them) or by electrical means, it is possible to inseminate a woman or an egg with sex-preselected sperm. The Japanese have almost perfected the latter method (Sydney Morning Herald 1984). Sex-selecting spermicides have also been used with mice. Campbell (1976) has pointed out that blue and pink diaphragms could soon be marketed. He also talks of the possibility of a man child pill. In North America, a company called Gametrics Limited has developed a sperm-washing technique which is 75 percent successful for selecting boys. This company has also patented the method (Fidall et al. 1979; Williamson 1976).

At first glance this technology may seem to be another way of giving people greater choice in terms of their children. But for women there are great dangers as many studies have shown that most societies are male-preferring (Holmes et al. 1981). With the introduction of these techniques the sex-ratio balance is likely to be severely disrupted. And in countries where couples are allowed more than one child, the number of first-born sons could dramatically increase. The danger here is that first-borns have been shown in general to have more advantages over later-borns and to be generally more motivated, more assertive, independent, and high in self-esteem. We would therefore be building the traditional sex-role stereotypes into a biological determinism. Males would be more stereotypically masculine, and second-born females more stereotypically feminine.

Indications are that people would use this technology. Even within educated groups the majority of people would choose male offsprings as first-borns. Few people prefer females; rather most of

Table 1

Possible Positive and Negative Consequences of Sex Preselection

Positive	Negative
1. Avoidance of sex-linked disease	1. Mainly the rich will benefit
2. Girls will especially feel wanted	2. Wherever a strong boy preference, girls will be present in fewer numbers.
3. Balance two child family	3. Concentration of first- and second-born characteristics in boys or girls
4. Enhance happiness in families	4. Imbalance of sex ratio and social dislocation
5. Reduce population in less-developed nations	5. Precedent for genetic engineering, eugenics
6. Enhance family planning	6. Increase conflict between sexes
7. Increase human control over genetics	7. Possibility of abuse by totalitarian state
8. Increase status of women	8. Impact of expectations on child

those who do not indicate a male preference are disinterested in the sex of the child (Fletcher 1983). In addition, Hartley and Pietraczk (1979) found in a group of 2138 North Americans a "wide spread acceptance of ongoing biomedical research to perfect preselection methods" and a strong indication of intent to use such methods were they to become available. In addition, advertisements often appear encouraging people to select their child's sex. One even appeared in MS magazine, in April 1984, entitled "Choosing Your Baby's Sex." People were encouraged to write for a "revolutionary new kit" which would increase the odds 80–90 percent for selecting the child's sex. Table 1 clarifies the positive and negative consequences of sex preselection. It is based on Fletcher's (1985) table with some additions.

On the positive side, then, it is assumed that because most societies are male preferring, those born girls will feel specially wanted. People will easily limit family size instead of trying for a boy or a girl after two or three of the one sex. Families will also be happier because there will be no disappointment at the birth of a "wrong" sex child. The overpopulated countries which are more strongly male-preferring will be able to control their population more easily through making "choice" available.

Some have suggested that women's status will rise. Because of her scarcity woman will be "highly valued." However, she will be valued for sexual and breeding purposes rather than for her intrinsic worth as a person. "When women are scarce and men readily available," write Guttentag and Secord (1983: 2), "a protective morality develops that favors monogamy for women, limits their interactions with men, and shapes female roles in traditional domestic directions." They also give examples of the creation of a subclass of prostitutes to satisfy the sexual desires of men, especially those unable to marry.

On the negative side, only the rich may have access to the technology. I would add that as with IVF, single, lesbian, minority, and poor women may also have difficulty affording the technology or gaining access to it. The imbalance of the sex ratio has been hypothesized as leading to a rise in "male" values: aggression, sexual pressure on women, alcoholism, and violence. As Campbell (1976: 88) wrote: "More of everything, in short, that men do, make, suffer, inflict and consume." The British scientist Postgate (1973) has suggested that women's right to work will need to be curtailed, and polyandry would develop. Some societies "might treat their women as queen ants, others as rewards for the most outstanding (or most determined) males" (Herlands 1981). In fact, it is likely that "choice" of sexual partner will not be allowed as men demand and take sexual satisfaction and breeding rights from the diminishing numbers of women. It is possible that the female suicide rates would escalate, as was reported in earlier histories about female infertility.

Women are the most exploited, manipulated, oppressed, and brutalized group in the world, yet we have the numbers. What would our status be as a vastly outnumbered group? And how many women would be prepared to accept the world where only their value as breeders and sexual objects would be recognized?

And finally, in all these discussions the experience of the child who grows to adulthood as the result of predetermined sex is rarely discussed. They would carry the burden of their parents' desires and expectations as they are attached to a particular sex. As with children born of AID and IVF programs, a great deal of stress will be placed upon them to "perform" in order not to disappoint their parents and make them wish they had "chosen otherwise."

Future Fixes

Some technologies are currently being discussed within the medical literature and may be in experimental stages. I will consider just a couple of these in order to explore the point that a rationale is being developed for further forays into the more futuristic aspects of reproductive technology.

Cloning. This technology can be used to duplicate members of either sex. It bypasses sexual reproduction by using one of a number of available methods: nuclear transplantation, chemically induced self-replication, development from single blastomeres, or egg fusion (Murphy 1985). The new individual created has an identical genetic constitution to that of its clone. Frogs have been successfully cloned, and most scientists predict that it is possible in humans. One experiment on human cloning has been discussed (Walters 1982). Asexual production of this type still involves using the egg of the woman.

The potential use of cloning has caused considerable debate. The child created or the "clonee" could be psychologically traumatized by the nature of their conception and their likeness to the parent. This lack of identity could result in a lack of a sense of uniqueness of self which makes up the human character. It should be of concern that some medical scientists advocate cloning as an end to some social problems. Professor William Walters, a member of the Monash IVF team, has written:

> In any case it is not necessarily desirable to emphasize the self, when one considers this in the light of the teachings of Buddha, Jesus Christ and other religious leaders, who were at pains to teach the necessity of eradication of feelings of self...it could be argued that clonees could cooperate better with one another and others precisely because of this lack of the sense of self. (Grossman 1971: 42)

Here is a rationale, then, for cloning. But cloning would place doubt on the experience of parenthood. It would be an alienating experience for both male and female partners. It would deny the value of the individual. Yet Grossman can comment with a certain glee that cloning shows that an individual "previously unique and mortal, may be rid of its uniqueness and have immortality conferred on it." The experiment, he says, is "dazzling" (Lederberg 1966). But perhaps one of the most telling comments has come from an article by Lederberg, the American Nobel laureate in medicine, who wrote in 1966 that "we would at least be able to enjoy being able to observe the experiment of discovering whether a second Einstein would outdo the first one" (Lederberg 1966: footnote 2). We can only wonder if the "experiment" that is the cloned person would share his delight. These comments do, however, give the person in the general community a clear idea of some of the things which are going on in the minds of scientists.

Twinning. This technique involves splitting the embryo into two at an early stage of its development. The two halves can then regenerate themselves to produce two identical offspring. This technique has been used considerably in the animal area, particularly with sheep. It is now possible to carry out this procedure in human beings, though it has not been done so far to our knowledge. What results from this possibility is that together with the freezing technique, one embryo could be frozen and the other one implanted. Two identical twins could then be born one or two or three years apart. Alternatively, the second embryo may be implanted in a second woman so the two identical embryos would be borne and birthed by two different women. Recently in Australia a situation similar to this has occurred. However, in the Australian situation the embryos were not from the same egg. Nevertheless, from one harvest of eggs the woman bore two children, eighteen months apart, who would normally have been twins (Herlands 1981). Again the impact of these procedures on the sense of self of the child created has been neglected.

Ectogenesis. This is a scientific word for the growth of a fetus outside the human body, without the need of a womb at any time. Herlands (1981) has written of work at Stanford University in the United States where researchers are creating an artificial womb. Oxygen and nutrients are pumped into it, and young human fetuses which are products of spontaneous abortion have been sustained for 48 hours. We do not know if the women who had to abort were aware of this. Lamb fetuses have been sustained by other researchers for several days in this way (Buuk 1977).

These attempts should not seem so dramatic when we consider the fact that today very young premature babies are being kept alive in incubators from 24 weeks onwards. From the other end of the process we can see that fertilized embryos have been kept alive in vitro up until at least the fourteenth day. Research scientists now want to extend that period. A notable example of this is the push of medical professions in England to extend the suggested fourteen-day limit on experimentation of embryos to at least thirty days.

The current problem with maintaining an embryo and then fetus outside a woman's body is the imitation of the placenta, which is needed to supply nutrients and to eliminate waste products. One obstacle to further work in this area has been said by Buuk (1977) to be a lack of national commitment (that is, money) to the task.

Again, a set of rationales for this "glass womb" has also been provided. Grossman lists these clearly: fetal medicine would be improved; the child could be immunized while still inside the "womb"; the environment would be safer than a woman's womb; geneticists could program in some superior traits "on which society could agree"; sex preselection would be simple; women could be permanently sterilized; and men would be able to prove for the first time who is the father of the child. As he claims: "Natural pregnancy may become an anachronism....the uterus would become appendix-like" (Grossman 1971: 49). And we know what happens to the appendix!

Although a glass womb would allow some women to continue to work or to continue to progress within their chosen area of life without either the difficulties or encumbrances of pregnancy or the time that pregnancy takes from a woman's life, many would miss the special relationship between a woman and a child who is carried within her body. In addition, for many women in countries throughout the world, the obliteration of the need for them as breeding mechanisms would further endanger their survival.

In addition, we do not know what it would be like to be an adult who had never been carried in a woman's womb or had never experienced birth. Adrienne Rich has written:

> All human life on the planet is born of woman. The one unifying, incontrovertible experience shared by all women and men is that months-long period we spent unfolding inside a woman's body....Most of us first know both love and disappointment, power and tenderness, in the person of a woman, we carry the imprint of this experience for life even into our dying. (Rich 1977: 11)

We cannot predict the impact on people of being "of ectogenesis delivered." We cannot estimate what relationship the child would feel to her/his "parents." The concept of self-identity and family continuity would be changed. Women should ask the question: would the loss of the experience of pregnancy and birth as uniquely female and for some as a power base be worth the "liberation" from pregnancy and childbirth?

ISSUES IN REPRODUCTIVE TECHNOLOGY

It is clear that women who are infertile and in need are being used in these experimental procedures as living laboratories. This creation of "woman as laboratory" is leading to methods of divorcing parts of the woman from the whole. For example, doctors now talk about the "uterine environment" or "the womb" as entities in their own right. The logical extension of this process has been the development of surrogate motherhood. Unfortunately, there is no space here in which to investigate the dilemmas and pitfalls involved in this process. I have outlined elsewhere the dangers to women in the creation of commercial surrogate agencies (Rowland 1986b). The language of surrogacy itself is part of this process of woman-splitting. The surrogate mother, for example, is no surrogate at all but is in fact the biological mother. By calling her a surrogate, commercial agencies can more easily divorce her from her child. We know now about the pain of relinquishing for women who gave up their children for adoption. Many of them grieve over a thirty-year period (Winkler and Van Keppel 1986). I believe that through surrogacy we are now creating the next generation of grieving women. In addition, the "surrogate" experience can be very harmful to the infertile couple who enter into this contract. It may also be very harmful to the child, who, as the object of a commercial deal, is in fact sold into slavery. And as Krimmel (1983: 5) comments: "It is human nature that when one pays money, one expects value."

It is important to mention surrogacy here because some of the values that are inherent in this process are also part of the reproductive technological fix. In the United States of America, particularly at the present, reproductive supermarkets are being established in which many of these technologies are mixed with the surrogate process. This has already occurred with respect to, for example, superovulation of the surrogate so that she would produce twins or the use of in vitro fertilization with a donated embryo to avoid connections between the biological mother and the child she is to relinquish. The suggestion here is that the genetic component is the only thing which is important to a woman, and that the carrying of the child for nine months is similar to the carrying of a parcel from the post office! Surrogacy can also be used in association with sex predetermination and surrogate embryo transfer. It is the final and grossest exploitation of women and their bodies.

There are good reasons why women should be anxious about this new technology. The relationship of women historically to the medical profession has not been a positive one (Ehrenreich and English 1978). The experiences of women with the contraceptive pill, Depro provera, and the interuterine device, the Dalkon Shield, lead us to the justifiable conclusion that women are seen by the medical profession and its commercial associates as good fodder for experimental procedures.

The medical profession itself has gained more and more control over birth, and part of the motivation behind the women's health movement has been to regain the right to have children in the manner which women themselves choose. But the mistreatment, manipulation, and mutilation of women through obstetrics and gynecology continue. Hysterectomy has reached proportions so high in Australia that the Doctors Reform Society has condemned it. In the United States, where about 800,000 hysterectomies a year are performed, Cynthia Cook estimated that a woman born today has only a 50/50 chance of keeping her uterus (Cook and Dworkin 1981). Between 15 and 30 percent of these operations, she contends, are unnecessary. In Silent Knife, Cohen and Estner (1984) show that today up to 30 percent of births in the United States are by caesarean delivery. Rates have doubled over the last fifteen years, despite the fact that it has not lowered infant mortality rates as it was supposed to do. Medical technology has not always "freed women," and we need to ask now whether the new technologies will. What makes them so different that they will suddenly give women more control and freedom over their lives?

In addition, scientists do not indicate willingness to exercise restraint. Discussions are now going on concerning "genetic therapy" or rather genetic manipulation and engineering. Outrageous ideas such as the crossing of a human with an ape have been discussed. Geoffrey Bourne, chancellor St. George's University School of Medicine in Grenada, West Indies, has said: "I believe that it would be very important scientifically to try to produce an ape-human cross...and I hope someone in a position to do it will make the attempt." Although some scientists have expressed concerns on ethical grounds about doing this, Stephen Seager, Chief of the Reproductive Physiology Unit at the National Institutes of Health, Veterinary Resources Branch, suggested that human females might serve as "hosts" for embryos of chimpanzees or gorillas. He did not think there would be any birth difficulties; and when seeking volunteers for such a "hosting," Dr. Seager said, "I think you could find women who are serious conservationists who want to help animals" (Morgan 1985: 259).

A major issue within all of this debate is the commercialization of reproductive technologies. The booming of reproductive supermarkets in the United States is one example of the misuse of the technology for pure financial gain. In Australia, in a climate of great public debate and concern, Monash University has established IVF Australia, a commercial company. Commercialization of the technologies mean that the scientists are now governed to a large extent by a profit motive. This represents a strong threat to academic freedom and a danger that information and processes will not be freely available for scientific scrutiny. In spite of the fact that universities are publicly funded in Australia, commercial interests will now control public access to information, with the result that public control and scrutiny will no longer be a viable possibility. Many medical researchers themselves are very concerned about this move into the commercial arena. As Willard Gaylin, a medical ethicist, says, it represents "an erosion of the concept of service in medicine...none of us are thrilled by the drift toward commodity orientation" (Morgan 1985).

This commodity orientation is leading us to view the child as a product. And the product must be perfect and, as far as possible, consumer designed. For the first time technology is encouraging people to create children to suit the need of adults. This is quite clearly related to the middle-class consumption ethic: money can buy anything. Issues of race and class exploitation are a strong concern within this area. Access to these technologies is severely limited to those who can afford it. It is also quite clear from the discussion of surrogacy in Corea's book (1985) that the surrogate agencies are exploiting poor women and are involved in the importing of third world women for the purpose of producing pure white babies for the American market.

We need to take a clear look at the values underlying this work. There is a strong lack of acceptance of mortality and death, of infertility, and of the imperfect child. In addition, the needs of the individual are being used to create technologies which pose a threat to society as a whole. Suddenly people talk about the "right" to have a family. But the needs and rights of an individual must always be balanced against the welfare of the greater social group.

And finally, what of the basic questions of helping the infertile? Although reproductive technologies are purportedly directed toward helping the infertile, they seem not to have been very effective, or else helpful in only a very special sense. Very little money, if any, goes toward preventative measures regarding infertility. Education about infertility and how to avoid it needs to be expanded, and there is need for expanded research on the causes of infertility. Specialized counseling should be available to couples who are infertile so that they can choose from a range of options. This search for solutions to infertility should not be reduced to technological fixes but should include noninvasive methods (e.g., massage). It is the scientists who need the reproductive technology to advance their knowledge and status, not the infertile. Instead, more research resources are needed for noninvasive solutions to infertility.

Women particularly need to take a very close and critical look at these technologies. Although they might be presented as "new choices" for the individual, their consequences in narrowing opportunities for women as a social group should also be considered. Does the desire, the need, the wanting of choice have no boundaries? There must be a time when the rights of one group impinge so strongly on those of the majority that social control is needed. Then the terminology of rights becomes meaningless. Powledge (1983) would argue that the principle of freedom of choice must be second to that of "fairness" and equal treatment.

It may be that the stress on choice gives the medical profession more, not less, control in the reproductive technology area. The "right" to choose the sex of your child, the "right" to use donor ova, the "right" to have a surrogate mother, and the "right" of the medical profession to service these rights have been used to ensure a lack of government and social intervention. Gordon (1979) has pointed out that we cannot always distinguish personal need for the product from the "needs" defined for us by social policy. In this instance we have to look at the root of the driving force which leads many women to involve themselves in such painful and exhausting enterprises as in vitro fertilization.

Hanmer and Allan (1982) have said that women act as agents of male individual and social power. We continue to collude to our own disadvantage. We need to challenge our own thinking and the current technology without eroding the hard-won gains we have made in reproductive choice. So the question is, in the end, does the new technology mean a transfer of power to women as a social group? Or are they methods by which a male-dominated research sector in the sciences gains more control over reproduction and procreation, thus alienating women more and more from their own bodies and from the processes of reproduction? It may be worthwhile to keep in mind Roberta Steinbacher's (Holmes et al. 1981: 189, note 89) comments on the contraceptive pill and relate them here to reproductive technology:

Who invented it, who manufactures it, who licensed it, who dispenses it? But who dies from it?

Notes

[1]Personal correspondence from a woman who runs an infertility self-help group in Australia—confidential.

References

Annas, G., 1984. "Surrogate Embryo Transfer: The Perils of Patenting," Hastings Centre Report (June): 25–26.

Avidan, A. and D. Avidan, 1976. "Artificial Insemination by Donor: Clinical and Psychological Aspects," Fertility and Sterility 27: 528–32.

Birkenfeld, A., 1984. "Effect of Clomiphene on the Uterine and Oviductal Mucosa," Journal of In Vitro Fertilization and Embryo Transfer 1, 2: 99.

Burton, B., 1985. "Contentious Issues of Infertility Therapy—A Consumer's View." Paper presented at the Annual Meeting of the Australian Family Planning Association, March.

Bustillo, M. and J. Buster, 1984. "Non-Surgical Ovum Transfer as a Treatment in Infertile Women," Journal of the American Medical Association 251, 9: 1171–73.

Buuk, J., 1977. "Ethics of Reproductive Engineering," American Biology Teacher 39, 9: 545–47.

Cahn, E., 1966. "Drug Experiments and the Public Conscience," pp. 368–72 in L.L. Cahn (ed.) Confronting Injustice: The Edmond Cahn Reader. Boston, MA: Little Brown.

Campbell, C., 1976. "The Man Child Pill," Psychology Today (August): 86–91.

Cohen, N.W. and L.J. Essner, 1984. Silent Knife—Caesarean Prevention and Vaginal Birth After Caesarean. South Hadley, MA: Bergent Garvey.

Collins, J., W. Wrixon, L. Janes and J.E. Wilson, 1983. "Treatment-independent Pregnancy Among Infertile Couples," The New England Journal of Medicine 309, 20: 1201–06.

Cook, C. and S. Dworkin, 1981. "Tough Talk About Unnecessary Surgery," MS (October): 43–44.

Corea, G., 1985. The Mother Machine. From Artificial Insemination to Artificial Wombs. New York: Harper and Row.

Corea, G. and S. Ince, 1985. "IVF A Game for Losers at Half of US Clinics," Medical Tribune 26, 19: 11–13.

Easlea, B., 1981. Science and Sexual Oppression: Patriarchy's Confrontation with Woman and Nature. London: Weidenfeld and Nicolson.

Easlea, B., 1982. Fathering the Unthinkable: Masculinity, Scientists and the Nuclear Arms Race. London: Pluto Press.

Eck-Menning, B., 1977. Infertility: A Guide for the Childless Couple. Englewood Cliffs, NJ: Prentice Hall.

Ehrenreich, B. and D. English, 1978. For Her Own Good: 150 Years of the Experts' Advice to Women. New York: Anchor Books.

Fidall, L., D. Hoffman and P. Keith-Spiegel, 1979. "Some Social Implications of Sex-Choice Technology," Psychology of Women Quarterly 4, 1: 32–42.

Fletcher, J.C., 1983. "Ethics and Public Policy: Should Sex Choice Be Discouraged?" in N. Bennet (ed.) Sex Selection of Children. New York: Academic Press.

Gordon, L., 1979. "The Struggle for Reproductive Freedom: Three Stages of Feminism," in Z. Eisenstein (ed.) Capitalist Patriarchy and the Case for Socialist Feminism. New York: Monthly Review Press.

Grossman, E., 1971. "The Obsolescent Mother, A Scenario," The Atlantic 227: 339–50.

Guttentag, M. and P. Secord, 1983. Too Many Women? The Sex Ratio Question. Beverly Hills: Sage.

Hanmer, J. and D. Allen, 1982. "Reproductive Engineering: The Final Solution?" Feminist Issues 2: 53–75.

Hartley, S.F. and L. Pietraczk, 1979. "Preselecting the Sex of Offspring: Technologies, Attitudes and Implications," Social Biology 20: 232–46.

Haseltine, F.P., 1984. "Psychological Interviews and Assessments of Couples Participating in In Vitro Fertilization," Journal of In Vitro Fertilization and Embryo Transfer 1, 2: 113.

Henriet, B., L. Henriet, D. Holhoven and V. Seynave, 1984. "The Lethal Effect of Superovulation on the Embryo," Journal of In Vitro Fertilization and Embryo Transfer 1, 2: 86.

Herlands, R., 1982. "Biological Manipulations for Nurturing Mammalian Embryos," pp. 231–40 in H. Holmes, B. Hoskins and M. Gross (eds.) The Custom-Made Child? Women Centered Perspectives. Clifton, NJ: Humana Press.

Holmes, H., B. Hoskins and M. Gross (eds.), 1981. The Custom-Made Child? Women Centered Perspectives. Clifton, NJ: Humana Press.

Horin, A., 1984. "Feminists Critical of the Test Tube Production Line," National Times (May 25–31): 6.

Hoskins, B. and H. Holmes, 1985. "Technology and Prenatal Femicide," pp. 237–55 in R. Arditti, R.D. Klein and M. Shelley (eds.) Test-Tube Women: What Future For Motherhood? London: Routledge and Kegan Paul, Pandora Press.

Jones, H., 1983. "Variations on a Theme," editorial, Journal of the American Medical Association 250: 2182–83.

Kishwar, M., 1985. "The Continuing Deficit of Women in India and the Impact of Amniocentesis," in G. Corea (ed.) Man Made Women: How New Reproductive Technologies Affect Women. London: Hutchinson, Explorations of Feminism.

Klein, R.D., 1984. "Taking the Egg From One and the Uterus From the Other," Development: Seed of Change 1984 1: 92–97.

Kovacs, G., P. Dennis, R. Shelton, K. Outch, R. McLean, D. Healq and H. Burger, 1984. "Induction of Ovulation with Human Pituitary Gonadotrophins," The Medical Journal of Australia (May 12): 575–79.

Krimmel, H., 1984. "A Case Against Surrogate Parenting," in C. Levine (ed.) Taking Sides: Closing Views on Controversial Bio-Ethical Issues. Guilford, CT: Dushkin.

Lederberg, J., 1966. "Experimental Genetics and Human Evolution," Bulletin Atomic Scientists 22: 4–11.

Mao, K. and C. Wood, 1984. "Barriers to Treatment of Infertility by In Vitro Fertilization and Embryo Transfer," The Medical Journal of Australia (April 28): 532–33.

Mazor, M., 1979. "Barren Couples," Psychology Today 12: 101–12.

McIntosh, P., 1985. "In Vitro Twin Born 16 Months After Sister," The Age (October 2).

Morgan, R., 1985. The Anatomy of Freedom. Oxford: Martin Robertson.

Murphy, J., 1985. "From Mice to Men? Implications of Progress in Cloning Research," pp. 76–91 in R. Arditti, R.D. Klein and S. Minden (eds.) Test-Tube Women: What Future For

Motherhood? London: Routledge and Kegan Paul, Pandora Press.

Pfeffer, N. and A. Woollett, 1983. The Experience of Infertility. London: Virago Press.

Porter, R.N., W. Smith and I.L. Craft, 1984. "Induction of Ovulation for In Vitro Fertilization Using Buserelin and Gonadotropins," The Lancet (December 1): 1284–85.

Postgate, J., 1973. "Bat's Chance in Hell," New Scientist 5: 11–16.

Powledge, T., 1983. "Towards a Moral Policy For Sex Choice," in N. Bennett (ed.) Sex Selection of Children. New York: Academic Press.

Rich, A., 1977. Of Woman Born. Motherhood as Experience and Institution. London: Virago.

Rowland, R., 1982. "An Exploratory Study of the Child-Free Lifestyle," Australian and New Zealand Journal of Sociology 18, 1: 17–30

Rowland, R., 1985a. "Reproductive Technologies: The Final Solution to the Woman Question?" in R. Arditti, R.D. Klein and S. Minden (eds.) Test-Tube Women: What Future for Motherhood? London: Routledge and Kegan Paul.

Rowland, R., 1985b. "Motherhood Patriarchal Power, Alienation and the Issue of Choice in Sex Preselection," in G. Corea (ed.) How New Reproductive Technologies Affect Women. London: Hutchinson.

Rowland, R., 1985c. "A Child at Any Price? An Overview of Issues in the Use of the New Reproductive Technologies and the Threat to Women," Women's Studies International Forum 8, 6: 539–46.

Rowland, R., 1986a. "Of Woman Born, But for How Long? The Relationship of Women to the New Reproductive Technologies and the Issues of Choice," Signs. A Journal of Woman in Culture and Society (forthcoming).

Rowland, R., 1986b. "Surrogate Motherhood: Who Pays the Price?" Mimeo.

Schultz, R., 1978. The Psychology of Death, Dying and Bereavement. Reading, MA: Addison Wesley.

Soules, M., 1985. "The In Vitro Fertilization Pregnancy Rate: Let's Be Honest With One Another," Fertility and Sterility 43, 4: 511–13.

Sydney Morning Herald, 1984. "Doctors Clash at Meeting," 25 May, p. 1.

Sydney Morning Herald, 1985. "He's 'Daddy' Of Them All," 3
     February.
The Australian, 1983. "Parents May Be Able to Choose Child's
     Sex," 23 May.
Veevers, D., 1980. Childless by Choice. Toronto: Butterworths.
Walters, L., 1983. "Ethical Aspects of Surrogate Embryo
     Transfer," editorial, Journal of the American Medical
     Association 250, 16: 2183.
Walters, W., 1982. "Cloning Ectogenesis and Hybrids: Things to
     Come?" pp. 110–18 in W. Walters and P. Singer (eds.) Test-
     Tube Babies: A Guide to Moral Questions, Present
     Technologies and Future Possibilities. Sydney, Australia:
     Oxford University Press.
West, R., 1984. "IVF Researcher Quits Over Reprehensible
     Techniques," The Age (May 18): 1.
Whitlock, F., 1984. "Test-Tube Miracle Workers Attacked," The
     Australian (May 25): 1.
Williamson, N., 1976. Sons and Daughters: A Cross-Cultural
     Survey of Parental Preferences. London: Sage.
Winkler, R. and M. Van Keppel, 1984. Relinquishing Mothers in
     Adoption: Their Long-Term Adjustment. Australia:
     Melbourne Institute of Family Studies, Monograph No. 3.
Wood, C., 1984. "In Vitro Fertilization—The Procedure and Future
     Development," Proceedings of the 1984 Conference on
     Bioethics. Melbourne, Australia: St. Vincent Bioethics
     Center.
Woodfall, J., 1984. The Age (May 15).

PART II

PERSONAL RIGHTS: ROLE CHOICE

CHAPTER 5

CHILD CARE

Greer Litton Fox
Jan Allen

Throughout this analysis of child care in the contemporary United States, we returned inevitably to three underlying conclusions. The quality of child care in the U.S. reflects at heart an ambiguity of attitudes about the value of children, the relegation of child care to women, and cultural conflict about the appropriate roles for women.

Our review is divided into three parts. We start with an examination of recent data on the demand for and supply of child care, its quality, caregiver characteristics, and the role of private and public sector agencies in securing or failing to secure high-quality child care at reasonable cost for all families who need it. This is followed by an analysis of individual responses in coping with needs for child care. Finally, cultural configurations are examined which give rise to and support the maintenance of the current child care picture in the U.S.

The Catch-22 mechanisms that are operative here can be summarized as follows:

- Women who fail to have children and thus fail to need child care are deviant.
- Women who have children and need child care are deviant.
- Women who have children, need child care, and fail to secure child care for them are deviant.
- Women who have children, need child care, and secure child care for them are deviant.

Clearly, only the woman who stays at home with her children enjoys the full moral approbation of society. Other women are faced with varying degrees of implicit censure for their gender role and lifestyle choices.

Women's economic roles in the wage economy can be capped by the failure of a society to provide opportunities for safe, adequate, and affordable care for children, and all the more so if child care is defined as solely a mother's responsibility. It is when labor force participation is not a choice and the child care options are severely limited—a situation facing most employed American mothers—that one can see most sharply the societal ambivalence about the value of children and our chilling readiness to apply harsh moral sanctions for women's "deviant" choices.

DIMENSIONS OF THE PROBLEM
Need for Child Care

The demand for child care has grown along with the labor force participation of women. The eightfold increase in labor force participation of working mothers from 1940 to 1975 (Hill 1977) has been followed in the last decade by a 50 percent increase in the number of working women with children under age 18. Today over three-fifths of all mothers, almost twenty million women, are in the labor force and the majority (71%) are employed full-time (U.S. Bureau of Census 1984a). Increasing most rapidly is the labor force participation rate of married mothers with preschool children. Hayghe (1984) reports that 47 percent of women with children under the age of one and 60 percent with children aged 3 to 5 are in the labor force.

There are 5.5 million children 13 years and younger, including 1.8 million children under age 6, who live in one-parent families in which the parent works (U.S. Bureau of Census 1984a). The percentage of female heads-of-household needing child care is even greater than that of married working mothers; 79 percent of divorced women with children are employed or looking for work (Hayghe 1984). Children from single-parent households are also more likely to be poor than those in two-parent families, suggesting that affordability of child care is of particular concern for employed single mothers.

Other groups for whom the need for child care has been demonstrated include 2.4 million children under age 13 with one or both parents looking for work (Grossman 1981); over half a million children born each year to teenage mothers, half of whom have not completed high school (National Center for Health Statistics 1981); over 4 million handicapped preschool and school-age children (Children's Defense Fund 1982); one million children in families under stress needing emergency child care as an alternative to more expensive foster or institutional placement (U.S. Department of Health and Human Services 1980); and 1.8 million school-age "latch-key" children (Children's Defense Fund 1982). Finally, the needs of adolescents for supervision and contact with adults after school hours must be counted among the demands for child care. The child care needs of adolescents are rarely defined as such, quite unlike the situation in Scandinavian countries, for example, where it is assumed that children up to age fifteen need various kinds of care.

Most families with children need some supplemental and/or professional child care; however, the need for child care varies with the demographic characteristics of the family. Child care responsibilities appear particularly important when comparing groups of employed women by number of children. In female-headed families 78 percent of women with one child work, but only 43 percent of women with 4 or more children work. In two-parent families 70 percent of mothers with one child work; 50 percent of mothers with 4 or more children work (U.S. Bureau of the Census 1984a).

Female heads-of-households, low-income women, and professional women have reported the particular difficulties of finding or maintaining employment when child care is unavailable or only available at costs which they cannot afford (Levine 1981). Among unemployed mothers of young children, 36 percent with family incomes below $15,000 report that the lack of child care at a reasonable cost is a primary barrier to looking for work (U.S. Bureau of the Census 1983). Child care cost and availability, and governmental policy which affects services, are a primary influence in labor force participation for many women.

Availability of Child Care

The supply of child care lags far behind the demand. For example, for the 10 million children under age 6 who have employed mothers, there are only 900,000 center-based slots and 5.2 million family day care home slots (Divine-Hawkins 1981). Care for infants and toddlers is even more difficult to find; for the over 3 million children under age three with employed mothers there are 122,000 licensed center slots (Children's Defense Fund 1982). In fact, there were fewer day care slots in licensed programs in 1982 than 40 years ago (Clarke-Stewart 1982).

The 1970s brought a dramatic increase in the number of national child care chains, but they only account for 6 percent of the market. Churches accounted for one-third of the group child care programs by 1984 (Lindner 1985). Many states have exempted church-sponsored child care from licensing regulations as the demand for child care far exceeded the existing supply (Fenn 1983). The 1980s thus far have brought a 200 percent increase in the number of employers providing work-place day care for employees. Thus, in several sectors child care facilities have increased rapidly in the 1980s, but there has been a decline in publicly funded day care, so the net change has not resulted in an increase of slots.

Quality of Care

Assessing the quality of care is particularly complex. Even when parents seek information from "experts" such as their pediatrician, few of the experts who recommend day care settings have ever visited them and know little about their quality (Clarke-Stewart 1982; Bradbard and Endsley 1980). Among child development professionals, there is general agreement about what constitutes quality child care; researchers have emphasized the importance of child-staff ratios, group size, and caregiver training in child care. However, there are no enforced federal guidelines for standards of quality in child care, and state guidelines for licensing suggest only minimal standards.

Greenman (1984) suggested that policymakers, parents, and professionals avoid a critical analysis of quality in child care for several reasons. Child care attempts to meet so many diverse goals, such as enhancing children's intellectual and psychological development, strengthening families, educating and training parents, providing health services and preparing children academically for school, that it is difficult to determine success and resolve quality issues related to such a broad mission. Also, the struggle for quantity has often taken precedence over the struggle for quality, and raising regulatory standards to improve quality threatens to raise child care costs to parents or close programs. Moreover, Greenman suggests that questioning the quality of care creates anxiety and guilt for parents who must use nonparental child care and undermines attempts to establish day care as a positive alternative to familial care. The explosion of a variety of child care options has produced pressure to establish criteria for "quality" care. Further pressure for criteria has resulted from the reports of child sexual and physical abuse in day care, from research findings about the outcomes from early childhood education, and from the recognition of the need for selection and training of providers.

Child Care Provider Characteristics

Research has demonstrated that child care provider characteristics are among the most important determinants of day care quality (Roupp 1979). Few studies are available to document professional and personal characteristics of providers; the profiles available must be used with an understanding of their limitations.

Eddleman and Gulley (1982) surveyed the employment and education histories and working conditions of 291 employees in Title XX funded child care centers and family day care homes in 27 counties of southern Illinois. The majority of child care workers were female (98%), white (83%), ages 20–39 (68%), and married (58%). Almost a quarter of the respondents chose not to answer questions related to education; of those that did, 10 percent had less than a high school education, 33 percent had a diploma or GED, 3 percent had an associate degree, 7 percent had a college degree, and 1 percent had a graduate degree. The majority of caregivers had had no classes in child care or development in either high school (79%) or college (61%). The most frequent training reported by workers was personal reading (59%) and baby-sitting experience (62%).

Salary and working conditions for employees were reported as poor in the Eddleman and Gulley (1982) survey. Among the 64 percent who provided salary information, only 3 percent reported paid health insurance; 5 percent worked for less than minimum wage, and 33 percent received minimum wage. The modal annual family income for providers was $5,000 to $10,000. A multistage study reported that the average median income of child care workers in 1982 was $10,155 (up from $5,100 in 1975), approaching the 1975 median income of elementary school teachers ("Wage Woes" 1983).

Eddleman and Gulley also reported that most of the child care workers surveyed either moved from position to position frequently or entered and left the profession after a short period of time. According to Bureau of Labor Statistics, child care workers have higher turnover rates than most other workers in the country. "Workers in day care centers, nursery schools, Head Start, and other child care professions left work at a 41.7 percent rate in a 12-month period in 1980–81." Only dishwashers, peddlers, and gas pumpers leave their jobs at higher rates ("Wanted: Experienced Teachers" 1984: 1). The same Bureau of Labor Statistics report projected the growth rate for preschool teachers in the 1990s would be 38 percent to 44 percent, compared to a total labor force growth rate of 23 percent to 28 percent, suggesting that the demand will be far greater than the supply of qualified child care providers into the next decade.

A somewhat different picture of worker characteristics is provided by a 1983 survey of child care workers conducted by the National Association for the Education of Young Children (NAEYC 1984). Questionnaires were included in the NAEYC's national publication mailed to 43,000 members and 5,000 nonmembers. Usable responses were received from 2,800 members and 1,000 nonmembers. Because the sample was drawn from readers and members in a professional organization whose salaries, educational levels, and level of professional identification are high, this survey yields information on child care workers with the most professional preparation and orientation.

The majority of child care workers in the NAEYC study were female (85%), white (90%), over age 30 (60%), and with some college work in early childhood education (59%). Despite their educational qualifications and professional identification, the majority of the teachers earned between minimum wage and $7.50 an hour; the majority of directors earned $5.00 to $10.00 an hour.

The largest survey of child care workers' income and characteristics is provided by the Bureau of the Census (1984b). In 1979 there were over a half million paid child care workers (other than in private households). The majority were female (93%), 6 percent had an eighth-grade education, 60 percent had 1–4 years of high school, 30 percent had 1–4 years of college, and 3 percent had some graduate training. The mean annual income for both full-time and part-time employees was $3,675 (mean hourly wage of $3.13) for female child care workers and $6,669 (mean hourly wage of $4.55) for male child care workers. For employees who worked full-time the annual salary was higher, yet the hourly earnings were lower. Mean annual income was $6,124 (mean hourly wage of $2.67) for females and $10,575 (mean hourly wage of $4.52) for males.

The Bureau of Census reported that among 106,000 employed child care workers in private households, 17 percent had an eighth-grade education, 62 percent had 1–4 years of high school, 20 percent had 1–4 years of college, 1 percent had some graduate training. The mean annual income for both full-time and part-time employees was $2,415 (mean hourly wage of $2.17) for females and $4,366 (mean hourly wage of $3.92) for males. Year-round full-time female child care workers had a greater economic disadvantage than males or part-time employees. Their mean annual income was $4,360 (mean hourly wage of $1.90); full-time male employees had an annual income of $9,337 (mean hourly wage of $4.07).

The small number of private household child-care workers included in these data indicates the informal, transitory, almost invisible nature of private and family day care home services. It is difficult to profile these providers; even states which have laws requiring the licensing of family day care homes have difficulty identifying, much less monitoring, these services.

The data presented about the education and training of child care providers are particularly relevant to our previous discussion of child care quality. The National Day Care Study (Roupp 1979) identified vocational education and training in child development and care as one of the most important, feasible, and inexpensive determinants of higher-quality child care. Even the limited information available about child care workers' training suggests the tremendous need for expanded training and educational opportunities for both center-based and home-based providers.

Although comprehensive information on child care workers in this country is lacking, it is probable that the fact that they primarily are women explains their poor economic status. The "demographic nightmare" confronting millions of women, then, is that child care is a barrier to economic equity for some women and a cause of economic inequity for other women whose labor force participation as minimally paid child care workers subsidizes the services they provide (Kaufman 1984). Moreover, employees, particularly females who work full-time, subsidize the services they provide to an even greater degree than employees who work part-time or those who enter and leave the profession frequently.

Governmental Regulation of Child Care (Licensing and Certification)

There are at least four types of governmental regulations about minimal standards of quality that child care providers must meet before lawfully providing services: licensing, zoning, building and fire safety, and health and sanitation regulations. Of these, day care licensing is "the cornerstone of regulatory administration for day care" (Morgan 1984). Licensing standards usually are established by a designated state agency through public hearings and a task force of parents and child care professionals. Licensing standards are a form of consumer protection for children and their families; child care providers not meeting the standards are denied a license to lawfully provide services. Although in some professions licensing implies quality, licensing in day care assures only minimum standards. And while in the 1970s there was evidence that state day care licensing was improving (Johnson 1980), more recent indications show weakening in the standards and their enforcement.

Currently all states have standards for licensed day care centers. The standards, however, vary from state to state. For example, requirements for child-staff ratios for groups of four-year-olds vary from 20:1 in two states to 5:1 in one state (Johnson 1980). States also vary in the frequency and completeness of enforcement. In Louisiana, for example, compliance for all of the standards is voluntary; other states recently have substituted an "honor system" for routine inspection and monitoring of child care facilities. Under such an honor system child care centers register with a central agency, but centers are not routinely monitored except when complaints are made against the center or when random spot checks occur. Some states exempt casual or drop-in care and mothers-day-out programs from monitoring and regulation. Without monitoring and periodic inspection abuses may go uncontrolled for extended periods.

Family day care homes provide an important, often convenient, and less expensive alternative to center-based care for many parents. But unlike day care centers, many family day care homes are not licensed or monitored by the states. Licensing, certification, and registration, listed in decreasing order of state involvement and monitoring, are examples of regulatory concepts in family day care. Thirty states license family day care homes, twelve states use registration, and three states license and register homes. In five states there is no monitoring of family day care homes except for those in which certified slots are purchased for low-income families through the Social Services Block Grant program (Adams 1982, 1984).

A review of state child care regulatory systems reveals standards which require only minimum quality, which vary from state to state, and which are enforced through infrequent monitoring. Parents who desire quality child care services must rely on a system of governmental intervention that is severely restricted in its support of parents' needs and demands.

There is even less governmental support for certifying the credentials of those working in day care centers or homes. Ten states require a four-year college degree for at least one category of center staff, the director or head teacher, for example. Only three states, however, specify that the degree be in early childhood education or child development. Twenty-six states require the Child Development Associate (CDA) credential of some center staff; the CDA is a competency based credential available to candidates 16 years or older who have had work experience with children and parents and informal or formal training in early childhood education or child development. From 1978 to 1981, fourteen states dropped the academic degree as a requirement for child care workers; only three states increased the academic requirement provisions for child care center staff (Collins 1983). These requirements apply only to center-based care; governmental regulation of family day care providers do not generally address worker training.

Public Programs for Child Care

Governmental involvement in child care in this country has been complicated by efforts to implement other public policy programs, often in a context of conflicting values, through day care legislation. For example, when mothers were needed in the labor force during World War II, Congress passed the Lanham Act to meet the child care needs of mothers working in defense plants. Child care was needed for only the length of the war, and makeshift centers were arranged. "They had only to be better than a locked car, and by that criterion they did succeed" (Rothman 1979).

Providing child care in the context of family assistance was one of the most controversial proposals of recent decades, and it illustrated the complexity of value conflicts in public policy. The Manpower Training Act announced in 1969 by Nixon was designed to provide funds to train low-income and unemployed mothers and day care for their children; the link between child care and welfare reform was obvious. Services were available to welfare mothers who agreed to go to work.

Some critics were angered by Nixon's vague notion of day care which they argued was simply custodial care (Steinfels 1973). Opposition to Nixon's Family Assistance Plan resulted in the introduction of several other day care bills. Senator Walter Mondale introduced a bill calling for $2 billion to plan, develop, and operate "comprehensive physical and mental health, social, and cognitive development services necessary for children" (Keyserling 1972). A similar bill was introduced in the House by John Brademas; a compromise version of the two was passed by Congress on December 6, 1971. Conservatives attacked the bill as a tool to "sovietize children" that sounded "dangerously like Nazi eugenics" (Roby 1975). On December 9 Nixon vetoed the bill, denouncing its "family weakening implications" and declaring it "the most radical piece of legislation to emerge from the 92nd Congress." He stated that "for the federal government to plunge headlong financially into supporting child development would commit the vast moral authority of the national government to the side of communal approaches to childrearing over against the family-centered approach" (Congressional Record 1971). This position is consistent with the ideology that childrearing is the exclusive responsibility of the nuclear family. Social welfare policy, which defines the family, not its members, as its legitimate target, is rooted in the patriarchical tradition. From this perspective it is politically unacceptable to address children's rights apart from parents' rights.

Mondale, Brademas, and Jacob Javits renewed the struggle in 1975 with the introduction of the Child and Family Services Act, whose purpose was to provide free day care to low-income families and to maximize parent participation and control in child care decisions. The Act was not passed by Congress. Senator Alan Cranston introduced another bill in January 1979 "to provide assistance in the provision of child care services for children living in a home with working parents" ("Hearings held on Cranston Child Care Bill" 1979). As with previous attempts to pass child care legislation, the Cranston bill was labeled radical, socialistic, and feminist-inspired. Hearings and related action on the bill were canceled in March, 1979.

Currently federal involvement and support for day care is implemented in direct expenditures—Grants to States for Social Services, Work Incentive Program (WIN), Child Welfare Services, and Head Start—and indirect support—Dependent Care Tax Credit, Aid to Families with Dependent Children (AFDC), and the Dependent Care Assistance Program (Phillips 1984). As with other social services, day care support by the federal government is particularly vulnerable. Economic declines are often accompanied

by both curtailment of governmental support for child care and
declines in real family income. As a result, the cost of child care to
families is increased when they are least able to afford it.

A prime example of this increased cost to children, families,
and even society occurred with recent cuts in Title XX Grants to
States. In many families children were left unsupervised, in low-
quality care, or with a parent who left the labor market and
sacrificed income. Recent cuts in other programs portend the
development of vastly different services for families of varying
income levels and a continued debate on the values and beliefs
relevant to governmental intervention in child welfare.

RESPONSES TO THE CHILD CARE DILEMMA

From the above review of child care availability, quality,
provider characteristics, certification and licensing standards, and
history of public policy regarding funding of child care, we have
established the following: The very great demand—which is
increasing for children under age three—has not been matched by
available placements for children, particularly in licensed center-
based care, either through the private sector or through public
sector initiatives. Indeed, it is ironic that there has been such a
retreat from society-wide, systematic solutions to child care
dilemmas during a period in which converging demographic trends—
increasing labor force participation by women, the shift in women's
work histories to more nearly match those of men in terms of year-
round, full-time employment with no time out for childbearing and
childrearing, and the increasing probability of marital disruption
during one's lifetime—have made child care a necessity for the
majority of American children.

Coping at the Individual Level

Response to the structurally produced strain from the lack of
child care occurred not at the systemic level but at the level of the
individual family unit. There is evidence of much creativity on the
part of individuals in meeting their parenting obligations to provide
a safe caregiving environment for their children.

Few children are in full-time, group care arrangements that
extend over the full work-day, work-week, and work-year. For
instance, according to recent Current Population Survey data on
nursery school attendance for children aged three to six, fewer than

one-third of children in this age group are attending full day nursery school or kindergarten. Unfortunately, there are no data available through our national data systems (U.S. Bureau of the Census, National Center for Health Statistics, National Survey of Education) or through private sector survey firms that can tell us precisely where children too young for nursery school are cared for during the day. Surprisingly, the need for data on care contexts of very young children was not mentioned in a recent report on statistical needs related to children (Child Trends 1984), nor is this need addressed in revisions to the Current Population Survey schedule for the Child Care Supplement, fielded annually (Siegal, personal communication, 1985).

Further clouding the picture of care contexts for children is the fact that there is little good information about day care homes. Day care homes, as noted earlier, are the least stable, the least subject to external review and scrutiny by local and state licensing bodies, and the least likely to be run by persons trained in child development or group care techniques.

Schedule Splicing. Apparently, most families make patchwork arrangements for the care of their children, piecing together a variety of caretakers and environments over the course of a day and week. Reliance on relatives, neighbors, and paid sitters is common (Waite 1981). The use of several types of family and community services, particularly by part-time workers, mothers with older preschool children in group care, and by families in which the father is the primary caregiver, suggests a need for child care services which are convenient to families and flexible in scheduling (U.S. Bureau of the Census 1983).

Child development professionals continue to point to children's needs for security and consistency in caregiving environments at every age but especially for children under six (Clarke-Stewart 1977). It is unsettling at best that few children of working parents have the luxury of a consistent environment over time. Whitbread (1979) reports that 30 percent of the working mothers in her survey had made changes in the care arrangements of their children at least once in the previous two years because of concerns about the undependability and poor quality of care their children were receiving.

Shift Work. Another response individual adults have made to the discrepancy between their need for childcare and its availability is to turn to shift work, such that at least one parent is home (often asleep) with children while the other is at work. Shift work scheduling among two-earner families is another example of familial stretching as the family system attempts to adapt itself to the inflexible demands of the economic system (Presser and Cain 1983). Alternative work arrangements that facilitate needs for child care are flex-time schedules and job sharing. Both options require support of employers, and both are increasingly available in larger corporations.

Reduced Family Size. From the fertility literature there is evidence that women who work have fewer children in response to the demands of the workplace; that is, their childbearing is reduced over what it might have been in the absence of employment roles in order to accommodate their labor force participation (Waite and Stolzenberg 1976). Cramer (1980), for instance, has shown effectively that the perceived incompatibility of continued labor force participation for women with more than one child has had a dampening effect on fertility decisions in the long run. Further, from anecdotal data it would appear that timing decisions relative to first and later births are made in partial response to child care cost and availability factors. Younger couples may postpone births to build up the economic resources needed for quality child care. Similarly, timing and number decisions about second or later births may be made on the basis of perceived availability of child care (Kamerman 1985). Finally, Lehrer and Kawasaki (1985), in a national sample of married, employed women, found that there was a link between child care arrangements and intended fertility.

Life Course Manipulations. Another common response of women to the structural incompatibility of simultaneous participation in the labor force and in family life is the postponement of labor force entry or of career preparation and participation until children are of school age or older. This pattern was reflected in the very high rates of labor force entry or reentry by women aged 30–50 (whose children were most likely to be of school age) during the 1970s. However, these patterns of late entry or entry/drop-out/reentry have been superseded by the shift in women's work histories to more nearly resemble those of men in terms of early entry and persistence in the labor force over time, regardless of childbearing (Barrett 1979). As shown earlier, the changes over the past decade in the labor force participation patterns of married women with children under six years old are striking. This group has been least likely to participate in the paid labor force, but by 1985 fully 63 percent of married women with children under six were employed (U.S. Bureau of the Census 1985b).

It seems clear that individual men and women, in couples or singly, use the resources available to them in meeting child care needs. They "vote" so to speak with their time—both day-to-day (shift work) and life-course time—their bodies (through fertility decisions), their resources of relatives, friends, and income in an attempt to deal with the care of their children.

Societal-Level Responses

The Failure of Free Market Mechanisms. Our review has also attempted to show that because of low profitability, free market mechanisms have failed to generate an adequate supply of child care placements to meet the demand. High quality means low profit margins because of the high cost of quality care. No one— investors, taxpayers, government officials, or even parents— appears willing to shoulder the costs involved in adequate worker training and salary, safe facilities, and necessary monitoring systems.

The reluctance to pay for care of adequate quality generates its own problems. For instance, it creates a caste of exploited women workers in child care. Kamerman (1985: 269) maintains that current child care policies in the U.S. have resulted in a "...service in which the cost burden is carried largely by underpaid caregivers, who are overwhelmingly female." Our earlier discussion of caregiver characteristics confirms this conclusion.

The Failure of Public Policy. Finally, the review has demonstrated the failure of public policy at the societal level. Ultimately, the ambivalence of public attitudes about the importance of children, the definition of child care as a woman's problem to be handled however she can, and the perception that child care is problematic only for women who are deviant—that is, women who work outside the home—are important factors contributing to the abysmal public record on child care policy in this country. Uncovering some of the underlying reasons for the failure to respond to this serious public issue is the subject of the third part of this chapter.

GENDER ROLE DEFINITIONS AND CHILD CARE

The seriously deficient state of child care in the U.S. reflects a peculiar aversion to anything other than familial patterns of care for children. Underlying this aversion are several gender-linked definitions of normative and nonnormative roles and behaviors. Ultimately, these definitions are intimately tied to configurations in the traditional family, which are based upon sex role segregation and age-based stratification. These include the following generalizations each of which will be briefly discussed.

Childbearing justifies women.
Women should bear more than one child.
Quality mothering is independent of family size.
Men's parenting is secondary to wage earning roles.

Ready availability of child care would reduce the motivation for childbearing and childrearing and therefore destroy the family.

Childbearing Justifies Women. Childbearing justifies a woman's place in family and society. To have children is normative; not to have children is considered deviant for women. Women who opt for a childfree lifestyle are subject to moral sanction and are stereotyped as selfish, unfeminine, and threatening (Veevers 1973). In her studies of childfree women, Veevers cites the common experience among her respondents of childbearing pressure from parents, friends, and significant others.

Houseknecht (1979) suggests that childlessness as a fertility outcome is a product of two separate processes. A few women choose a childfree lifestyle early in their lives and construct their lives around this choice. She found that most childfree women, however, begin as postponers and then never get around to making up for lost time, so that their childfree status is less a product of conscious choice than of happenstance.

Fox et al., in their discussion of fertility socialization, speculate that among young children "childbearing" is equated with "woman." They suggest that "It is probable that as part of learning about sexuality (including sex role learning) in infancy and very early childhood, children come to differentiate men and women in terms of their ability to bear children, and thus to link the property of 'womanness' to childbearing" (22). Girls, in particular, would develop very early an expectation for their own future childbearing (Fox et al. 1982).

Regardless of whatever else she may do, it is generally believed that a "good" woman will have children. This earning of moral worth through childbearing is more subtle in industrialized countries than in countries in which it is a more explicit part of the value system; but it is present nonetheless. Relative to child care, it suggests that not having children as a way of accommodating to the lack of fit between economic and personal spheres is not a morally acceptable option.

Interestingly, recent surveys of fertility intentions of American women suggest that increasing proportions of the younger cohorts of women will remain childless. Using an analog of life-table analysis, the Census Bureau projects that almost one-quarter (24.3%) of white women who are childless at age 19 in 1980 and over one-third (36.7%) of white women who are childless at age 24 in 1980 will remain childless over their lifetimes. The corresponding figures for black women are 9.1 percent and 17.6 percent respectively (U.S. Bureau of the Census 1985a).

Clearly there is a lag between moral values and behaviors relative to norms regarding the meaning of childbearing to women's identity and worth. It is a truism in the social science literature on mores, folkways, and societal sanctions that persons on the outskirts of acceptable behavior cannot count on societal resources to support their behavior.

One Child Is Not Enough. A corollary to the child bearing principle is that women should bear more than one child. The only child is stereotyped as a forlorn and brattish creature (Falbo 1979; Blake 1981) despite research evidence to the contrary. Indeed, in both child development and family research, evidence abounds of the positive benefits to both the child and to the adult parents of the one-child family (Zajonc 1976). Nonetheless, the two-child family continues to be the preference of most American couples, followed by choices of three rather than one child (U.S. Bureau of the Census 1985a).

Because women with small families are far more likely to be in the labor force than those with two or more children (Waite 1981), the linking of deviant fertility behavior (zero or one child) with deviant work roles (working for pay outside the home) makes it easier to ignore needs for child care services for all women. The relative absence of societal resources for nonnormative behavior applies here as well.

Quality Mothering Is Independent of Family Size. Regardless of the shift to smaller families, the demands for quality mothering have not changed. In his analysis of the link between fertility and labor force participation of women, Sweet (1982) identified the expectation that women who work are not exempt from the role demands associated with the traditional wife/mother role. Further, although women may adjust to the demands of the work role by having smaller families, the expectations for "good" mothering are the same irrespective of family size.

Thus some of the economies that are effected through fertility reduction (as, for example, the lower child care costs of two versus more than two children or the reduced hassle of coordinating efforts to respond to needs of fewer rather than more children) are not matched by corresponding accommodations in the normative definition of adequate mothering. That is, mothers of only one or two children are expected to perform the same kinds of activities— such as volunteer roles in their children's school or their extra-academic activities—as mothers with larger families. The principle sustained is that women's mothering is not to be compromised by wage earning.

Popularization of the "Superwoman" syndrome suggests that a competent woman should be able to have above average children, manage a well-kept home, prepare the family meals, hold an executive job, dress well, be beautiful, well groomed, sexually attractive, and smile. In other words, women who have chosen additional roles are expected to handle their multiple roles effortlessly and should not expect to be excused from high standards of performance in traditional roles.

The identification of the "Superwoman" who combines well the stroking, caretaking, and economic provider roles is an important part of the mystification of the current reality of women's lives. Nowhere is it discussed how Superwoman manages child care (or any of her other functions); she simply does, silently, effortlessly, uncomplainingly, and without any drain on societal resources.

Nonmaternal Child Care Is Harmful. This statement suggests that there is no substitute for a mother's care for her small children. Several popular volumes on child development suggest the harm that will come to small children by spending large amounts of time with alternative caregivers (Fraiberg 1977; White 1981). Additionally, many social surveys of adult attitudes toward child care for children under six reflect similar beliefs. They routinely document disapproval of a woman's working outside the home while her children are small, the belief that out-of-home care is harmful to small children, and the like (Scanzoni 1978; Retert and Bumpass 1974). A recent national survey of attitudes toward work and family found, for instance, that majorities of teens and adults agreed with the statement that "When both parents work, children are more likely to get into trouble" (General Mills 1981).

It matters little that incidence of respiratory illness was the only major difference found in research comparing children in group care and children in home care. Experts point out that it is the quality of care rather than its source or location that determines the effect of child care on children (Scarr 1984).

It may be, of course, that a wider range of differences would be found if research were more plentiful on children in less than adequate facilities or in day care homes. Such studies are difficult and expensive; most of the research on children in group care settings is conducted in university-based lab school programs because of the ability of universities to underwrite the studies' costs, and because of the greater acceptability of evaluative research by university lab school directors. However, the most important factor contributing to the paucity of adequate research in this area is that federal research priorities generally ignore the need for research in this area.

The implications of the belief that nonmaternal child care is harmful are many: for one, a woman who would knowingly harm her children by leaving them in the care of others is by definition a bad mother. In other words, simply by securing the safety and well-being of their children by placing them in alternative care contexts, women are deviant. It is perhaps worth stating here that women and men who need and seek child care are socialized in the culture that we are describing. This means that in addition to the difficulty of finding and paying for good child care (not to mention the logistical problems that are associated with it), parents—and especially mothers—must confront the fact that there is little moral, normative support for their efforts.

It follows that blame for any harm that actually does befall children either directly or indirectly can be placed squarely at the feet of the person responsible for the care of the children, and that is their mother. One can begin to see why there is such reluctance to propose and support national policy for children and child care. Most simply put, if child care for young children is harmful, then it follows that facilitation of alternative care is poor public policy.

Interestingly, the use of alternative caregivers in the home is a common pattern among well-to-do and upper-class families both here and abroad. Nannies, maids, au pairs, governesses, and mother's helpers are familiar institutions. The difference between these personnel and today's caregivers lies not in their function, training, or relationship with children but rather in the function of the mother who employs them. So long as caregivers are used to enhance women's performance of their wife-mother roles rather than to substitute for it, then the alternative caregiver is acceptable. In other words, assistance in caring for children in the home is not deviant so long as it enables the woman to intensify her role performance in traditional spheres.

Men's Parenting Is Secondary to Wage-Earning Roles.
Men may perform as backup caregivers, but men's fathering is secondary to their economic provider functions. Men's wage-earning role is not to be compromised by parenting; to do so is deviant.

Even when participation in parenting is facilitated, there is indication that few men take advantage of the opportunity for fuller engagement in the parenting role. Bohen (1984) cites confirming evidence from Sweden, which as a matter of public policy has embarked on perhaps the boldest effort to ensure sex equality. Since the lack of alternatives for care for children is recognized as one of the most significant barriers to sex equality in the marketplace in the U.S. (U.S. Commission on Civil Rights 1981), the Swedish experience with parenting leaves is an important one. According to Bohen (1984: 266), after six year's experience with a parental-leave policy, "...Swedish men were using only about 15% of the time available to them—even though their time away from work is compensated at 90% of their wage." Bohen points to sex wage differentials as a major reason for the lack of use of the parenting policy by men. Women earn less than men; a couple deciding on which parent should stay home usually opted for the wife. But more than economic rationality is involved. Bohen (1983: 41) also reports that Swedish men believed that those taking father's leaves fell in three categories: (1) worked in low level occupations in which job disruption has no long-term career consequences, (2) were forced into it by controlling wives, (3) were members of the new intelligentsia with well-educated wives in comparable job status and engaged in alternative life styles.

In the U.S. the experience with parenting leaves has been similar. Bohen (1983) reports that only a handful of U.S. employers offer parenting leave to employees, generally surrounding the time of childbirth. According to a report from the Children's Defense Fund (cited by Bohen), even when parenting leaves are available, few men have taken advantage of parenting leaves. Similarly, a survey of 104 human resources officers of Fortune 1300 corporations and of 56 labor leaders showed that three-fifths of the former and two-fifths of the latter group felt that paid paternity leaves would not benefit employees and their families (General Mills 1981).

Even during periods of unemployment when the availability of time to care for children no longer is a factor in parenting, there is evidence that men continue to define childrearing as primarily the wife's responsibility. The Economic Stress and Coping Study of more than 600 households in the Detroit (MI) SMSA during the early 80s recession showed that fathers did not increase the amount of time spent in parenting activities during periods of unemployment; unemployed women, however, reported that "having more time with the children" was one of the positive aspects of unemployment (Fox and Sheldon 1983).

It is important to recognize the gap between attitudes and practice on the matter of paternal participation in child care. A national survey of a cross section of American adults showed that large majorities disagree with the statement "Raising children should be the responsibility of the mother, not the father, whether or not she works." Almost 9 out of 10 persons surveyed registered their disagreement (General Mills 1981). However, when parents are queried about their parenting time and activities in the home, it is clear that women are the parents more involved with child care. More importantly, when working parents are called upon to disrupt their work days because of needs of their children (sickness, doctor's appointments, special events), it is women workers rather than men workers who respond.

Almost a decade ago Pleck (1977) wrote of the differential permeability of male versus female work and family roles. His analysis is still apt. Men's family roles are permeable to work demands; women's work roles are permeable to family demands. If anything has changed over the past decade, it is the decreasing degree of permeability of women's work roles and women's greater inability to respond to family needs as their jobs have become more similar to those of men.

The reluctance of fathers to define care of their own children as their (as opposed to their wife's) primary responsibility contributes to the problem of defining care of other people's children as a citizen's responsibility. Instead, we are much more likely to define another woman's children as her own problem and thus are reluctant to support an overall societal approach to problems of child care.

Ready Availability of Child Care Threatens the Family.

Underlying recent proposed federal legislation (Family Protection Act) is the concern that too much child care or child care too readily available on a societal scale will lead to the abandonment of the natural female role—that of mother. This concern is also notable in the minority report on the child care hearings. In their addendum to the report of the Select Committee on Children, Youth, and Families of the U.S. House of Representatives (1984: 159) on child care, Representatives Coats, Bliley, and Vucanovich write:

> The Committee heard from many witnesses who listed the shortfalls in the current child care network and the need to expand these resources. Regrettably, very little attention was focused on an option which holds a lot of promise for many women—reducing the need for child care.
> ...As it stands now, economically and socially, many mothers feel pressured to work. Economic and social incentives for mothers who want to be at home would at least present women with a fair balance of opportunity—the first genuine "choice" they've had in a long time.

Whether the choice of motherhood as the main role and home as the major locus of adult women's activity is forced or merely fostered by the lack of child care resources in a society, the advocates of these positions are inaccurate in their analysis of how private behaviors have been shaped by public policies. For, as was suggested earlier, the motherhood role is reduced not by the ready availability of good child care but by its absence. Because of the difficulty in securing and paying for high-quality care for more than one or at most two children, couples have adjusted their fertility plans and performance downward as an accommodation to the situation (see Lehrer and Kawasaki 1985, for example).

Further, time-use studies have suggested that the mothering time of employed women is reduced by some eleven hours per week compared to that of housewives, and that it is not made up for by the husbands of these women (Walker and Woods 1976). The lack of good child care for preschoolers and after-school placements for older children does not push their mothers out of the labor force; rather, it simply reduces the number of hours per week children spend in the company of adult caregivers. In essence, children are bearing the brunt of the burden for a structurally inconsistent system. Only a society with ambivalent attitudes about the value of childhood and children could support the emergence and persistence of such a "solution" to work-family interface problems.

In our society family privacy is a strong and pervasive value. The protection of the "family" over against "society" has been a goal of much social legislation in U.S. history. One of the outcomes of this orientation is the privatization of many family functions that in other societies are defined as a collective responsibility. Child care is one of these responsibilities. Our society stands in sharp contrast to most of Europe, Australia, and much of Asia, where proper child socialization and child care are viewed as a community responsibility rather than that of the family alone (Sarri 1985; Bronfenbrenner 1970). The benefits to society of an adequate supply of affordable, quality child care suggest that child care responsibilities should be viewed as a societal responsibility as much as a parental one.

PROGRAM AND POLICY IMPLICATIONS

Excellent analyses and program agenda exist in the area of child care, and it is not necessary to recreate or repeat them here (Kamerman 1980; Kamerman et al. 1983; Levine 1981; U.S. Department of Labor 1982). As an alternative, we make the following modest observations:

The debate over child care must be taken out of the moral arena. Earlier, we attempted to pull out the underlying presumptions about women and their appropriate roles in order to examine the moral bases of the failure of child care policy in this country. As we tried to show, the ambivalent attitudes toward children and their care are tied intimately to our feelings about the nature of families, of women, and of men.

Others have found that when child care is defined as a necessity for women who work without choice, the resistance is eliminated. For instance, Kamerman (1985: 265) cites a survey conducted by the Public Agenda Foundation as follows:

When child care is removed from the realm of morality and expressed instead as a practical problem...rather than a trade-off between women's rights and children's needs, Americans agree that the child care problems of working families are critical problems that must be tackled.

The hidden costs of a poor system of child care alternatives must be counted. These include costs in lost productivity of employees due to child care breakdowns and inadequate arrangements. The Women's Bureau suggests that reliable child care arrangements can reduce tardiness, absenteeism, job turnover, and industrial accidents due to divided attention of anxious employees (U.S. Department of Labor 1982). Similarly, Fernandez (1985), in an analysis of 5000 employees at a major U.S. corporation, shows that the work-family conflicts of workers reduce corporate productivity and that child care problems in particular have a negative impact on employee performance. Fernandez recommends that corporate employers provide a wide variety of child care assistance alternatives, including flexible work options, referral services, training programs, subsidized day care and job sharing (1985). It may well be that the best strategy for generating support for systematic child care policy in this country will be effective cost-benefit analyses documenting dollar costs of productivity short-falls due to child care difficulties of employees.

The costs of an inadequate system of child care to children must also be tallied for the long run. Included are long-term effects of poor care or care ill suited to their needs, the fear and loneliness that accompanies the self-care of children, lost opportunities of socialization through curtailed exposure to adults, and the risks of poor or no supervision of children. Although we have not dealt specifically with the needs of adolescents in this chapter, it is obvious that an outcome of long hours of unsupervised time for older children is the increased opportunity for participating in harmful behaviors such as alcohol and drug abuse, smoking, and sexual intercourse. For example, it should not be surprising that adolescents who are sexually experienced report that their usual location for sexual intercourse is their own or their partner's home, in the afternoon after school when no one else is at home (Zelnik and Kantner 1980). Although other countries such as Sweden have included adolescents' needs in national attempts to provide child care, in this country we struggle with preschool and school-age needs for care and virtually ignore older children.

Costs to families are also involved. For example, families meeting child care needs through staggered work schedules pay for this arrangement with reduced opportunities for parents to spend time together. The anxiety, stress, and tension that accompany the search for child care are commonly reported as are the continuing concerns for the child's ultimate well-being (Powell 1980). For parents, child care means loss of control over the life of one's child at an age earlier than that to which we were accustomed, that is, at the time of mandated school enrollment. Exacerbating the problem of loss of control is the difficulty for families to establish a systematic extension and compatibility of their parenting style with that of caregivers when child care arrangements are short term and a variety of caregivers fluctuate into and out of the parenting/ caregiving arena of a family's life. Other studies have suggested that part of the price working parents pay for child care services include psychological tensions between caregiver and parent and stress due to parental dissatisfaction with the specific care received by their child (Whitebrook 1984; Rapoport and Rapoport 1976). Lindner (1985) has concluded that these costs—to employers, to children, and to families—of our "national policy of child carelessness" are expensive in human and economic terms and extract a toll that we as a nation cannot afford.

Finally, we would observe that a forceful articulation is needed of the value of children to a society and of a society's broad responsibility to all of its children. In one of the clearest and most dispassionate analyses of the systematic transfer of societal resources away from children over the past decade, Preston (1984) documents the deterioration in the quality of life, health, and well-being of children in this society. He concludes that our society has ceased to acknowledge its collective interest in the welfare of children, at heart a disinterest in the future welfare of the commonwealth.

Preston (1984), Skolnick (1983), and others have argued that recent legislative and administrative attempts to eliminate numerous federal and state programs designed to safeguard and enhance child well-being and to return a variety of responsibilities for child welfare back to the family have occurred not because of the family's ability to meet those responsibilities, but because "...the constituency for children in public decisions simply appears too feeble to fight back. In short, we may be returning responsibilities to families not because they are so strong but because they are so weak" (Preston 1984).

Such analyses suggest that a national agenda for supportive services for families and children is sorely needed. For all its faults, the 1980 White House Conference on Families did in fact generate such an agenda, and foremost among its recommendations was a partnership of business and government in the support of family-oriented policies.

We suggest that issues of child care can most effectively be addressed as part of a broader set of needs of families for supportive services. Comprehensive services to children and families would include not just child care but health care, nutrition, education, and concern with psychological and emotional well-being. Excellent child care could be the first step toward circumventing problems of abuse, neglect, and later individual personality and social disorders. Although Head Start serves a select population of children, findings from a long-term assessment of program costs and benefits are instructive: for each dollar cost of the program, approximately four dollars are averted in expenditures for future social services, including juvenile incarceration (Weikart et al. 1978).

CONCLUSION

Is there reason for optimism relative to issues of child care? Is there reason to expect an amelioration of the current situation? We can offer a tentative "yes" to these questions. For one, more families now experience the need for child care, and their expectations for care are more sophisticated perhaps than was the case earlier. For another, more employers recognize the difficulties facing their employees with children. Both corporate and union interest in employer-assisted child care alternatives is growing.

Third, increased media attention to the problem of child sexual abuse, with concern focused particularly on children in group care settings, has had the perhaps counterintuitive effect of increasing public awareness of and demand for high standards of group care, on the one hand, and on the other of recognizing the relative safety of group care as compared to care in a child's own family or in day care home situations. The consumer interest in higher quality care can translate into public pressure for more adequate licensing standards, more adequate monitoring, more adequate training for caregivers, and even greater willingness to pay for better care.

Finally, there is evidence that child care issues are increasingly present on the political agenda. The Select Committee on Children, Youth and Families of the U.S. House of Representatives conducted hearings on child care during the session of the 98th Congress. Greater attention is being paid to child care issues in the collection and dissemination of national data holdings (Child Trends, Inc. 1984). Challenges by women's political organizations to own child care as an issue of special significance to women are appearing in the literature (Kamerman 1985; Pogrebin 1983). And in various communities across the country there is evidence of experimentation with community resources, including schools, to provide child care services before, after, and during the regular school day.

The bottom line in the matter of child care, however, is an issue of values. As a society, we have consistently shied away from serious and systematic approaches to the provision of child care because of beliefs about the nature of women and the value of children. Until our value system catches up with the new realities of family life in this society—what Preston refers to as "the earthquake that shuddered through the American family in the past 20 years"—so that we can clearly design social structures that are workable, until that time the burden of adjustment and coping will continue to fall on those most vulnerable.

References

Adams, D., 1984. "Family Day Care Registration: Is It Deregulation or More Feasible State Public Policy?" Young Children 39, 4: 74–77.

Adams, S.D., 1982. National Survey of Family Day Care Regulations, Statistical Summary. ERIC Document Reproduction Service No. 220 207.

Barrett, N.S., 1979. "Women in the Job Market: Occupations, Earnings, and Career Opportunities," in R.E. Smith (ed.) The Subtle Revolution. Washington, DC: The Urban Institute.

Blake, J., 1981. "The Only Child in America: Prejudice versus Performance," Population and Development Review 7, 1 (March): 43–54.

Bohen, H.H., 1983. "Corporate Employment Policies Affecting Families and Children: The United States and Europe." New York: Aspen Institute for Humanistic Studies.

Bohen, H.H., 1984. "Gender Equality in Work and Family: An Elusive Goal," Journal of Family Issues 5, 2 (June): 254–72.

Bradbard, M. and R. Endsley, 1980. "The Importance of Educating Parents to be Discriminating Day Care Consumers," pp. 189–200 in M.S. Kilmer (ed.) Advances in Early Education and Day Care, Vol. I. Greenwich, CT: JAI Press.

Bronfenbrenner, U., 1970. "Two Worlds of Childhood: U.S. and U.S.S.R." New York: Russell Sage Foundation.

Child Trends, Inc., 1984. Improving National Statistics on Children, Youth, and Families. Washington, DC.

Children's Defense Fund, 1982. The Child Care Handbook. Washington, DC: Children's Defense Fund.

Clarke-Stewart, A., 1977. Child Care in the Family: A Review of Research and Some Propositions for Policy. New York: Academic Press.

Clarke-Stewart, A., 1982. Daycare. Cambridge, MA: Harvard University Press.

Collins, R., 1983. "Child Care and the States: The Comparative Licensing Study," Young Children 38, 5: 3–11.

Congressional Record, 1971. December 2, E12897.

Cramer, J.C., 1980. "Fertility and Female Employment: Problems of Causal Direction," American Sociological Review 45, 2 (April): 397–432.

Divine-Hawkins, P., 1981. Family Day Care in the United States: Executive Summary. Washington, DC: U.S. Department of Health and Human Services, Administration for Children, Youth, and Families.

Eddleman, E.J. and S.B. Gulley, 1982. "The Child-Care Provider: A Profile and Implications for Training," Early Child Development and Care 10: 113–24.

Falbo, T., 1979. "The Only Child: A Review," in G.K. Whelan (ed.) Family Relationships. Minneapolis, MN: Burgess.

Fenn, D., 1983. "Day Care Chains," Working Woman (August): 104, 106, 108.

Fernandez, J.P., 1985. Child Care and Corporate Productivity: Resolving Family/Work Conflicts. Lexington, MA: Lexington Books.

Fox, G.L., B.R. Fox, and K.A. Frohardt-Lane, 1982. "Fertility Socialization: The Development of Fertility Attitudes and Behavior," in G.L. Fox (ed.) The Childbearing Decision. Beverly Hills, CA: Sage Publications.

Fox, G.L. and A.W. Sheldon, 1983. "The Impact of Economic Uncertainty on Children's Roles Within the Family." Paper presented at the Society for the Study of Social Problems Annual Meeting, Detroit, MI, August.

Fraiberg, S., 1977. Every Child's Birthright: In Defense of Mothering. New York: Basic Books.

General Mills, 1981. The American Family Report 1980–81: Families at Work. Minneapolis, MN.

Greenman, J.T., 1984. "Perspectives on Quality Day Care," pp. 3–20 in J.T. Greenman and R.W. Fuqua (eds.) Making Day Care Better. New York: Teachers College Press.

Grossman, A.S., 1981. "Working Mothers and Their Children," Monthly Labor Review 104, 5: 3.

Hayghe, H., 1984. "Working Mothers Reach Record Number in 1984," Monthly Labor Review 107, 12: 31–34.

"Hearings Held on Cranston Child Care Bill", 1979. Young Children 34, 3: 62.

Hill, C.R., 1977. "The Child Care Market: A Review of the Evidence and Implications for Federal Policy," pp. 133–36 in Policy Issues in Day Care. ERIC Document Reproduction Service No. ED 149 861.

Houseknecht, S.K., 1979. "Timing of the Decision to Remain Voluntarily Childless: Evidence for Continuous Socialization," Psychology of Women Quarterly 4, 1: 81–96.

Johnson, L. and Associates, 1980. Comparative Licensing Study. Washington, DC: U.S. Department of Health, Education and Welfare. Administration for Children, Youth, and Families.

Kamerman, S.B., 1980. Parenting in an Unresponsive Society: Managing Work and Family. New York: Free Press.

Kamerman, S.B., 1985. "Child Care Services: An Issue for Gender Equality and Women's Solidarity," Child Welfare 44, 3 (May-June): 259–71.

Kamerman, S.B., A.J. Kahn and P.W. Kingston, 1983. Maternity Policies and Working Women. New York: Columbia University Press.

Kaufman, B., 1984. "The Feminization of Poverty: A Case Study of Policy Formation," The Networker 5, 2.

Keyserling, M.D., 1972. Windows on Day Care: A Report on the Findings of the National Council of Jewish Women of the Day Care Needs and Services in Their Communities. New York: National Council of Jewish Women.

Lehrer, E.L. and S. Kawasaki, 1985. "Child Care Arrangements and Fertility: An Analysis of Two-Earner Households," Demography 22, 4 (November): 499–513.

Levine, J., 1981. "Child Care and Equal Opportunities for Women." Washington, DC: U.S. Government Printing Office.

Lindner, E., 1985. "Danger: Our National Policy of Child-Carelessness." Paper presented at the meeting of the National Association for the Education of Young Children, New Orleans, LA, November.

Morgan, G., 1984. "Change Through Regulation," pp. 163–84 in J.T. Greenman and R. W. Fuqua (eds.) Making Day Care Better. New York: Teachers College Press.

National Association for the Education Statistics, 1981. "Advance Report of Final Natality Statistics, 1979," Monthly Vital Statistics Report 30, 6.

Phillips, D., 1984. "Day Care: Promoting Collaboration Between Research and Policymaking," Journal of Applied Developmental Psychology 5: 91–113.

Pleck, J.H., 1977. "The Work-Family Role System," Social Problems 24, 3: 417–27.

Pogrebin, L.C., 1983. Family Politics. New York: McGraw-Hill.

Powell, D., 1980. Finding Child Care: A Study of Parents' Search Process. Detroit: Merrill-Palmer Institute.

Presser, H. and V. Cain, 1983. "Shift Work Among Dual-Earner Couples with Children," Science 219: 876–79.

Preston, S.H., 1984. "Children and the Elderly: Divergent Paths for America's Dependents," Demography 21, 4 (November): 435–57.

Rapoport, R. and R. Rapoport, 1976. Dual-Career Families Re-examined. New York: Harper and Row.

Retert, S. and L. Bumpass, 1974. "Employment and Approval of Employment Among Mothers of Young Children." Working Paper, University of Wisconsin.

Roby, P., 1975. "Child Care—What and Why?" in P. Roby (ed.) Child Care—Who Cares. New York: Basic Books.

Rothman, S.M., 1979. "Other People's Children: The Day Care Experience in America," The Public Interest 54: 11–28.

Roupp, R., J. Travers, F. Glantz, and C. Craig, 1979. "Children at the Center." Final report of the National Day Care Study. Cambridge, MA: Abt Associates.

Sarri, R., 1985. "Child Welfare and Family Policy." Paper presented at the Conference on Rethinking Child Welfare, Hubert Humphrey Institute of Public Affairs, University of Minnesota, MN, June 20.

Scanzoni, J.H., 1978. Sex Roles, Lifestyles, and Childbearing. New York: Free Press.

Scarr, S., 1984. Testimony before the U.S. House of Representatives Select Committee on Children, Youth, and Families, September 5.

Siegal, P.W., 1985. U.S. Bureau of the Census, Personal Communication, September.

Skolnick, A.S., 1983. The Intimate Environment. Boston: Little, Brown and Co.

Steinfels, M.S., 1973. Who's Minding the Children? New York: Simon and Schuster.

Sweet, J.A., 1982. "Work and Fertility," in G.L. Fox (ed.) The Childbearing Decision. Beverly Hills, CA: Sage Publications.

"The Sexual Abuse Issue: How Can Child Care Providers Respond?" 1984. Child Care Information Exchange 34: 20–24.

U.S. Commission on Civil Rights, 1981. Child Care and Equal Opportunity for Women. Washington, D.C.

U.S. Department of Commerce, Bureau of the Census, 1983. Child Care Arrangements of Working Mothers: June 1982. Current Population Reports, Series P-23, No. 129.

U.S. Department of Commerce, Bureau of the Census, 1984a. Families at Work: The Jobs and the Pay. Bulletin 2209.

U.S. Department of Commerce, Bureau of the Census, 1984b. Earnings by Occupation and Education. PC80-2-8B, May.

U.S. Department of Commerce, Bureau of the Census, 1985a. Future Fertility of Women by Present Age and Parity. Current Population Reports, Series P-23, No. 142.

U.S. Department of Commerce, Bureau of the Census, 1985b. Household and Family Characteristics: March 1984. Current Population Reports, Series P-20, No. 398.

U.S. Department of Health and Human Services, 1980. Public Assistance Statistics.

U.S. Department of Labor, 1980. Marital and Family Characteristics of Workers. Bureau of Labor Statistics News Release USDL 80-767, December 9, Table 4.

U.S. Department of Labor, 1982. Employers and Child Care: Establishing Services Through the Workplace. Women's Bureau, Pamphlet 23.

U.S. House of Representatives, Select Committee on Children, Youth, and Families, 1984. Families and Child Care: Improving the Options.

Veevers, J.E., 1973. "Voluntarily Childless Wives: An Exploratory Study," Sociology and Social Research 57, 2: 356–66.

"Wage Woes," 1983. Child Care Employee News 2, 3: 1–2.

Waite, L.J., 1981. "U.S. Women at Work," Population Bulletin 36, 2.

Waite, L.J. and R.M. Stolzenberg, 1976. "Intended Childbearing and Labor Force Participation of Young Women: Insights from Nonrecursive Models," American Sociological Review 45, 2: 397–432.

Waldman, E., 1983. "Labor Force Statistics from a Family Perspective," Monthly Labor Review 106 (December): 16–20.

Walker, K. and M. Woods, 1976. "Time Use: A Measure of Household Production of Family Goods and Services." Washington, DC: American Home Economics Association.

"Wanted: Experienced Teachers," 1984. Child Care Employee News 3, 3: 1–2.

Weikart, D., A.S. Epstein, L. Schweinhart, and J.T. Bond, 1978. The Ypsilanti Preschool Curriculum Demonstration Project: Preschool Years and Longitudinal Results. Ypsilanti, MI: High/Scope Educational Research Foundation.

White, B., 1981. "Viewpoint: Should You Stay Home With Your Baby?" Young Children 37, 1: 11–17.

Whitbread, J., 1979. "Who's Taking Care of the Children?" Family Circle (February 20): 88.

Zajonc, R.B., 1976. "Family Configurations and Intelligence," Science 192: 227–36.

Zelnik, M. and J.F. Kantner, 1980. "Sexual Activity, Contraceptive Use, and Pregnancy among Metropolitan-area Teenagers: 1971–1979," Family Planning Perspectives 12: 230–37.

CHAPTER 6

WOMEN AS CAREGIVERS OF THE ELDERLY: CATCH-22 DILEMMAS

Nancy R. Hooyman
Rosemary Ryan

Family care of dependent older relatives is a critical issue for both social welfare policy and for feminist practice. With fiscal restraints and increased emphasis on private responsibility for long-term care, public expectations are growing for families to provide custodial care for older relatives without compensation for their services. Within this context, the term family caregiving is misleading, since women—primarily wives for men and daughters or daughters-in-law for women—provide over 80 percent of the care—care often taken for granted as a labor of love (Steinitz 1981; Troll 1982). The probability is also great that the person receiving care will be a woman, typically a widow over age 80 with at least one chronic illness. Although some men are caregivers, the involvement of most men tends to be indirect, such as managing finances and home maintenance. Men generally assume primary responsibility for hands on care only when a female relative is unavailable (Horowitz and Dobrof 1982; Brody et al. 1984b; Brody et al. 1984a). Because health care of the elderly depends on women's invisible and unpaid labor, it is also a feminist issue. Women of all ages are interdependent in devising ways to insure their autonomy in old age and to prevent excessive sacrifices among women who provide care to older generations.

The Catch-22 dilemmas faced by women as caregivers of the elderly are the focus of this chapter. A primary bind for women is that they are socialized for caregiving roles accepted as natural, but denigrated by our society. Those who refuse to perform these responsibilities, either because of employment, personal preference, exhaustion, or other family demands, receive little professional, familial, or public support for their choice. Instead, women who deviate from expectations to provide care often experience ambivalence, inadequacy, and guilt. Faced with pervasive societal and professional expectations about caregiving, most women do not reject care responsibilities toward older relatives, however. Those who attempt to combine their care responsibilities along with employment, often at great personal cost, also receive little public support through social services or financial compensation. Either way, women who do not make their caregiving duties primary tend to be defined as deviant in our society.

Yet even those who give first priority to caregiving tasks are frequently punished by poverty and powerlessness. Their lack of lifelong earnings and limited retirement options, for example, produce a double jeopardy for their economic status in old age. Many women face the Catch-22 of being forced to choose between performing their caregiving obligations at the cost of their financial security or deviating from societal expectations to pursue employment-related stability, often at the expense of their own physical and emotional well-being.

Although this chapter focuses on caregiving performed by middle generation women for older generations, it recognizes that caregiving is not a single time-limited episode but spans the life course, often intermixed with paid labor force participation. Caregiving in middle age for an older relative may perpetuate a caregiving career begun with motherhood and extend into old age responsibilities of caring for disabled husbands. Most middle-aged caregivers, for example, provide assistance to more than one older relative along with caring for dependent children (Brody 1985). Although the particular constellation of caregiving demands varies by generation, the societal denigration of caregiving serves to perpetuate women's powerlessness throughout their lives.

This chapter first examines how the ideology and nature of caregiving, along with the historical and societal definitions of caregiving as women's primary role, lock women into socially powerless positions. The demographic and social trends that intensify the Catch-22 dilemmas for female caregivers of the elderly are then reviewed. Next, we discuss detrimental consequences of caregiving roles for women, including the increase in their institutionalized economic dependency with age; the emotional burdens of care; and women's internal barriers to accepting others' help. Finally, this chapter points out how current social and health care policies serve to discourage and even penalize women who care for older relatives. Alternative approaches are suggested to enhance the rewards of caregiving and to reconcile the interests of younger and older generations of women. The chapter concludes that long-range solutions are needed to reintegrate women's and men's private and work lives, rather than maintaining social programs based on traditional assumptions of women's roles that perpetuate an exploitative gender-based division of labor.

THE BINDS FACED BY WOMEN AS CAREGIVERS

The burdens for women as caregivers of the elderly are best understood in the broader context of the binds created by the primacy of women's caregiving roles throughout their lives, and how these isolate them from mainstream activities and values. Women are socialized to a value system of responsiveness and care that is antithetical to marketplace norms of competition and financial gain. They are expected to perform unpaid work that underpins the economy yet is peripheral to the economy as defined by men. Their life's work is thus regarded as nonwork, unrecognized and undervalued in our society.

The ambivalence with which our society views caregiving serves to lock women into powerless positions. On the one hand, wives, mothers, or daughters are expected to be self-sacrificing, nurturing to their families, and caring for their homes. Yet caregiving tasks are assumed to require minimal effort, with women caregivers presumed to have unlimited free time. Our society does little to acknowledge that household and caregiving responsibilities constitute at least a full-time job.

The dual nature of caregiving, composed of both expressive and instrumental behaviors (Graham 1983), also perpetuates the powerlessness of those for whom caregiving is primary. Caregiving is romanticized and honored for meeting fundamental needs for love and affection within the family, needs which presumably cannot be met by paid care providers. Yet caregiving is also viewed with contempt, in part because it does not resemble the time-regulated, task-structured work of industrial production (Cott 1977). Providing human services for family members—whether visiting a homebound parent, driving a child to school, or caring for a disabled spouse—is vital to the maintenance of social bonds, but not defined as work. Caregiving tasks involve maintenance services and being present on 24-hour call to give time and attention to others, rather than the production of tangible and visible goods.

Being held responsible for other family members, regardless of the performance of any specific task, can be psychologically exhausting. A primary cause of such exhaustion is that the psychologically responsible caregiver experiences most relationships as nonreciprocal, constantly giving more support than she receives.

Interacting with a sick child, a preoccupied husband, or a cognitively impaired parent can fail to satisfy even the most altruistic, especially when the care demands are unremitting. Caregivers of Alzheimer's patients, for example, find the most burdensome tasks to be those which require constant vigilance (Morcyz and Blumenthal 1980). Most caregivers of the elderly experience a "support gap," giving more support than they receive (Belle 1982).

In addition, caregiving chores, performed in relative isolation from other adults, are generally not visible and thus not recognized nor rewarded. Caregiving work is more likely to be noticed by others when performed poorly than when done well. The dual nature of caregiving also intertwines the physical drudgery of providing personal services with concern for a loved one's well-being, emotionally tying women to those they assist (Waerness 1983). A woman cannot simply walk away from an incontinent parent or a paralyzed husband as she might from a poorly paid job.

The time-extended process and nature of care for older relatives produce additional dilemmas. With few behavioral norms and models for elder care, our society does little to prepare women for this nearly universal role. In contrast to the extensive childrearing literature, for example, guidelines on caring for older relatives are scarce. Compared to caregivers of children who can expect growing competence and independence, caregivers of the frail elderly, especially those diagnosed with dementia, face only increasing dependence, decline, and relentless physical care tasks, in some instances for more than 20 years (Brody 1985). They may cope for years with little rest, their sleep continuously interrupted by a wandering parent or an incontinent husband, knowing that this situation will not improve with time. Caregiving for elders has been given less status and power than caring for children, because of the low regard generally accorded to the old and disabled in our society. Despite the lack of preparation and rewards, women are expected to know automatically how to be long-term caregivers and are blamed for failing to meet societal expectations if their older relatives are neglected, abused, or institutionalized.

Although most women embrace the traditional norm that families should care for older relatives, and that married daughters should adjust their employment in order to do so (Brody et al. 1984b), many women are confronted with new expectations to work outside the home. Double duty has become the norm for most women. Increasingly, both those who give higher priority to employment than to family responsibilities or those who opt out of paid work altogether are considered deviant in our society. Thus another bind for women, particularly during middle age, is the expectation to "do it all," to juggle the competing marketplace demands of employment with the unpaid, low status, and emotionally binding work of caring for both nuclear and extended family members. Yet few public supports exist for those who attempt to "do it all," either through day care for children and adults, in-home support services, respite programs, tax breaks, or subsidies. In fact, with the current emphasis on private responsibility, policy makers tend to view family care as the most efficient, inexpensive option for providing services to the elderly, without considering the costs to the caregivers. A model of progress prevails that places increasing economic responsibility on women without reducing their role as the mainstay of family life in the home. As a result, many women end up physically or emotionally exhausted from their multiple demands, hidden victims of our current social and health care system.

Women who know their own limits and seek alternatives for their relative's care, such as institutionalization or in-home support services, may be labeled by professionals as unloving, selfish deviants and instilled with guilt and self-doubt. In fact, a husband or son of a disabled older person is more likely to be provided with in-home services, such as visiting nurse, than is his female counterpart, partially because it is presumed that caregiving is not his inherent responsibility. While caregiving for women is an expected duty, for men it is more likely to be regarded as an unexpected expression of compassion. Accordingly, hospital discharge planners usually contact wives, daughters, and daughters-in-law first, assuming that they will be able and willing to provide care (Polansky 1985). Discharge planners, for example, may advise a daughter that "she would not want to place her mother in a nursing home because she would always feel guilty," without assessing the daughter's needs and preferences (Brody 1985). When professionals follow the path of least resistance and shield men from caregiving, they may perpetuate traditional gender-based inequities in caregiving as well as women's powerlessness. Few women have the personal strength to deviate when daily faced with such gender-specific standards.

DEMOGRAPHIC AND SOCIAL TRENDS

The number of women caught in these Catch-22 dilemmas as providers of long-term care will increase substantially in the next few decades due to demographic and social trends. In the past century changes in mortality and fertility rates and patterns of migration have contributed to dramatic increases in the absolute number and proportion of older people. In 1900 approximately three million persons aged 65 and over comprised four percent of the population. By 1980 an estimated 25 million persons age 65 and older constituted 11.8 percent of the population, with those age 75 and over the fastest growing segment. These old-old, who currently comprise 38 percent of the aged population, are most likely to suffer chronic illnesses and disabilities that make them dependent on others. Therefore, even if the norms of family responsibility have not altered substantially over the years, the probability of having to act on them has increased dramatically (Brody 1985).

The increase in life expectancy has also resulted in a major demographic shift in the growth of the multigenerational family. Older people with children comprise four-fifths of the elderly population, a proportion unchanged over the past 20 years. Of these, approximately 94 percent have grandchildren and 46 percent have great-grandchildren. Among adult children, over 80 percent of middle-aged couples have at least one living parent, compared to fewer than half at the beginning of the century (Uhlenberg 1980). As a result, middle-aged children frequently care for two older generations, along with their own dependent children. With technological and medical advances, these trends will continue, with caring for dependent relatives becoming a normative life experience (Brody 1985).

Another crucial demographic factor is that the proportion of elderly relatives has increased faster than the pool of younger family members available to provide care. The current cohort of frail older people reached childbearing age during the Depression. They had markedly low marriage and birth rates, resulting in few adult children to assist with their care in old age. People now entering old age, who gave birth to the baby boom generation, have more children to look to for care. But this increase in the number of potential caregivers is temporary. The next generation returned to the historical pattern of successively declining birth rates. Families thus are increasingly characterized by four generations, by the frailness of the oldest of these generations, and by proportionately fewer younger members to shoulder responsibilities for the growing number of older people. Given these demographic trends, as women advance from 40 years of age to their early 60s, those with surviving parents or parents-in-law are more likely to spend time caring for and living with older relatives. In addition, 90 percent of middle-aged women, many of whom are single parents, have dependent children (Lang and Brody 1980). The anticipated "empty nest" is thus being filled by frail elderly as well as by grown children who cannot afford to leave or who return home.

While faced with multiple caregiving responsibilities from both younger and older generations, more middle-aged women also hold paid jobs. Sixty percent of married women ages 45 to 54 and 42 percent of those aged 55 to 64 are employed (U.S. Bureau of Labor Statistics 1984). Although growing numbers of women work because of career commitments or self-fulfillment, the majority, especially single parents, are employed out of economic necessity. Women's paid employment generally does not reduce their hours of assistance to dependent family members, even though their jobs often provide neither the flexibility nor the income to cushion the effects of these additional demands on their lives (Stroller 1983). As women assume new commitments, their leisure or discretionary time shrinks, not their other obligations (Bernard 1979; Robinson and Thurnher 1979).

Given the ramifications of these changes for the long-term care of the elderly, a critical question is why the U.S. social welfare system treats family caregivers, primarily women, as unpaid service providers. Why is our societal failure to reward caregiving efforts tolerated? Part of the answer lies in how societal expectations of women as caregivers of dependents have developed historically, making it difficult for women over time to deviate from such expectations.

HISTORICAL DEVELOPMENT OF SOCIETAL EXPECTATIONS FOR CAREGIVERS

The caregiving responsibilities traditionally assumed by women did not become social norms and the core of their life's work until after the Industrial Revolution. Women's caregiving became invisible when industrialization made paid labor outside the home the only way to produce something of value. A moralistic ideology of "separate spheres" or the "cult of domesticity," which appeared around 1820, held caregiving to be women's mission to save civilization from moral ruin in the new industrial age. While men controlled the technology, women were to preserve the values of love and nurturing within the home, "removed from the arena of pecuniary excitement and ambitious competition" (Cott 1977). Homelife became an antidote to marketplace competition rather than a central force in shaping society. The conflicting value systems of the old and new social order were thus resolved along lines of gender: men would compete, women would nurture.

Advocating domesticity as a way to enhance women's influence, Catherine Beecher stressed that life's "highest calling"—motherhood—required scientific training, similar to male professions. Beecher and other midnineteenth-century feminists argued for women's moral superiority, "based on their highly developed capacity for self-sacrifice" (Hayden 1981). Since all they owned and earned belonged to their husbands, women were without other means and motives for self-seeking. The only means for extending their influence with the men who controlled their lives was to assert the moral superiority of self-sacrifice (Cott 1977). Caregiving was women's private responsibility, reinforced by high regard for the private sanctity of home life. For the first time in the history of Western civilization, women thereby gained moral leverage over men.

It has been argued that women in preindustrial times had more power as equal economic producers, but that their power eroded as economic production moved out of the home and women stayed behind. While women's contributions were essential to the economic survival of preindustrial households, men nevertheless controlled family finances, property, and custody of the children (Flexner 1973). Patriarchal values and men's physical presence in the home supported the male prerogative to dominate their families (Degler 1980). The fact that industrialization drew men out of the home, along with the growing belief that women's isolation from the marketplace made them morally superior, actually created opportunities for women to exercise more power at home.

From a modern day feminist perspective, the cult of domesticity has been characterized as a patriarchal ploy to maintain women's unpaid and subservient position in the home. It meshed conveniently with the emerging capitalist view of social utility and order, by maintaining and reproducing a viable work force and blunting the brutality of the new industrial system (Bernard 1979). Placing responsibility for workers' emotional needs within the family freed entrepreneurs from affectional concerns, permitting them to pursue profit and serving to support male dominance in society (Cott 1977); Ehrenreich and English 1979; Finch and Groves 1983; Scott 1984). In the long run the cult of domesticity created negative consequences for women by limiting their full participation in life outside the home.

Twentieth-century hindsight, however, fails to explain why our foremothers embraced domesticity with enthusiasm. Viewing it as a male ploy discounts the intensity of people's belief that only the home, as a sanctuary for the old values of love and caring, could save humanity from marketplace inhumanity. The modern view also fails to appreciate the sense of autonomy that women in the mid-1800s felt as they gained freedom from patriarchal bonds within their own separate sphere of influence.

Despite the sincerity of these early feminists, the ideology of separate spheres penalized women by defining labor force participation as deviant for married women of all classes. Except for black married women, only about 10 to 15 percent of minority immigrant women and 5 percent of white middle-class women worked outside the home until World War I. Further, as family income rose, married women in all ethnic groups dropped out of the labor force (Degler 1980). Middle-class married women who fell on hard times often worked surreptitiously because their poorly paid employment cost them the respectability of full-time motherhood. Poor married women and widows not only faced the shame of having to work but could not compete favorably against younger single "girls." They were forced to take the dirtiest, most dangerous, and lowest paying jobs to support their families (Rothman 1978). The ideology of separate spheres also reduced the range of appropriate women's jobs to only those that resembled domestic functions. Because their caregiving responsibilities. were defined as primary, women were considered unsuitable applicants for jobs involving training, continuous labor force participation, or upward mobility. In 1880, for example, 80 percent of nonfarm working women were teachers, domestics, clericals, sales personnel, or workers in clothing manufacturing (Rothman 1978).

Since the Industrial Revolution, efforts to expand women's rights and roles repeatedly met with opposition based on fears that egalitarianism would destroy the family. Women gained access to education, suffrage, and paid employment only as people were convinced that an expansion of women's sphere would enhance rather than undermine their caregiving and would extend women's moral influence into public life (Degler 1980; Flexner 1973; Rothman 1978).

The perception that mothers' paid labor force participation was deviant began to shift in the 1960s, when government officials became concerned that the economy was not growing fast enough. The first President's Commission on the Status of Women developed recommendations for enabling "women to continue with roles as wives and mothers while working and making a maximum contribution to the world around them" (Executive Order 10980).

> Modern woman, on discharging her homemaking obligations, is faced with a variety of needs and opportunities for activities outside the home. Their needs often are related to the needs of her family, and her assumption of responsibility for helping to meet them is, in essence, an extension of her homemaking role. (Commission Report on Home and Community 1963: 1)

As women's caregiving duties have extended into the marketplace, their responsibilities have multiplied, without a compensatory reduction in the psychological demands and the physical work of caregiving nor an increase in public supports. For example, a 1984 study found that both employed and not employed women provided nearly equal amounts of care to their dependent mothers (Brody et al. 1984b). Regardless of their employment status, personal preference, and abilities, major portions of women's lives are consumed by caring for dependents. Some of the detrimental consequences of this pattern are next examined.

DETRIMENTAL CONSEQUENCES OF THE CAREGIVING ROLE FOR WOMEN

Although this section deals specifically with the deleterious effects of caregiving, caregiving values per se are not under scrutiny. The importance and necessity of caregiving work are taken as givens. And for many women—and some men—family caregiving is their preferred life's work. Our critique is directed at the structurally based assumption that caregiving is women's unpaid work, an assumption that perpetuates the powerlessness of female caregivers and blocks their access to socially valued resources.

A primary negative consequence of caregiving is structural economic inequality. Society's denigration of the invisible work of caregiving is played out in women's lower economic status throughout life, and especially in old age. Years spent out of the full-time paid labor force to care for others are not compensated by private pensions or social security, even though caregiving services are essential to the economy and to the family. Women's status as unpaid caregivers and underpaid employees are closely interconnected. For example, women's paid jobs tend to be regarded as secondary income sources, providing low pay and inadequate retirement benefits. The ultimate penalty is that a woman who has performed socially expected caregiver roles frequently faces poverty upon her husband's death or divorce, when she cannot draw on his income or status. The poverty of many middle-aged and older women derives from the fact that their economic position has depended on their relationship or lack of one with a man and the provisions he has made for them on his death or divorce. Most women are unable to count on either survivors benefits from their husband's pensions or on alimony payments in exchange for years devoted to caregiving. In fact, the feminization of poverty might more appropriately be labeled the growing irresponsibility of men, who control the sources of economic and political power (Amidei 1985).

After devoting their lives to attending to others' needs, many women then face years of living alone on a low or poverty-level income, with inadequate medical care and health insurance, in substandard housing, and with their welfare resting on the presence, willingness, and ability of younger female relatives. Outliving their husbands, women predominate in nursing homes, part of a woman's industry, with poor women as residents and other poor women as attendants. A growing number of women in nursing homes are painfully realizing that "motherhood and apple pie are sacred in our society, but neither guarantees security in old age" (Sommers 1975). Instead, gender stratification in youth produces economic stratification in old age.

Structural barriers to reentering the paid work force are a second negative economic repercussion from leaving the marketplace to care for dependents. Model employees are expected to enter the labor force around age 20, work in the same occupation continuously for 45 years, and then retire. This ideal may approximate many men's experiences, but it is alien to the discontinuities and later age of full-time employment characteristic of women's work lives. Work interruptions for six months or more for marriage, childrearing, and elder care place women at a competitive disadvantage; for example, married women currently aged 45 to 64 have lost an average of 37 percent of their potential work years due to work discontinuities, which thereby limit their earnings and retirement benefits (Rix 1984). Furthermore, women socially isolated by their caregiving experiences frequently lack the educational qualifications, self-confidence, and knowledge of resources conducive to securing decent paying jobs. Employers who discount women because of their age, sex, and limited education are generally unwilling to give them credit for caregiving experience, because work in the home is viewed as nonwork and without monetary value. Many employers also still hold the "cheap labor reserve theory" that women are supported by men and do not need to work. Presumably capable of only unskilled jobs, women often settle for low-paying positions that require little specialized training and afford limited opportunities for advancement. These factors converge to keep most women in an economically precarious position even though their marketplace responsibilities have increased (Minkler and Stone 1985).

Women who attempt to combine employment with caregiving responsibilities often find that their paid work further reflects and intensifies their caregiving roles. Many middle-aged women with multiple caregiving demands predominate in public service jobs, such as teaching, nursing, social work, and clerical and service occupations—all of which require an ability to respond quickly to others' needs. Such service positions usually do not permit the flexibility to take time off during the day to attend to ill dependents, but instead require a deduction in pay for missed time. If women in lower status jobs need to feign illness as a cover for helping a family member, they may experience the additional pressure of close scrutiny for their use of sick time. Earning approximately 64 cents for each dollar earned by men, women generally do not have extra money to purchase support services, such as respite care, in-home assistance, or even labor-saving appliances to ease their care responsibilities. If divorced or widowed, women facing the care of parents and former in-laws are also often struggling just to support themselves.

The minority of women who are in higher status professional jobs may possess more income and greater work time flexibility to adjust for caregiving demands. Ironically, utilizing these choices may put them at a disadvantage for promotions next to male colleagues who do not take time off for family tasks. Women who juggle work and family are frequently viewed as less reliable workers because they cannot shift their home responsibilities to someone else. Unable to count on a spouse to entertain a client or have the boss over for dinner, they are deviant in terms of marketplace standards. They cannot draw on the shadow labor—supplied mostly by women—that enables the salaried work force—primarily male—to keep the workplace running. Even among those successful in the business and professional world, caregiving responsibilities tend to shape women's identities, compelling them to juggle both time and psyche. Career-oriented women, for example, have to cope with the antithetical expectations of old and new social orders: to be businesslike and efficient at work and nurturing and warm at home. Many of the conflicts women currently experience between nurturing others and striving for success derive not only from constraints of time and energy but also from attempting to blend fundamentally different value systems.

As more women have become long-term labor force participants, they have struggled to bridge the separate spheres, but their domestic responsibilities have not diminished. The sex-based division of labor has eroded, but in a lopsided fashion, with more women assuming the role of economic provider, but fewer men becoming caregivers (Vanek 1983). Time use studies have consistently found that women perform the majority of tasks in the home. Likewise, the number of hours that women spend on housework has not decreased in the United States nor Great Britain for the past 50 years (Finch and Groves 1983). Whether women work for pay will not affect the distribution of domestic chores as long as the convention persists that they are primarily responsible for what happens in the family.

Employed women who retain primary caregiving responsibility are less free to involve themselves fully in their paid jobs. Consequently, they often end up feeling they are not performing any job well. They may try to resolve such conflicts by quitting work or reducing their hours. For example, three generations of women in a 1984 study agreed that a working woman should pay someone to care for her parents rather than leave her job, but nevertheless expected working married daughters rather than sons to adjust their employment in order to provide care (Brody et al. 1984b). Of the employed daughters in a subsequent study, 26 percent were considering quitting their jobs or had reduced their working hours to meet care demands (Brody et al. 1984b). In a national survey of over 3000 units in which relatives cared for disabled elders, only 25 percent of the female caregivers were in the labor force compared to half their male counterparts. Many women had tried to combine the two responsibilities but had subsequently quit their paid jobs to provide care (Soldo and Myllyluoma 1982). This action, however, does not remove the underlying source of conflict—the societal expectations for women to give priority to others' needs—nor end the gender-based division of labor.

Sex-based inequities in pay are one reason that women disproportionately leave the marketplace to provide care. Because women earn less, forgoing or reducing their income rather than their husband's is often the most practical adaptation. The higher the caregivers' income, the more likely they are to remain full-time in the labor force, since the opportunity costs of leaving are higher (Soldo and Myllyluoma 1982). Without adequate community alternatives for elder care, however, employment's financial and psychological rewards are unlikely to compensate women for the stresses generated by prolonged elder care combined with work (Brody et al. 1984b).

Financial considerations only partially explain who sacrifices employment for caregiving. Most men simply do not perceive caregiving as their work and therefore are less likely to quit their jobs or reduce their hours to provide care (Waerness 1983). Even when unemployed, men still tend to view themselves primarily as breadwinners. Unemployed husbands in England, for example, spent more time on traditional male tasks, such as fixing the car, than their employed peers, but did not substantially increase the time given to housework and child care (Finch and Groves 1983). Unlike many women, most men have not bridged the separate spheres of work and home.

Socialized since childhood to sacrifice their own interests and respond to others' needs, women often have difficulty setting limits to expectations from employers, work, mates, and family members as well as from themselves. If a family member is ill or in need, the emotional pull to be helpful generally takes precedence over intellectual demands to complete pressing work. Most women will drop a project at work to attend to family needs, while men more easily insist that they are too occupied. At work and at home, men tend to be the symbolic fathers, too busy to be disturbed. Women remain available and nurturant, even when at work. When women caregivers, who set their priorities in terms of others, are asked "What about you?" they often respond with silence, admitting that they have never thought about meeting their own needs (Brody 1985). Women's employers and family members tend to reinforce these gender-based inequities by their expectations of "superwives, supermoms, and superdaughters" who can work for pay, drive carpools, respond to others' illnesses, and still have time to exercise and entertain.

Internalizing a sense of themselves as caregivers, women are also more likely than their male counterparts to find care demands stressful. Even when women and men share care tasks equally, women are more likely to experience caregiving as burdensome (Horowitz and Dobrof 1982). Men are less likely than women to feel personally responsible for their parents' emotional well-being or to experience guilt from not doing more (Robinson and Thurnher 1979). In a 1984 study of three generations of women, for example, three-fourths of the middle-generation women felt guilty about not doing enough, even though these women provided considerable care (Brody et al. 1984a). Men are better able to distance themselves physically and emotionally, focusing primarily on their economic responsibilities.

Women are further restricted by their own internalized barriers against letting go of caregiving responsibilities, setting limits on their helping, or accepting others' aid. Created by societal definitions of deviance, these barriers serve to perpetuate women's powerlessness within caregiving roles. Many female caregivers believe they should be able to do everything themselves, as proof of their love, competence, or marriage vows. Accepting others' help is thus viewed as an admission of weakness or failure.

Although we maintain that women's caregiving roles restrict them from enjoying power equal to that of men outside the home, caregiving relationships can provide some women with a negative power advantage. Feminist literature, such as My Mother/Myself, Our Mother's Daughters, and Of Woman Born, presents images of mothers as powerful figures (Chodorow and Contratto 1982). Similarly, some women find that the only relationship in which they can exercise control is through caring for dependents. Caregiving may be a sole basis of identity, especially for wives of disabled husbands with few other sources of power and meaning. Family members or professionals who offer assistance may be bewildered by caregiver's simultaneous complaints about inadequate help along with her refusals to abdicate responsibilities. Yet a caregiver's need to control intrusions into her territory may result in her exhaustion as well as others' withdrawal of assistance.

Not surprisingly, women who forego employment and who sacrifice personally to provide elder care frequently become depressed and isolated (Brody 1981; Fengler and Goodrich 1979; Horowitz and Dobrof 1982). Experiencing a narrowing of their life space and confined by their round-the-clock care tasks, caregivers may feel helpless to control their lives. Unable to take the time even to walk around the block or to drive to the grocery, many caregivers feel they are literally prisoners in their own homes. As noted above, such emotional burdens intensifying over time can lead to family conflicts, institutionalization, neglect or abuse of the older person, and the caregiver's stress-related illnesses (Kraus et al. 1976; Brody and Masciocchi 1978; Teresi 1980). One reason that many women become victims of stress is that caregivers' rights to public support have not been legitimized within existing social policies. How social policy affects the gender-based distribution of caregiving responsibilities is next examined.

SOCIAL POLICY, STRUCTURAL INEQUALITY, AND CAREGIVING

Promoting the well-being of women as caregivers of the elderly has not been a goal of U.S. social welfare policy. Instead, their interests are accorded a low priority in the distribution of societal resources, reflecting our society's devaluation of both women caregivers and the elderly. Social and health resources are generally allocated on the basis of the care recipient's needs, not the family care system. For example, the United States is one of the few industrialized nations that does not provide a stipend to family caregivers of older people, compared to more than sixty countries with attendant allowances (Gibson 1984). Recent concern with caregiver welfare is often justified as a means to low-cost elder care rather than a primary goal of aging policy. As more services have been cut, primarily women are being forced to deal with the health and social service system's deficiencies. The next few years will be critical for determining the conditions under which older people will live and women's choices regarding caregiving will contract or expand.

Historically, U.S. social welfare policy has been organized on the premise that the family has primary responsibility for caring for dependent persons. The state has generally intervened only after the resources of the older person and the family have been exhausted or the family has proven itself incapable of meeting certain standards of care, as in instances of elder abuse. For example, a 1980 California ruling on Title XX funds prohibited in-home supportive service to frail elders who had an "able and available" spouse (Newman 1980). Likewise, a two-tier entitlement policy has been suggested, with one tier providing comprehensive services for older people without family supports while the second level allows only modest benefits to those with close relatives, creating differential treatment depending upon family ties (Frankfather et al. 1981; Kane 1985). Such proposals further privatize responsibility rather than raising the fundamental policy question of whether and under what conditions the responsibility for elder care ought to remain private. In the absence of consistent funding for support services for caregivers, the state creates and legitimizes the dependency of both women as caregivers and older people as recipients of care. A basic question of social justice is also ignored: how so much can be demanded of individuals who suffer the misfortune of having relatives become impaired.

Privatization was institutionalized around the 1930s in the filial responsibility laws of 25 states. Although rarely enforced, these laws require financially able children to contribute to their parents' long-term support. More importantly, a growing number of states have recently reintroduced family responsibility amendments requiring adult children to contribute a portion of nursing home costs prior to application for Medicaid (Estes 1983). These amendments are intended to deter wealthy families from "dumping" their parents in nursing homes, a rationale that does not accord with the reality that most families turn to institutionalization only as a last resort. Such demands for filial responsibility mask social irresponsibility. They label adult children, primarily women, as unloving deviants if they institutionalize their relatives, scapegoat them for the escalating long-term care costs, and place the legitimate needs of two or three generations of women in conflict with one another (Brody 1985).

Policymakers concerned with cost containment argue that services to family caregivers supplant families' efforts. Such arguments artificially frame formal services as antithetical to informal family supports. For example, a 1982 General Accounting Office report criticized in-home health programs as a cost-inefficient way to perform custodial functions deemed appropriate to family caregivers (Sommers 1983). Service providers have sometimes justified targeting scarce in-home services to elderly who are without family supports as a cost-effective approach (USRCE 1982). Yet services have been found to strengthen families' caregiving capacities rather than encouraging an abdication of care (Horowitz and Dobrof 1982; Zimmer and Sainer 1978). Alternatively, older people whose caregivers are experiencing greater burden and stress have been shown to use more community services, suggesting that targeting services to reduce caregiver burden would be a more cost-effective approach (Boss and Noelker 1985).

Despite the growing documentation of the need for services to relieve caregivers, most social policies serve to discourage or, in some cases, to punish families' care efforts. For example, Medicaid and Medicare, the major health care reimbursement mechanisms, fund primarily institutional care, not in-home services nor respite and day care (Newman 1980; Estes 1983). The home care services that are funded by Medicaid are determined by income, not by the older person's level of functional disability, even though the older person's increasing disability is a major predictor of caregiver stress (Brody 1985). Female caregivers of elders who are ineligible for Medicaid, but not wealthy enough to hire private assistance, generally have to shoulder care responsibilities alone. Caregiving wives who "spend down" their assets in order to be eligible for Medicaid-supported services face the risk of destitution after their husbands' deaths. Consequently, most caregiving wives bear the financial burden of home care in addition to the unestimated value of their nonpaid work. Women caring for severely disabled husbands who deplete their resources in order to qualify for Medicaid-covered nursing home care also face shrinking alternatives in this current cost-containment era. For example, regulations to limit nursing home expansion are closing nursing home doors to those most in need of skilled care—the "heavy care" Medicaid patients, such as Alzheimer's victims (US GAO 1983; Brody 1985).

Incentives for family caregivers have been debated in Congress since 1965. These debates imply that families need to be induced to perform what they have already done for years. Financial incentives, such as more liberal tax credits and deductions and tax free stipends, have been proposed to offset home care costs but have several limitations. Based on marketplace mentality, financial incentives fail to address caregivers' nonrational and nonmonetary motives for providing care. They also ignore caregivers' preferences for concrete supportive services and relief rather than for financial aid (Horowitz and Shindelman 1980; Sussman 1979).

Another limitation is that proposed changes in tax credits would benefit only employed caregivers who can afford to hire private in-home help. They would not assist those who most need financial support—low-income wives and daughters without sufficient income to cover the up-front costs of care and wait for a subsequent refund. Such tax credits would also not provide relief from burdensome daily care tasks to unemployed, full-time caregivers. Concerned with enhancing incentives for the provision of cost-effective family caregiving, one analyst examined the possibility of making tax credits available to nonemployed caregivers. However, he recommended retention of the work requirement because altering it "might lead to demands that such a credit be allowed for any expenses associated with a dependent's care" (Nelson 1982). Tax credits are being debated as mechanisms tied to the regulation of women's labor force participation, but not as unregulated reimbursement for the expenses of providing care. As such, they may serve to further control women rather than to provide relief.

In recent years a number of states have instituted programs financed by Medicaid funds to provide in-home care to low-income elders who would otherwise reside in nursing homes at government expense. Under such programs relatives who meet program restrictions can be paid as providers of in-home care. The purpose of the program, however, is not to promote caregiver welfare but cost containment, since the cost of in-home care is assumed to be less than that of nursing home placement.

Policies and programs have not only failed to support family caregiving efforts but also have reinforced traditional gender-based inequities in caregiving responsibilities. For example, some publicly funded education and training programs for family caregivers seem to imply that personal inadequacy is the source of caregiver burnout. Likewise, increased efficiency at task performance is presumed to be an antidote to the stresses created by multiple demands. An example is the recommendation of better time management (Clark and Rakowski 1983). Such an approach, however, attempts to impose criteria of efficiency on processes governed by standards of quality. Economizing on the amount of time required to change an incontinent person's bedding does not substantially minimize the stress of performing this task several times a night. Nor do models of efficiency offer solutions to the constant vigilance required by a cognitively impaired person's wandering. Efficiency is a misplaced standard for caregiving. As a dominant societal value, however, it implies that female caregivers are the cause of their stress, and that women can reduce their sense of burden by becoming "superwomen" who better manage their time and multiple demands. Under such conditions, education and training interventions may actually increase the caregiver's stress.

The growing professionalization of the aging field also does not necessarily benefit family caregivers. With advanced training, professional providers tend to become more involved with their discipline's technology than with low paying, low status caregiving jobs. Those with the greatest status, prestige and power generally spend the least amount of time with the recipients of care (Waerness 1983; Estes 1979). Their professional orientation biased toward rational scientism and efficiency may make them less qualified to plan and deliver basic care than are family caregivers. Yet their credentials give them the power to shape, from a distance, caregiving norms and standards. When professionals act as experts who advise caregivers, they run the risk of compounding care demands by undermining caregiver confidence. Rather than provide relief, they may inadvertently increase caregiver stress through unrealistic expectations and standards for care. For example, a caregiver who is already feeling overwhelmed may not have the time nor the energy to learn new care techniques presented by professionals. Professionalization has also contributed to service bureaucratization. As a result, caregiving work increasingly requires an ability to maneuver specialized agencies, thereby adding yet another care expectation without releasing women from their hands-on responsibilities.

FUTURE DIRECTIONS

The assumption that family caregivers' welfare should be a central goal of social and health policy, not a means to low cost care, is fundamental to our discussion of policy and program changes. Even though caregivers are not motivated primarily by financial gain, the link between caregiving and economic hardship cannot be ignored. Therefore, monetary compensation for caregiving is an important first strategy, although fraught with the paradox of financially rewarding nonmonetary values. An attendant allowance can help expand caregivers' options to purchase respite services and other concrete supports, even though the amount of money per caregiver is small. To avoid the gender inequities inherent in the allowances given only to unmarried women in some Western European countries, caregiver allowances should be a recognized right for performing a service to society, regardless of the care provider's marital or occupational status. Otherwise, such allowances can serve to reinforce women's position as the allegedly "natural" carer in the family.

Although more services to provide caregiver support and relief have become available recently, many of these are offered through short-term demonstration programs. While important first steps, if such efforts lack stable public funding and are limited in duration, they may not ease caregivers' burdens over the long haul. For example, day care and respite services, of benefit to both older people and their caregivers, are widely advocated by both professionals and caregivers. Although such programs provide an essential break from continuous round-the-clock care, they still may imply that women caregivers, refreshed by their short break, will continue to be primarily responsible. In addition, the fundamental imbalance of caregiving responsibilities will not be addressed if such services are provided by female volunteers or unskilled, minimum wage women, leaving unpaid and underpaid women serving the elderly. Without a major shift in the organization of caregiving services, women with economic resources will confront a bind they have always faced: gaining freedom from caregiving chores at the expense of women with less money. In order to redistribute caregiving responsibilities across gender lines and out of the private sphere, support and relief services need to be publicly funded, widely available for substantial time periods, and provided by employees who are adequately compensated for their important caregiving work.

Although educational and training programs are incremental approaches to caregiver welfare, they can serve some functions to reduce caregiver stress. Such programs can inform caregivers of the limited community services that do exist, thereby enhancing service accessibility. They can also provide caregivers with information about their relatives' illnesses and potential problems, thus reducing some of the uncertainty of care demands. One of the greatest benefits is the mutually supportive relationships that develop when caregivers have a chance to talk together. However, to avoid reinforcing the notion that caregivers need only acquire more skills and information to solve their care dilemmas, caregivers must have a voice in formulating the care standards of educational programs as well as concrete assistance in meeting them.

When caregivers with a strong sense of personal responsibility resist using outside services, professional counseling skills may enable them to accept services, such as respite or day care. Professionals need to clarify their own values regarding family responsibility and recognize that answers about the best form of care vary with both the caregiver's and care receiver's needs. Although institutional placement may be counter to the professional's inclination, such long-term options may be the best choice when at-home care is unhealthy for the caregiver and care receiver. In such instances professionals need to help the caregiver resolve feelings of guilt and anxiety. Frequently, the most appropriate professional role may be to help the caregiver do less, not to do more, and to accept what she cannot do as well as what she can do (Brody 1985). Unfortunately, such counseling services for caregivers are oftentimes not reimbursable, which highlights another needed policy change.

Support groups are another mechanism for affirming caregivers' efforts and providing them with new sources of meaningful activity and influence. As they share their insights to help solve others' problems, support group members generally become more aware of their competence. They also become more cognizant of the importance of taking time for themselves, setting limits on their helping, and developing other pursuits. Support groups encourage an active stance toward problems. Even if difficulties cannot be eliminated, caregivers' attitudes toward problems usually change. For example, when members hear about others' angry outbursts or impatience, they may modify their expectations for themselves, recognizing human fallibility. Support groups that focus only on individual competence and responsibility can conceivably divert society from developing and funding critical services. However, support groups can also serve consciousness-raising functions, increasing members' awareness of gaps in services to which they are entitled and encouraging their involvement in public education and legislative advocacy. Such political efforts can serve to influence policies in ways to reward caregiving work.

A long-range challenge for social welfare policy and for feminism is how to mainstream caregiving values as a central force in shaping society. Caregiving values must become public values, rather than be divided along economic and gender lines. Traditional values of family responsibility must be given equal footing with marketplace values in shaping the course of a society built around human needs. Accordingly, if unpaid work were established as a legitimate economic category, it would have its own criteria of value and own rewards for both men and women (Scott 1984). The fundamental solution to the inequity of women bearing the burdens of care is the reintegration of women's and men's private and work lives (Ehrenreich and English 1979). Such reintegration would enable women to pursue their own marketplace aspirations while achieving an equitable share of caregiving responsibilities.

To move toward a more equitable sharing of care responsibilities, practitioners need to identify concrete ways to involve male family members in caregiving tasks. For example, hospital discharge planners must not automatically phone daughters or wives, but instead include sons, brothers, and husbands in their initial contacts. Professionals need to be trained to be sensitive to how they inadvertently reinforce gender-specific roles and women's inclinations to try to "do it all" through subtle pressures on women or their failure to expect more from male family members.

Traditional assumptions of caregiving roles also must be challenged in the workplace. We have argued that women in the labor force earn less than men because of the primacy of their caregiving roles. Research conducted in England suggests that men who assume primary childrearing responsibilities also suffer a drop in income. Although less likely than single mothers to fall below the poverty lines, reductions in single fathers' income are attributable to some of the same factors that affect women's pay: shifts to less demanding and lower paying jobs, loss of overtime pay, absenteeism to care for ill children, and a drop in social ties with business or professional associates that had served to increase income in the past (Rossi 1985). The economic penalties of caregiving work transcend sex and must be addressed by policy changes, such as Social Security credit for caregiving work in the home, or earnings sharing of Social Security benefits.

The separate spheres assumption that exonerates the workplace from responsibility for family care must be challenged. Business benefits from family caregiving. For example, families supply the corporate sector with a work force and a market for manufactured goods. Rather than penalizing workers' involvement in family life, businesses could support it through benefit packages that include the options of day care and in-home services for employees' older relatives. The growing number of Employee Assistance Programs could provide counseling and referrals to appropriate support services.

Workplace modifications are also necessary to enable men and women to more equitably share caregiving tasks and thus integrate their public and private lives. Narrowing the gap between men's and women's wages is an essential first step to weaken the economic impetus for women to automatically sacrifice their jobs when at-home caregivers are needed. The second is to assure that equal family-related benefits are available to both men and women.

The work setting could be restructured to better accommodate family responsibilities of both men and women through flex time, part-time jobs with full benefits, job sharing, a shorter work-day, and leaves to provide care. Smaller scale, more humane, nonhierarchical, and decentralized work sites would facilitate a greater flexibility between work and home. Finally, redistributing work, education, leisure, childrearing, and kin keeping across the life span would provide both men and women with more discretionary time throughout their lives. For example, sabbaticals and part-time options might be offered in young and middle adulthood when a person is most likely to be pressured by care responsibilities along with more educational and career development opportunities for the increased leisure time of old age.

Finally, the caregiving trends and burdens described above compel us to raise the question: why not extend the principle now inherent in the economic provider role to the caregiving role? Our society embraces the concept of social insurance against financial disaster. Unemployment and disability insurance and Social Security are accepted as entitlements to protect people from undeserved economic hardships. Similarly, why not insure against the possibility of giving round-the-clock care for chronically ill relatives or becoming the dependent person requiring others' care to survive. This would mean developing a social insurance in support of long-term caregiving and against the tragedies of physical or cognitive impairment. This direction is counter to our societal value on individual responsibility and our human tendency to hope that we will be lucky and not face years of caring for a dependent relative. Yet the demographic and social trends indicate that growing numbers of us will not be lucky but will face the burden of long-term care. The challenge for both policy makers and feminists is to redefine how our society, in the form of social policy, will assume its responsibility to both the growing number of caregivers—usually women—and care receivers—generally women. Clearly, funding priorities would have to be shifted to restructure caregiving work more equitably. We maintain that such a redistribution is essential to insure the autonomy of both older and younger generations, enabling older people to remain independent with a full array of entitlements to humane care, and younger caregivers to have the choice not to devote years to care of disabled relatives.

References

Amidei, N., 1985. "Women and Powerlessness: A Feminist Perspective." Paper presented at the Women's Symposium, Annual Program Meeting of the Council on Social Work Education, Washington, DC.

Boss, D. and L. Noelker, 1985. "The Influence of Family Caregivers on Elder's Use of In-Home Services: An Expanded Conceptual Framework." Paper presented at the 38th Annual Meeting of the Gerontological Society of America, New Orleans, LA, November.

Belle, D., 1982. "The Stress of Caring: Women as Providers of Social Support," in L. Goldberger and S. Breznitz (eds.) The Handbook of Stress. New York: Free Press.

Bernard, J., 1983. "The Good-Provider Role: Its Rise and Fall," in A. Skolnick and J. Skolnick (eds.) Family in Transition, 4th ed. Boston: Little, Brown.

Bernard, J., 1979. "Policy and Women's Time," pp. 303–27 in J. Lipman and J. Bernard Sex Roles and Social Policy. Beverley Hills, CA: Sage Publications.

Brody, E., 1981. "Women in the Middle and Family Help to Older People," The Gerontologist 21, 5: 471–80.

Brody, E., 1985. "Parent Care as a Normative Family Stress," The Gerontologist 25, 1: 19–30.

Brody, E.M., P.T. Johnson and M.C. Fulcomer, 1984a. "What Should Adult Children Do for Elderly Parents? Opinions and Preferences of Three Generations of Women," Journal of Gerontology 39, 6: 736–47.

Brody, E.M., M. Kleban, P. Johnson, and C. Hoffman, 1984b. "Women Who Help Elderly Mothers: Do Work and Parent Care Compete?" Paper presented at the 37th Annual Scientific Meeting of the Gerontological Society of America, San Antonio, TX, November.

Brody, S.J. and C.F. Masciocchi, 1978. "The Family Caring Unit: A Major Consideration in the Long-term Support System," The Gerontologist 18, 6: 556–61.

Chodorow, N. and S. Contratto, 1982. "The Fantasy of the Perfect Mother," in B. Thorne and M. Yalom (eds.) Rethinking the Family: Some Feminist Questions. New York: Longman.

Clark, N. and W. Rakowski, 1983. "Family Caregivers of Older Adults: Improving Helping Skills," The Gerontologist 23, 6: 637–42.

Cott, N., 1977. The Bonds of Womanhood: Woman's Sphere in New England, 1780–1835. New Haven: Yale University Press.

Degler, C., 1980. At Odds: Women and the Family in America from the Revolution to the Present. New York: Oxford University Press.

Ehrenreich, B., 1983. The Hearts of Men: American Dreams and the Flight from Commitment. Garden City, NY: Doubleday.

Ehrenreich, B. and D. English, 1979. For Her Own Good: 150 Years of the Experts' Advice to Women. Garden City, NY: Anchor Press.

Estes, C., 1979. The Aging Enterprise. San Francisco: Jossey Bass.

Estes, C., L. Gerard and T. Arendell, 1985. "Gender Gap: Economics of Aging for Women." Paper presented at the Annual Meeting of the Western Gerontological Society, Denver, CO.

Estes, C., R. Newcomer and Associates, 1983. Fiscal Austerity and Aging. Beverly Hills, CA: Sage Publications.

Fengler, A. and N. Goodrich, 1979. "Wives of Elderly Disabled Men: The Hidden Patients," The Gerontologist 12, 2: 175–83.

Finch, J. and D. Groves, 1983. A Labour of Love: Women, Work and Caring. London: Routledge and Kegan Paul.

Flexner, E., 1973. Century of Struggle. New York: Atheneum.

Frankfather, D.L., M.J. Smith and F.G. Caro, 1981. Family Care of the Elderly: Public Initiatives and Private Obligations. Lexington, MA.

Gibson, M.J., 1984. "Women and Aging." Paper presented at the International Symposium on Aging, Georgian Court College, Lakewood, NJ, October 19.

Graham, H., 1983. "Caring: A Labor of Love," pp. 13–30 in J. Finch and D. Groves, A Labour of Love: Women, Work and Caring. London: Routledge and Kegan Paul.

Hayden, D., 1981. The Grand Domestic Revolution: A History of Feminist Designs for American Homes, Neighborhoods, and Cities. Cambridge, MA: MIT Press.

Horowitz, A. and R. Dobrof, 1982. The Role of Families in Providing Long-Term Care to the Frail and Chronically Ill Elderly Living in the Community. Final Report to the Health Care Financing Administration.

Horowitz, A. and L. Shindelman, 1980. "Social and Economic Incentives for Family Caregivers." Paper presented at the 33rd Annual Scientific Meeting of the Gerontological Society of America, San Diego, CA.

Kane, R.A., 1985. "Long-term Care Status Quo Untenable? What Is More Ideal for Nations Elderly?" Perspectives in Aging 14: 23–26.

Kraus, A.S., R.A. Spasoff, E.J. Beattie, D.E.W. Holden, J.S. Lawson, M. Rodenburg, and G.M. Woodcock, 1976. "Elderly Application Process: Placement and Care Needs," Journal of the American Geriatrics Society 24: 165–72.

Lang, A.M. and E.M. Brody, 1983. "Characteristics of Middle-aged Daughters and Help to their Elderly Mothers," Journal of Marriage and the Family 45: 193.

Minkler, M. and R. Stone, 1985. "The Feminization of Poverty and Older Women," The Gerontologist: 351–58.

Morcyz, R. and M. Blumenthal, 1980. "Late-life Brain Disease and Family Burden," Community Support Service Journal II, 4: 1–8.

Nelson Jr., J.R., 1982. "Tax Subsidies for Elderly Care." Unpublished paper. Washington, DC: Center for the Study of Social Policy.

Newman, S.J., 1980. "Government Policy and the Relationship between Adult Children and their Aging Parents: Filial Support, Medicare and Medicaid." Unpublished paper. Ann Arbor, MI: Institute for Social Research.

Polansky, E., 1985. "A Feminist Analysis of Hospital Discharge Planning: Women as Caregivers of Disabled Family Members." Paper presented at the Women's Symposium, the Annual Program Meeting of the Council on Social Work Education, Washington, DC.

President's Commission on the Status of Women, 1963. Report of the Committee on Home and Community. Washington, DC: U.S. Government Printing Office.

Rix, S., 1984. Older Women: The Economics of Aging. Washington, DC: Women's Research and Education Institute.

Robinson, B. and M. Thurnher, 1979. "Taking Care of Aged Parents: A Family Cycle Transition," Gerontologist 19, 6: 586–93.

Rossi, A., 1985. "Gender and Parenthood," in A. Rossi (ed.) Gender and the Life Course. New York: Aldine.

Rothman, S., 1978. Women's Proper Place: A History of Changing Ideals and Practices. New York: Basic Books.

Scott, H., 1984. Working Your Way to the Bottom: The Feminization of Poverty. London: Pandora Press.

Soldo, B.J. and J. Myllyluoma, 1982. "Caregivers Who Live With Dependent Elderly." Unpublished article.

Sommers, T., 1975. "On Growing Old Female: An Interview with Tish Sommers," Aging (November/December): 11.

Sommers, T., 1983. "Cost of Care: What Do We Do With Grandmother?" Gray Panther Network (September/October): 5.

Steinitz, L., 1981. "Informal Supports in Long-term Care: Implications and Policy Options." Paper presented to the National Conference on Social Welfare.

Stroller, E.P., 1983. "Parental Caring of Adult Children," Journal of Marriage and the Family 45: 851–58.

Sussman, M.B., 1979. Social and Economic Supports and Family Environments for the Elderly. Fiscal Report to the Administration on Aging, AOA Grant *90-A-316, 3, January.

Teresi, J.A., J.A. Toner, R.G. Bennett, and D.E. Wilder, 1980. "Factors Related to Family Attitudes Toward Institutionalizing Older Relatives." Paper presented at the 33rd Annual Scientific Meeting of the Gerontological Society, San Diego, CA, November.

Troll, L.E., 1982. "Family Life in Middle and Old Age: The Generation Gap," The Annals of the American Academy of Political and Social Science 464 (November): 38–47.

Uhlenberg, P., 1980. "Death and the Family," Journal of Family History 5: 313–20.

U.S. Bureau of Labor Statistics, 1984. "Employment and Earnings," Table 3. January.

U.S. General Accounting Office, 1983. "Medicaid and Nursing Home Care: Cost Increases and the Need for Services are Creating Problems for the States and the Elderly." Washington, DC: U.S. General Accounting Office, October 21.

Urban System Research in Engineering, 1982. "In-home Services and the Contribution of Kin: Substitution Effects on Human Care Programs for the Elderly." Washington, DC.

Vanek, J., 1983. "Household Work, Wage Work, and Sexual Equality," in A. Skolnick and J. Skolnick (eds.) Family in Transition, 4th ed. Boston: Little, Brown.

Waerness, K., 1983. "Caring as Women's Work in the Welfare State." Unpublished manuscript. Bergen, Norway: University of Bergen.

Zimmer, A. and J. Sainer, 1978. "Strengthening the Family as an Informal Support for their Aged: Implication for Social Policy and Planning." Paper presented at the 31st Annual Meeting of the Gerontological Society, Dallas, TX.

CHAPTER 7

WIFE BATTERING: A SOCIAL DEVIANCE ANALYSIS

Bonnie E. Carlson

In recent years the problem of woman battering, also known as spouse abuse or domestic violence, has come to the attention of scholars and human service professionals. Traditionally, social science has viewed violence as an indication of the deterioration of the social order and individual perpetrators as deviant (Dobash and Dobash 1977–78). Because deviance definitions are always culturally and historically based, attempts to comprehend wife battering are best viewed in the sociohistorical context of patriarchy. There is ample evidence of a long and well-established historical tradition of socially accepted male violence against women in the family:

> Western tradition until the 19th century contained strong prescriptive rules concerning husbands' use of physical force, including beatings and sometimes murder, to keep their wives in line. Dobash and Dobash, in extremely thorough analyses, have traced the continuing presence in literature, law and ethical treatises of statements of a husband's right and even duty to punish his wife's transgressions from her marital responsibilities with physical force. Wifebeating was no simply deviant behavior that was tolerated, but rather for centuries was considered to be a desirable part of a patriarchal family system. (Greenblat 1984: 236)

In fact, only about one hundred years have transpired since American men lost the legal right to use physical violence to control their wives. Before that, men were permitted to beat their wives, indeed were obligated to control them through the use of physical force. This tradition dates back to the eighth century B.C. when the first marriage laws were established by the Romans. It was considered a husband's moral duty to control his wife's behavior and punish her misbehavior. After Roman times these norms prescribing husband domination in the family were carried on by the early Christians, codified in the Bible and eventually adopted by the state as well as the Church (Dobash and Dobash 1977–78). In a historical sense, then, any violation of the norm of male supremacy might elicit community-supported violence from a husband, although extreme violence (use of weapons, public beating, or infliction of serious injury, for example) was proscribed. Husband beating, on the other hand, was apparently quite rare, and women who violated this norm were seriously sanctioned for their behavior (Dobash and Dobash 1981).

Thus there is agreement that wife beating has been considered normative behavior historically, and men who beat their wives have not been defined as deviant by most members of the community (Pagelow 1981b). Instead, it can be argued that women have come to be viewed as deviant in the domestic violence encounter. Initially they are seen as deviant because they have violated important social rules. Later they are again viewed as deviant as a result of their responses to having experienced violence at the hands of their spouse. Ultimately this process gives rise to a range of negative consequences, including stigmatization and being relegated to generally devalued social status. The extent to which battered women have been almost universally blamed for their victimization is but one manifestation of this process.

This chapter attempts to demonstrate the value of applying a social deviance model to our understanding of spouse abuse. This application will be somewhat unusual in that deviance theory has generally been used to explain the behavior of offenders rather than victims. The chapter will attempt to show how a social deviance model can help explain woman battering in two ways. First, it will be argued that deviance emanating from sex-role violations contributes to wives being physically abused as their husbands try to coerce them into conforming to the traditional female role. Later, after they have experienced abuse, women again are considered to be the deviant party if they do not respond to the abuse in ways society deems appropriate. What is defined as "appropriate" will vary with the circumstances. Sometimes appropriate behavior would be defined as changing one's behavior, that is, conforming and acting more like a "good wife." However, if the abuse is serious and viewed as "undeserved," an appropriate response in the eyes of society might be separation and divorce, and/or arrest. To the battered wife it may seem like she can't win. She is criticized by outsiders for not leaving and further abused by her husband (or the authorities) for trying to leave.

The interactionist deviance perspective adopted here, exemplified by such theorists as Schur (1971), Lemert (1978), Erikson (1964), and Becker (1963), is well suited to an analysis of domestic violence. This perspective assumes deviance to be a status conferred on an individual by another individual rather than a property inherent in a particular act or person. Thus, since deviance is socially defined and created, neither people nor behaviors are intrinsically deviant, although certain personal characteristics may predispose one to being labeled or typed as deviant. Rather, it is the social interpretation of a behavior that is important in determining deviance. Finally, although definitions of deviance tend to vary across time and place, generally deviance is determined by those who are powerful in the interaction, in this case men (Schur 1984).

SEX ROLES, DEVIANCE, AND WOMAN BATTERING

Widom (1984) has observed that our understanding of deviance is affected by gender in several important ways:

> First, sex roles have been cited as causal factors in theories of why people engage in crime and deviant behavior. Second, assumptions and societal expectations about appropriate sex role behavior influence the diagnosis and labeling of certain actions as deviant or criminal. Finally, gender affects the response to such behaviors by society. (185)

In addition, since they tend to be less powerful and of lower social status than men, women are more easily labeled as deviant and have even been said to serve as "all-purpose deviants." Being a woman, in that sense, has been said to be an inherently stigmatizing experience that serves to perpetuate women's subordination to men (Schur 1984).

Our knowledge about the complex causes of domestic violence is increasing rapidly. Although most of the investigations to date have focused on factors at the individual and interpersonal levels, powerful macrolevel factors also are known to play an important contributing role in family violence (Straus 1977). One of those macrolevel factors, as pointed out by feminist scholars of family violence, is sex-role or gender norms, that is, differential expectations for values, attitudes, and behaviors as a function of one's gender. These norms serve as important standards against which women and men are evaluated through application of various sanctions (Schur 1984).

Sex-role norms dictate that the "good wife" behave in a certain manner, especially vis-a-vis her husband. She should maintain a comfortable, smooth-running household and ensure that children are well behaved. In addition, she should be attentive, deferential, and submissive in relation to her husband, avoiding the appearance of independence or assertiveness. Certainly any show of physical aggression, especially against her husband, would violate sex-role expectations for female behavior. If the deviance model applies, we should find certain kinds of outcomes when wives behave in ways inconsistent with prevailing sex-role norms. According to deviance theory, norm violations tend to trigger forces aimed at making the violator conform to expected standards of behavior. Thus, when women do not behave like the male ideal wife, we would expect to see efforts by husbands, those most directly affected by failure to be a "good wife," to make their wives conform. What actually happens when wives fail to fulfill the female sex-role ideal?

It is clear that female behavior that departs from sex-role standards does not inevitably elicit a violent response from husbands. Undoubtedly some men feel more strongly than others about the importance of femininity for women and masculinity for men, as demonstrated by research on sex-role attitudes. But even men who do feel strongly about their wives conforming to the feminine ideal have at their disposal a number of potential means to induce them to conform, only one of which is physical violence. For example, they might choose to discuss the source of dissatisfaction, withdraw inside themselves, withhold affection, or leave the family temporarily or permanently.

Thus sex-role violations do not automatically lead to husband violence, and a complex set of variables undoubtedly interacts to ultimately determine whether a husband will resort to physical force to gain his wife's sex-role compliance. One of these variables is his subjective definition of the male sex role and its demands and privileges. If his version of the male sex role is the traditional one, it will tend to include the need to dominate his female partner, even to the point of using physical force if necessary (Coleman 1980). For whatever set of complex reasons, with some frequency many husbands resort to physical force as a form of social control, regardless of the complex factors typically found in these incidents.

Several types of research lend support to the argument that

sex-role infractions by wives are especially likely to elicit aggressive responses by their husbands. Greenblat studied the perceptions of appropriate circumstances associated with marital violence held by a sample of 80 men and women. She found that the modal justifications cited by both men and women pertained to fulfillment of the wife role. Unfaithfulness in the sexual realm was especially likely to be seen as warranting a violent response (Greenblat 1984). Research on the causes of spouse battering also indicates that many of the events leading to violent marital conflict are related to the husband's dissatisfaction with his wife's performance of her role. For example, arguments about children, sex, jealously, and financial management, often considered the wife's province, are most likely to lead to violence, especially in blue-collar families where sex-role norms are most entrenched (Carlson 1977; Rubin 1976; Straus, Gelles, and Steinmetz 1980). Coleman found that two of the three major causes identified by a group of male batterers pertained to the female sex role: dissatisfaction with her performance as a wife and mother and jealousy over suspected liaisons with other men, sometimes reaching "delusional proportions" (Coleman 1980).

Finally, the historical evidence for violations of sex-role norms being a major source of conflict leading to wifebeating is even more compelling. Infidelity was viewed as a particularly egregious offense and was even considered grounds for death in Roman times. In addition to adultery, wives were also punished for alcohol consumption and appearing in public, especially if "unveiled" (Dobash and Dobash 1977–78, 1981). Dobash and Dobash also indicate that even in the 1800s married women had no legal rights, and a husband could still chastise his wife legally for such things as "assertion of independence [and] wanting to retain control of her property after marriage...."

Thus there is a substantial body of evidence supporting the assertion that sex-role norms, or rather their violation, contribute to the tendency to use violence against wives. In light of the fact that such norms are changing, an important related issue concerns whether sex-role standards for women's behavior will continue to be a significant source of vulnerability to family violence.

PERSISTENCE OF GENDER-BASED STANDARDS

It is widely agreed that sex-role expectations and standards are changing, albeit slowly, with a variety of new roles and experiences available to both women and men. However, gender norms remain very strongly entrenched, and women continue to be significantly more supportive of egalitarian norms in both the public and private spheres than men, even among those born after the feminist movement was well under way. A recent study examined support for sharing of the breadwinner role in the family and equal job opportunities for men and women among black and white tenth-graders from lower-, middle- and upper-class backgrounds (Figueira-McDonough 1985). Among males of any race and class, the mean level of support for sharing the breadwinner role did not even reach the midpoint on a five-point scale, although support was somewhat greater among females. Support for equal job and leadership opportunities was higher for both genders. These and other findings on attitudes regarding sex roles suggest that support for egalitarianism is stronger in the public than the private sphere (Herzog and Bachman 1982).

Such changes notwithstanding, the push for equality has not resulted in an end to or observable decrease in violence against women, either within or outside of the family. This is true despite the fact that the egalitarian marital relationships said to be more prevalent today are thought to be less likely to be associated with violence than relationships dominated by one partner (Yllo 1984). How do changing sex-role norms at the macrolevel affect marital relations?

Paradoxically, the case can be made that the press for equality by women has actually exacerbated conflict between the sexes in the short run because there is less agreement on their respective roles. This is consistent with Erikson's (1964) observation that deviance is most likely to occur when rules regarding behavior are ambiguous or contradictory: As the individual tries to avoid breaking one rule, he or she may well violate another. In this way deviance and the responses to it perform a boundary-defining function by identifying behavior considered unacceptable based on community standards. From this perspective deviance is "normal" and inevitable. When other women observe the negative consequences experienced by battered women, they learn just how far they can go before incurring sanctions. In this sense what happens to abused wives affects the status of all women. Thus battered women can be seen as providing a service for all women by helping to establish the boundaries of acceptable behavior for their sex.

There is additional evidence that the trend toward a relaxation of rigid sex-role standards gets played out in the power relationship within a couple. The "ultimate resource" theory of family power, a variant on exchange theory (Allen and Straus 1980), addresses issues of gender, power, and resources in relation to marital violence. According to this formulation, the spouse with the greater resources should be the more powerful. Taking into account access to resources and cultural expectations about the distribution of marital power, this will generally be the male (Blood and Wolfe 1960).

However, "the presumption of male superiority must be validated by superiority in resources" (Straus 1976: 63). What happens when the female partner has greater resources, a clear violation of sex-role expectations? When the male partner cannot demonstrate superiority in resources such as education, income, or occupational prestige, he may resort to the "ultimate resource" to maintain his dominant power position: physical force (Goode 1971). That is, violence occurs when a man feels pushed to the limit and "stripped of his defenses" (Coleman 1980). Anecdotal sources such as the staff in battered women's shelters have noted an unusually high incidence of relationships in which the female partner is of higher status than the male on at least one dimension such as education, occupation, or less commonly, income. Carlson (1977) corroborated this observation in her sample of battered women seeking services, especially with regard to education. Even though both partners may have relatively little education, frequently the female partner has more. This clearly has implications for how power is distributed within the couple. O'Brien (1969) similarly found a disproportionately high incidence of couples where the wife's status was higher than her husband's in his study of violence in divorcing couples.

If this theory has validity as a partial explanation for violence against women, then the more women tend to gain equality in society and the family, the more vulnerable they may be to physical abuse in the home. There is support for this hypothesis. Research on the impact of status inconsistency and incompatibility on a marital relationship suggests that progress toward equality tends to increase women's vulnerability to violence, although once equality has been achieved, violence may be less likely. When a wife has higher social status than her husband in terms of her education, occupation, or income, the odds of her experiencing violence at the hands of her husband increase, at least within the lower-to-middle socioeconomic range.

> Particularly high risks are found when the woman's
> occupation is incompatible with her partner's job. Couples in
> which the woman has a job that is higher than anticipated in
> view of her partner's occupation are...more than twice as
> likely to experience life-threatening violence...(Hornung,
> McCullough, and Sugimoto 1981: 688).

In addition, women who were overachievers, not in relation to
their husbands but based on their occupational achievements in
relation to their education, were more than five times as likely to
experience life-threatening violence than women whose
achievements were consistent with their preparation, irrespective of
the couple's social class standing (Hornung et al. 1981). Apparently,
many men have very strong negative feelings about women who
have unexpectedly high achievements or superiority in domains
society values highly. It cannot be determined from the Hornung et
al. data whether the status inconsistency itself leads to male
violence or whether overachieving women share certain
characteristics that "provoke" violence from their male partners.
However, since overachieving women are not the only status-
inconsistent women who are at higher risk of abuse, it would seem
to be this incompatibility rather than special traits that is causal.

The status inconsistency effect is of particular concern
because there is every reason to expect that women will continue to
make progress toward equality in the family and in society. In no
area is this more apparent than labor force participation, a major
avenue to upward mobility, along with higher education, for women.
Although women have not made great strides toward equality with
men in terms of income, the differential in rates of labor force
participation between men and women is narrowing as women leave
for work each day in record numbers. This is in many ways
changing the texture of the American family as husbands must
come to terms with the implications of not having a full-time wife in
the home.

There is reason to suspect that increased labor force
participation rates for women are related to marital violence.
Disagreements over whether the wife will work, and the
circumstances surrounding her employment if she does work, are
known to be a source of conflict potentially leading to violence
(Rubin 1976). Despite the fact that most women work primarily
out of economic necessity and their families benefit directly from
their earnings, it is still considered deviant for a wife to share the

breadwinner role in many sectors of society, regardless of her motivation for working. In addition, employment of the wife and lack of economic dependency on the husband have been found repeatedly to be predictors of women leaving violent marital relationships (Gelles 1976; Hilberman 1980; Hornung et al. 1983; Roy 1977; Strube and Barbour 1984). For example, one recent study using a rather large sample of battered women found employment status of the wife to be the best individual predictor of a woman's leaving (Strube and Barbour 1984). Perhaps husbands' resistance to wives' employment reflects an awareness that access to an independent source of income is associated with wives' ability to choose to stay or leave the marriage.

Another manifestation of the resilience of gender-related deviance standards is the extent of victim blaming experienced by battered women despite almost a decade of educational efforts. Although there seems to be increased awareness of woman battering, understanding of the problem is still limited, and victim blaming persists. These attitudes are prevalent not only in the general public but also among many human service professionals charged with helping abused women. One recent study found that although husbands were viewed as more responsible for physical abuse, wives were also seen as quite responsible by judges, probation officers, social service workers, emergency room staff, police, shelter workers, and social workers (Davis and Carlson 1981). Stereotypes of victims abound, many of which interfere with women's efforts to resolve family violence. The author has encountered numerous professionals who even today believe that all battered women are masochistic, with a need to be mistreated that will lead to other abusive behaviors if the violence is eliminated.

Finally, despite changing sex-role norms women continue to be viewed as overwhelmingly responsible for their families' welfare and well-being. Social change notwithstanding, Cloward and Piven (1979:663) note that the "psychobiological ideology of women's nature, of the correlative female obligation to family and to a role of family service, has remained hegemonic, seemingly rooted in the natural world itself." Although most men report being more invested in their families than in their work (Pleck 1985), the quality of the marital relationship and children's behavior continue to be seen as the woman's domain, direct reflections of her performance as wife and mother. This is especially likely to be true when the wife has low marital power due to her educational status, her lack of employment outside the home, or when the husband's income is either very high or very low (Ericksen, Ericksen, and Yancey 1979). And when things do not go well in this arena, it is the wife who gets scapegoated (Klein 1981). When a woman reveals to the authorities a home environment incompatible with the myth of the idealized happy family, she exposes herself as a failure and increases her chances of being labeled as deviant by the community (Pagelow 1981a).

So because women are viewed as inherently responsible for children and often believe that children must have two parents in the home to develop normally, they do what the "good wife" is supposed to do—they "endure rather than deviate" (Cloward and Piven 1979), trying to keep the family intact, even when doing so endangers their personal safety. Many have role models in their families of origin for enduring physical abuse at the hands of their male partners. The mother role, too, implies selflessness and putting aside what one desires personally for the good of the children. Whereas men have traditionally left their families with almost complete impunity, providing them with neither economic nor emotional support, women who even temporarily leave their children while fleeing from imminent danger risk being called inadequate mothers. Ultimately, they can lose custody of their children as a result of actions taken on their own behalf that violate traditional sex-role norms. Once again, women experience Catch-22 as sex-role norms again play a role in perpetuating women's violent victimization in the family.

DEVIANCE AND DEPRIVATION OF RIGHTS AND RESOURCES

After the domestic violence encounter, women and men are again viewed differently. After marital violence has occurred and is revealed to those outside the family, the wife again tends to be labeled as the deviant participant. How do we know this? One of the ways in which we know that battered women have been labeled or typed as a consequence of the abuse is that behavior that was heretofore considered unremarkable or normative comes to be seen as requiring a justification. Generally, remaining in a marriage is regarded as normative and is not seen as demanding an explanation or "account" (Scott and Lyman 1968). However, in the case of the battered woman, the burning question in everyone's mind, from the next door neighbor to the police officer and psychiatrist, is "Why does she stay?" (Loseke and Cahill 1984). Although the experts do not agree on why battered women fail to leave physically abusive relationships, there is virtual consensus that staying in many cases is not a good thing—"unreasonable, normatively unexpected and therefore deviant" (Loseke and Cahill 1984: 298).

Once again, battered wives experience Catch-22. If staying requires an explanation and is seen as clearly deviant, then leaving must be normative—except that what is usually regarded as normative is remaining in the relationship. What is the significance of the explanation or account? According to Loseke and Cahill, there are two kinds of accounts: justifications and excuses. The nature of the account reflects just how trapped the battered woman is. Justifications are explanations that acknowledge some responsibility on the part of the actor but do not accept the attribution of deviance. For example, one justification for remaining in a violent family situation might be that the victim came from a family where such behavior was considered normative and did not perceive alternatives for herself. Consequently, she did not act in ways that might end the violence. Excuses, on the other hand, deny personal responsibility but acknowledge that the behavior in question was deviant. An excuse for not leaving a violent marital relationship might be that a woman was fully aware that she was experiencing abuse but was terrified that she or her children would be killed if she attempted to leave. As a result, she made no real efforts to do so. Regardless of whether she resorts to a justification or an excuse, she must account for why she does not leave and is perceived as deviant in yet another instance of Catch-22.

If the social deviance model applies, again we would expect to see other kinds of consequences resulting from the labeling process. Ultimately imputations of deviance are perhaps most important precisely because of these negative consequences. Once women have been abused, irrespective of how they subjectively define the experience, they must confront the problem of what to do about the violence and its aftermath. This might include physical injury and the need for medical attention, paralyzing fear or other emotional trauma, the need to deal with frightened, upset children, and so forth. What can the battered wife do? Although there are a number of possible courses of action, virtually all of them may lead to further deviant labels, particularly if the victim exposes the marital disagreement and violence to those external to the family.

One course of action already mentioned is essentially to do nothing. For centuries women have remained with their families and endured violence without seeming to take any deliberate action at all. Although this would seem to be the alternative most consistent with female sex-role norms and therefore most likely to be rewarded or at least tolerated, in reality even passivity and resignation often lead to labels carrying negative mental health implications. This is especially true as the public and professionals have become more informed about the problem and as services such as domestic violence shelters have developed. Many, including professionals, ask, "Why doesn't she just leave?" the clear implication being that any woman who tolerates violent behavior must be sick, crazy, etc. Unfortunately, leaving is not always feasible and, more importantly, does not guarantee an end to the violence.

Another course of action consists of remaining in the violent situation but calling in external authorities when the violence gets out of control. This might consist of contacting neighbors, extended family members, mental health professionals, and/or the police. One possible consequence of this course of action is that it can lead to public identification of the victim as a "battered woman" and subsequent labeling, especially if it occurs more than once. This in turn carries a number of possible negative consequences, elaborated below. In any event, based on battered women's reports, these efforts are also unlikely to be successful in terminating the violence, further reinforcing the victim's helplessness and powerlessness.

Another alternative is to remain in the situation but not passively. Some women elect to respond to violence in an aggressive manner. This may be the alternative that most fundamentally violates the female sex-role ideal in that aggression and violence are universally seen as being incompatible with femininity (Widom 1984). According to one current typology, violence can be of two types. Instrumental or social violence is goal-oriented and normative, that is, socially acceptable; expressive or asocial violence, which is not goal-oriented, is said to be deviant. Although male violence can be of either type, female violence is virtually always considered to be expressive or deviant (Ball-Rokeach 1980). Within this framework male violence against women can be justified as long as it is intended to accomplish a certain goal, whereas for women violence and deviance are virtually synonymous, another Catch-22 for women. Consequently, violent husbands are rarely if ever viewed as deviant for using physical aggression against their wives, unless it is excessive, largely because they are not violating social rules. Rather, it could be argued that through their violent behavior they are actually living up to the sociocultural stereotype of masculinity (Pagelow 1981a).

Battered Wives Who Kill

The most extreme instance of female aggression against a male partner is, of course, homicide. Despite the popular misconception that women today are more likely to kill, female homicide rates have remained fairly stable and account for about 13 percent of all homicides. There are two general categories of justification or defense that might be used by a woman who has killed her abusive partner: impaired mental state, including diminished capacity, extreme emotional disturbance, and mental incapacity (insanity); and self-defense (Kaas 1982; Schneider and Jordan 1981). Demonstrating impaired mental state results in the charge of murder in the first degree being reduced to a lesser charge, such as murder in the second degree or manslaughter, but does not lead to an acquittal. Perhaps for this reason, the use of the self-defense justification, the only "complete" defense, i.e., one that results in an acquittal, has increased "explosively" in the past few years (Frank 1984).

How successful has self-defense been as a justification for battered women who have killed their abusive partners? The first instance of self-defense being used with success was in Ibn-Tamas vs. United States, 407 A.2d 626 (D.C. 1979) (Burns 1980). Since Ibn-Tamas self-defense has sometimes been successfully employed but on other occasions has not been a viable defense strategy. A major reason for this lack of success is that many, perhaps most, battered woman murder cases do not meet the criteria for use of the self-defense justification (Vaughn and Moore 1983). The burden of proof lies with the defendant to prove that (1) she did not instigate the assault and was not the first party to resort to violence; (2) she reasonably believed that she was in imminent danger of death or serious physical injury; and (3) she reasonably believe that deadly force was necessary to repel the attack by her partner (Kaas 1982; Vaughn and Moore 1983). In addition, some jurisdictions impose on defendants the "duty to retreat." This means that the reasonable man has the obligation to leave the scene if doing so could have prevented the use of force, unless the incident occurs in one's own home, which is usually the case with battered women (Vaughn and Moore 1983). As pointed out by Walker, "the key to women's self defense, then, lies in the definition of what perceptions are reasonable for a female victim of violence" (Walker, Thyfault and Browne 1982: 3, emphasis added).

It has been difficult to prove the reasonable belief in the imminent danger criterion because frequently the woman has killed her partner after, not during, an abusive attack. Thus, to support the claim of self-defense an important strategy has been the introduction of expert testimony to demonstrate the existence of a "battered women's syndrome." The key element of this syndrome from a legal standpoint is an altered belief system resulting from a long history of abuse and multiple attempts to terminate it, such that the woman comes to believe that no escape was possible and that she was thus in imminent danger at the time of her homicidal act. Such testimony is said to be necessary to "dispel the average juror's misconceptions concerning a battering relationship" (Kaas 1982: 840).

The problem with this strategy is that many courts have denied the admission of expert testimony on the battered women's syndrome on a number of grounds (Kaas 1982; Kultgen 1982; Walter et al. 1982). These include the belief that such testimony is irrelevant, would prejudice the jury, is not offered by a qualified expert, is based on conclusions not arrived at through appropriate methodology, and so forth. The challenge for defense attorneys has been to convince the courts that such testimony is legitimate and is admissible. It appears that the courts are increasingly likely to admit testimony on the battered woman's syndrome, as suggested by a number of cases since Ibn-Tamas where the woman was acquitted on the basis of self-defense (see, for example State vs. Harwood, Santa Clara Cty. Ct. 1981; other successful cases include Marlene Roan Eagle in South Dakota and Miriam Greg in Montana, cited in Schneider and Jordan 1981). More common, however, is the trend toward overturning prior convictions on appeal, based on the admissibility of expert testimony on the battered women's syndrome (Walker et al. 1982). (See, for example, State vs. Smith, 247 Ga. 612, 277 S.E. 2d 678, 1981, or State vs. Wanrow, 88 Wash. 2d 221, 559 P.2d 548, 1977.)

What are the implications of these recent legal decisions for á social deviance analysis of wife battering? The defense options for a battered woman driven to homicide are very limited, and each in its own way comes with a Catch-22. A successful impaired mental state defense may avoid a prison sentence but instead lead to mandatory hospitalization, hardly an acceptable outcome for a woman who is not mentally ill. This has led Schneider and Jordan to conclude that "an impaired mental state defense should be considered only as a last resort, <u>with full awareness of its social implications</u>" (Schneider and Jordan 1981: 29, emphasis added).

Traditionally, self-defense has been recognized as a legal right under the specified circumstances outlined above. However, "the law clearly does not permit a woman to protect herself to the same extent that a man may protect himself," largely because of its sexist assumptions (Schneider and Jordan 1981). The circumstances of many battered women who commit homicide do not correspond closely to the criteria stipulated by the law for justification (Vaughn and Moore 1983). Thus, to employ self-defense successfully and be acquitted, the defendant must admit to being a victim of "battered woman's syndrome"—another Catch-22. Once again battered women are trapped.

A final and quite threatening alternative is for a woman to leave the violent family situation temporarily or permanently (Cloward and Piven 1979). By doing so the woman not only further violates sex-role norms prescribing her place in society but, more importantly, breaches the implicit marital contract that says, "I allow you to possess me in return for the privilege of running your home, bearing and rearing your children, and being supported by you" (Pagelow 1981a). Chances are, the wife will pay a high price for this affront in the form of many obstacles and little assistance if she attempts to end the violence. If she takes her children with her, she risks being accused of depriving them of a father, reflecting the myth of the inherently dysfunctional single-parent family. But the stigma she incurs will be even greater if she leaves her children behind in a desperate attempt to free her life of violence, since such behavior is clearly seen as "unnatural" and certainly unfeminine and quite deviant.

The "Catch-22" quality of the abused wife's choices is apparent. Pagelow summarizes this process by saying

> The point is, rules are broken when a woman accuses her spouse of battering, and those "rules" according to Becker were created by social groups who apply them to particular people and label them "deviant"....These rules demand that women stay at the side of their spouses, even if staying may be to the disadvantage of women. (282)

Thus, regardless of what action or inaction is taken by an abused wife, she is likely to be typed as deviant and may incur significant personal costs as a result, an outcome generally not experienced by male victims (Pagelow 1981a; Schur 1984). How can the "effectiveness" of the deviant labeling of battered women be explained? According to Rubington and Weinberg (1978), there are several reasons why the social typing of deviants is so successful, all of which are relevant to the case of domestic violence. First, fundamental social rules, namely those that dictate relations between the sexes, are violated. In addition, labeling is facilitated insofar as those performing the actual labeling are of higher social status than the female victims being labeled by virtue of being predominantly male. Lastly, there is an incentive to label because the labeling audience—police, court officials, agency officials, and others—stands to benefit from the social typing process, which reinforces their power and higher social status. In addition, by discrediting the victim official audiences are relieved of the need to respond to the victim's appeals for help. Thus gender and gender-role definitions are inextricably linked to criteria for social deviance.

Three possible consequences of effective social typing have been identified, all of which apply in the case of woman battering: typecasting, recasting, and self-fulfilling prophecy (Rubington and Weinberg 1978; Schur 1971). These consequences are especially noteworthy because they tend to impede battered women's efforts toward resolving violent family situations (Pagelow 1981a). Social typing and the associated stigmatization further erode women's already secondary power position relative to men, reinforcing their subordinate status. This in turn makes it even more difficult to terminate the violence because the act of exposing the husband triggers powerful social pressures toward conformity, that is, staying in the relationship (Dobash and Dobash 1981).

One of the first things to occur following social typing is that others' perceptions of the deviant individual change in predictable ways (Schur 1984). That is, the deviant label carries with it new expectations for behavior. In typecasting the deviant stereotype becomes so well accepted that both the audience and the deviant herself respond in predictable, automatic ways (Rubington and Weinberg 1978). A number of special characteristics are also attributed to the deviant class, for example, low self-esteem, passivity, masochism, and so forth, despite the actual variation known to exist on these characteristics both within the group and outside it. Thus all members of a particular deviant category tend to be viewed as similar to one another and different from those not so labeled. Often their histories are reconstructed to be consistent with their new deviant identities, a process Schur (1971) calls retrospective interpretation. The generally unstated assumption is that such associated characteristics, to the extent that they exist, predate and "explain" the abuse. Much of the research on woman battering has just such a focus. However, it may be equally plausible to assume that they are the result rather than cause of the violence. Loseke and Cahill (1984) argue quite persuasively that battered women are vulnerable to "victimism," that is, being perceived primarily in terms of one's role as some type of victim. Battered women tend to be viewed largely in relation to the occurrence of violence in their marriages and are assumed to be special and different because of this. In reality they are quite like the rest of women in regard to many behaviors said to occur because they are battered women, such as being reluctant to terminate an unsatisfactory relationship. Although a "profile" development approach that tries to identify distinctive characteristics of battered women may have potential heuristic value, it also can contribute to the development of misleading stereotypes about classes of victims. In the end they may be further stigmatized.

Another consequence of changes in perceptions of and attitudes toward a particular class of deviants is a response that conveys the community's disapproval of those who challenge its standards. In recasting (Rubington and Weinberg 1978) the audience applies pressure on the deviant to reform her behavior and conform to existing community norms. This punitive attitude gets conveyed repeatedly to female victims of violence seeking help outside the nuclear family as they inevitably encounter a variety of negative institutional responses ranging from complete indifference to outright hostility. Battered women report they are told that nothing can be done, that they are undeserving of help, and that it is their own fault, all of which convey the message that they should go home and be good wives. The very systems and institutions that must be utilized by women to free their lives of violence can be very unresponsive to their needs, in part because many are committed to the norms being challenged.

There is ample evidence of institutional resistance to aiding abused women attempting to leave a violent home. For example, until recently in New York State, a woman was eligible for services of the Family Court, where most domestic assault cases are handled, only if she met two conditions: she was legally married to the assailant and was committed to working toward a reconciliation with him. In terms of service eligibility, previous attempts to resolve the problem and the batterer's behaviors were viewed as irrelevant in the eyes of the court. In addition, some Family Court judges are still reluctant to grant women orders of protection, an essential precondition for many to starting a new life with some minimum hope of legal protection from the batterer. Thus women are given a powerful message about where they belong.

Perhaps this type of institutional response should not be surprising insofar as those who represent the criminal justice, medical, social service, and mental health systems were all socialized into the same traditional sex-role norms that serve to maintain women's subordinate position in the family and society (Widom 1984). These predominantly male agents of social control agencies act as powerful deviance definers and labelers. For example, formal sanctions against husband-to-wife violence do exist today in most communities. However, they have had a limited impact on family violence because even where sanctions exist, they tend to be only selectively enforced, a feature characteristic of other types of deviance as well (e.g., Becker 1963; Straus 1976). Agents of the criminal justice system, including police officers, court personnel, and judges, have tremendous discretion and play a decisive gate-keeping role in determining what constitutes a domestic violence "case" in any given locality, whether a warrant will be sought and served, and so forth. An event usually experienced as a crisis in the life of the individual may be regarded as a routine, even trivial matter for the institution (Schur 1971).

There are other examples of policies that impede access to resources. Oftentimes the helping agency's operating policies or procedures are informal and unwritten, confusing the client and making it difficult to demonstrate how discretionary policies or interpretations of policy impose barriers to service. An example of such a policy is the so-called "cooling-off period" between a violent incident and the signing of a complaint against the assailant that is informally required by some police agencies. Not surprisingly, few victims of violence are willing to wait a week or more to file a written complaint, particularly if they live with the assailant. Other police agencies have been known to rely on "stitch rules" in deciding whether to issue a warrant, which would be granted only if the complainant's injuries were severe enough to require a certain number of sutures (Straus 1977). Insofar as such actions discourage women from leaving their partners, they may have a stabilizing effect on the community. However, although the status quo is maintained, organizational actions or inactions may unquestionably have a punitive impact on the discredited individual.

One of the more insidious effects of the labeling process is its impact on the victim's self-concept. As Kirk points out, the "labeling process entails a ritualized public lowering of status that reconstitutes a person's total social identity" (Kirk 1972: 31). Since self-concept in part reflects interactions with and perceptions of others, being labeled as deviant will have obvious ramifications for how the victim views herself, a process called self-fulfilling prophecy (Rubington and Weinberg 1978) or role engulfment (Schur 1971). It has been observed that "the categorical identity of battered women is a deeply discrediting one..." (Loseke and Cahill 1984: 309). Stigmatization and internalization of society's negative judgments encourage the deviant to see herself in pejorative terms. The hostile and disapproving attitudes encountered during attempts to extricate herself from the violent environment disparage a woman's self-worth and contribute to social isolation. These assaults on self-concept make it even more difficult to take constructive action, especially if others resist her actions or believe that she is to blame.

Thus the social-psychological impact of labeling encourages the wife-victim to get caught up in the deviant role of battered wife and to reorganize her behavior around the role. Once self-definitions, behaviors, and even personality are altered as a result of societal reactions to initial norm violations, "secondary deviation" occurs (Lemert 1978). In the face of secondary deviation, disavowal of deviance becomes difficult, especially when powerful others believe behavioral change is impossible or unlikely (Schur 1971). This is a concern for battered women in light of recent research demonstrating that service providers, especially those with advanced education, believe that battered women, especially those from the lower class, will have substantial difficulty preventing future violence (Davis and Carlson 1981). On the one hand, this may be a realistic appraisal of the situation. On the other hand, such a view may be overly pessimistic and may communicate to abused women that their plight is hopeless and immutable. And yet, almost any battered women's shelter could provide stories documenting women's triumphs over seemingly insurmountable problems. Even more problematic in the Davis and Carlson (1981) research was the tendency of some respondents, especially the highly educated, to focus on those factors least amenable to change—not stress or specific precipitating behaviors but rather characterological factors, that is, the "kind of person" each partner is. This finding appears to accurately reflect the thinking of current "experts" who may not agree on why battered women have difficulty resolving violence but do agree that their problems are related to the type of persons they are, for example, dependent, passive, or socially isolated (Loseke and Cahill 1984).

SUMMARY

It has been argued that sex-role definitions of the ideal wife and husband tend to contribute to the causation and maintenance of marital violence. This is said to occur in two ways, both of which are mediated by deviant labeling. First, the wife's behavior is interpreted by the husband as a violation of the female sex-role ideal. This infraction is perceived as deviant and requiring corrective action, which may take the form of physical force. If a violent reaction by the husband is encountered repeatedly, some type of response on the part of the wife is demanded. However, as she attempts to cope with the violence in various ways, ranging from denying that anything is wrong to more proactive strategies, she will again be labeled as deviant for revealing a defective home and/or rejecting the wife role. As a consequence, she will tend to encounter negativity and resistance if she makes efforts to end the violence. Thus women are twice labeled as deviant—before and after the violence. And they experience Catch-22 situations almost by definition, regardless of whether they do or do not attempt to terminate the violence.

IMPLICATIONS FOR FUTURE RESEARCH AND ACTION

The chances of ameliorating violence against women are slight in the absence of fundamental changes in cultural norms that prescribe inequitable relations between the sexes. No longer can it be considered socially acceptable for men to view women as objects to be possessed and used for their own benefit. Research on associations between gender roles and measures of adjustment strongly suggests that the stereotyped ideals for highly masculine men and highly feminine women are neither possible to achieve nor mentally healthy. If we want to eradicate couple violence, both male and female roles must be redefined and broadened to include a wider range of characteristics and to be more responsive to situational demands. Although change of this sort is occurring, little is being done on a broad scale to consciously facilitate such changes, and those experimenting with sex roles often pay a high emotional price for their actions.

Much can be done in the areas of gender roles and violence. Although most of the research on domestic violence conducted thus far has been focused on factors at the individual level, a social deviance analysis strongly suggests that contextual factors at the macrolevel have an overriding effect on relations between husbands and wives. In addition to trying to learn more about how battered women differ from women who are not battered, we must commit ourselves to a better understanding of how social structural factors function to keep women in their place. For example, although we know that family violence and social class are related, we lack an understanding of the specific aspects of poverty that tend to be associated with violent conflict. Similarly, we know little about why some people seem quite flexible and adaptable in their approach to sex roles whereas others are more rigid, traditional, and reluctant to change.

Because family violence is not likely to end overnight, we need to learn more about the effectiveness of a whole range of programs and services targeted for marital violence. All the psychotherapy in the world will not solve the problem of battered women in the absence of other interventions aimed at the deeper roots of the problem, rather than its manifestations. And there are practical as well as theoretical limitations to the psychotherapeutic approach to the amelioration of wife abuse. Several problems exist. For example, psychotherapy tends to be employed only after the family violence has become a chronic problem, and thus after much destructive labeling has occurred. In addition, it is very difficult, as shelter staff have pointed out, to engage a woman in individual, couple, or family counseling without the implication that she bears substantial responsibility for her victimization. Also, the labeling and subsequent victimization of women by no means end when a woman seeks professional intervention. But regardless, battered wives have been seeking assistance and counseling and will continue to do so. What can be done to ensure that the quality of psychotherapeutic services available to victims of wife abuse helps rather than perpetuates their victimization?

Several strategies can be and are being employed. First, to combat victim blaming and the widespread perception that individual factors such as personality defects largely account for abuse, what Davis and Carlson have called "kind of person" explanations, we need to continue to do research that identifies the other complex causes that contribute to family violence. In addition, to dispel myths about why wife battering occurs we need to disseminate the results of that research to all categories of professional and paraprofessional staff who will be called on to assist victims of wife abuse. But we also need to especially target certain categories of professionals, such as social workers, clinical and counseling psychologists, for specialized education and training aimed at identifying knowledge, attitudes, and values that are helpful rather than destructive to those who seek their services. The belief that intrapsychic factors are at the root of family violence, while ignoring the role of stress and societal and economic factors, is an example of a potentially destructive belief.

It is equally important to learn more about interventions at the community and societal levels to answer questions such as: What kinds of communities are more receptive to providing services for abused spouses? What kinds of approaches are most effective in mobilizing services in resistant communities? How can people's consciousness about violence in the family be raised so that they see the personal and social costs of exerting force on loved ones?

References

Allen, C.M. and M.A. Straus, 1980. "Resources, power, and husband-wife power," pp. 188–208 in M.A. Straus and G.T. Hotaling (eds.), The Social Causes of Husband-Wife Violence. Minneapolis: University of Minnesota Press.

Ball-Rokeach, S.J., 1980. "Normative and Deviant Violence from a Conflict Perspective," Social Problems 28: 45–62.

Becker, H.S., 1963. Outsiders. New York: Free Press.

Blood, R.O. and D.M. Wolfe, 1960. Husbands and Wives. New York: Free Press.

Burns, L.P., 1979. Expert testimony relating to subject matters of battered women admissible on issue of self-defense—Ibn-Tamas v. United States, 407 A.2d 626 (D.C.).

Carlson, B.E., 1977. "Battered Women and their Assailants," Social Work 22: 455–60.

Cloward, R.A. and F.F. Piven, 1979. "Hidden Protest: The Channeling of Female Innovation and Resistance," Signs 4: 651–69.

Coleman, K.H., 1980. "Conjugal Violence: What 33 Men Report," Journal of Marital and Family Therapy 6: 207–13.

Davis, L.V. and B.E. Carlson, 1981. "Attitudes of Service Providers Toward Domestic Violence," Social Work Research and Abstracts 17: 34–39.

Dobash, R.E. and R.P. Dobash, 1977–78. "Wives: The 'Appropriate' Victims of Marital Violence," Victimology 2: 426–42.

Dobash, R.P. and R.E. Dobash, 1981. "Community Response to Violence Against Wives: Charivari, Abstract Justice and Patriarchy," Social Problems 28: 563–81.

Durkheim, E., 1951. Suicide. New York: Free Press.

Ericksen, J.A., W.L. Yancey and E.P. Ericksen, 1979. "The Division of Family Roles," Journal of Marriage and the Family 41: 303–13.

Erikson, K., 1978. "Notes on the Sociology of Deviance," pp. 25–29 in E. Rubington and M.S. Weinberg (eds.) Deviance: The Interactionist Perspective. New York: Macmillan.

Figueira-McDonough, J., 1985. "Gender, Race, and Class: Differences in Levels of Feminist Orientation," Journal of Applied Behavioral Science 21: 121–42.

Frank, C., 1984. "Drive to Kill: 'Battered Women' Strike Back," American Bar Association Journal 70: 25–26.

Gelles, R.J., 1976. "Abused Wives: Why Do They Stay?" Journal of Marriage and the Family 38: 659–68.

Goode, W.J., 1971. "Force and Violence in the Family," Journal of Marriage and the Family 33: 624–36.

Greenblat, C.S., 1983. "A Hit is a Hit is a Hit...or Is It? Approval and Tolerance of the Use of Physical Force by Spouses," pp. 235–60 in D. Finkelhor, R.J. Gelles, G.T. Hotaling, and M.A. Straus (eds.) The Dark Side of Families: Current Family Violence Research. Beverly Hills: Sage.

Herzog, A.R. and J.G. Bachman, 1982. Sex Role Attitudes Among High School Seniors: Views About Work and Family Roles. Research Report Series. Ann Arbor, MI: Survey Research Center, Institute for Social Research, The University of Michigan.

Hilberman, E., 1980. "'The Wife-beater's Wife' Reconsidered," American Journal of Psychiatry 137: 1336–47.

Hornung, C.A., B.C. McCullough, and T. Sugimoto, 1981. "Status Relationships in Marriage: Risk Factors in Spouse Abuse," Journal of Marriage and the Family 43: 675–92.

Kaas, C.K., 1982. "The Admissibility of Expert Testimony on the Battered Woman Syndrome in Support of a Claim of Self-defense," Connecticut Law Review 15: 121–39.

Kirk, S.A., 1972. "Clients as Outsiders: Theoretical Approaches to Deviance," Social Work 17: 24–32.

Klein, K.D., 1981. "Violence Against Women: Some Considerations Regarding its Causes and its Elimination," Crime and Delinquency 27: 64–80.

Kultgen, R.A., 1982. "Battered Woman Syndrome: Admissibility of Expert Testimony for the Defense," Missouri Law Review 47: 835–48.

Lemert, E.M., 1978. "Primary and Secondary Deviation," pp. 411–13 in E. Rubington and M.S. Weinberg (eds.) Deviance: An Interactionist Perspective. New York: Macmillan.

Loseke, D.R. and S.E. Cahill, 1984. "The Social Construction of Deviance: Experts on Battered Women," Social Problems 31: 296–310.

O'Brien, J.E., 1969. "Violence in Divorce-prone Families," Journal of Marriage and the Family 32: 692–98.

Pagelow, M.D., 1981a. "Secondary Battering and Alternatives of Female Victims to Spouse Abuse," pp. 277–300 in L. Bowker (ed.) Women and Crime in America. New York: Macmillan.

Pagelow, M.D., 1981b. "Sex Roles, Power, and Woman Battering," pp. 239–77 in L. Bowker (ed.) Women and Crime in America. New York: Macmillan.

Pleck, J., in press. Working Wives, Working Husbands. Beverly Hills: Sage.

Roy, M., 1977. "A Current Survey of 150 Cases," pp. 25–44 in M. Roy (ed.) Battered Women: A Psychosociological Study of Domestic Violence. New York: Van Nostrand.

Rubin, L.B., 1976. Worlds of Pain: Life in the Working-class Family. New York: Basic Books.

Rubington, E. and M.S. Weinberg, 1978. Deviance: An Interactionist Perspective, 3rd ed. New York: Macmillan.

Schneider, E.M. and S.B. Jordan, 1981. "Representation of Women Who Defend Themselves in Response to Physical or Sexual Assault," pp. 1–39 in E. Bochnak (ed.) Women's Self-Defense Cases: Theory and Practice. Charlottesville, VA: Michie.

Schur, E.M., 1971. Labeling Deviant Behavior: Its Sociological Implications. New York: Harper and Row.

Schur, E.M., 1984. Labeling Women Deviant: Gender, Stigma, and Social Control. New York: Random House.

Scott, M.B. and S.M. Lyman, 1968. "Accounts," American Sociological Review 33: 46–62.

Straus, M.A., 1976. "Sexual Inequality, Cultural Norms, and Wife-Beating," Victimology 1: 54–70.

Straus, M.A., 1977. "A Sociological Perspective on the Prevention
    and Treatment of Wifebeating," pp. 194–239 in M. Roy
    (ed.) Battered Women: A Psychosociological Study of
    Domestic Violence. New York: Van Nostrand.
Straus, M.A., R.J. Gelles, and S.K. Steinmetz, 1980. Behind
    Closed Doors: Violence in the American Family. New York:
    Anchor Books.
Strube, M. and L.S. Barbour, 1984. "Factors Related to the
    Decision to Leave an Abusive Relationship," Journal of
    Marriage and the Family 46: 837–44.
Vaughn, E. and M.L. Moore, 1983. "The Battered Spouse Defense
    in Kentucky," Northern Kentucky Law Review 10: 407–26.
Walker, L.E., R.K. Thyfault, and A. Browne, 1982. "Beyond the
    Juror's Ken: Battered Women," Vermont Law Review 7: 1–
    16.
Widom, C.S., 1984. "Sex Roles, Criminality, and
    Psychopathology," pp. 183–217 in C.S. Widom (ed.) Sex Roles
    and Psychopathology. New York: Plenum.
Yllo, K., 1984. "The Status of Women, Marital Equality, and
    Violence Against Wives: A Contextual Analysis," Journal of
    Family Issues 5: 307–21.
Ziegert, F., 1983. "The Swedish Prohibition of Corporal
    Punishment: A Preliminary Report," Journal of Marriage and
    the Family 45: 917–26.

PART III

ECONOMIC RIGHTS

CHAPTER 8

WOMEN IN THE LABOR FORCE: POSITION, PLIGHT, PROSPECTS

Mary Frank Fox

The increase in women's participation in the labor force is so dramatic as to be called the "single most outstanding phenomenon of our century" (Lindsy 1976). Because women's labor force participation affects each aspect of life, from marriage, fertility, and divorce patterns to demand for supportive services in the economy, the greatest changes of the twentieth century may result not from the conquest of space, atomic energy, or the depletion of resources but from the tremendous increase in the proportion of women working outside the home (Fox and Hesse-Biber 1984; Rozen 1979).

At the turn of the century, fewer than 20 percent of American women were in the labor force[1] (see Figure 1). Because they were concentrated in particular pockets of the community— young, single women from working-class families, blacks, immigrants—these women workers were even less visible to the rest of the community than their small (20%) proportion would indicate (Rozen 1979). Until the outbreak of World War II, women's participation in the labor force grew very slowly. In the war years, however, women began to enter jobs created by mounting war production and a shortage of male workers; and by 1945, almost 30 percent of American women were working outside the home.

Just after the war, production industries shut down, veterans returned to work, and women's labor force participation declined. But the war had disrupted traditional roles, lifted the social prohibition about married women working, and most importantly, resulted in expansion of the economy and significant changes in its sectors. In response, women's participation grew, slowly in the 1950s, steadily in the 1960s, and sharply in the 1970s, so that by 1980 a clear majority of American women were in the work force (see Figure 1).

During these postwar decades the great gains in women's labor force participation were accomplished by the entry into the work force of married women and later mothers of young children. In 1940 (and earlier decades) young single women predominated among female workers. Figure 2 shows that in 1940, 48 percent of the 20-to-24-year-olds were in the work force, while the participation rate of each older group declined successively. In 1950 the peak rates of young women prevailed, but the rates for older women increased as married women over 35 entered or reentered the work force in these years. By 1960 we see that the labor force participation of women between 35 and 54 shifted yet further upward, with more women returning to the work force as their children grew older (Figure 2). All of this was but a prelude, however, to what happened in the 1970s and 1980s.

First, throughout the 1970s women added to the work force at an average rate of one million annually and accounted for nearly three-fifths of the total increase in the civilian labor force in these years. Second, while in earlier decades women frequently stopped working when they married and especially when they had children, between 1970 and 1980 the labor force participation of women in prime childrearing ages—25 to 34—increased by an astounding 20 percentage points. The profile of the average female worker changed from a young single woman or an older woman with grown children to a married woman in her early thirties with preschool or school-aged children. Looking at Table 1, we see that in 1965 less than one-third of married women were working; in 1980, 50 percent were in the labor force. In 1965 a quarter of mothers with preschool children were at work; by 1975 the proportion was 38.6, and by 1980, 45.6. The labor force activity of mothers continues at record pace: In 1985, 54 percent of women with preschool children and 70 percent of those whose youngest child was between 6 and 13 were at work (U.S. Department of Labor 1985). These represent dramatic compositional changes in the labor force.

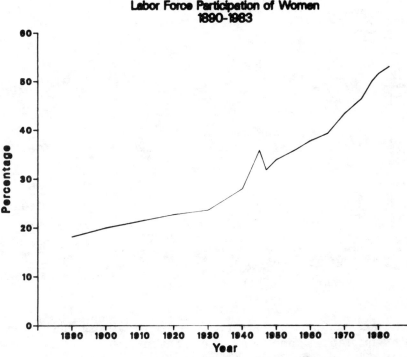

Figure 1

**Labor Force Participation of Women
1890-1983**

HOW DID IT HAPPEN AND WHAT DOES IT MEAN?

The rise in female labor force participation is tied to the changing structure of the American economy. Recovery from the World War II effort resulted in expansion of the economy and significant sectoral changes—namely, growth in health, education, clerical, and service sectors, decline in agricultural employment, and decline in the ratio of blue- to white-collar jobs. The demand for labor was then high in the service and white-collar areas characterized as "women's work" (Oppenheimer 1970). This demand for workers to back up production, staff offices, teach students, and provide services exceeded the supply of young, single females; married women began to fit the bill. Declining birth rates and rising divorce rates also contributed to women's increased

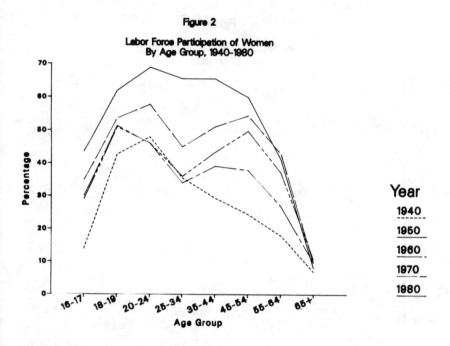

Figure 2

Labor Force Participation of Women
By Age Group, 1940-1980

participation (although the cause-and-effect relationships between the demographics and work participation are uncertain). In addition, higher educational attainment, rising expectations, and a political climate of the 1960s and 1970s questioning traditional gender values and assumptions helped transform women's participation in the economy.

With women's rising levels of education, later marriage, and lower fertility, it is likely that they will continue to enter the labor force in yet greater numbers. The projections are that by 1995 the labor force participation of women age 25–34 will increase to 90 percent (Keyserling 1984). Responses to national surveys indicate that women view employment as central to their lives and that they would choose employment even if they could live without earned income (Kamerman and Kahn 1981). This, plus the recent pattern of female labor force participation across the whole life cycle (Figure 2), points to a trend of permanent or lifetime labor force commitment and attachment for women—similar to that of men.

Table 1

Labor Force Participation Rates of Married Women and Mothers
(with and without spouse present), Select Years 1950–1980

Year	Mothers with Children			Married (spouse present)
	Under 18 years	6–17 years only	Under 6 years*	
1950	21.6%	32.8%	13.6%	23.8%
1955	27.0	38.4	18.2	27.7
1965	35.0	45.7	25.3	30.5
1975	47.4	54.8	38.6	44.4
1980	56.6	64.4	46.6	50.1

*May also have older children.

Source:

Data for 1950–1975: US Department of Labor, Women Workers Today.
                     Washington, DC: Government Printing Office, 1976.

                     US Department of Labor, Employment and Training Report
                     of the President. Washington, DC: Government Printing
                     Office, 1982.
        1980: "US Women at Work," Population Bulletin 36, 2.
               Washington, DC: Population Reference Bureau, 1981.

Women's Labor Force Location and Rewards

In itself female labor force participation is no cause for celebration. Women are concentrated in a limited number of low-paying jobs and locations with few chances for influence or advancement. This sex segregation and segmentation of the labor force is one of the most stable and striking features of the American workplace (Ilchman 1984: vii).

First, whole industries are segregated by sex. Metal and coal mining, fisheries, horticultural services, logging, construction, and railroad industries are each composed of a work force that is more than 90 percent male. While no industries are so overwhelmingly female (partly because even in female typed areas, men hold the upper level and managerial positions), the direct sales industries, employment agencies, convalescent institutions, libraries, apparel, and fabricated textile manufacturing industries are each more than 75 percent female (Reskin 1984: 2).

More broadly, men and women are concentrated into different segments (or internal markets) of the labor force (Bluestone 1970;

O'Connor 1973). Men are located in markets with advanced technology, large capital investments, unionization, and higher profits—areas like petroleum, chemicals, and utilities. Women, on the other hand, are more likely to be located in the "secondary" market segment, characterized by low capital investment, little unionization, irregular personnel practices, and low profit margins— industries such as textiles, garment making, and food processing which offer poor pay, few fringe benefits, and limited advancement opportunities. Garment making, for example—a heavily female dominated industry—is characterized by small firms, little capital investment beyond fabric and sewing machines, small and uncertain profits because of intense competition and changing tastes in fashion, and in turn, low pay, seasonal work, and few advancement opportunities (Baker 1978).

Along with industries and labor market segments, occupations are also segregated by sex. Women are concentrated in retail, sales, clerical, and service occupations (Table 2)—with three-quarters of all working women in occupations in which 75 percent of their fellow workers are female. One-quarter of all working women are concentrated in just five jobs—secretary, household worker, bookkeeper, elementary school teacher, and waitress. If we add typist, cashier, nurse, and seamstress to this list, we account for fully 40 percent of all female workers (Blau 1978).

Even when men and women work in the same general occupation for the same employer, they are frequently assigned different job titles, with different duties, responsibilities, and opportunities (Bielby 1985). For example, in the sewing divisions of auto industries, white men have the lighter, high-paying jobs, guiding automated cutting machines, changing sewing machine parts, and driving tractors. Women have the hard but lower paid jobs involved in sewing and lifting upholstery (Roby 1974). In their study of 393 California establishments with 62,000 employees, Bielby and Baron (1984) found that only 10 percent of the workers were in job titles that had both men and women assigned to them.

Of late, the popular media has made much of the entry of women into previously male-dominated occupations—and, at a gross level, the data do point to changes in the sex segregation of certain occupations. So, for example, while women constituted 4 percent of lawyers in 1970, that proportion rose to 12.4 percent in 1980, and more notably, the proportion of women in law school grew from 8 percent to 33 percent in the same decade (Epstein 1981). In academia the proportion of women faculty rose from a low of 22 percent in 1960^2 to 28 percent in 1970 and 34 percent in 1980. Among bank officers and managers, women's rate of participation grew from 13 percent in 1960 to 18 percent in 1970 and 34 percent in 1980 (Reskin and Phipps 1985). The aggregate proportional changes are also remarkable for other occupations such as pharmacy, where women more than doubled their proportion from 12 percent to 24 percent between 1970 and 1980 (Phipps 1985a). And of all occupations, one of the greatest proportional changes has been for insurance adjusters and examiners, where women constituted 12 percent of the occupation in 1960, 26 percent in 1970, and 60 percent in 1980, thus representing a turnaround from a male- to female-dominated occupation (Phipps, 1985b).

But by themselves these aggregate data conceal more than they reveal. First, professional jobs represent a small proportion of the female labor force. Less than a quarter of employed women are in managerial and professional areas; and more significantly, of those who are in these classifications, the greatest proportion are in elementary and secondary school teaching or nursing. Second, case studies suggest that the women recently hired in previously male dominated occupations are being assigned to devalued functions, low-paying positions, and less autonomous roles, and thus that, internally, the occupations are being resegregated by sex. Hence, while women have tripled their proportion in law in the last two decades, their prospects in the profession remain to be seen. The legal profession is being eroded by both an oversupply of law graduates and a growth in the proportion of legal work done in a routinized fashion (Carter and Carter 1981). And the women in law are concentrated in government practice, estate and trust work, and matrimonial cases, where their contact with powerful clients—corporations, banks, investment houses—is limited (Epstein 1981).

In academia, likewise, women are increasing their proportion of doctoral degrees awarded at a time when the market is already "glutted" with Ph.Ds. Furthermore, the areas in which women represent the largest proportion of new doctorates (English, foreign languages, social sciences) are those fields with the greatest surplus of candidates and most limited job opportunities. Women are entering academia when the chances for secure, well-paid, prestigious positions are probably more dismal than they have been at any time in American academic history (Carter and Carter 1981). And when women do obtain jobs, they are in the lowest and most marginal ranks. Across fields and institutions, women are one-third of the assistant professors but only one-fifth of the associate professors, and just one-tenth of the professors. It is, instead, at the subprofessional (lecturer, instructor) ranks that we find disproportionate concentrations of women, who are almost half the faculty at these marginal ranks (Fox 1984).

In the 1970s the Office for Federal Contract Compliance targeted the banking and insurance industries for affirmative action and antidiscrimination regulations. Partly as a result, women rose to 34 percent of bank officers and financial managers over the decade. But like law or academia, banking is stratified, and the newly hired and "promoted" women are being physically and functionally segregated within the occupation. Women rarely manage high profit departments such as loans or investments; they are absent from the main banking offices; are located, instead, in the small, suburban ("shopping center") branches that multiplied during the '70s; and as a group, they earn only 53 percent of what is earned by male bank managers for full-time work (Reskin and Phipps, forthcoming).

As noted, two of the most dramatic compositional changes in women's occupational participation are found in pharmacy and insurance. But here, again, aggregate changes alone do not reveal the internal segregation and ranking in the occupations. While women's participation in pharmacy doubled between 1970 and 1980, women pharmacists work disproportionately in lower paying settings, in nonmanagerial roles, and in deskilled areas. The growing numbers of women in pharmacy are staffing hospitals and the proliferation of retail chain stores that now deliver pharmaceutical services. Moreover, within these chain stores, only 15 percent of the women are managers compared to 44 percent of the men. In independent pharmacies women are only 19 percent of the owners, managers, and assistant managers, compared to 61 percent of the men (Phipps 1985a).

Women in pharmacy are moving into a profession that has, in general, lost its former skills and functions. Prior to World War II pharmacists mixed (or "compounded") drugs prescribed by physicians. Over the next decades manufacturers began producing drugs in final form, and pharmacists increasingly just ordered and dispensed drugs (Phipps 1985a). As the profession dropped in status, skills, and entrepreneurial opportunity (owing to decline in independently owned pharmacies), women entered ranks no longer attractive to men (Reskin and Phipps, forthcoming). As Carter and Carter (1981) put it: "Women get a ticket to ride after the gravy train has left the station."

The processes of deskilling, devaluation, and resegregation are yet more striking among insurance adjusters and examiners—an occupation that changed from predominantly male to female in two decades. Insurance adjusters determine whether policies cover claims and stated losses, and traditionally have carried on the work outside the office, using reports, physical evidence, and witness testimony. During the 1970s, however, decisions and adjustments became more centralized and routinized, and claims are now dealt with by telephone, mail, and computer using standardized procedures (Phipps 1985b). Insurance examiners investigate and review claims for completeness, accuracy, and calculation of payments. Because of the computerization of insurance claims, the analytical part of the job has declined, and examiners now simply review claims on video display terminals using programs that calculate payments (Phipps 1985b).

In both insurance occupations then, the work is increasingly routinized, involving less discretion, negotiation, and analysis. As the job content has simplified and the status declined, women have moved into these positions. The men remaining in the occupations tend to hold the specialized adjustment positions with work outside the office, and as a group, male adjusters and examiners who worked full-time, year around in 1980 earned an average of $18,576 a year compared to women's $11,064 (Phipps 1985b).

Thus even with the seeming entry of women into primarily male dominated occupations, men and women remain concentrated by industry, by occupation, by firms, and by specific job titles. This becomes consequential, especially when we look to the earning differences of men and women. To cite the now commonly recognized figure: among full-time, year-round workers, the mean earnings of women are only 60 percent of men's, and that proportion has actually declined in the past 30 years. Significantly, a large proportion of that income difference owes to the labor force segmentation and segregation of women—and to the fact that jobs held by women pay less in part because they are held mainly by women (Treiman and Hartman 1981). As Treiman and Hartman's report of the National Research Council's Committee on Occupational Classification and Analysis points out, first, differentials in earnings of women's and men's jobs persist when the characteristics of workers (e.g., education, experience, training) are held constant. Second, differences in wages for women's and men's work have been regarded as "acceptable" until very recently, and these traditions are now built into wage structures. Moreover, as

Table 2

Employed Civilians by Occupation and Sex, 1984

Occupation	Men	Women
Managerial and professional	24.6%	22.5%
Technical, sales, and administrative support (clerical)	19.5	45.6
Service occupations	9.4	18.7
Precision, production, craft, and repair	20.2	2.4
Operators, fabricators, and laborers	21.2	9.6
Farming, forestry, and fishing	5.1	1.2
TOTALS	100.0%	100.0%

Source: U.S. Department of Labor, Bureau of Labor Statistics. Employment and Earnings 32 (January, 1985): Table 21.

we discuss further below, at the level of specific firms, studies show that women's jobs pay less than men's even when they require comparable (or higher) levels of skill, effort, and responsibility. While part of the earnings gap between men and women is a function of women's limited access to higher paying industries and firms and to inequitable pay for the same jobs, a substantial portion of the gap is also due to the higher pay scales for job classifications held primarily by men. Deprivation of resources (pay, prestige, power) is linked then to the composition, and definitions, of female compared to male domains.

WOMEN, WORK, AND DOUBLE-BINDING CRITERIA

Along with these deprivations in occupational location and rewards, traditional definitions of male, female, and sex-appropriate domains create other tensions, strains, and "institutionalized deviance" (no-win, double-binding) criteria for women at work. First, women are victimized by conflicting cultural values and roles. Traditionally, women's socialization has been directed toward virtue and acceptance in family and personal relationships, rather than competition and success in worldly accomplishment (Fox and Hesse-Biber 1984). Yet society rewards those who achieve and succeed and it pays merely lip service to those who are noble and nurturant. Consequently, women who devote themselves to nourishing and nurturing gain few extrinsic rewards; despite rhetoric to the contrary, our society accords childbearing and caring low esteem and gives little recognition to those who do this work (Lott 1974). But at the same time, women who seek status and stature in the world at large often lose in virtue and acceptance (Barnett and Baruch 1978). This is a double-binding, no-win predicament.

Second, reliance on a male model for work and employment has resulted in the postulate that the work attitudes and behavior of men are "normal" and those of women, by implication, "deviant" and "abnormal" (Acker 1976, 1978). So, for example, it is women who are compelled to learn male values through such programs as "assertiveness training." Men, however, are exempt from any parallel program in "civility" or "humanism" that might equip them with these more female-centered skills and values (Marciano 1981).

Third, women's family roles impose onerous demands and constraints—both at home and at work. Despite the dramatic increase in women's labor force participation, the allocation of household responsibilities has, in comparison, changed very little (see Hofferth and Moore 1979). Women have not relinquished house for market work; they have simply added one role to the other. Men, on the other hand, spend little time in housework— whether their wives are employed or not (see Hofferth and Moore 1979; Pleck 1981). The duties that men have to their families have been primarily their occupational involvement and achievement, and a man is thought to best serve his family by advancing his career. And of course many of these men have available to them supportive partners who provide the feeding and fueling that makes this work involvement possible.

But with sex role values that stress the dominance of men's employment needs and opportunities and with the disproportionate allocation of housework and child care, the family role competes with, rather than complements, women's occupational role. Domestic responsibilities vie for resources which must be allocated between home and work, and women are confronted with burden and overload in both spheres (Fox and Hesse-Biber 1984). Given demands from all sides of life, women face choices and obstacles rarely encountered by men. They may need to limit the hours they work, the jobs they can take on, and the leisure and recreation they can afford. And with accumulating and sometimes unmet demands, women frequently feel guilt and a sense of failure in living up to standards (Johnson and Johnson 1977).

This is compounded by the structure and demands of employment institutions that remain geared to a traditional family model of two parents, with husband as full-time employee and wife as full-time homemaker—a model which, in fact, characterizes only 6 percent of American homes (Moroney 1978; Pifer 1978). Even when the woman is the main wage earner in the household, the man is still regarded as the "provider" and the woman the "secondary" partner available for backup on the homefront.

In managerial and professional occupations, for example, work demands are so high as to run far beyond the nine-to-five work-day into weekends as well. This relentless pace is possible because employing institutions have traditionally assumed and depended upon the presence of a spouse to provide care, service, and backup at home. In blue-collar, clerical, and service occupations, work schedules requiring fixed starting hours and providing little or no release time for childbearing, caring, and domestic demands have also been based on a family model with a full-time homemaker assumed to be available to deal with school hours and breaks, home deliveries, and children's illnesses. Similarly, extensive travel demands of employing institutions and policies of frequent transfers have relied on a family model with the woman as a supportive, secondary partner available to respond to the demands of a "primary" employee. With a (55%) majority of women now in the labor force, and more than half of mothers with children under six working outside the home, these outmoded practices of employing institutions create stresses and problems— conflicts, binds, and unavoidable failure or "deviance"—for women in their home and work roles.

SOME RESOLUTIONS

Traditional assumptions about work and family roles are no longer tenable and indicate a need for response and adjustment in family, employment, and other institutions. At the least we need: a salary policy of equal pay for work of comparable effort, skill, and responsibility; open lines of mobility from clerical and other sex-typed jobs with low ceiling on pay and prestige; introduction of flexible work schedules; and child care benefits and services that provide alternative ways for adults of both sexes to manage work and home without damage to themselves and the children.

Women's low earnings are linked to their location in female sex-typed jobs. To improve their earnings, one option is women's integration into nontraditional jobs. But the sex segregation of the workplace is so complete that, in order to accomplish equal distribution of the sexes across occupations, two-thirds of all men and women would have to change jobs (Hartman and Reskin 1983; Remick and Steinberg 1984). Integration would require men entering women's jobs as well as the other way around—and given the low rewards of female-typed jobs, incentives are limited for doing so. Further, the sheer numbers involved prohibit full integration as a solution; and as Remick and Steinberg (1984: 294) point out, "only a small portion of the million typists can become one of the 800,000 carpenters." Finally, as we have discussed, when women have entered male occupations, resegregation by job function and status has resulted.

The fundamental issue is that work done by females (and minorities) has been systematically undervalued because it is done by women. Controlling for comparable levels of tasks, behavior, and functions on the job, two dozen different studies by states and municipalities show consistently that the female-dominated job titles command 5 to 20 percent less than male job titles with comparable "factor points" (Perlman and Grune 1982). With the majority of women (and men) in sex-typed jobs, and with the earnings of women's work systematically depressed by sex composition itself, comparable worth is then a critical job equity issue of the '80s.

To actually achieve "equal pay for equal work," jobs must be analyzed and evaluated according to neutral principles and payed according to comparable levels of effort, skill, and responsibility. Neutral assessment can be problematic, however, because the values assigned to jobs have been driven by current labor market values, so that work with numbers, for example, is assigned more "factor points" than work with people and personal relations (see Remick 1984). More fundamentally, the issue of comparable worth is controversial because it challenges assumptions about the relative worth of different groups—and more specifically, assumptions about the intrinsically greater worth of male compared to female labor. Comparable worth is also controversial because it threatens to increase costs (as have child labor laws, federal minimum wage regulations, and the whole evolution of laws on wages and hours in labor history). It meets the resistance of critics who say that comparable worth will destroy "the free market"—despite the fact that the government not only interferes in the "free market" through the Fair Labor Standards Act, the Occupational Health and Safety Act, or Title VII of the Civil Rights Act, but also through the protection of corporations by provision of funds, for example, to Chrysler, Amtrack, and Lockheed to prevent their bankruptcy (see Remick and Steinberg 1984). The point remains that as long as the work force continues to be sex segregated, and as long as women's work is systematically undervalued, equity will depend on neutral assessment of jobs and equal pay for work of comparable value.

Among women in the labor force, the largest proportion are clerical workers. The status of clerical work is then central to the economic status of women. Along with neutral assessment of the work, and payment commensurate with effort, skill, and responsibility, these positions must also be located on paths of mobility and opportunity. At present clerical work is surrounded by "dead space" of short promotion ladders and few possibilities for development. To advance the opportunities of clerical workers (and hence the largest proportion of employed women), tracks of mobility must be created both within clerical and into other jobs (Kanter 1976). The status of clerical workers also depends on internal modifications. Specifically, for a large number of clericals, the job is characterized as a personal relationship between secretary and boss—a paternalistic, patronizing association that needs to be rationalized with job descriptions and periodic appraisals, which reward the work done rather than the relationship formed.

Because domestic responsibilities fall primarily on women, and because child care services are so limited (as we discuss below), inflexible work schedules are another obstacle to a humane and sex-equitable workplace. In deliberation of work schedules, part-time employment is a prime consideration. Less than half of all female employees work full-time the year around.[3] The remainder work part-time for some or all of the year, or full-time for some fraction of the year (Bureau of Labor Statistics, Current Population Survey, March 1985). Some women work part-time by "choice" since, in the absence of adequate child care, it is the only way they can manage the needs of their children. Others do so because certain industries will only hire part-time—in order to avoid paying benefits such as health insurance.

Either way, part-time work carries heavy liabilities: low pay, little job security, and few benefits. Most part-time jobs are in the lowest paying areas—food services, clerical, retail sales, and household work. Yet a study of professionals and executives by the Department of Health, Education, and Welfare shows the feasibility of less than full-time employment in higher status positions. After selecting 22 employees on a part-time basis, HEW found that these part-timers were highly productive employees, who had few problems with their jobs or their supervisors (U.S. Department of Labor, Employment and Training Administration 1977). The feasibility of part-time work in higher status, more lucrative positions becomes more understandable when we consider that managers, for example, are frequently traveling, at conferences, and actually away from the office and those they supervise for significant portions of time.

Beyond part-time employment, the particular arrangement of hours at work is also an issue for equity in the workplace. For those who must accept responsibility for children and their schedules, "flex-time" can be a help. Under "flex-time" arrangements an employee must be at work during certain "core hours" (say, 9:30 am to 3:00 pm), but the particular starting and stopping times at the beginning and end of the day are discretionary, so long as total hours add up to the terms of employment. Other scheduling possibilities include arrangements for 80 hours of work during a given two week period without adherence to an eight-hour day, or the option to do portions of work at home (see Fox and Hesse-Biber 1984). None of these options really reduces women's overload per se, nor do they shift responsibilities more equitably within the home; but they do help reconcile the conflicts and manage the burden.

A root of these burdens is the inadequacy of child care services in our society. The child care system in the United States is basically a "nonsystem" (Joffe 1983)—an amalgam of some public programs, some private programs, and mostly unlicensed informal arrangements. As much as 90 percent of day care is, in fact, provided by unlicensed facilities of vastly varying quality (Joffe 1983); and the U.S. Commission on Civil Rights (1981) report on Child Care and Equal Opportunities for Women estimates that some 32,000 preschoolers and 2 million school age children are caring for themselves.

Among Western, industrialized nations (including France, Federal Republic of Germany, German Democratic Republic, Hungary, and Sweden), the United States is the only country without a national policy of child care benefits (such as maternity benefits or child care allowances) or services (care for infants, toddlers, and children) (Kamerman and Kahn 1981). The price of "nonpolicy" is a lack of standards, goals, and guidelines for child care. Furthermore, nonpolicy is essentially a tacit support for norms about traditional roles, and division of labor, of men and women—norms that legitimize the allocation of home and child care to women, whether they are employed or not (Fox and Hesse-Biber,

1984). The consequence is another double-binding constraint on women's status. The dual burdens draw on women's time and resources so as to make them less competitive (thus potential "deviants") at work, and reciprocally their disadvantaged labor force status can depress and restrict their employment aspirations.

Work does not exist in a vacuum. Women's status at work reflects and connects with their position and plight in other institutions—the family, as well as education, polity, and economy (Fox and Hesse-Biber 1984). As long as women are allocated disproportionate responsibility for home and children, and as long as the labor is undervalued and unsupported, that, too, will restrict women's opportunities at work and in society.

Why haven't social institutions kept up with changing labor force behavior? Partly it is a familiar pattern of institutions trailing behavior. But beyond that, institutions lag because it is profitable for them to do so and costly not to do so. Pay equity, adequate child care, and rearrangements of the workplace entail costs for public and private institutions. At present, women are providing high-quality, low-cost labor—while forced to assume the strains and burdens themselves. In the process women are quelled by double-barreled Catch-22 criteria—conflicting values and norms, male models of work and employment, onerous domestic demands, and employment structures geared to a traditional (and largely nonexistent) family model, among other factors. These create "institutionalized deviance" (no-win) binds for women at work that both reflect their depressed status and serve to perpetuate it.

Notes

[1] The labor force includes all those who are employed or actively seeking employment.

[2] The proportion of women faculty was actually higher in 1920 (30%) and 1940 (27%) than in 1960 (Reskin and Phipps 1985).

[3] Two-thirds of men are employed full-time, year around.

References

Acker, J., 1976. "Introduction: Women and Work," International Journal of Sociology 5 (Winter): 936–45.

Acker, J., 1978. "Issues in the Sociological Study of Women's Work," in A. Stromberg and S. Harkess (eds.) Women Working: Theories and Facts in Perspective. Palo Alto, CA: Mayfield.

Baker, S. H., 1978. "Women in Blue-Collar and Service Occupations," in A. Stromberg and S. Harkess (eds.) Women Working: Theories and Facts in Perspective. Palo Alto, CA: Mayfield.

Barnett, R. and G. Baruch, 1978. The Competent Woman: Perspectives on Development. New York: Irvington.

Bielby, W. and J. Baron, 1984. "A Woman's Place is With Other Women," in B. Reskin (ed.) Sex Segregation in the Workplace. Washington, DC: National Academy Press.

Bielby, W., 1985. "Undoing Discrimination: Comparable Worth and Job Integration." Paper presented at conference on "Ingredients for Women's Employment Policy," Albany, NY.

Blau, F., 1978. "The Data on Women Workers, Past, Present, and Future," in A. Stromberg and S. Harkess (eds.) Women Workers: Theories and Facts in Perspective. Palo Alto, CA: Mayfield.

Bluestone, B., 1970. "The Tripartite Economy: Labor Markets and the Working Poor," Poverty and Human Resources: 15–35.

Carter, M. and S.B. Carter, 1981. "Women's Recent Progress in the Professions, or Women Get a Ticket to Ride After the Gravy Train has Left the Station," Feminist Studies 7 (Fall): 477–503.

Epstein, C.F., 1981. Women in Law. New York: Anchor Books.

Fox, M.F., 1984. "Women and Higher Education: Sex Differentials in the Status of Students and Scholars," in J. Freeman (ed.) Women: A Feminist Perspective. Palo Alto, CA: Mayfield.

Fox, M.F. and S. Hesse-Biber, 1984. Women at Work. Palo Alto, CA: Mayfield.

Hartman, H. and B. Reskin, 1983. "Job Segregation: Trends and Prospects," in C. Chertos, L. Haignere, and R. Steinberg (eds.) Occupational Segregation and its Impact on Working Women. Albany, NY: Center for Women in Government.

Hofferth, S. and K. Moore, 1979. "Women's Employment and Marriage," in R. Smith (ed.) The Subtle Revolution: Women at Work. Washington, DC: Urban Institute.

Ilchman, A.S., 1984. "Preface," in B. Reskin (ed.) Sex Segregation in the Workplace. Washington, DC: National Academy Press.

Joffe, C., 1983. "Why the United States Has No Child-Care Policy," in I. Diamond (ed.) Family, Politics, and Public Policy. New York: Longman.

Johnson, C.L. and F. Johnson, 1977. "Attitudes Toward Parenting in Dual-Career Families," American Journal of Psychiatry 134: 391–95.

Kamerman, S. and A. Kahn, 1981. Child Care, Family Benefits, and Working Parents: A Study in Comparative Policy. New York: Columbia University Press.

Kanter, R.M., 1976. "The Policy Issues: Presentation VI," in M. Blaxall and B. Reagan (eds.) Women and the Workplace. Chicago: University of Chicago Press.

Keyserling, M., 1984. "The Status and Contribution of American Women to the Economy—1950–1983," Proceedings of the National Conference on Women, the Economy, and Public Policy, Washington, DC, August.

Lindsy, R., 1976. "Women Entering the Job Market at an Extraordinary Pace," New York Times (September 12): 1, 49.

Lott, B., 1974. "Who Wants the Children?" in A. Skolnick and J. Skolnick (eds.) Intimacy, Family, and Society. Boston: Little, Brown.

Marciano, T.D., 1981. "Socialization and Women at Work," National Forum 61 (Fall): 24–25.

Moroney, R., 1978. "Note From the Editor," Urban Social Change Review 11, 1/2: 2.

O'Connor, J., 1973. The Fiscal Crisis of the State. New York: St. Martins Press.

Oppenheimer, V.K., 1970. The Female Labor Force in the United States. Berkeley, CA: University of California Press.

Perlman, N. and J.A. Grune, 1980. "Preliminary Memorandum on Pay Equity." Working paper no. 2. Albany, NY: Center for Women in Government.

Phipps, P., 1985a. "Preliminary Case Study of Pharmacists." Unpublished paper, the University of Michigan.

Phipps, P., 1985b. "Preliminary Case Study of Insurance Adjusters, Examiners, and Investigators." Unpublished paper, The University of Michigan.

Pifer, A., 1978. "Women and Working: Toward a New Sociology," Urban and Social Change Review 11: 3–11.

Pleck, J., 1981. "The Work-Family Problem: Overloading the System," in B. Forisha and B. Goldman (eds.) Outsiders on the Inside: Women and Organizations. Englewood Cliffs, NJ: Prentice Hall.

Remick, H. and R. Steinberg, 1984. "Technical Possibilities and Political Realities," in H. Remick (ed.) Comparable Worth and Wage Discrimination. Philadelphia: Temple University Press.

Remick, H. (ed.), 1984. Comparable Worth and Wage Discrimination. Philadelphia: Temple University Press.

Reskin, B., 1984. "Introduction," in B. Reskin (ed.) Sex Segregation in the Workplace. Washington, DC: National Academy Press.

Reskin, B. and P. Phipps, forthcoming. "Women in Male-Dominated Professional and Managerial Occupations," in A. Stromberg and S. Harkess (eds.) Women Working: Theories and Facts in Perspective, 2nd edition.

Roby, P., 1974. The Conditions of Women in Blue Collar, Industrial, and Service Jobs: A Review of Research and Proposal for Research Action and Policy. New York: Russell Sage Foundation.

Rozen, F.S., 1979. "Women in the Work Force: The Interaction of Myth and Reality," pp. 79–102 in E. Synder (ed.) The Study of Women: Enlarging Perspectives of Social Reality. New York: Harper and Row.

Treiman, D. and H. Hartman, 1981. Women, Work, and Wages: Equal Pay for Jobs of Equal Value. Washington, DC: National Academy Press.

U.S. Commission on Civil Rights, 1981. Child Care and Equal Opportunities for Women. Washington, DC: Government Printing Office.

U.S. Department of Labor, 1977. "Employment Standards Administration," Women and Work. R&D Monograph 46. Washington, DC: Government Printing Office.

U.S. Department of Labor, Bureau of Labor Statistics, 1985. "Labor Force Activity of Mothers of Young Children Continues at Record Pace." Washington, DC: Bureau of Labor Statistics.

CHAPTER 9

WELFARE DEPENDENCY AS THE LANGUAGE OF SOCIAL CONTROL

Deborah K. Zinn

THE EXACERBATION OF POVERTY

At midnight on September 30, 1981, hundreds of thousands of working women who were recipients of supplementary benefits under Aid to Families with Dependent Children (AFDC) throughout the United States were unwillingly emancipated. They were granted "independence" from the welfare system by a political act which was espoused to be in their best interest. It was asserted that they would be "better off" if they were on their own without the benefits which they were receiving from welfare.[1] The mechanism of their emancipation was the Omnibus Budget Reconciliation Act of 1981 (OBRA). This law contained a number of provisions which cumulatively ensured that AFDC recipients who were working full-time would no longer be eligible for supplementary AFDC benefits, Medicaid, or child care (Zinn and Sarri 1984). As such it represented a dramatic reversal in the evolution of social policy initiated in 1935 aimed at improving the well-being of poor children and their caretakers. In the name of combating welfare dependency, OBRA eliminated the objectively least dependent but still needy group from AFDC, thereby punishing them by withdrawing one-fifth of their incomes, Medicaid,[2] child care,[3] and other supplemental housing and work-related benefits. This automatically made them more dependent on their employers, their relatives, and their exhusbands if the well-being of their children was to be maintained. It thrust these families deeper into poverty at a time when the society was experiencing the most serious economic recession since the 1930s (U.S. House of Representatives 1983).

Why were these families, the most independent of AFDC recipients, who only received supplementary benefits, made the scapegoats for reform in the AFDC program? This is the question that this chapter will attempt to answer.

POVERTY IN THE UNITED STATES

Because several chapters in this volume address the increasing impoverishment of women and children in the United States, I will only highlight its major characteristics so that the discussion and analysis of welfare dependency will be placed within that context. Poverty increased significantly in the United States in the 1980s, but especially noteworthy is the fact that poverty is increasingly concentrated among women and children, primarily those in single-parent-female-headed households (Pearce and McAdoo 1981; McAdoo and Parham 1985). Nearly one in seven Americans is now poor, but among female-headed families nearly one in two is poor (Center for Budget Priorities 1985). Although female-headed families constitute only one-fifth of all families with children, 51 percent of all poor children lived in such families with the percentages far higher for black and Hispanic children (U.S. House of Representatives 1985). These female-headed families are poor regardless of inclusion of nonincome transfers such as Food Stamps or Medicaid, alimony, child support, or their own earnings.

Women and children's poverty escalated in the United States in the 1970s and 1980s because women were forced to depend more exclusively on their own earnings or else rely on steadily declining social welfare benefits. Ironically, paralleling this growth in poverty has been the rapidly increasing labor force participation of women with children. Among Western industrial countries the United States is now second only to Sweden in the rate of female labor force participation. As of September 1985, 70 percent of women with school-age children were in the labor force, and 63 percent of those with preschool children were working outside the home (U.S. Department of Labor, Bureau of Labor Statistics 1985). However, increased entry has not been accompanied by higher wages or benefits, resulting in little alleviation of poverty through work. Moreover, these women are said to be "welfare dependent" if they seek public resources to aid in meeting needs for rearing their children, yet these children are a most essential resource for the future of society. Thus it is essential to examine the concept of dependency because of its importance in U.S. ideology regarding welfare.[4]

WOMEN AND DEPENDENCY

Employing a perspective articulated by Edelman (1971, 1977) welfare dependency is examined here as political language—language which allows politicians, bureaucrats, academics, and the public to communicate in a summary, evocative, yet abstract way about policy. Political language, by invoking accepted norms and values, sanctifies action and reassures the public that policy actions are in accordance with its political interests. Given a pluralistic political environment, political language must be abstract, vague and simplistic enough to coalesce varying perspectives while reinforcing fundamental support for the political system and trust in its ability to deal with major social problems (such as war or poverty) (Edelman 1964, 1971, 1977; Gamson and Lasch 1981; Burton 1985).

Dependency is a powerful component of political language in welfare policy, but its influence is indirect. The impact of the concept of dependency is at the level of problem definition—poverty is transformed from a condition of need for which the social group assumes responsibility into "welfare dependency" (Rein 1967). Dependency imagery was a consistent part of the political language of income support programs for children and their families even before the passage of the Social Security Act of 1935 (Abbott 1966). As a consequence, dependency has now become an unchallenged, underlying assumption guiding research and policy change in federal and state family policy directed toward poor, single females and their children (Moynihan 1986; U.S. Dept. of HHS 1986).

But, if the concept of dependency is a guiding force in problem definition, what is its nature, i.e., what exactly do people mean by dependency? How does it come to be so central to the debates on family policy? Dependency is a natural and necessary human condition, an everyday, day-in-and-day-out phenomenon. We depend on each other for our basic needs: on farmers for food; on the city for clean water; on our friends and relatives for love and support. As Memmi (1984) has noted, none of us is wholly self-sufficient; we all live in circumstances of partial dependence.

Although all of us are dependent at various times in our lives, independence is the preferred ideology guiding national policy and individual actions in the United States (Riesman 1951). Capitalist society is built on concepts of individualism, independence, and self-interest as much as on free markets and competition. A closer analysis of national ideology reveals that while it apparently supports universal independence, it ascribes dependence to women.[5] According to American cultural norms, women are—and should be—dependent while men are—and should be—independent. This ascription automatically gives a superior position to men since dependence is devalued overall. Women should be dependent; the question is, on whom?

Women with children have a special relationship to dependence: they are dependent, yet they have dependents. Women of color are often considered to be even more dependent. Despite evidence to the contrary (for example, the statistics that show that black women have higher labor force participation rates than white women: USDOL, BLS 1985), black women are perceived as less willing to work and more willing to sit back and receive governmental benefits, i.e., be dependent.

The dependency of poor women with children takes on a different cast when they receive governmental benefits. When this occurs, dependency, which might otherwise be seen as a normative female condition, becomes deviant or evidence of laziness and dishonesty (Schur 1983). Therefore governmental policies created to regulate the relationship of these families with the welfare state have clear control objectives. For example, the rationale for making the poor work for their benefits (Workfare) has the overt intent of "correcting" the psychological attitudes and behavior of recipients— if these lazy people are forced to work, they will learn good habits and the value of the dollar. The obvious inference is that poverty is self-created and that the low levels of benefits and controlling procedures are strategies of rehabilitation.[6] This interpretation obfuscates the fact that benefit levels and procedures are preserved to maintain economic need as an "incentive" to low-wage work and to minimize the cost of welfare benefits to taxpayers, thereby frustrating any real efforts at income redistribution to reduce income inequality.

There are three major components of a dependency relationship: the dependency target, those in the dependent roles, and the services that are provided by the dependent for the target. For our analysis the dependency target is defined as those individuals or entities who utilize or consume the services of the person defined as dependent. This relationship for women is different from the "normal" market relationship between producer and consumer because the dominant construction of reality assigns them to the private sphere. The impact of this prevailing and distorted view of women as marginal to market participation in the valuation of their work is well documented (see Fox chapter, "Women in the Labor Force," in this volume).

The practical necessity of dependence and the ideology of independence are at loggerheads. This contradiction places women in an especially vulnerable position: they are coerced into dependent roles through socialization and then denigrated because they violate the ideology through acts of their own volition or those required in order to survive. Some (Gilder 1981) argue that women are meant to be dependent and cite the glorification of motherhood as supporting evidence. But mothers are economically beggared despite the ideological rhetoric. Mothers who head families are four times as likely to be in poverty as are male heads of families.

Control is inherent in dependency as is most obvious in child-parent relationships. In the case of adult women the dependency consumer wants to ensure that services will be available when needed. Thus he seeks to do whatever is necessary in social, political, or economic spheres to maintain the dependency because it serves his interests and well-being. For example, it is often noted that anyone would like to have a "wife" with all the service that such a status connotes, but no one wishes to be a "wife."

WELFARE DEPENDENCY

For poor mothers the necessity/ideology contradiction has even graver consequences than it does for women in general because they are at the nexus of the full complement of dependency relationships (e.g., gender, race, class). Examination of the dynamics of these interactions is essential to an understanding of poverty as deviance (Schur 1983). Public policies governing poor women receiving AFDC provide visible evidence of the mechanisms and nature of these dependency relationships. Therefore examination of welfare dependency can inform our knowledge about the increasing feminization of poverty.

Use of the concept welfare dependency as a condition to be avoided at all costs unless one is wholly destitute or without any social resources enables the political and economic forces in society to reinforce traditional male dominance and control in the family. This is so because the value of independence it reinforces is in fact operationalized as family, not individual independence. Given the cultural prescription of dependence for wives and children within the family, this ultimately means independence for the male head of the family. This ideology is also tied to the view of the family as an economic unit in which the father is the provider. Obviously there is no place in such a framework for female-headed single-parent households, so that status is by definition deviant and to be discouraged and avoided. This position, however, flies in the face of the high rate of divorce and separation, the current labor force participation of women, the increasing demand of society for low-wage workers in the service sectors, and the fact that most blue-collar two-parent families require both spouses to be wage earners if they are to remain above the poverty level (U.S. Bureau of the Census 1985).

The hidden but controlling web of dependency relations can be exposed through an analysis of the mediating role that language and social policy play between necessity and ideology. Language is a powerful tool of control. The stigmatizing language of welfare dependency protects the necessary dependency relationships so as to reinforce the dominant male role as provider while decreasing the value of the female's service and, therefore, the economic bargaining position of poor women. One need only consider the great difficulty that women have encountered in attempting to receive any economic acknowledgment for years of work as homemaker.[7]

The intended outcome of the negative label of welfare dependence is to make those who are dependent deviants who need to be punished (Erickson 1966; Hutter and Williams 1981). But if normatively women are expected to be dependent, why should their position in a dependent role be considered deviant? In programs for women such as AFDC, the concept implies "misplaced dependence." According to American norms, women should be dependent within the family, but the unit as a whole should be independent; therefore dependency by women and children on the state is misplaced.

One key to unlocking the puzzle of how independence rhetoric actually reinforces the dependency of women is to examine the use of language during the historical formation of welfare policy—OBRA then becomes only the most recent AFDC policy shift motivated and rationalized by the intent of eliminating welfare dependency. Examination of the historical usage of the language of welfare dependency and changes in welfare policies governing women or welfare relationships with their families, employers, and the state will show the direct policy consequences of this ideology and political language.

In sum, a central contention of this chapter is that the concept of welfare dependency can only be interpreted through an understanding of AFDC recipients as performing needed services for the state, their families, and/or the economy. Furthermore, these services require that women on welfare be in a dependent position. Ideal wives and mothers are dependent, not independent. Ideal female employees are low paid, low in power, and deferring so that they cannot bargain for higher wages and benefits. Ideal reserve laborers, from the perspective of the state, support the capitalist system, have children, remain unemployed during economic recessions, and do so at the lowest levels of support. The operation of the eligibility system governing AFDC is a concrete example of the stringency with which these controls are enforced. One need only examine the daily newspaper to see the inordinate public concern about the welfare fraud of AFDC recipients when far greater fraud in the Medicaid, Medicare, and nursing home industries is seldom investigated.

DEPENDENCY TARGETS

In order to develop a conceptual framework to guide the historical content analysis of welfare policy, it is necessary to delineate the dependency targets. The dependency target is the person/institution that provides (or is expected to provide) financial support in exchange for consumption of services provided by those in the dependent roles. These subcategories of consumers are termed targets because welfare policies propel women into selected dependent relations. As we will see in the historical analysis, the construed salience of these targets will shift over time, and women will be forced to pursue alternate relationships during different historical periods.[8]

There are seven potential dependency targets for women on welfare:

1. self
2. men
3. relatives
4. employers
5. professionals
6. the state
7. anyone but the state

Each target is defined below, and the relationship among policy, women on welfare, and the target explored.

1. Self-dependence. In the language of welfare legislation, self-dependence is usually synonymous with termination of aid, regardless of the recipient's resulting income level. Self-dependence cannot be equated with independence because independence implies a functional level considered adequate by society's standards.[9]

Therefore, if women are forced by AFDC policy to work under conditions detrimental to the care of their children, they are not independent. Or, if the only employment choices of women on welfare are jobs that pay minimum wage (i.e., subpoverty-level income), they remain trapped in poverty and cannot be considered independent.

Likewise, if women remain in male-female relationships under the threat of destitution, they are not independent. Using similar logic, as long as welfare benefit levels are below the poverty line, then receipt of welfare benefits cannot be interpreted as independence. The basic point is that those without access to the necessary resources to function adequately in a given society cannot be considered independent. The concept of independence implies a degree of free choice which is nonexistent in situations of scarce resources. If all that is available to poor mothers is the choice between insufficient benefits or jobs without benefits and paying minimal wages—both conducive to poverty—then they are in fact trapped in a Catch-22, no-win situation without real choice. Furthermore, the very possibility of establishing interdependent exchanges (be it processes of reciprocity or economic bargaining) becomes nonexistent when the power of the parties is extremely asymmetrical. This is true both in the marital relationship as in the marketplace, where the powerlessness of poor mothers can be extreme.

The correspondence between independence and self-dependence is too often an unrealized objective of poor women. Defining independence as the availability of choices that allow women to support themselves and their families above the poverty level would give control back to women within an accepted social reality of interdependence. This would make reality and ideology congruent and the relationships between the dependency consumer and producer one among power equals.

2. Men. The consequences of having men as dependency targets vary. If men were ideal, willing, and available targets, many women would not be on assistance but would be supported by men—either within the intact family or through child support. But men may be a poor choice of target. Today, with increasing rates of marital dissolution, men are unpredictable marriage partners; and as Trczynski (1985) shows, women are reluctant to rely solely on the expectation of support from their spouse or partner—even for the care of children. The reciprocity implied in the traditional gender division of labor has lost its meaning, with tragic consequences for many single mothers. The widespread failure of fathers to pay child support (Weitzman 1984) and the quasi-universal rule of mother custody characterize a situation in which men appear to have been exempted from their role as providers while the traditional child care role of women remains unaltered. That men's income tends to increase substantially after divorce and women's income declines dramatically is a self-evident outcome of this situation (Weitzman 1984).[10] The recent proposals by Moynihan (1986) and others encourage return to the traditional two-parent family, with the mother apparently being the one who is expected to return to the traditional domestic caregiver role.[11] Moynihan recognizes that welfare legislation cannot resolve the poverty situation of these families if the fathers lack access to provider roles. The high rate of unemployment among young minority males is a case in point for which there are few concrete proposals for change.[12]

Although the children's father may be the preferred target, any man in the house will do, since welfare administrators expect him to support the family when they remove a woman from AFDC eligibility.

Remarriage to a wage-earning male is the most effective socially supported way for a woman to remove herself from AFDC roles and move out of the poverty range (Ross and Sawhill 1975; Moscovice and Craig 1985). This alternative can be contrasted to ending welfare receipt due to employment of the mother, which usually means a continuation of poverty (Bane and Ellwood 1983; Bane 1984). Therefore, albeit indirectly, sex discrimination in the workplace encourages women's dependence on men because they are often better off financially, depending on the income of a male rather than on their own income alone. For example, in 1984 the median husband-wife family (wife not in labor force) earned $23,582 (or $34,668 with the wife in the labor force); the male householder without a wife present earned $23,325, and the female householder with no husband present earned $12,803 (USDOL Census Bureau 1985).

3. Relatives. The kin network is an established source of aid for families in time of need (Stack 1974). However, the extent of dependence that is realistically possible is limited, particularly among low-income families. Studies on help and exchange among kin in Western industrialized societies indicate that patterns of help persist but that they are not continuous (Kelly 1983; Litwak 1960; Jones 1981; McLanahan et al. 1981; Ladner 1971; Litwak and Figueira 1970). Relatives may respond with help in a crisis, but such help is normatively defined both by recipients and givers as transitional and not without cost to the recipient. The verified stronger mutual helping patterns in some black communities are interpreted as carryovers of extended rural family structures which have survived the great urban migration of the 1950s. However, more recent information suggests high levels of isolation for many single parent black families in urban communities (Kamerman 1985). Extended families have historically played crucial roles at times of mass migration and crisis, but their ties tend to weaken after the first generation (Tilly 1978).

4. Employers. All employees depend on their employers; however, this dependence does not carry negative connotations. Why? Two factors affect the perception of employer-employee relationships. First, in a society valuing work highly, employment has necessarily a positive connotation. Second, the assumption permeating work relations is that they are characterized by a free interchange: the employee needs wages—the employer needs labor. These two factors are often in conflict.

Employment is too often equated with independence. However, as mentioned previously, independence is limited to circumstances in which women heading families have choices that raise them above poverty level. Low wage levels for women proscribe a direct correlation between employment and independence (Smith 1984).

Dependency of low-wage workers increases during economic downturns. The recession in the early 1980s alone increased poverty by ten percent and significantly decreased the bargaining power of workers and their ability to resist wage and benefit concessions (U.S. House of Representatives 1984b: 40). As Piven and Cloward (1971: 55) point out, during recessions employers have greater control that can be bargained for reductions in wages and benefits because employees do not have alternative employment.

5. *Professionals*. Professionals can also be dependency targets. Although social work professionals often profess to encourage their clients to become independent and to terminate client-professional relationships, the professional rhetoric must be distinguished from actual practice. Professionals and professional associations have a vested interest in the continuation of services and continued dependency. Cloward and Piven (1972) have argued that welfare professional bureaucracies have two major goals: to expand for the benefit of the professionals and to control recipients so as to assure political approval. Hasenfeld (1978) and Lipsky (1980) also noted the power asymmetry of the professional-client roles and argued that it compounded the dependence of recipients.

Edelman (1977) discusses the issue of "helping" and how the term is applied differentially: Social Security beneficiaries aren't "helped," but lower status welfare recipients are. This issue is very closely linked to power. If one needs "help," the assumption is that power and control will be relinquished in order to gain needed assistance. This issue arises during the historical periods when professional services are touted to be the solution to "welfare dependency."

6. *The State*. The state is considered to be a dependency target as a result of the initiation and continuation of the AFDC program. However, the adequacy and, therefore, the desirability of the state as a target of dependency are politically at issue as evidenced by the fact that in no state are AFDC benefits alone adequate to raise a woman and her children above the poverty level (Zinn and Sarri 1984; U.S. House of Representatives 1983). The punitive character of welfare functions as a symbolic strategy of perpetuating the laissez-faire fantasy of nonstate intervention. By equating state dependency with welfare dependency other forms of state dependency can be purged easily from the negative label (e.g., business and farm subsidies, tax exemptions, Social Security).

7. *Anyone but the State*. This target represents the position that almost anyone or anything, including illness and lack of health care for family members, is better than receipt of welfare from the state (Gilder 1981; Anderson 1978). Control is applied in a negative way. This means encouraging dependency on any or all of the above targets except the state. The denial of opportunity to rely on the state controls the life chances of welfare recipients by denying them adequate food, shelter, and medical care (given that racial and sexual discrimination and unemployment continue).

EXAMINING THE POLITICAL LANGUAGE OF WELFARE DEPENDENCY FROM 1935 TO 1981

These dependency targets are the major object of analysis for the remainder of the chapter. Using content analysis of historical documents, the major changes in AFDC will be traced from 1935 to 1981.

How can the case be made for viewing the concept of "welfare dependency" as the language of control? One way is to examine the language used by policymakers while setting AFDC policy to see if it reflects control. These controls over women on welfare ensure that women remain in dependency relationships with socially acceptable dependency targets and reduce the value of the service provided through denigration. The cavalier attitudes in U.S. society about caregiving generally are illustrative of societal valuation of women's domestic services. Furthermore, the success of the control strategies can be measured by AFDC policies and their consequences for poor women.

The language of dependency meets the political needs of policymakers by calling upon accepted norms and values to reassure publics that policy actions are in accord with their political interests.[13] Analysis of representative written documents reveals the language used by politicians and others to influence legislation that has changed the lives of AFDC recipients. Documents include: the House and Senate bills that were proposed and ultimately passed, committee reports and hearings records, laws themselves, presidential statements related to the bills, reports of congressional and presidential advisory commissions, and policy-related research and commentary. Table 1 identifies the principal items of legislation to be analyzed.

The Social Security Act of 1935

Dependency was very much on the minds of the policymakers who fashioned the Social Security Act of 1935. Franklin Roosevelt concluded that the government would have to assume responsibility for dependencies formerly accommodated through family and community.

> ...security was attained in the early days through the interdependence of members of families upon each other and of the families within a small community upon each other.

Table 1

AFDC Policy Changes and Shifting Dependency Targets

Year	Legislation	Focal Dependency Targets
1935	Social Security Act	State
1950	Social Security Amendments	Men/relatives
1956	Social Security Amendments	Professionals
1962	Public Assistance Act	Professionals
1967	Social Welfare Amendments	Employers
1981	Omnibus Budget Reconciliation Act	Anyone but the State

The complexities of great communities and of organized industry make less real these simple means of security. Therefore, we are compelled to employ the active interest of the Nation as a whole through government in order to encourage a greater security for each individual who composes it. (quoted in Stevens 1970: 61)

This was partially accomplished by the Social Security Act: A BILL TO ALLEVIATE THE HAZARDS OF OLD AGE, UNEMPLOYMENT, ILLNESS, AND DEPENDENCY... (U.S. House of Representatives 1935: i) in which dependency was broadly construed:

The bill is designed to aid the States in taking care of the dependent members of their population, and to make a beginning in the development of measures which will reduce dependency in the future. It deals with four major subjects: Old-age security, unemployment compensation, security for children, and public health. These subjects are all closely related, all being concerned with major causes of dependency. Together they constitute an important step in a well-rounded, unified, long-range program for social security. (Stevens 1970: 146)

The Aid to Dependent Children program, one component of the Social Security Act of 1935, provided financial assistance to needy children. Although the language of the statute was sex-neutral, in practice ADC families were headed almost exclusively by

women (Congressional Quarterly Service 1965: 5). Because
parental unemployment was not grounds for receipt of federal aid
through ADC, men were in effect excluded from becoming
beneficiaries (U.S. Senate 1935).

Welfare dependency was salient to professionals and
politicians during the era in which the Social Security Act was
passed. Traditional male/female authority relationships were
maintained through creating a distinction between male and female
dependency: between social security insurance for males, while also
providing for their dependents; and public assistance for women,
which would ostensibly allow them to continue their work and
subordinate status in the home. Public assistance policies for
women and children ensured low benefits and considerable state
discretion, thus reinforcing women's traditional dependence upon
men and making it clear that dependency upon the state was not to
be a viable option for a family that wished to have its minimal
needs met. Although wage discrimination against women was cited
as a factor for keeping mothers in the home, many women found
that they had to work in order to supplement ADC benefits. Black
women were often forced to work by ADC regulations (Bell 1965).

Professionals also began vying to become a dependency target
and to receive governmental recognition of this status. A battle to
have the ADC program placed under the administrative purview of
the Children's Bureau (controlled by social workers) rather than the
Social Security Board and the Bureau of Public Assistance (BPA)
was waged, but the BPA gained administrative control (Brown
1940: 467–68). However, the losses of professionals were recouped,
to some extent, by the requirement of the BPA that state plans
address the services that state agencies intended to provide (Bell
1965: 153).

Aid to Dependent Children in the 1940s

The 1940s brought no significant policy changes to the ADC
program. However, the newly instituted public assistance
programs, of which ADC was only one, did not escape the attention
of the public or political leaders.[14] Winifred Bell characterizes the
early 1940s as a time when punitive state administrative practices,
such as using "suitable home" or "fit mother" policies as the basis
on which to prevent blacks or unmarried mothers from qualifying
for assistance, were beginning to change. However, during the
postwar period, a "tide of criticism flowed over ADC" (Bell 1965).

Social upheaval due to racial tension, unemployment, and mobility led to a barrage of criticism. Complaints, primarily directed toward assistance received by blacks and unwed mothers, reversed the positive trends that had begun a few years earlier (Bell 1965: 57). Also, it became increasingly clear that the public assistance programs, formerly seen as stop-gap measures needed only until insurance programs covered all in need, were here to stay. The idea of the 1930s and early 1940s that public assistance would gradually disappear was accepted unwillingly, as evidenced by attacking ADC with charges of client fraud and administrative mismanagement.

Social Security Amendments of 1950

President Truman introduced the Social Security Amendments of 1950 with this statement recognizing the "Withering away Fallacy":

> It is my strong belief that it is a responsibility of the Government to provide this protection, and to provide it in a manner that is consistent with our ideals of independence and self-reliance—through the already established and tested principle of contributory social insurance....
>
> The effects of our failure in recent years to carry out this philosophy are already dramatized by the increase in the public assistance rolls. (quoted in Stevens 1970: 360)

The most significant change in ADC policy in the 1950 amendments was the inclusion of caretakers of children (mostly mothers) as beneficiaries for whom the federal government would match state expenditures. The reason for this change is disputed.

From a political language perspective, the focus of attributions of dependency shifted from "natural" dependents (children) to "suspect" dependents—adults. Concurrent with the inclusion of the caretaker relative, the "NOLEO" (Notice to Law Enforcement Officials) regulation was passed making it mandatory "that public welfare agencies notify law enforcement officials whenever aid was granted in behalf of a child who had been deserted or abandoned" (Burns 1951: 470).

Joel Handler (1972: 32) interprets the NOLEO amendment as arising from two factors: the societal norm that fathers should support their children and the desire of the federal and state governments to cut welfare costs. I contend that the government went to these administrative extremes to enforce the dependency of women on men. This would explain why women had to act when the wrong-doing was male. The distinction is subtle but important. If the focus had been on male responsibility, why did not the government take the more stringent proposed action of making abandonment of dependents (usually by men) a federal crime for men of all economic strata?

The "substitute parent" policy[15] found in many states during the 1950s reinforced the argument that the acceptable target is not simply "fathers" but men. Many states extended the substitute parent policy to include men who were occasional visitors to the family; Michigan counted "male boarders" as substitute parents (Bell 1965: 85–86), despite recognition that maintaining a boarding house was a traditional means by which poor women earned a living (Kessler-Harris 1982). The enforcement of these provisions became increasingly punitive, as will be shown in the section below on 1962 policy changes. Both NOLEO and substitute parent policies enforced dependency on men and directed dependency away from the state.

Employment was another way to shift the dependency target from the state. A 1952 study by the American Public Welfare Association, an organization composed of public welfare administrators, reported that 39 percent of the homemakers on ADC worked while receiving benefits (Blackwell and Gould 1952: 55). Because of the silence of federal regulations on the treatment of earnings (not to come until 1967), states. could determine the relationship between earned income and the grant amount. Often earnings reduced the grant dollar for dollar; employment earnings were cited as the termination reason for 25 percent of ADC recipients (Blackwell and Gould 1952: 82). However, the study also found that income levels, after termination from welfare, continued to be extremely low:

> Median income per person for the total sample was a little less than $30.00 per month.... We are convinced that, generally speaking, income levels of ADC families are too low for proper conservation of the human resources represented in this million and a half ADC children. (Blackwell and Gould 1952: 97)

In sum, the Social Security Amendments of 1950 changed the focus of dependency from children to women. With this shift also came new federal and state policies enforcing men as an alternative dependency target to the state. Low benefit levels continued to discourage dependency upon the state. Women's relationship to other dependency targets, employers and relatives, for example, remained unchanged by ADC policy.

A 1951 article (reprinted in 1960) by Helen Harris Perlman, a respected social worker, provides a useful transition between the policy changes in 1951 and the ADC changes in the Social Security Amendments of 1956. Perlman's article begins with the recognition that dependency is a "bad word," defuses myths about dependency, and concludes with the role of social workers in public assistance. Perlman establishes a distinction between economic and psychological dependency, stating that receipt of assistance necessarily implies the former but not the latter. However, she states that the economically deprived situation of ADC families often leads to life circumstances resulting in psychological dependency:

> Therefore the adequacy or inadequacy of a welfare program— its mean or decent meeting of basic human needs—will have a potential influence in creating, abetting, or preventing psychological dependency. (1960: 330)

Perlman then infers that the locus of the problem is within the individual—who needs to be "stimulated" to resolve his or her problems. Perlman makes no mention of the social work role of advocacy or policy-level intervention; the worker helps the client use existing resources. Perlman's writing presages the dilemma of dependence on professionals: Do professionals encourage independence (defined as selection among options for adequate income support) or simply dependence on professionals?

Social Security Amendments of 1956

The Senate, in its report on the Social Security Amendments of 1956 (Stevens 1970: 500), draws a very clear connection between the provision of welfare services and welfare dependency. The Senate also provides an operational definition of rehabilitative services:

> Individuals who receive assistance are materially affected by the extent to which appropriate welfare services are provided

by assistance agencies. Services that assist families and individuals to attain the maximum economic and personal independence of which they are capable provide a more satisfactory way of living for the recipients affected. To the extent that they can remove or ameliorate the causes of dependency they will decrease the time that assistance is needed and the amounts needed.

President Eisenhower echoed this connection when signing the newly passed law:

Another Administration proposal placed increased emphasis, in public assistance programs, on services to help more needy people build toward independence. The law initiates new programs of grants to train more skilled social workers and to support research in ways of helping people overcome dependency. (Stevens 1970: 504)

The comments of the administration, as well as those of Helen Perlman, reflect the individual approach to the amelioration of welfare dependency. A representative of the Bureau of Public Assistance also takes this approach in citing success cases when providing testimony to encourage Congressional support of social services (U.S. House of Representatives 1956: 16):

The aid-to-dependent-children program is full of examples of the kind of situation which requires self-support and self-care services to strengthen family life. When a mother applies for ADC and tells the public-welfare worker that her husband has deserted her, the welfare worker has a choice in dealing with the family. The matter can be considered solely on the basis of eligibility for aid-to-dependent-children by verifying the fact that the husband has deserted and that he is not in the home and contributing to the support. On the other hand, the worker can inquire more closely as to where the husband is likely to be, what were the reasons for his desertion, and to set up a plan for locating the father and trying to put together the broken family.

In analyzing these statements from a dependency perspective, one thrust of services was to enhance family life—by encouraging women to reexamine their dependency relationships with men; another, to encourage women to depend on any target other than the state by using the bootstrap approach to self-sufficiency; and a third, to ensure that the social work profession would benefit through the provision of these services and through direct assistance to social work education.

The 1960s and the Public Assistance Act of 1962

The early 1960s brought a significant change in the political environment of the United States and important changes in the AFDC program as well. The liberalizing movement of the sixties was slowly beginning. John Kennedy was President; Michael Harrington "discovered" poverty in 1962; the Civil Rights Movement continued; and the War on Poverty started.

An important addition to public welfare came with the inclusion, albeit time-limited and only at state option, of unemployment as a category of eligibility for public assistance in 1961.[16] The beginning of this program, titled Aid to Dependent Children-Unemployed Parents, was a significant step in making the ADC program available to men.[17]

The main argument for beginning the ADC-UP program was the belief that the female focus of ADC encouraged family breakup (Patterson 1981: 130). An alternative interpretation is that the program strengthened the male as a target of dependency. By the 1960s ADC, originally intended for widows, had a preponderance of families in which the mothers were separated or divorced. With ADC-UP public policymakers took a half-hearted step toward encouraging the patriarchical male-female dependency relationship—even if the dependency target was, by definition, unemployed and unable to support his family. Better to shore up the family temporarily than to have women turn permanently from men to the state for support.

The welfare amendments of 1962 were part of liberalizing trends occurring with a renewed recognition of the role of the federal government in reaching long-term solutions to poverty. Hope for achieving this goal arose from the rapid economic growth that was contributing to an overall feeling of national well-being.

President John Kennedy, in several speeches, shifted the political language of welfare programs from negative connotations of dependence to the positive qualities of independence:

The goals of our public welfare programs must be positive and constructive—to create economic and social opportunities for the less fortunate—to help them find productive, happy and independent lives. (ACIR 1980: 49)

However, more conservative overtones were heard in his State of the Union address in 1962:

To help those least fortunate of all, I am recommending a new public welfare program, stressing services instead of support, rehabilitation instead of relief, and training for useful work instead of prolonged dependency. (cited in Burgess and Price 1963: 155)

The 1962 welfare amendments changed the name of ADC to Aid and Services to Needy Families with Children. In most states, and in federal language, the acronym changed to AFDC, Aid to Families with Dependent Children. The connection to dependency was made clear by the title of the part of the law concerning AFDC: "Improvement in Services to Prevent or Reduce Dependency" (U.S. House of Representatives 1962: 30). The Ad Hoc Committee on Public Welfare, appointed by Secretary Abraham Ribicoff, reinforced this connection. Its first recommendation was "accelerated and intensified rehabilitative services aimed at reducing family breakdown and chronic dependency and helping families become self-supporting and independent..." (U.S. House of Representatives 1962: 72).

Dependency on the services of professionals highlights the issue of powerlessness that arises from welfare dependency.

Social services, when they are effective, can result in a highly coercive system. Effective, in this sense, means that a program has something to offer that a poor person wants.... But when something of value is at stake, poor people become very dependent on the officials who are in control.... These problems, of course, are increased when services are tied to income maintenance.... Formal notions of what is 'voluntary' may have little meaning for poor people in need. (Handler 1972: 55)

Dependency continued to be a central concern in debates about public welfare (Moynihan 1968). However, this concern was now linked to the increasing unemployment and lack of economic opportunity in the black community. The release of the "Moynihan Report" in 1965 stirred considerable controversy and is important from the perspective of political language. The report, because of its treatment of public welfare, is also significant to our concern with dependency. One section of the report is entitled "The Breakdown of the Negro Family Has Led to a Startling Increase in Welfare Dependency."

Three aspects of the report are of interest: race, matriarchy, and illegitimacy. Race is of interest because of its special relationship to dependency. Blacks had been historically discouraged from engaging in state dependency to the extent that whites did. Motivated by exploitation, whites, who controlled welfare programs, often forced black women to work. However, despite continued allegations of laziness, more black than white welfare recipients worked.

> Significantly more Negro than white homemakers were employed during the ADC period for each age grouping of children both in urban and rural areas. In urban areas from 30 to 55 percent of the Negroes worked and in rural areas from 57 to 75 percent worked when children were in various age groups. (Burgess and Price 1963: 30)

Moynihan cited matriarchy among black families as evidence of the deterioration of the family that the availability of welfare benefits had encouraged. Patriarchy was challenged by the availability of welfare monies for black women. When women established family forms contrary to the patriarchical norm—and used federal money to do it—Moynihan expressed disapproval by invoking the negative concept of welfare dependency. If the independence of women had been socially acceptable and attainable, much of Moynihan's argument would have been moot. Moynihan's arguments only gained credibility when seen against the backdrop of a society that viewed families headed by women as deviant.

Moynihan also failed to consider the extremely low wages available to black women, particularly in southern states. Even these low wages, however, were too high to make them eligible for any welfare benefits because the state level of need regarding eligibility for AFDC was also far below that needed for survival. The exposure of serious malnutrition among black children in the South in the 1960s was a predictable outcome of the intolerable situation.

From a dependency target perspective, the third factor Moynihan emphasizes, illegitimacy, blatantly challenges the societal mandate that women be dependent on men. By eschewing legal, father-child relationships, women defy traditional dependency relationships. When they do this, society responds by creating a social problem and enforcing sanctions such as denial of welfare benefits, eviction, or permanent removal of the children from the mother. If the violators are black women, sanctions are even greater (Bell 1965: 67–75).

From the perspective of public language, the Moynihan Report retreated to negative symbols. I would contend that this was one reason for the racial backlash against the report. Blacks were no longer willing to have a white castigate their life styles (see Rainwater and Yancy 1967: 395–426).

Through the midsixties, dependency on men and anyone but the state continued to be encouraged by federal policy. Self-dependency continued to be discouraged by low AFDC benefit levels and economic discrimination against women. Substitute parent policies ("man-in-the-house"), enforcing women's reliance on men, reached their zenith in the mid-1960s. The following quote from a California study demonstrates the administrative lengths to which welfare administrators went to enforce dependency.

> Under the normal procedure one investigator goes to the front door, another to the back door (to make certain that the man does not escape that way), the door bell is rung, the investigators identify themselves, and ask if they may come in. They may say they want to look for a man, or they may say they are "making a routine check and want to see the conditions of the home and how the children are being cared for." The investigators then go through the house looking in closets, drawers, attics, medicine chests, children's bedrooms, and under the bed. They look not only for the man but for evidence of clothing, toilet articles, and personal effects that would indicate a man is living there. The search is usually made between 10 p.m. and 4 a.m. Most investigators prefer to wait until the house is dark as they say this increases the possibilities of catching a man in bed and makes for a stronger fraud case. (cited in Steiner 1966: 121)

These practices were to be declared unconstitutional by the Supreme Court in 1968 (Steiner 1971).

Professionals also had received funding that promoted them as a dependency target, funding that would ultimately result in a dramatic increase in their numbers. However, professionals eventually failed as target in two fundamental ways. Most importantly, from the perspective of politicians, they failed to reduce the welfare rolls despite promises about the effectiveness of services.[18] Second, the social work profession abandoned public welfare. Despite the contention of a few social work leaders, the bulk of the social work profession had no desire to work with low-priority and low-income clients but rather with the middle class and in mental health activities. Promised professionals were not available to provide services to the poor (Steiner 1971).

Social Welfare Amendments of 1967

The quest for the appropriate target shifted to the employer with the 1967 welfare amendments. Despite evidence showing that welfare recipients already worked (Burgess and Price 1963; Schiller 1978), the 1967 amendments contained a number of provisions to further encourage work.

Statements by Wilbur Cohen, Under-Secretary, Department of Health, Education and Welfare, and Senator Abraham Ribicoff (Democrat, Connecticut) illustrate the connection between work and dependency that motivated these amendments during Senate Finance Committee hearings:

> Senator Ribicoff. I would assume from what you [Cohen] say—you are the developing this, Mr. Cohen—that you feel probably the most important phase of the entire dependency and poverty element in this country is jobs and job training.
> Mr. Cohen. I would not say the only important one. I think the—
> Senator Ribicoff. The most important.
> Mr. Cohen. Well, I think it is very important, but I think it should be part of a broader context of making these families independent. In this, work and training is a central part.
> Senator Ribicoff. Well, you take not only the problem of welfare but the problem of the American city that is so much in the fore, the high unemployment rates among the Negroes in the ghettos, about one out of every three. It seems that almost everyone who has looked at this entire field comes up with the conclusion that the No. 1 priority is probably jobs.... (U.S. Senate 1967: 264)

With the passage of these amendments, the Work Incentive Program (WIN) was started as a job training and placement service for welfare recipients. State welfare agencies had the option to decide which welfare recipients would be required to participate in the WIN program. In 1971 federal requirements were changed to specify that all women, except those with children under the age of six, must participate in WIN. This child-based criterion is interesting from a dependency perspective. The socially approved dependency needs of children under six overcame the negative sanctions for adult welfare dependency.

An earnings exemption of the first $30 of earnings and one-third of the remainder (disregarded when calculating the amount of grant reduction that would occur due to increased income) was also a work incentive. This ensured that women on welfare who worked would be financially better off than women who did not. Penalties for quitting a job or refusing training without good cause were also included in the legislation (Congressional Quarterly Service 1969: 775).

The government's efforts to encourage dependency upon employers did not take into consideration the situation in the labor market. Not only were jobs often impossible to find, available jobs encouraged continued dependency due to low wages and poor benefits (Levitan et al. 1972).

President Nixon introduced his own welfare reform plan, the Family Assistance Plan (FAP), in 1971. This plan, based upon a low income guarantee with heavy emphasis on work, was attacked from the right and the left. The National Welfare Rights Organization, at its peak in the early 1970s, strongly opposed the bill because of inadequate income levels. Eventually the bill was defeated (Piven and Cloward 1971).

No new AFDC policy thrusts, from a dependency perspective, occurred in the AFDC program from 1967 to 1981. In 1975 child support enforcement was given a federal boost when an office was created within the Department of Health, Education and Welfare to oversee state operations. Also the matching rate for child support activities was raised from 50 to 75 percent, thus encouraging states to hire staff dedicated to child support enforcement alone (U.S. Congress, Joint Economic Committee 1975: 141). Also in 1975 a new service program (Title XX of the Social Security Act) removed service funding from Title IV-A, the public assistance title, and liberalized the income eligibility criteria. This was a move toward "universal services"—federally-funded, comprehensive services for citizens of all income levels. However, the dependency link remained even within this broadened scope. One of the five Title XX goals was "achieving or maintaining self-sufficiency and reduction or prevention of dependency..." (U.S. Senate 1978: 541).

President Jimmy Carter proposed the Program for Better Jobs and Income (BJIP) in 1978. The plan called for the creation of public employment that might have, dependent upon its programmatic features, made the state a more desirable dependency target, as it had been as a result of the unemployment programs of the 1930s. Critics complained that the plan was too expensive. The bill finally died.

Neither FAP, BJIP, nor the service or child support amendments added new dependency targets. Therefore, by 1980 when Ronald Reagan was elected president, past attempts to shift the welfare dependency target from the state, to men, to professionals, to employers had all failed to reach the liberal goal of ameliorating poverty or the conservative goal of eliminating AFDC.

However, from 1935 until 1981 there was a gradual increase in the standard of living for persons on public assistance (Patterson 1981: 200; U.S. House of Representatives 1983). Even in the relatively conservative Republican administrations of Dwight Eisenhower and Richard Nixon, welfare programs were incrementally expanded. This trend was to come to an abrupt halt with the election of Ronald Reagan and a shift in dependency targets. The language and the policies of the AFDC program were to change significantly.

Omnibus Budget Reconciliation Act of 1981

Two prominent conservatives, author George Gilder and economist Martin Anderson, provide the theoretical framework for the welfare changes sponsored by President Ronald Reagan. Anderson presents his theses in his book Welfare (1978). His second thesis deals with the Dependent Americans:

> The virtual elimination of poverty has had costly social side effects. The proliferation of welfare programs has created very high effective marginal tax rates for the poor. There is, in effect, a "poverty wall" that destroys the financial incentive to work for millions of Americans. Free from basic wants, but heavily dependent on the State, with little hope of breaking free, they are a new caste, the "Dependent Americans."

Seven steps guided Anderson's proposal for practical welfare reform:

1) Reaffirm the needy-only philosophical approach to welfare and state it as explicit national policy.
2) Increase efforts to eliminate fraud.
3) Establish and enforce a fair, clear work requirement.
4) Remove inappropriate beneficiaries [e.g., strikers and college students] from the welfare rolls.
5) Enforce support of dependents by those who have the responsibility and are shirking it.
6) Improve the efficiency and effectiveness of welfare administration.
7) Shift more responsibility for welfare from the federal government to state local governments and to private institutions. (1978: 199–64)

Anderson's theses and steps for welfare reform can be understood within a dependency frame of reference that Anderson himself recognizes as fundamental:

The basic principle involved here is one of dependence versus independence. If a person is capable of taking care of himself, he is independent and should not qualify for any amount of welfare. To the extent that a person is dependent—that is, to the extent that he cannot care for himself—to that extent he qualifies for welfare. If he can earn part of what he needs, then he has an obligation to work to that extent. (Anderson 1978: 162)

Anderson, however, begs the question of who should be dependent on whom and uses the concept of dependency as political language to justify his policy recommendations.

George Gilder, in Wealth and Poverty (1981), emphasizes the debilitating effect of welfare on males.

For many years defenders of welfare have acknowledged that the system was harsh on intact poor families. The answer, it was widely agreed, was to extend benefits to families with unemployed fathers. This was done in twenty-six states and, to the surprise of some observers, had no effect on the rate at which poor families broke down. The reason was clear. As under the guaranteed-income plans tested in Denver and

Seattle, the marriages dissolve not because the rules dictate it, but because the benefit levels destroy the father's key role and authority. He can no longer feel manly in his own home....

Nothing is so destructive to all these male values as the growing, imperious recognition that when all is said and done his wife and children can do better without him. The man has the gradually sinking feeling that his role as provider, the definitive male activity from the primal days of the hunt through the industrial revolution and on into modern life, has been largely seized from him; he has been cuckolded by the compassionate state....

In the welfare culture money becomes not something earned by men through hard work, but a right conferred on women by the state. (1981: 114–15)

Gilder's welfare reform proposal has two parts: "Welfare benefits must be allowed to decline steadily in value as inflation proceeds...," and "a sensible program would be relatively easy on applicants in emergencies but hard on clients who overstay their welcome. Ideally such a system should be supplemented with child allowances given to every family, of whatever income, for each child" (1981: 125–26).

Anderson's and Gilder's statements and policies lend themselves to analysis from the dependency perspective. Anderson speaks out for dependency on anyone but the state. Fathers should support their children; mothers and fathers should work—if they don't they will become "Dependent Americans." Anderson, unlike those who use the language of dependency to justify increases in welfare programs, states that dependency will be reduced by eliminating opportunities to be dependent. If there are no welfare programs, no one can be dependent upon them.

Gilder comes to the same policy conclusion, but from the contention that opportunities for dependency on the state undermine the role of the male. Dismantling welfare programs would restore the normal patriarchical order. Assistance that is provided should be to children within nuclear families.

The Reagan administration used the language and strategies of these two conservative thinkers to justify welfare reform contained in the Omnibus Budget Reconciliation Act of 1981 (OBRA).[19] Mandatory changes included:

- ...limit[ing] AFDC eligibility to families whose gross incomes do not exceed 150 percent of their state's AFDC needs standard...
- reducing disregards that are applied to earned income before an individual's AFDC benefits are determined;
- limiting these disregards to four months; after four months, the AFDC grant is reduced dollar for dollar for every dollar earned (except for earnings spent on work expenses such as child care and transportation)....
- deeming stepparent income available to an AFDC child and reducing the child's grant accordingly, whether or not the income is actually available and regardless of whether the child can legally compel the stepparent to provide support.... (Children's Defense Fund 1981: 2-3)

Working women terminated due to OBRA lost all AFDC benefits, Medicaid, and child care benefits. A typical New York AFDC mother and two children lost $246 per month; income declined from $806 per month prior to OBRA to $560 post-OBRA (Joe et al. 1984: 21). These figures do not include the value of Medicaid (which covers preventive as well as hospital care) or child care.

My interpretation of OBRA policies is that they encouraged dependency on anyone but the state. OBRA policies variously encouraged dependency on men (stepparent policy), on relatives (many women who were terminated moved in with their families to reduce expenses) (Joe et al. 1984), and on employers. Increased dependency upon the employer was common; OBRA primarily terminated working women. These women were more dependent upon their employers because they no longer had the option to rely on AFDC. Furthermore, these women were more dependent on employers who had demonstrated a lack of interest in their well-being by paying them low wages and providing few benefits. Recognition of this exploitation occurred in recent hearings on the Poverty Rate Increase (U.S. House of Representatives 1984: 76). A poverty expert answered in the affirmative when asked this question by Representative Fortney Stark (California):

Did it ever occur to you that some of the people in those States [with low benefit levels] might want to keep people dependent because it keeps domestic and family help readily available?

The only (other than the "state") target not encouraged by OBRA was professionals. This was predictable as the Reagan administration viewed professional services as part of the welfare system that had to be reduced or eliminated. A shrinking of the age span for the accepted dependency of children also occurred with OBRA. Children 18 to 21 and in school were no longer allowed to receive benefits; children 16 to 18 received benefits only if they were in school; and mothers of children between three and six could be required to participate in work programs. Because social disapproval of women's dependency on the state is tempered by the presence of children for whom they are to care, OBRA decreased the opportunity for familial receipt of benefits by changing children's dependency relationship to the state.

Conservative Nathan Glazer captures the essence of Ronald Reagan's policy strategy, the enforcement of traditional norms, through an example of the relationships of welfare women and male dependency targets:

> Various changes introduced into the welfare system indicate in which direction the administration was moving and how it was implementing its ideology.... But the Reagan administration was not trying to provide an incentive for family stability. Rather, it wished to promote stability by imposing a norm; that a man living with a woman and her children had an obligation to support the woman with whom he lived as husband, and the children with whom he lived as father.... (Bawden 1984: 231–32)

However during the 1980s, the ultraconservative political environment has guided policies toward the reinforcement of societal norms: those who can work must work; only the most destitute should receive public assistance; families are responsible for their own economic and social needs; men should support their wives and families. In line with this, AFDC policies, through the Omnibus Budget Reconciliation Act of 1981, have shifted women's dependency to men, relatives, and employers, in short, to anyone but the state —while in no way encouraging true economic independence of women.

In summary, the most basic finding is that welfare dependency has been used as political language by all categories of policymakers throughout all phases of the AFDC program from 1935 to the present. Therefore this confirms the importance of welfare dependency as political language.

Furthermore, despite the seeming ambiguity of the concept of welfare dependency, there was a strong correlation between use of the term dependency and the use of other terms connoting negative psychological characteristics.

The following citations provide convincing evidence of this:

...[many people] view public aid recipients as the undeserving beneficiaries of society's largess, as living a good life while being lazy and dependent. (Beeghley 1983: 10)

"Poverty Across Generations: Is Welfare Dependency a Pathology Passed from One Generation to the Next?" (Hill and Ponza 1983)

In the identification of dependency with sin or unfitness there was some exception made always for the "worthy poor,"...but the "worthy" seemed hard to find.... (Wright 1931)

But by the early 1960's the stereotype was likely to evoke visions of "hard core" black welfare mothers with hordes of illegitimate children. It was no wonder that people who in one breath favored aiding the "needy" gulped again and blamed "lack of effort" for welfare dependency. (Patterson 1981: 110)

They lived in God only knows what misery. They ate when there were things to eat; they starved when there was lack of food. But, on the whole, although they swore and beat each other and got drunk, they were more contented than any other class I have happened to know. It took a long time to understand them. Our Committees were busy from morning until night in giving them opportunities to take up the fight again, and to become independent of relief. They always took what we gave them; they always promised to try; but as soon as we expected them to fulfill any promises, they gave up in despair, and either wept or looked ashamed, and took to misery and drink again—almost, so it seemed to me at times, with a sense of relief. (quoted in Banfield 1974: 142)

Alice Boyce, the supervisor of counselors [in a Supported Work Program],...[says] "What I find mostly is students not thinking that far ahead," she says, echoing the views of

Edward Banfield. But she, too, blames dependency. "That's the welfare syndrome." (Auletta 1982: 242)

What they [persons in a "dependency relationship"] personify is poverty, delinquency, or other forms of deviance. They are in need of help, but help in money, in status, and in autonomy must be sharply limited so as to avoid malingering. (Edelman 1977: 74)

The words speak for themselves: pathology, sin, laziness, lack of effort, drunkenness, violence, malingering, lack of financial incentive. The "welfare dependent" are characterized as having serious psychological problems in the writings of policymakers, researchers, and politicians of all political viewpoints.

A historical review shows that in 1935 the limited Aid to Dependent Children program focused primarily on widows whose legitimate dependency targets (husbands) were unavailable. In 1950 changes were made to ensure that nonwidows receiving assistance notified law enforcement officials so that child support could be pursued. In 1956 and 1962 social services were perceived to be the answer to the problem of welfare dependency—making welfare recipients temporarily dependent on service professionals would make them independent in the long run. In 1967 (reinforced by amendments in 1971) the solution to the dependency problem was seen in transferring women, particularly women with children over the age of six, to the economy where they would be employed and no longer dependent on the state. Finally, in 1981 with OBRA, a variety of strategies was adopted to shift women from reliance on the state. This is characterized here as encouraging dependency on anyone but the state. Multiple dependency targets were simultaneously reinforced. Increased emphasis on child support, employment, and dependence on informal networks were all stimulated directly or indirectly by policy changes.

CONCLUSIONS: CHOICE AND ADEQUACY OF TARGETS

Before turning to new policy proposals, let us use the criteria of choice and adequacy to review why past welfare policies and targets have not encouraged independence. Women have continually been forced by governmental policy to accept men and relatives as dependency targets; for example, child support enforcement by governmental agencies, such as the Internal

Revenue Service, is increasingly taking away the option of women to choose their source of support. Employers as targets do not meet the adequacy criterion. As shown by the high proportion of working female-headed families in poverty, about half do not earn enough to support their families (Bane and Ellwood 1983). Professionals become control agents when providing individually oriented services within a welfare system providing inadequate benefits. Finally, the state (AFDC program) is not a viable target; none of the fifty states provides AFDC benefits that raise women and children on AFDC out of poverty (U.S. Commission on Civil Rights 1982: 5–7).

How could independence as a social policy goal be achieved? Fundamentally, the choices of women are constrained by sexism; the choices of black women by racism and sexism. However, if sexism and racism are reduced, there are three targets that have the potential for becoming true income alternatives: men, employers, and the state.

The major criticism of men as targets is based on issues of choice and control. The dependence of women with children on men should not be forced by the state (or traditional norms) or indirectly by discrimination in the labor market. Even after marriages dissolve, women are forced into continuing dependency relationships with their husbands if they are to receive support from the state; the failure of the child support stratagem has been well documented (Weitzman 1984; Ehrenreich and Piven 1984; Kamerman 1985). Proactive strategies would attempt to prevent marital breakup resulting from the lack of earning power of working class men and women. For example, Martha Hill cites the increased earnings capacity of black men as a necessary strategy to improve the economic well-being of black families with children (1983).

Women's employment in low-paying, sex-segregated jobs perpetuates their inability to support themselves and their families. Strategies, such as job evaluation based upon the comparable-worth principle or integrating women into higher-paying, male-dominated occupations are solutions that could redress the trend toward the feminization of poverty. Employer- or community-provided child care, more comprehensive coverage by medical insurance, and the provision of other benefits traditionally supplied by employers in the primary economic sector could also alleviate economic hardships faced by women with children (GAO 1985; Duncan 1984; Goodwin 1983; Ozawa 1982; Kamerman 1985).

Finally, the state is currently an adequate target only for limited sectors of the population. For example, Social Security raises many elderly persons from poverty; and unemployment compensation provides temporary relief, often at adequate levels, for unemployed workers. These programs are much more likely to meet the characteristics of the primary welfare sector, as defined by Pearce and McAdoo (1981). In the primary sector benefits are a right, coverage is universal and consistently implemented across states, and benefits are adequate to raise a family or individual out of poverty. The AFDC program would have to come much closer to meeting these criteria if it were to become a target of choice.

The societal shifting of women from one dependency target to another and the recent concommitant reduction in the adequacy of the targets form a closing circle in which women are caught. Some analysts (e.g., Gartner et al. 1982) characterize the recent treatment of AFDC women as exemplifying an antifeminist movement opposed to the changing roles of women. The conservative writings of George Gilder (1981) lend special credence to this interpretation as Gilder is one of the foremost proponents of retaining women's subordinate position in the home and family.

The organizational framework of the dependency/independency perspective provides a useful structure for policy recommendations. The basic recommendation is that there must be choice among adequate targets. Choice will come through changes in the political environment. Women must be allowed and encouraged to choose. Adequacy means that dependency consumers must provide fair exchange for the services that they receive from women. This applies to all sectors: the economy, the family, and the state.

The approach must be comprehensive in order to allow women to select options according to their preferences. This would also avoid undesirable side effects that occur when choices are constrained and individual behavior must change to conform. For example, AFDC policies have long been criticized for promoting family breakup with policies that denied benefits to intact families, but few of these studies have investigated the reasons why these families break up.

The hope is that once the internal contradictions between welfare dependency rhetoric and the actual increase in dependency that results from welfare policies are recognized, that these contradictions can be eliminated and the cycle of shifting dependencies broken.

But, unfortunately, to go full circle to the beginning of this chapter, this change depends on a more realistic view of all types of interdependency and for the independence ideology to be challenged. A difficult task.

Notes

[1]Most discussions of the causes of poverty focus on individual versus economic and structural causes although different authors may have slightly different terminology. However, OBRA points out the need for a third major category of causation—political causation of poverty and/or welfare status. Nothing changed within these individuals, nothing changed in the economic structure; but thousands moved out of poverty (just as their movement into welfare eligibility began with the creation of the policy changes in 1968, which also can be viewed as political causes).

[2]Note that this was a violation of the law because many recipients continued to be eligible for Medicaid but were terminated nonetheless, as I shall discuss later.

[3]Eligibility through Titles IV-A or Title XX of the Social Security Act.

[4]The concept of dependency is central to Charles Murray's (1984) critique of welfare programs. He argues that welfare programs, rather than need, increase dependency. This stands in sharp contrast to the arguments of earlier writers such as Alva Myrdal (1968) and Robert Moroney (1980), who conceive of welfare as a response to physical and social needs. In fact, the concept of dependency is alien to their formulation of family policy.

[5]It should also be noted that dependency resulting from illness or a handicap is generally accepted or at least tolerated because it is believed that the individual cannot alter her/his situation or is not responsible for it. However, in the 1980s this belief has been placed in jeopardy with requirements that the mentally ill and the handicapped participate in programs such as Workfare and be moved to independent living with little or no services or supervision.

[6]These policies and practices are still heavily influenced by the Elizabethan Poor Laws of the sixteenth century. The concept of lesser eligibility asserted that no one receiving benefits should ever receive as much as the lowest level wage earner; otherwise people would have incentives to be lazy. Even the recent tests of negative income tax programs had vestiges of this now obsolete policy.

[7]Public policy concern about the "displaced homemaker"

exemplifies public recognition about the plight of some of these women who are left without resources or entitlement to pensions after years of service as an unpaid homemaker.

[8]The metaphor of "target" is not intended to imply that individual women are hurled willy-nilly toward any of the above targets, but that policies have effects that often supercede individual choices. Targets can also actively influence their attractiveness as consumers of dependency. For example, employers can offer greater or lesser wages. Therefore neither targets nor women on welfare are passive.

[9]Women are not self-dependent if they and their families are at risk; families are assumed to be at risk if they have incomes below the poverty level. These low levels of income, despite families' perceptions of adequacy, place them in vulnerable positions in the short run (if a family member becomes seriously ill) and in the long run (if members must forego preventive services such as dental care or education).

[10]The Kenneally legislation (PL. 98–378, 98 Stat 1305, Aug. 16, 1984) enforces parental support of children and is expected to increase the dependability of fathers as children's providers, but it remains to be seen if this legislation will be effective, especially among low-income persons.

[11]In his new statement of family policy recommendations, Moynihan says, "A credible family policy will insist that responsibility begins with the individual, then the family, and only then the community, and in the first instance the smaller and nearer rather than the greater and more distant community" (194).

[12]Others such as Mandell (1975) argue that the methods for enforcing men-as-targets are often counterproductive and ineffective. Men who divorce are likely to remarry and start new families which command the majority of their resources. Obviously, this can be seen as irresponsible behavior, but change through long-term resocialization is necessary, not just court action. When child support is enforced through court action, women must take actions which are antagonistic and which often result in adverse relations between father and children, or they may even exacerbate family violence, as Beisel (1984) has suggested.

[13]In another political sphere the discussions about tax reform and budget deficits include extensive use of political language to justify one course of action over another.

[14]The others were Old Age Assistance and Aid to the Blind.

[15]"By welfare edict in some states even a casual man in the

mother's life became a 'substitute parent' whose presence meant that children were not 'deprived of parental support,' irrespective of whether the man had an income, spent it in behalf of the children, or was in any way legally responsible for their support" (Bell 1965: 76). If a substitute parent were present, a child would no longer be considered dependent, and thus not quality for ADC.

[16]The Aid to Dependent Children-Unemployed Parents program was extended by Congress as part of the Public Assistance Act of 1962.

[17]As in the definition of a dependent child, use of the term parent should not be confused with the intent of the legislation. ADC-UP was primarily directed toward families headed by men; this was expressly reflected in state statutes that restricted the program to male-headed families (U.S. House of Representatives 1962: 112).

[18]It should be noted that other societal forces such as the War on Poverty and the Welfare Rights Movement worked in direct contradiction to the provisions in welfare legislation. The former increased the welfare rolls through a combination of advocacy and changing administrative policies (Piven and Cloward 1971).

[19]David Stockman, head of the federal Office of Management and Budget called Gilder's book "Promethean in its intellectual power and insight. It shatters once and for all the Keynesian and welfare state illusions that burden the failed conventional wisdom of our era" (Gilder 1981: jacket).

References

Abbott, E. (ed.), 1966. Public Assistance. New York: Russell and Russell.

Advisory Commission on Intergovernmental Relations, 1980. The Federal Role in the Federal System: The Dynamics of Growth. Washington, DC: Government Printing Office.

Advisory Committee on Public Welfare, 1966. Having the Power, We Have the Duty. Washington, DC: Government Printing Office.

Anderson, M., 1978. Welfare: The Political Economy of Welfare Reform in the United States. Palo Alto, CA: Hoover Institute.

Auletta, K., 1982. The Underclass. New York: Random House.

Bane, M.J., 1984. Slipping Into and out of Poverty: The Dynamics of Spells. Cambridge, MA: Urban Systems Research and Engineering.

Bane, M.J. and D.T. Ellwood, 1983. The Dynamics of Dependence: The Routes to Self Sufficiency. Cambridge, MA: Urban Systems Research and Engineering.

Bawden, D.L. (ed.), 1984. The Social Contract Revisited. Washington, DC: Urban Institute Press.

Beeghley, L., 1984. "Illusion and Reality in the Measurement of Poverty," Social Problems 31: 322–33.

Bell, W., 1965. Aid to Dependent Children. New York: Columbia University Press.

Bernstein, B. and W. Meegan, 1975. The Impact of Welfare on Family Stability. New York: New School for Social Research.

Blackwell, G. and R.F. Gould, 1952. Future Citizens All. Chicago: American Public Welfare Association.

Brown, J., 1940. Public Relief: 1929–1939. New York: Holt.

Burgess, M.E. and D. Price, 1963. An American Dependency Challenge. Chicago: American Public Welfare Association.

Burns, E., 1951. The American Social Security System. Boston: Houghton Mifflin.

Burt, M. and K. Pittman, 1985. Testing the Social Safety Net: Impact of Changes in Support Programs During the Reagan Administration. Washington, DC: Urban Institute.

Burton, C., 1985. Subordination: Feminism and Social Theory. Boston: Allen and Unwin.

Center for Budget Priorities, 1985. "Poverty Rate Shows Disappointing Drop: Income Inequality Widens." August 27 release.

Children's Defense Fund, 1981. A Child's Defense Budget. Washington, DC: Children's Defense Fund.

Cloward, R. and F.F. Piven, 1972. The Politics of Turmoil. New York: Vintage.

Congressional Quarterly Service, 1965, 1969, 1973, 1977, 1981. Congress and the Nation, vols. 1–5. Washington, DC: Government Printing Office.

Duncan, G.J. (ed.), 1984. Years of Poverty, Years of Plenty. Ann Arbor, MI: Institute for Social Research, University of Michigan.

Edelman, M., 1964. Symbolic Uses of Politics. Urbana, IL: University of Illinois Press.

Edelman, M., 1971. Politics as Symbolic Action. Chicago: Markham.

Edelman, M., 1977. Political Language: Words That Succeed and Policies That Fail. New York: Academic Press.

Ehrenreich, B. and F. Piven, 1984. "The Feminization of Poverty," in I. Howe (ed.) Alternative Proposals for America from the Democratic Left. New York: Pantheon.

Erickson, K., 1966. Wayward Puritans. New York: Wiley.

Gamson, W. and K. Lasch, 1981. "The Political Culture of Social Welfare Policy," in S. Spiro (ed.) Evaluating the Welfare State. New York: Academic Press.

Gartner, A., C. Green and F. Riessman (eds.), 1982. What Reagan Is Doing To Us. New York: Harper and Row.

Gilder, G., 1981. Wealth and Poverty. New York: Basic Books.

Goodwin, L., 1983. Causes and Cures of Welfare. Lexington, MA: D.C. Heath.

Handler, J., 1972. Reforming the Poor: Welfare Policy, Federalism and Morality. New York: Basic Books.

Harrington, M., 1962. The Other America. Baltimore: Penguin Books.

Hasenfeld, V., 1978. "Client-Organization Relations: A Systems Perspective," pp. 184–206 in R. Sarri and Y. Hasenfeld (eds.) The Management of Human Services. New York: Columbia University Press.

Hill, M., 1983. Trends in the Economic Situation of U.S. Families and Children. Ann Arbor, MI: Institute for Social Research, University of Michigan.

Himmelfarb, G., 1984. The Idea of Poverty. New York: Alfred A. Knopf.

Hutter, B. and G. Williams, 1981. Controlling Women: The Normal and the Deviant. London: Croom Helm.

Joe, T., R. Sarri and M. Ginsberg, 1984. Working Female-Headed Families in Poverty: Three Studies of Low-Income Families Affected by the AFDC Policy Changes of 1981. Ann Arbor, MI: Center for Political Studies, Institute for Social Research, University of Michigan.

Jones, B., 1981. "Mental Health and the Structure of Social Support." Ph.D. dissertation, University of Michigan.

Kamerman, S., 1985. "Young, Poor and a Mother Alone: Problems and Possible Solutions," pp. 1–38 in H. McAdoo and T.J. Parham (eds.) Services to Young Families. Washington,DC: American Public Welfare Association.

Katz, M.B., 1983. Poverty and Policy in American History. New York: Academic Press.

Kelly, R., 1983. "Welfare Dependency Under Depressed Labor Market Conditions," Journal of Urban Affairs.

Kessler-Harris, A., 1982. Out to Work. New York: Oxford University Press.

Ladner, J., 1971. Tomorrow's Tomorrow: The Black Woman. Garden City, NY: Doubleday.

Levitan, S., M. Rein and D. Marwick, 1972. Work and Welfare Go Together. Baltimore: Johns Hopkins Press.

Lipsky, M., 1980. Street-Level Bureaucracy: Dilemmas of the Individual in Public Services. New York: Russell Sage.

Litwak, E. and J. Figueira, 1970. "Technological Innovation and Ideal Forms of Family Structure in an Industrialized Democratic Society," pp. 348–96 in R. Hill and R. König (eds.) Families East and West. Paris: Mouton.

Mandell, B. (ed.), 1975. Welfare in America. Englewood Cliffs, NJ: Prentice Hall.

McAdoo, H. and J. Parham (eds.), 1985. Services to Young Families: Program Review and Policy Recommendations. Washington, DC: American Public Welfare Association.

McLanahan, S., N. Wedemeyr and T. Adelberg, 1981. "Network Structure, Social Support and Psychological Well-Being in the Single-Parent Family," Journal of Marriage and Family (August): 601–12.

Memmi, A., 1984. Dependence. Boston: Beacon.

Moroney, R., 1980. Families, Social Services and Social Policy. Washington, DC: U.S. Department of Health and Human Services.

Moscovice, I. and W. Craig, 1983. Meeting the Needs of the Working Poor: The Impact of the OBRA. Minneapolis, MN: Center for Health Services Research, University of Minnesota.

Moynihan, D. (ed.), 1968. On Understanding Poverty. New York: Basic Books.

Moynihan, D., 1986. Family and Nation. New York: Harcourt Brace Jovanovich.

Murray, C., 1984. Losing Ground. New York: Basic Books.

Myrdal, A., 1968. Nation and Family, 2nd ed. New York: Harper.

Ozawa, M.N., 1982. Income Maintenance and Work Incentives. New York: Praeger.

Palmer, J. and I. Sawhill (eds.), 1982. The Reagan Experiment. Washington, DC: Urban Institute Press.

Patterson, J., 1981. America's Struggle Against Poverty: 1900–1980. Cambridge, MA: Harvard University Press.

Pearce, D. and H. McAdoo, 1981. Women and Children Alone and in Poverty. Washington, DC: National Advisory Committee on Economic Opportunity.

Perlman, H.H., 1960. "Are We Creating Dependency?" Social Service Review 34: 323–33.

Piven, F.F. and R. Cloward, 1971. Regulating the Poor. New York: Pantheon.

Rainwater, L. and W. Yancy, 1967. The Moynihan Report and the Politics of Controversy. Cambridge, MA: MIT Press.

Rein, M., 1967. "The Strange Case of Public Dependency," Trans-Action (April/March): 16–23.

Riesman, D., 1951. The Lonely Crowd: A Study of Changing American Character. New Haven: Yale University Press.

Ross, H. and I. Sawhill, 1975. Time of Transition. Washington, DC: Urban Institute Press.

Sarri, R. (ed.), 1984. The Impact of Federal Policy Changes on AFDC Recipients and their Families. Ann Arbor, MI: University of Michigan, Institute for Social Research, Center for Political Studies.

Schiller, B., 1978. "Lessons from WIN: A Manpower Evaluation," Journal of Human Resources 8: 505–23.

Schur, E., 1983. Labeling Women Deviant: Gender Stigma and Social Control. Philadelphia: Temple University Press.

Smith, J., 1984. "The Paradox of Women's Poverty: Wage-Earning Women and Economic Transformation," Signs 10: 291–310.

Stack, C., 1974. All Our Kin. New York: Harper and Row.

Steiner, G.Y., 1966. Social Insecurity: The Politics of Welfare. Chicago: Rand McNally.

Steiner, G.Y., 1971. The State of Welfare. Washington, DC: The Brookings Institution.

Steiner, G.Y., 1981. The Futility of Family Policy. Washington, DC: Government Printing Office.

Stevens, R. (ed.), 1970. Statutory History of the United States: Income Security. New York: McGraw-Hill.

Tilly, C., 1978. "Migration in Modern European History," in W.H. McNeil (ed.) Human Migration: Patterns, Implications, Policies. Bloomington: Indiana University Press.

Titmuss, R.M., 1958. Essays on 'The Welfare State'. New Haven: Yale University Press.

Trczynski, E., 1985. "Effect of Uncertainty and Risk on the Allocation of Time of Married Women." Ph.D. dissertation, University of Michigan.

U.S. Bureau of the Census, 1985. Money Income and Poverty Status of Families and Persons in the United States. CPR P. 60, No. 140. Washington, DC: Government Printing Office.

U.S. Commission on Civil Rights, 1982. Unemployment and Underemployment among Blacks, Hispanics and Women. Washington, DC: Government Printing Office.

U.S. Congress, Joint Economic Committee, 1972a. "Issues in Welfare Administration: Welfare—An Administrative Nightmare," Studies in Public Welfare No. 5 (Part 1). Washington, DC: Government Printing Office.

U.S. Congress, Joint Economic Committee, 1972b. "Supplemental Material," pp. 62–70 in Studies in Public Welfare No. 3. Washington, DC: Government Printing Office.

U.S. Congress, Joint Economic Committee, 1974. "Aid to Families with Dependent Children," pp. 140–70 in Studies in Public Welfare No. 20. Washington, DC: Government Printing Office.

U.S. Congress, Joint Economic Committee, 1975. Handbook of Income Transfer Programs: Studies in Public Welfare No. 20. Washington, DC: Government Printing Office.

U.S. Department of Health and Human Services, 1986. Request for Proposal to Study Welfare Dependency. Washington, DC: USDHHS, January.

U.S. Department of Labor, Bureau of Labor Statistics, 1985. "Labor Force Activity of Mothers of Young Children Continues at Record Pace," News USDL85–131, Sept. 19.

U.S. General Accounting Office, 1985. Evidence is Insufficient to Support Administration's Proposed Changes to AFDC Work Programs. Washington, DC: Government Printing Office, Aug. 25 Report to House Committee on Government Operations.

U.S. House of Representatives, 1935. Committee on Ways and Means, Hearings on Social Security. Washington, DC: Government Printing Office.

U.S. House of Representatives, 1962. Hearings on Public Welfare. Washington, DC: GPO.

U.S. House of Representatives, Committee on Ways and Means, 1956. Hearings on H.R. 9120 and H.R. 9091 and

H.R. 10238 and H.R. 10284. April 12, 13, 16, 19 and 20. Washington, DC: GPO.

U.S. House of Representatives, Committee on Ways and Means, 1983. Background Material on Poverty. Washington, DC: GPO.

U.S. House of Representatives, Committee on Ways and Means, 1985. Children in Poverty. Washington, DC: Government Printing Office.

U.S. House of Representatives, Committee on Ways and Means, 1984a. Hearings on Poverty Rate Increase, October 18-November 3, 1983. Washington, DC: GPO.

U.S. House of Representatives, Committee on Ways and Means, 1984b. Effects of the Omnibus Budget Reconciliation Act of 1981 (OBRA): Welfare Changes and the Recession on Poverty. Washington, DC: GPO.

U.S. Senate, Committee on Finance, 1935. Hearings on S. 1130, the Economic Security Act, January 22 to February 20, 1935. Washington, DC: GPO.

U.S. Senate, Committee on Finance, 1950. Hearings o H.R. 6000 (Parts 1-3). Washington, DC: GPO.

U.S. Senate, Committee on Finance, 1962. Hearings on the Public Assistance Act of 1962, May 14, 15, 16, 17, 1962. Washington, DC: GPO.

U.S. Senate, Committee on Finance, 1967. Hearings on the Social Security Amendments of 1967, September 20, 21, 22, and 26, 1967. Washington, DC: GPO.

U.S. Senate, Committee on Finance, 1972. Hearings on the Work Incentive Program. Washington, DC: GPO.

U.S. Senate, Committee on Finance, 1978. Social Security Act. Washington, DC: GPO.

Wallace, P., 1982. Black Women in the Labor Force: Cambridge, MA: MIT Press.

Weitzman, L., 1985. The Divorce Revolution. New York: The Free Press.

Wright, H.R., 1931. "Dependency," pp. 93-95 in Encyclopedia of the Social Sciences. New York: Macmillan.

Zinn, D., 1984. "Welfare Dependency as Political Language." Ph.D. dissertation, University of Michigan.

Zinn, D. and R. Sarri, 1985. "Turning Back the Clock on Public Welfare," Signs 10: 355-70.

PART IV

SOCIAL RIGHTS: EDUCATION

CHAPTER 10

THE IMPACT OF FAMILY AND SCHOOL ON ADOLESCENT GIRLS' ASPIRATIONS AND EXPECTATIONS: THE PUBLIC-PRIVATE SPLIT AND THE REPRODUCTION OF GENDER INEQUALITY

Diane Mitsch Bush

Despite change in the attitudes of American adults toward "appropriate" roles for women over the past fifteen years, the social organization of gender appears to have remained the same in essential ways. Most importantly, women as a group remain segregated in low-status, low-pay occupations (Waite and Hudis 1980; England 1984; Stallard et al. 1983). The current policy debate about sex segregation of occupations and about the major solution proposed to alleviate the problem, pay equity (or comparable worth), has focused in part upon the process whereby large proportions of working women currently end up in "traditionally female" jobs. Opponents of pay equity argue that women freely choose such occupations as clerical, domestic, or food service, whereas proponents of this policy to alleviate the impact of sex segregation contend that women are channeled into female occupations via gender role socialization and discrimination. In order to understand the process whereby women enter "traditional" or "nontraditional" occupations, we must comprehend the intersection of the public and private spheres in the life course of women. Specifically, an examination of the intersection of family and education during late childhood and through adolescence may provide us with insight into how a "Catch-22" may operate to narrow aspirations and expectations for girls during this crucial portion of the life course. Given evidence that attitudes regarding women's rights have changed during the 1970s and given a variety of policies aimed at guaranteeing educational and occupational sex equity, one might expect that gendered socialization at home and, especially, at school has changed in content and process. If such change is occurring, then sex segregation might lessen as this cohort of young people enters the labor force.

Therefore this chapter will examine the ways in which gendered socialization operates as a social control mechanism at home and at school during adolescence. Special attention will be devoted to change, or lack thereof, in content and processes of socialization within and between these two institutions. I will emphasize occupational aspirations and family expectations as the dependent variables: how they are formed, and how they have changed for recent cohorts, and perhaps most importantly, how the process whereby boys and girls form occupational aspirations has changed or remained the same. I will explore the implications of these questions for the reproduction of gender inequality and for policies which may lessen such inequality.

THE PUBLIC-PRIVATE SPLIT AND SOCIAL CONTROL OF WOMEN: CHANGE AND CONSISTENCY IN THE SOCIAL ORGANIZATION OF GENDER

The sex-gender system (Rubin 1975) in virtually all known societies is organized around the ideology that women's primary place is in the home and that the public sphere is a man's place (Rosaldo 1974; Chodorow 1974, 1978). Both the ideology and structure of the public-domestic split render women relatively powerless in both spheres. As Rosaldo (1974) points out, "authority" resides in the public sphere. Since women are partially or fully barred form it, they lack authority. In the domestic sphere authority resides with the father, although women may wield peculiarly feminine forms of power. Where they do so, such power is either ridiculed or painted as evil.[1]

With the development of capitalism, the home and workplace became more distinctly separated (Zaretsky 1976; Chodorow 1978; Eisenstein 1979). As a result, ideology regarding a "woman's proper place" reflected the public-private split even more sharply (Rothman 1979; Eisenstein 1979). The family came to be conceived of as the shelter from the harsh, impersonal world of industry.[2] While such ideology may have described the experience of middle-class white men, it left out the public powerlessness of the middle-class white woman and bore no relation to the experience of working-class or minority women (Sargent 1981; Siltanen and Stanworth 1984).

Nonetheless, capitalism and the specific mode of work organization associated with it, bureaucracy,[3] required workers and managers to be reproduced in both meanings of the word. Women's role in biological reproduction and their role as unpaid laborer in social reproduction provided persons suited physically and mentally for the world of the bureaucracy (Chodorow 1978; Sargent 1981). Recent historical accounts of the early 1950s point to that period as the high-water mark of the public-domestic split (Ehrenreich 1983). As capitalism continued to change during the late 1950s, through the 1960s, and accelerating during the 1970s (Bluestone and Harrison 1982), women's labor force participation burgeoned and family structure became more varied in the United States (Stallard et al. 1983; Ehrenreich 1983; Miller and Garrison 1982). The vast majority of jobs created by the shifts in the economy were clerical or service jobs (Bluestone and Harrison 1982; Stallard et al. 1983; Glenn 1984). Women's participation in these positions was justified by the contention that women were especially well-suited to those occupations. That is, the same set of traits once used to keep women in the home became justifications for drawing them into the workforce in low pay, low status, low authority jobs.[4] Yet, at the same time that women have moved into the labor force, they have continued to be responsible for the bulk of household labor (Duncan and Duncan 1978; Huber and Spitze 1983; Miller and Garrison 1982) resulting in the double day for working women. The public-domestic split has not lessened as women have entered the labor force. Rather the ideology and structure of "woman's place" have been transposed into the public sphere so that when women do participate in the economy and polity they still have less status and authority than men in both the domestic and public spheres (see Siltanen and Stanworth 1984).

Much recent public attention has focused on changes in attitudes regarding women's and men's roles since the 1970s. Even if the sexual division of labor has changed little in the home workplace, or polity, it is argued that attitudes have changed and that behavior will follow. This contention is a crucial one to examine for those concerned with how current cohorts of adolescents will experience adulthood. If attitudes of adults have changed, perhaps they are transmitting fewer sex-stereotyped beliefs and behaviors to their children. There is ample evidence that attitudes toward women's roles have changed during the past two decades (Mason et al. 1976; Thornton and Freeman 1979; Cherlin and Walters 1981; Thornton et al. 1983). However, all studies show a more marked shift toward egalitarian attitudes toward women's roles in the public than in the domestic sphere. Both sexes hold less sex-typed expectations for women in the workplace and in the polity than in the home.[5]

The Tightening of Social Control in Early Adolescence: Gender Intensification and the Public-Domestic Split

Since women's participation in the public sphere and attitudes of both women and men still reflect a social organization of gender based on the assumption that women's primary responsibility lies in the domestic sphere, it is not surprising that studies of current cohorts of adolescents reveal persistence of sex-typed attitudes and stereotypes about expectations (Lueptow 1980, 1981; Bush et al. 1978; Herzog et al. 1983; Bush 1985; Ruble 1983; Corder and Stephan 1984). As with adults, there are sex differences in role expectations. There is a decided tendency for boys to be more conservative than girls. Boys tend to be more likely to expect future wives to quit work after children are born, whereas girls are more likely to expect to combine work, marriage, and children (Corder and Stephan 1984; Herzog et al. 1983). When compared to girls in earlier cohorts, adolescent girls in the late 1970s and early 1980s are more likely to report that they intend to work full-time outside the home (Bush et al. 1978; Lueptow 1980). However, data on the question of whether their occupational aspirations remain sex-typed are sparse (Bush et al. 1978; Rosen and Aneshensel 1978).

It seems that a key to understanding how adolescent girls narrow their aspirations and expectations, even within a context in which some change is evident in roles and attitudes, is gender intensification at home and at school (Hill and Lynch 1983). A wide variety of theory and research (Maccoby and Jacklin 1974; Huston-Stein and Higgins-Trenk 1978; Weitzman 1979, 1984; Bush et al. 1978; Simmons et al. 1979; Eccles and Hoffman 1984; Block 1984) shows that sex-typed behaviors, beliefs, and expectations become more pronounced during early adolescence (ages 12–16), especially for girls (Bernard 1975; Bush et al. 1978; Block 1979, 1984; Weitzman 1979, 1984; Hill and Lynch 1984; Plumb and Cowan 1984). Girls begin to value popularity over competence and independence in seventh grade (Simmons and Rosenberg 1975;

Bush et al. 1978); in the junior high context they exhibit a drop in self-image between sixth and seventh grade (Simmons et al. 1979) and in academic performance (Weitzman 1984; Eccles and Hoffman 1984), especially in mathematics (Sherman 1980; Parsons et al. 1982b). Rosen and Aneshensel (1978) found that the proportion of girls who aspire to executive-professional occupations drops from seventh-eighth grade to eleventh-twelfth grade. Gender intensification suggests that parents, peers, teachers, and the adolescent girl herself begin to see the primary goal of adolescence as finding a suitable husband (Bernard 1975; Huston-Stein and Higgins-Trenk 1978; Stericker and Kurdek 1983).

Adolescent socialization for girls appears to be fraught with discontinuity and conflict. Expectations by significant others seem to change dramatically from grade school to junior high (Parsons et al. 1982a; Eccles and Hoffman 1984; Best 1983). Just as they are expected to become more concerned with boys, some data suggest that they discover that boys expect them to act in traditionally feminine ways (Best 1983; Herzog et al. 1983; Braito and Klundt 1984). Yet at the same time, they realize that these "feminine" behaviors are devalued, not only in their public world of school, but in the adult public world as well (Broverman et al. 1972; Siltanen and Stanworth 1984). While there is much conjecture about how this Catch-22 process serves as a social control mechanism (Schur 1984), few studies examine the intersection of both public and domestic spheres in the gender intensification process. Some findings focus on parents (Maccoby and Jacklin 1974; Block 1979; Parsons et al. 1982a), but there is debate about whether parents have different expectations for boys and girls in adolescence (see below and Block 1979, 1984). Yet other research concentrates primarily on school and peers (Simmons et al. 1979; Parsons et al. 1982b). As theorists and researchers have consistently pointed out, parents, peers, and school all exert influence on the child, and, moreover, the institutions of family and school are intertwined with economic and political institutions (Bowles and Gintis 1976; Chodorow 1978; Sargent 1981; Siltanen and Stanworth 1984).

Status Attainment Models, Gender Intensification, and Social Control

Most of the research on gender intensification emphasizes traits and role expectations, rather than specifically examining formation of occupational aspirations/expectations. In contrast, much of the relevant literature on the status attainment process fails to consider that gender intensification may render the models of the process, largely developed with male samples, invalid for female samples. In pathbreaking departures within the status attainment literature, Sewell, Hauser, and Wolf (1980) and Rosenfeld (1980) show that status attainment models are significantly different for adult men and women.

Even this research does not shed light on the relevant gender intensification processes, since it does not focus on adolescence as a distinct period in the life-course. Furthermore, studies are based on cohorts who experienced adolescence in the 1950s or early 1960s.

A FRAMEWORK FOR UNDERSTANDING THE REPRODUCTION OF GENDER INEQUALITY: THE INTERSECTION OF THE PUBLIC-DOMESTIC SPLIT GENDER INTENSIFICATION, AND THE FORMATION OF ASPIRATIONS AND EXPECTATIONS

The public-private (or public-domestic) split, gender intensification, and status attainment processes appear to interact to continue to define girls who aspire to high status, high authority, and higher paying occupations/careers as deviant in the adolescent world, therefore preventing some girls from pursuing their aspirations. Yet I have not considered the processes of social organization whereby these social control mechanisms operate. To do so, I will look at how the ideology and social organization of the public-private split, gender intensification processes, and aspects of formation of aspirations interact in the family and in school.

The Family as a Social Control Mechanism: The Maintenance of Sex Segregation

Virtually all theories of gender socialization begin with the family, but there is disagreement between various theoretical frameworks about the impact of different processes of socialization and about the relative importance of mothers and fathers. It is beyond the scope of this chapter to provide an adequate discussion of the various theories, findings, and debate (see Maccoby and Jacklin 1974; Block 1979, 1984; Weitzman 1979, 1984; Constantinople 1979; Katz 1979; Cahill 1979; Bush and Simmons 1981; Eccles and Hoffman 1984; Bush 1985, for either reviews and/ or debate). However, the following are some family socialization processes believed to result in gender differences: same sex modeling, same sex identification, gender differentiated reward contingencies, gender specific parental perceptions, goals, and expectations, direct teaching, and sexual division of household labor. Each of these is embedded in the public-domestic (private) separation, each may take on added, or diminished, significance at adolescence, and each is believed to play a role in the formation of aspirations, thereby affecting occupation and family choices.

The Public-Private Separation and Family Socialization

The social organization of gender in contemporary American society is still based on the premise of separation of public and private (domestic). One does not have to embrace every detail of Chodorow's (1974, 1978) feminist revision of psychoanalytic theory to agree with her contention that the fact that women are still primarily responsible for child care is the major reason that gender inequality is reproduced. She locates women's responsibility for "mothering" (assumed by themselves as well as by others) in both the historic and current social organization of gender within capitalist society.[6] The linchpin of this sex-gender system is the public-private separation which relegates women to the private, domestic sphere as caretakers and also renders them socially and politically inferior to men in the public sphere. This process is intensified in advanced capitalist societies because of the more marked separation between the family (private) and the economy and state (public) (see Chodorow, 1978: 179–81 and above). Thus the feminine qualities of nurturance and interpersonal connectedness become devalued at both the interpersonal and cultural levels, as well as in social theory itself (especially psychoanalytic theory, and see Gilligan 1982 for parallels in cognitive-developmental theory). In this way social structure, culture, and personality are reciprocally interconnected in the social organization of gender.

This social structure leads to different processes of socialization within the family for girls and boys. Because the mother is present and because she sees the daughter as similar to herself, girls develop via personal identification, a process characterized by expressive interaction and acceptance. Role learning for girls is particularistic and affective, characterized by connectedness and intimacy. Gender identity and gender roles are marked by affiliation and ties to the other for girls. In contrast, boys' gender identity and gender role development occur through positional identification largely because the father is "invisible" in contemporary society. Male role learning tends to be more abstract and formal, gleaned from cultural rather than personal images (this is especially so for anticipatory socialization for work roles).

Gender Intensification within the Family: Adolescent Socialization and the Public-Private Split

Because the boy must separate from his mother to build a gender identity and self-concept, masculine role learning in adolescence revolves even more around the denial of the feminine than childhood socialization. Much of socialization for boys, especially in adolescence, entails separation and negative identification with the feminine. Contrary to earlier theory, which maintains that the discontinuity in boys' socialization at adolescence makes development hard for them, Chodorow embeds two gender-distinct processes in the larger social structure and concludes that the process is more complex and difficult for girls than for boys. Even though gender role socialization for girls is continuous, it revolves around connectedness to others (first mother, then family of origin, then husband and children) to such an extent that clear ego boundaries are difficult to establish.[7] I would add that while gender role socialization in the private sphere is marked by continuity for girls, in the public sphere it is quite discontinuous and contradictory. As I will argue below, there is a sharp break between public expectations (especially at school) for preadolescent and adolescent girls.

Not only is there temporal discontinuity here, but the adolescent girl cannot help but see that feminine qualities, roles, and behaviors are devalued in the public sphere (Weitzman 1979; Broverman et al. 1972); indeed, they are defined as deviant (Schur 1984). Furthermore, while specific interpersonal roles and processes in the family context may be marked by separation and discontinuity for boys, there is an essential continuity to male role expectations and high valuation of the masculine in our culture (see Rosaldo 1974; Aries cited in Chodorow 1974: 54; Weitzman 1979). To be masculine is to be "normal" in the public sphere; thus the adolescent girl receives mixed and conflicting signals. She is expected to and desires to be feminine, that is, to concentrate on connections with others, especially boys. Yet these same characteristics are stigmatized in the boys' world. Chodorow links this dilemma back to the public-private split in the larger society with the following argument. The existing social organization of the family not only tends to reproduce women with the capacity and desire to mother, but it also leads to and produces men with characteristics appropriate for the bureaucratic organization of work in capitalist society and the desire to compete in that hierarchical work world. In her theorizing Chodorow (1978; see also debate in Lorber et al. 1981) is well aware that not all women have the psychological capacity nor desire to mother, and that all men do not necessarily have the "organization man" psyche. However, she does not explain "deviant cases." As I will demonstrate below, it is just such variation that we must understand if we are to change gender inequality.

Within Chodorow's framework fathers play a significant part in the socialization process in gender-specific ways. Similarly, a wide variety of research on gendered socialization shows that fathers and mothers affect boys' and girls' gender roles and attitudes quite differently (Maccoby and Jacklin 1974; Bearison 1979; Weitzman 1979). From childhood on, cross-sex activities and characteristics are strongly discouraged in boys (Weitzman 1979; Eccles and Hoffman 1984), and there is evidence that fathers are more concerned than mothers with "sex appropriate" behavior for both boys and girls (Block 1984; Weitzman 1984; Huston-Stein and Higgins-Trenk 1978).

In adolescence the concern with "masculine" behavior for boys appears to increase. Independence is encouraged more for boys than girls throughout childhood (Weitzman 1984; Eccles and Hoffman 1984); however, the gender difference in parents' behavior and in children's reports of parents' behaviors becomes greater in adolescence (Block 1984). Sexual maturity for girls seems to lead to closer supervision for them than for adolescent boys and girls (Eccles and Hoffman 1984; Hill and Lynch 1983).

Household division of labor appears to become more sex-typed in early adolescence (Best 1985; White and Brinkerhoff 1981). It is unclear whether this shift is due to parents' direct influence or whether adolescents select sex-typed chores. Nevertheless, a traditional division of labor in the family is correlated with traditional gender-role attitudes in the 1980s (MacCorquodale 1984).

Parental beliefs about children's abilities and expectations for future achievement continue to be gender specific (Weitzman 1979; Eccles and Hoffman 1984; Huston-Stein and Higgins-Trenk 1978;

Kaufman and Richardson 1983; Best 1983; Rosen and Aneshensel 1978). Parents' expectations about future achievement and their beliefs about children's current abilities appear to have more impact on girls' occupational aspirations than modeling processes (Parsons et al. 1982a; Saltiel 1985). This may be due to the fact that girls have few same-sex role models for achievement (Huston-Stein and Higgins-Trenk 1978), or to conflicts with mothers who are employed (Macke and Morgan 1978), or because role models are not as potent as commonly believed (Speizer 1981; Parsons et al. 1982a). Saltiel (1985) finds that significant others who are definers, rather than models for occupational roles, are more influential in formation of aspirations for adolescent girls. For boys models have more impact than definers. Parents are the most important source for definitions of both occupational roles and of the children's conception of self in relation to occupational roles. They rank higher than siblings, peers, teachers, and other acquaintances. For boys fathers are twice as important as mothers in providing information, but for girls both parents were equally important.[8]

When the influence of both parents is considered in light of evidence that parents attribute achievement to ability for boys and to effort for girls (Parsons et al. 1982a), the ramifications appear negative for girls. Even though objective measures of ability and effort in Parsons et al. (1982a) reveal no gender difference, parents perceive that girls must try harder to succeed. As Parsons's et al. (1982a) data show, this message is not lost on the girls. The findings show that girls are more likely to attribute success to effort, whereas boys see their success emanating from ability. Similarly, a variety of data from attribution studies show that girls attribute success to effort and failure to lack of ability (Stipek 1984; Gitelson et al. 1982).

The message conveyed (and accepted) by parents seems to be not simply that of sex typing of occupations but the more basic perception that success in both school and work will require more time and effort for girls than for boys. If this self-conception is built by girls at the same period in the life course when they begin to place great importance on attracting a boyfriend, later a husband, the impact may well be a lowering of occupational and educational aspirations.

At first glance these findings on parental expectations and attributions for their children's success appear to be at odds with data on mothers' labor force participation. In 1982, 70 percent of women with children aged 5–16 were working for pay

(U.S. Department of Commerce 1983). Thus one might argue that adolescent girls do have same-sex role models for occupations and careers. Further, one might expect that both parents' expectations for daughters' future labor force participation would include the expectation of full-time, paid employment. To assess the validity of these contentions as well as their implications, we must recall the current social organization of gender in the public and private spheres (see above). As suggested by Macke and Morgan's (1978) findings discussed earlier, simple presence of an employed mother does not necessarily lead to the wish for a career by adolescent girls. I contend that the primary reason for this result is current sex segregation of occupations. As a group, employed women are crowded into a small number of low-pay, low-status occupations. Although many female adolescents currently have a "role model" for employment, that model may well be a negative role model due to the conditions of many women's employment. Thus daughters of mothers employed in "pink-collar" jobs (Stallard et al. 1983) do not have a same-sex model for a "career" (i.e., a high-status, high-paying job) nor do they necessarily have a positive model for employment per se. Likewise, parents may believe that employment does not offer opportunities for mobility for girls due to actual experiences of employed mothers.[9]

Parental Influence and the Formation of Aspirations: Evidence from Status Attainment Research

When interpreted in this way, existing data on the influence of parents in adolescence points toward different processes of aspiration formation and status attainment for males and females. A wide variety of research shows that family variables have either less impact on aspirations or actual attainment for females than for males (Sewell et al. 1980; Schulenberg et al. 1984; Rosenfeld 1980; Wright 1979) or the opposite impact (Rosenfeld 1980). The most striking findings here concern family socioeconomic status. Sewell et al. (1980: 574) find that for men, family SES has a potent, positive effect on attainment, but for women there is no significant effect. Moreover, measures of ability and achievement have a substantially larger impact on attainment for men than for women. Both Sewell et al. (1980) and Rosenfeld (1980) illustrate that there is not one status attainment process which describes and explains people's experience, rather there are two distinct processes for men and women.

A major problem with status attainment research is that it does not utilize data which tap family interactions. Rather it relies on children's and parents' reports of attitude and behavior. Only one piece of research examines actual interaction patterns related to children's occupational plans. Ihinger-Tallman (1982) observed parents and 12–15-year-old children play a career choice simulation game (SIMCAR—see Ihinger-Tallman 1982 for explanation). Each family unit played the game; later, the child played it alone so as to estimate family influence on later individual decisions. Although there was no evidence that parents encouraged sons and daughters differently, there was a distinct gender difference in the effects of parental encouragement on sons' and daughters' achievement values. Parental encouragement had no significant impact on attainment values for girls. Parent-child interactions accounted for twice as much variance in son's attainment values than in daughter's. Ihinger-Tallman concludes that "the variables that affect the attainment value of young women continue to elude us" (1982: 554).

Corder and Stephan (1984) provide us with a clue to the puzzle generated by Ihinger-Tallman's findings and those from the status attainment literature (Sewell et al. 1980; Rosenfeld 1981). They hypothesize that for adolescent girls the formation of occupational aspirations and expectations is a twofold process. First, the adolescent girl decides on a possible combination of future family and work roles. After the family-work expectation process is completed, she makes choices relevant to an occupation. Corder and Stephan (1984: 398) point out that most studies of women's occupational plans, including status attainment research, focus on only the second stage. Since the first stage may dramatically restrict the available range of occupations, this process may explain why usual status attainment models are less successful in accounting for variance in female attainment. The first stage of the process coincides with the period of gender intensification. During early adolescence girls become aware that boys may not approve of career-oriented women (see also Rosen and Aneshensel 1978). Depending on the importance of opposite-sex significant others, this perception may lead to a traditional first stage decision. Corder and Stephan's (1984) data show that significant others who approve of girls' career aspirations have a positive effect upon aspirations to combine work and family roles. The implications of this finding become more important when considered in concert with Corder and Stephan's (1984) results regarding gender differences in plans for future family-work roles. About 70 percent of the females aspired to combine marriage, work, and children, but only 40 percent of males wished their future wives to do so. Furthermore, males believed that a husband whose wife does not work outside the home has more prestige than a husband whose wife is in the labor force. The opposite was true for females.

Not only are females' aspirations more contingent upon significant others, as Corder and Stephan and others have shown, but even in the late 1970s and 1980s these opposite-sex significant others do not wish them to pursue careers (Corder and Stephan 1984; Herzog et al. 1983). These data clarify part of the lack of explanatory power of status attainment models for the female attainment process. It is not simply the content and process of parents' encouragement which differs by gender of the child, but both the content of the message and the part played by significant others in the process are quite different. For example, status attainment research finds a positive impact of a high school (or college) lover or fiancee for men (Reitzes and Mutran 1980). Likewise, marriage has a positive impact on status attainment for men, but not women (Rosenfeld 1980).

There is an important link between these discoveries and those of other researchers regarding women's overall life course development (Bernard 1975; Rossi 1980; Gilligan 1982). The relationship between identity and intimacy in development is entirely different for women and men. Both Rossi (1980) and Gilligan (1982) show that the sequencing of the developmental tasks of identity formation and formation of intimate relationships are opposite for the sexes. Following Erikson (1950), Gilligan and Rossi agree that boys form their identities (including educational plans and occupational expectations—see Marini 1978) before forming intimate, lasting sexual relationships. In contrast, the adolescent girl holds her identity in limbo as she looks for the future husband whose identity will define hers. Just as Gilligan (1982) argues that theories of "human" psychological development had ignored women's distinct experience, subsuming it under models derived from male samples, so we are beginning to see that research on aspiration formation and occupational and gender-role socialization has assumed that the same constellation of factors which describe and explain male experience also account for female experience. The research reviewed above certainly dispels this notion. (See also Perun and Bielby 1981; Siltanen and Stanworth 1984.) It also points to ways in which both social science research and real life interaction continue to define adolescent girls who value future work roles over family roles as "deviant." In order to understand these social control mechanisms more thoroughly, we must examine the ways in which education, as an institution, interacts with the family in the context of the ideology and structure of the public-private split to promote gender intensification and restrict adolescent girls' opportunities.

THE PUBLIC-PRIVATE SPLIT, GENDER INTENSIFICATION, AND THE IMPACT OF SCHOOL ON FORMATION OF ASPIRATIONS

In many ways socialization processes at and in the school and family operate in additive fashion. Teacher-student and counselor-student interactions and their effects on boys and girls parallel and reproduce parent-child interactions and their effects. The social organization of the classroom and the school both reflect and reproduce elements of the ideology and social structure of the public-private separation, especially sexual division of labor. As with socialization content and processes within the family, socialization in school does not appear to have changed in essential ways, despite the passage of Title IX and some consciousness of sexism at school (Millsap 1983; Sandler and Hall 1982; Sadker and Sadker 1982, 1985). I will examine how teacher expectations may affect teacher-student interactions and, ultimately, adolescents' occupational aspirations. Part of this discussion will include brief exploration of attributions for achievement. Then I will briefly examine counseling and vocational education. Next, I will look at school organization and its impact upon adolescent girls.

Teacher Expectations and Student-Teacher Interactions

There is abundant evidence that teachers' expectations and behaviors are sex typed even though teachers may believe that they are sex neutral (Sadker and Sadker 1985, 1982; Parsons et al. 1982b; Sandler and Hall 1982). Tavris and Offer (1977) and others have argued that there is a "hidden curriculum" in schools, beginning with the earliest school experience. The hidden curriculum reflects the basic premise underlying the public-private separation: that women are, and ought to be, primarily suited for the requirements of the private sphere. Gender inequality seems to be reproduced in school in much the same way that existing inequalities of class and race are reproduced in school (Bowles and Gintis 1976; Persell 1977; Ryan 1976, 1982). As with hidden curricula for class and race, the hidden curriculum for gender is based in teacher expectations and behaviors, as well as social organization of school.[10]

Serbin et al. (1973) observed teacher behaviors toward boys and girls in nursery classrooms and found subtle differences in treatment of boys and girls. Girls were rewarded for proximity to the teacher, boys were not; girls were not encouraged to be independent of teacher in play activities, boys were. Even more interesting were differences in amount and quality of teacher attention. Boys received twice as much individual attention and more tangible and visible rewards than girls. When help was provided for boys, it took the form of showing how to solve a problem whereas help for girls entailed solving the problem for them. Teachers were not aware that they were treating boys and girls differently.

The parallels between Serbin et al.'s findings and the data on gender specific socialization in the family (above) are striking. Not only do adults in the home and at school treat children differently, but the direction and quality of the differences are the same in both contexts. Both parents and teachers encourage independence in boys and dependence in girls. Moreover, the adults are not aware that they are treating children differently.[11]

In grade school these differences persist and become more focused on academic achievement, especially in traditionally masculine fields such as mathematics. Dweck et al. (1978: 274), observing fourth and fifth grade classrooms, found for boys almost 94 percent of all positive feedback was directed to intellectual performance, for girls 79 percent of all positive feedback was related to intellectual performance. The sex difference is more marked for negative feedback for boys: 33 percent of negative feedback was related to intellectual performance; for girls 70 percent of negative comments were about intellectual aspects of work. Dweck et al. (1978) suggest that "positive evaluation is less indicative of ability for girls than for boys, and negative evaluation is less indicative of ability for boys." In a laboratory simulation of the classroom, Dweck et al. (1978) found that the female evaluation-contingency pattern led girls to attribute failure to ability rather than to other factors.

If, indeed, girls learn to attribute failure to ability, while boys attribute it to other factors, especially lack of effort, this could have a very negative impact on the two-stage aspiration formation process for girls. When we couple this process with parental expectations and patterns of encouragement (above) which imply to the female child that she will need superhuman effort to be successful, especially at "masculine" occupations, the potential for lowered aspirations is clear. Two questions emerge: (1) how generalizable are the Dweck et al. findings, and (2) how are teacher expectations and behaviors related to adolescents' expectations and aspirations?

With regard to the question of generalizability of attributions, there is a tendency for adolescent females to attribute failure to ability and success to luck, effort, or the ease of the task (Gitelson et al. 1982; Stipek 1984). However, some research does not find consistent gender differences (McHugh et al. 1982). Particularly with regard to luck attribution, even studies which argue that gender differences are not consistent show that males make stronger ability attributions (Frieze et al. 1982) and that girls, in comparison to boys, make unstable internal attributions for success and more stable internal attributions for failure (Parsons et al. 1982c). Specifically, girls give a higher rank to effort when ranking success attributions than did boys. Stipek's (1984) data on real classroom achievement tasks show that girls are more likely to attribute failure on "masculine" achievement tasks (e.g., here: math) to ability, but boys do not attribute failure on a "feminine" achievement task (spelling) to ability. Girls were somewhat more likely to attribute success to effort than boys. Girls who experienced failure were more likely to expect to fail again than boys who experienced failure. It appears that actual failure has more lasting impact on early adolescent girls' expectations, whereas boys are not affected as permanently. Early adolescent boys expect to do better on future tasks regardless of past performance than do girls (Stipek 1984; Gitelson et al. 1982).

How are teacher behaviors and teacher expectations related to these patterns of attribution and, ultimately, to expectations and aspirations? There is virtually no longitudinal research on this question; however, we may speculate on this question using cross-sectional data on gender and findings on the impact of teacher expectations on class and race inequality (Dusek and Joseph 1983). In early adolescence (grades 6–9) teachers were likely to tell high-achieving boys that they were competent but to tell high-achieving girls that their assignment was easy (Sandler and Hall 1982), and teachers interacted more often and in a more supportive fashion with male students (Sandler and Hall 1982; Sadker and Sadker 1985).

Not surprisingly, Sadker and Sadker (1985) found that in classrooms in which boys got more attention and more high quality interaction (e.g., higher order questions, more praise, urged to "try again"), that boys participated significantly more than girls. Moreover, when teachers watched videotapes of classrooms in which boys outspoke girls three to one, teachers insisted that girls participated more and were called on more. These findings are consistent with Becker's (1981 cited in Eccles and Hoffman 1984 and Weitzman 1984) finding that high school math teachers encourage boys more, joke with them more, and make positive public statements about their abilities. These findings are analogous to those for teacher expectations linked to class and/or race (Rosenbaum 1976).

Parsons et al. (1982b) directly examined the impact of such sex-typed teacher expectations and behaviors upon students' achievement, expectancies, and ability self-concepts. Boys for whom teachers had high expectations for future math achievement received significantly more praise than had high-expectancy girls. Moreover, high-expectancy girls had significantly lower self-concepts of math ability than high-expectancy boys. When ability self-concept was regressed on past performance and several teacher-student interaction measures, the independent variables accounted for a higher proportion of variance in self-concept for boys than for girls (Parsons 1982b: 332–333). Similarly, past performance and teacher-student interaction variables account for more variance in future expectancies for boys than for girls.

There is a striking similarity between these findings and the gender-specific models for status attainment (discussed above). Once again, the usual variables that predict expectations for boys predict very little for girls. This gender difference in both the effects of teacher expectations and behaviors upon student attitudes and the process of status attainment implies that unmeasured variables play a more important part in the formation of expectations and aspirations for girls and that models appropriate for describing and explaining male aspiration and achievement are not applicable to the female experience. Gender intensification processes within the school may be the key to explain both the formation of expectations and aspirations for girls in early adolescence and the gender differences in process and outcome.[12] There is little direct evidence of gender-specific change in teacher expectations or behavior between elementary and high school; however, the data are quite clear that between grade school and high school girls lower their aspirations (Kaufman and Richardson 1982; Rosen and Aneshensel 1978; Marini 1978), and their academic achievement, especially in mathematics, declines (Kaufman and Richardson 1984; Hill and Lynch 1983; Huston-Stein and Higgins-Trenk 1978; Maccoby and Jacklin 1974; Weitzman 1984), and their self-concept in the junior high school worsens (Simmons and Rosenberg 1975; Bush et al. 1978; Simmons et al. 1979).

Two additional areas in which there is surprisingly little research on gender intensification are counseling and vocational education. Since most counseling does not occur until junior high or high school, we may infer that interaction with counselors constitutes one change in early adolescence. A variety of evidence reveals that counselors and counseling materials continue to provide traditional, sex-typed information for girls about occupations and about combination of work and family roles (Weitzman 1984; Eccles and Hoffman 1984; Diamond 1974; Parker 1984). Gifted girls and boys are given very different advice and choices regarding future coursework, especially mathematics, college requirements, and occupations. This may account, in part, for the relatively large proportion of women who begin college without four years of high school math (Block 1984; Eccles and Hoffman 1984; Kaufman and Richardson 1982). However, some research suggests that other influences are far more important in such choices than counselors (Eccles and Hoffman 1984; Saltiel 1985).

Vocational education may be a far more potent influence on gender specific occupational aspirations and attainment than counseling, in part because it appears to have remained rigidly sex typed, and it is still the major road to mobility for working-class young people.[13] Before the passage of Title IX (Educational Amendments Act of 1972), vocational education was extremely sex-typed. There appears to have been some progress, but little real change has occurred. A 1983 investigation of New York City's vocational schools showed that school officials were largely ignoring guidelines for educational equity, citing sex-stereotyped "excuses" (Weitzman 1984: 185). Millsap (1983: 107) summarizes progress up through 1984: "...many states have provided more good intentions than programs to overcome inequities, and in some states even the mandated activities have not been undertaken." Moreover, she points out that Title IX has become a major target of the New Right. The Reagan Administration has filled National Advisory Council of Women's Educational Programs with New Right activists who oppose sex equity in education and has continued to attack the concept of sex equity both legislatively and judicially.

The Social Organization of School: The Public-Private Split, Gender Intensification and Aspirations in Gender-Together, and Gender-Separate Worlds

The expectations and actions of teachers, counselors, and directors of vocational programs do not operate in a vacuum to reproduce gender inequality within the context of the public-private. Rather, attitudes and behaviors of adults, and, as we shall see, peers, are located within the social organization of education. I will explore three facets of social organization of school which reproduce gender inequalities: sex-separate and sex-together modes of formal and informal organization, sex ratios and tracking, and possible effects of sex ratios on available models or schema.

Mixed and Separate Worlds in School. Thorne (1984) argues that boys and girls move in mixed-sex and sex-separate worlds in schools, not only in separate worlds as others have argued (Lever 1978). Her field observations of elementary school children for one year in California (1976–77) and one year in Michigan (1980) were focused upon the process of sex segregation as a gendered social relationship. When and how does gender affect group formation and interaction in various settings within the school? She found that when gender was invoked, either by school staff or by children themselves, it heightened interaction boundaries between the sexes and highlighted sex-stereotypic characteristics. While curricula and school space were not formally segregated, teachers, principals, and aides used gender as a primary basis for organizing daily activities. Girls' and boys' lines, girls' and boys' teams (both for academic and recess activities), and girls' and boys' "turfs" were all explicitly drawn upon in the daily routine. In virtually all instances, competition between the sexes was coupled with sex-stereotyped characterizations of individuals and of boys and girls in general. As would be predicted by symbolic interactionist (Cahill 1979), cognitive developmental (for review of Kohlberg, see Eccles and Hoffman 1984; Bem 1981), and eclectic theory (Bem 1981), the children often, but not always, sorted themselves by sex. It is within these interactions, mostly on the playground, that the devaluation of the feminine and fear of cross-sexed activity on the part of boys come out clearly. Particularly among the older children, the term "girl" was an epithet use by boys, while girls who moved competently in the boys' world (usually athletics) were accorded high status by both boys and girls.

Another theme that occurred in early grades, but increased in fifth grade, was heterosexuality as gender boundary maintenance. The charge of "liking" a member of the opposite sex was used to tease both boys and girls and to accentuate perceived sex differences in personality characteristics. Thorne (1984: 29) argues that as children reach early adolescence, that popularity with the opposite sex enhances status for girls, while boys' status among same-sex peers is not affected. Thus the public-private separation becomes inscribed in the informal social organization of school.

Thorne's research shows how deep the infusion of gender is in school. Sex-stereotyped division of labor seems to be emphasized by both children and adults, in both intended and unintended ways. Crucially, Thorne finds that comfortable interactions between the sexes take place when a principle of organization other than gender is explicitly invoked, usually by adults. For example, in one classroom mixed sex groups were set up for a task. Since the task was deemed important and not gender linked, gender considerations were momentarily set aside. Thorne's research implies that vigorous efforts must be made if gender distinctions are not to continue to be the prime informal basis for social organization in the school.[14]

Sex Ratios and Tracking. Thorne's research focuses on informal, unofficial processes which serve to reproduce the public-private separation and the sex-gender system within the school, often in unintended ways. In addition, there are a variety of official practices which may implicitly segregate by sex and narrow girls' opportunities. Although much research on inequalities by race and class have cited tracking (or ability grouping) as a major organizational feature of schools that perpetuates inequality in society (Bowles and Gintis 1976; Rosenbaum 1976; Persell 1977; but see Alexander and Cook 1982 for a different view), remarkably little research has been done in gender and tracking (see Saario et al. 1973 for one exception). Research on class, race, and tracking suggests that tracking operates to reproduce existing structural inequalities partly by damaging self-concept, partly via teacher expectations and partly by restricting access to advanced subject matter and higher education on bases other than ability (Rosenbaum 1976; Bowles and Gintis 1976). It is possible that the same mechanisms operate to keep large proportions of girls from attempting to pursue higher levels of achievement.

What little research there is on gender and tracking concentrates primarily on vocational training and mathematics. As noted above, Millsap (1983) and others (Weitzman 1984) have found that vocational tracks are highly sex segregated. It appears that lax enforcement of Title IX and the continued use of sex stereotypes by counselors and vocational teachers are major causes for the persistence of sex-segregated vocational education; however, much of the evidence is anecdotal.

Data on tracking in junior high and high school are even less clear. There is some evidence that teachers and counselors discourage girls from taking advanced mathematics courses (Eccles and Hoffman 1984; Weitzman 1984). Likewise, there is some disturbing evidence that girls have less access to computers, both in school and in informal play situations, than boys (Kiesler et al. 1983). However, there is some speculation that this lack of computer opportunity may be due to the fact that much educational software is "masculine"—it deals with competition, wars, or killing. Thus girls may self-select away from such activities.

Furthermore, there may be a sex-ratio problem with computers. Since use of terminals and attendance at computer camps are proportionally male dominated, girls may feel doubly uncomfortable in such situations. Not only are these activities defined as "masculine," but the fact of being "the only girl" makes normal interaction particularly difficult. As Kanter (1977) has shown with regard to the corporate workplace, when the proportion of a minority group increases, members of the group have fewer problems interacting. This same dynamic is probably present in advanced-track mathematics and science classes in junior high and high school, as suggested by research on proportions of women in college classrooms (Hall and Sandler 1982; Block 1984). Again, there is virtually no clear evidence on this issue.

Still, the crucial unanswered question is: how does gender affect track placement? Again, there is much conjecture and little solid research; indeed, sex is seldom a variable in current research on track placement or on the effects of tracking. One study which does include sex finds that gender effects disappear when ability measures are entered into a regression equation (Alexander and

Cook 1982). Indeed, these researchers argue that "access to the academic track is governed almost exclusively by the traditional academic criteria, and we see little indication of appreciable socioeconomic, racial, or gender bias in curriculum sorting processes" (Alexander and Cook 1982: 637). However, they go on to suggest that experiences during primary grades (including grades 6–7) may have set achievement trajectories firmly. This caveat, in concert with evidence that standard achievement tests (especially in math) are sex-biased (see Sherman 1980; Eccles and Hoffman 1984; Weitzman 1984 and footnote 12), that teacher expectations are sex-typed, and that girls' ability self-concepts are low regardless of performance, renders "the traditional academic criteria" cited by Alexander and Cook extremely suspect as "neutral" measures of female abilities. Therefore the finding that these criteria predict track placement does not necessarily indicate an absence of gender bias. Furthermore, given pervasive evidence that achievement, aspiration formation, and status attainment processes differ markedly for the sexes, Alexander and Cook and others who use sex as a variable in a structural equation model are not adequately testing for gender effects. Rather, an appropriate test would entail estimation for separate models for the sexes. Until this procedure was used in status attainment models (e.g., Marini 1978; Sewell et al. 1980), the gender difference in process was not recognized.

There is pervasive evidence that school organization, including tracking, class size, peer groups, and extracurricular activities, is related to a variety of difficulties encountered by girls as they move through junior high and high school. Epstein and Karweit (1983) find that having few female peers in ability groups (especially academic tracks) makes personal adjustment and achievement problematic for high school girls. Eccles and Hoffman (1984) agree that low sex ratios in the classroom may make high school difficult for girls. We contend (Bush et al. 1978; Simmons et al. 1979) that the social organization of junior high school places a premium on dating and opposite sex popularity for girls. This factor accounts for our finding that the move from sixth to seventh grade is significantly more stressful to pubertal girls who change from a k-6 school to junior high than for pubertal girls who remain in a k-8 school. Likewise, the importance of dating relationships for gender specific attainment processes may be seen in Reitzes and Mutran's (1981) finding that a heterosexual significant other in high school improves college grades for men but not for women.

Heterosexual relationships take a "central place" in the social organization of junior high. This emphasis is the heart of the gender intensification process for early adolescent girls; they, their peers, teachers, and counselors all appear to reflect and reproduce the ideology and structure of the public-private split.[15]

Sex Segregation of Jobs in Education: Models and Definers. Not only do junior high and high school girls feel pressure and desire to conform to traditional role expectations which highlight their place in the private sphere as their primary identity, but there are important changes from elementary to secondary school in the sex ratio of adults in various positions. While the majority of elementary school teachers are female, much larger proportions of secondary school teachers, especially in math and science, are male. In 1983, 97 percent of elementary school teachers were female, while 49 percent of secondary teachers were female (U.S. Department of Commerce 1983). Only one percent of all school superintendents are female (Millsap 1983). In higher education, women faculty are disproportionately represented among temporary instructors and underrepresented among tenured faculty (Sandler and Hall 1982). Given these data and Saltiel's (1985) finding that teachers are more influential as role models for adolescent girls than peers or other adults, we can see one more process whereby the sex-gender system is reproduced.

CONCLUSION

Huston-Stein and Higgins-Trenk (1978: 282–83) state that the development of nontraditional gender role expectations in adolescence

> probably requires at least one "unusual" influence, be it a parent, a school program, or a particularly potent peer or adult model. In the absence of "intervention" on some level the culture breeds a traditional female.

It is not only our culture, based as it is on the public-private split, but it is the social organization of gender in the public spheres of education, the economy and polity, and in the private sphere of the family which interact together to reproduce gendered inequality.

Throughout this chapter I have focused on the fact that processes, not simply content of socialization messages, differ by gender. Status attainment literature shows different, sometimes opposite effects of variables such as achievement, ability, aspirations, significant others, education, and marital status upon attainment for men and women. From this fact, along with the puzzle that variables such as prior performance, teacher expectations, or attributions account for far less of the variance in girls' achievement, it is clear that we know amazingly little about the formation of aspirations and plans for young women. Although it is a tiresome prescription because it is so often invoked, the call for more research is especially important here. Rexroat and Shehan (1984) show that the process which predicts labor force participation for women who are 35 years old in 1980 differs considerably between those women who at age 22–23 had planned active labor force participation at age 35 and those who at age 22 had planned to be homemakers at age 35. Their findings highlight the importance of plans made in adolescence for later life work/-family roles. When we consider their findings in light of the Corder and Stephan (1984) research discussed above as well as our own (Bush et al. 1978; Simmons et al. 1979), we have reason to be concerned about the prospects for current cohorts of adolescents. The majority of girls in this cohort wish to, and think they will be able to, combine work and family roles. Yet in early adolescence girls who are pubertal and dating have great difficulty combining these roles with others within the junior high context (Bush et al. 1978; Simmons et al. 1979). They cite pressure from boys as the major problem. When we consider that the boys in our sample seem to be making demands on the girls directly and that the boys sampled in a variety of research cited above (Corder and Stephan 1984; Herzog et al. 1985; Braito and Klundt 1984) have very different expectations for future wives than these "future wives" have for themselves, the stage is set for conflict. Such conflict may well lead to individual changes in juggling family-work roles which could lead to a breakdown in the Catch-22 cycle, or it could lead to feelings of personal distress which become attributed to inadequacies in the self. Such conflict among individual men and women is due to the existing social organization of gender and may result in change in the sexual division of labor, provided that a variety of avenues for change remain or become open.

First, real changes in the division of labor in families will only be possible when women have equal opportunity in the labor market and when child care is no longer organized as the responsibility of women. As others (Chodorow 1978; Barrett 1980; Sargent 1981) have noted, there is an essential Catch-22 here: the public sphere will not change unless the private sphere does, and vice versa

(Rosaldo 1974). Pogrebin (1983) points out that "family policy" and "labor policy" are inseparable. If they are connected, then policy making must take that fact into account.

Second, we need more public education for both parents and teachers about sexism in socialization process, not simply in content. The research I discussed shows clearly that parents and teachers are quite often unaware of gender-specific attitudes and behaviors which have very negative effects on adolescence. Since the passage of Title IX, a variety of teacher education projects have been initiated (Sadker and Sadker 1982; Parker 1984; Diamond 1975). However, there has been a reticence to discuss family policy in this regard. Schools could provide the impetus here. Much of the research discussed in this chapter suggests specific policies within schools that will shortcircuit the reproduction of gender inequalities:

1) in-service training of principals, teachers, and counselors (see Sadker and Sadker 1982).
2) units on occupations, pay equity, single parents, working women in elementary, junior high, and high school. Having successful women give presentations might be very helpful (Parker 1984).
3) promotion of more women to authority positions within schools (Millsap 1983).
4) vigorous enforcement of Title IX (Sandler and Hall 1982; Millsap 1983).

Obviously, such recommendations will raise the ire of the New Right and other antiwoman political forces. As Millsap (1983) points out, we must not assume that gains won (e.g., Title IX) are permanent, nor can we underestimate the power of antifeminist backlash. At the same time we must remember that, according to survey data cited above, the majority of Americans endorse sex equity in education, the economy, and the polity.

The very inertia of the existing social organization of gender is a key component in the reproduction process. We can see stability in the lack of theory and research on the actual experience of current cohorts of adolescent girls. The gaps in theory and research on female development are incredible, but so are recent advances. These advances mirror the potential for change in the sex-gender system. We have begun to unravel the intricate and contradictory processes which contribute to women's continued oppression. That is the first step toward changing the social organization of gender inequalities.

One question, of course, is what kind of change is desirable. This issue is raised implicitly by both Gilligan (1982) and Chodorow (1978). Gilligan links the fact that men tend to fear intimacy and women fear separation to distinctly "male" and "female" bases for moral judgments. The distinctive "female" concerns with connection and responsibility lead the professional women interviewed by Gilligan to different career dilemmas and decisions than those faced by men. Given the socialization processes described by Chodorow and the outcomes revealed in Gilligan's research, as well as much recent feminist theory and commentary, it appears that the adolescent and adult woman is, indeed, caught in a Catch-22. Either she must "act masculine" to succeed in a career, or she must make the sacrifices required by acting "deviant" (Schur 1984) and face the possibility of failing at her career. Another option, often discussed in the fear of success literature (Horner 1968; Gilligan 1982; Kaufman and Richardson 1983), is that she will opt for success in the private sphere. All of these so-called options assume that the social structure and organization of the public sphere, especially work, remain hierarchical and dominated by "masculine" values and interaction styles.

There is another possibility. Kanter's (1977) research suggests that when the ratio of women (or any other minority group) in the workplace rises, women will feel more able to act according to their values of connection. Moreover, her research on American corporations shows that both employee satisfaction and efficiency are heightened by a more decentralized organizational structure (Kanter 1977, 1983). As her work and that of others (Sargent 1984; Miller et al. 1979; Gerson 1985) show, many large corporations are currently opting for what Gilligan (1982) would call a "weblike" structure. Whether such changes will have a positive impact on opportunities for women is an empirical question. This question and others related to formal organizations are important ones to examine in light of the impact of the social organization of the public and domestic spheres on women's and girls' lives. As much theory and research discussed in this chapter point out (Rosaldo 1974; Kanter 1977; Chodorow 1978; Gilligan 1982; Rossi 1980; Huber and Spitze 1983; Miller and Garrison 1982; MacCorquodale 1984; Bush 1985), both the public and private spheres must change for women to realize greater opportunity and escape the Catch-22 of the reproduction of gender inequalities.

There is little doubt that change in the reproduction of gender inequalities will produce ripples, if not waves, throughout the entire society. Conversely, it is clear that real change in women's oppression cannot occur unless there is broad change within a variety of social institutions. The keys to such change are a solid understanding of how reproduction processes operate currently in both public and private sectors and continued reflection upon what an equitable social structure might look like.

Notes

[1]One form of the latter is the fear of and revulsion at women's sexuality, ranging from the madonna-whore dichotomy, to menstrual taboos, to a wide variety of pronouncements through the ages on the evils of "carnal lust" in women.

[2]Late nineteenth and early twentieth century sociologists built such concepts as Gemeinschaft/Gesellschaft, primary-secondary groups (Cooley 1908), and particularistic-universalistic modes of social organization (Weber 1947) on the increasingly distinct separation between home and work, between the world of the personalistic, intimate relations and the world of impersonal, distant social interactions. These conceptions of social organization correspond to psychological conceptions of agency-communion (Bakan 1966), separation-connection (Chodorow 1974, 1978; Gilligan 1982), and affiliation-achievement (McClelland, others cited in Eccles and Hoffman 1984). Parsons and Bales (1955) linked the sociological and psychological aspects of the dichotomy in theorizing about husband-wife roles and the place of the family in industrial society. Chodorow (1978) revised this theory to render it more representative of women's experience.

[3]Weber's (1947) model of bureaucracy can be understood as a conceptual opposition to the European patriarchy with its emphasis on personal characteristics and qualities as the bases for judgment. Indeed, Weber pointed to value rationality as the key component for effective decision making. Later, both Piaget (1932) and Freud (1966) remarked that the female psyche lacked these traits; therefore women were not able to make rational effective decisions in the public sphere. Gilligan's (1982) discussion of distinctly different bases for moral judgment for men and women challenges Freud and Piaget's contentions about women's moral inferiority, but in so doing she challenges Weber's notion that value rationality and bureaucratic hierarchy are, by definition, preferable modes of conception and action.

[4]It is intriguing to note that clerical work was once considered suitable only for men and that male traits were cited as crucial to clerical jobs (see Glenn 1984; Hartman 1979).

[5]The issue of social desirability as a response set has not been adequately examined (Crowne and Marlowe 1964). In the late 1970s and early 1980s, many adults may feel constrained to agree that women should have equal opportunity.

[6]This is the major point of departure from psychoanalytic theory empirically; normatively it is a distinct addition to the functionalist tradition in family sociology from which Chodorow draws.

[7]Chodorow (1974: 57–60; 1978: 177, 179) points out, as many feminist theorists have, that women are socially defined by their relations to others (e.g., women's class position is generally defined by that of their husband; women's successes have often been seen as "by proxy," that is, in terms of the successes of their children) and that women's adult roles have a diffuse, unbounded quality (e.g., the old adage that "women's work is never done") (see also Bakan 1966). She gives a poignant example of the way in which this lack of differentiation from others (what Bakan, 1966, calls communion) results in women assuming responsibility for situations over which they have no control: "Since our awareness of others is considered our duty, the price we pay when things go wrong is guilt and self-hatred. And things always go wrong. We respond with apologies...long after the event is forgotten—and even if it had no causal relation to anything we did to begin with. If the rain spoils someone's picnic, we apologize. We apologize for taking up space in a room, for living" (Tax cited in Chodorow 1974: 59, italics Chodorow's).

[8]Some research suggests that fathers' nontraditional expectations have greater impact on girls' achievement than do mothers' expectations (Block 1984; Perun and Bielby 1981), but fathers are less likely than mothers to hold nontraditional expectations for girls or boys as discussed above (see Block 1984).

[9]It is important to separate parents' gender-specific expectations for children's future occupations from expectations about school achievement and attributions of ability.

[10]The "hidden curriculum" is anything but hidden in readers and textbooks used in the schools (Weitzman 1972, 1979, 1984; Pescosolido and Grauerholtz 1985; Eccles and Hoffman 1984). Girls and women are either invisible or, if shown, are portrayed as passive, dependent, and nurturant. The same generalizations may

be made about other media, especially television, as shown by a number of content analyses (Weitzman 1984; Eccles and Hoffman 1984). As for other teaching materials, standardized tests often use only male pronouns to refer to doctors, the President of the United States and characters in examples are sex-stereotypic (Weitzman 1984).

[11]One reason for this may be the lack of attention to issues of sex equity in teacher training materials. Sadker and Sadker (1980) found virtually no mention of sexism in the classroom in the top selling teacher-education texts.

[12]Sherman (1980) and Block (1984) show clearly that gender-role expectations are correlated with the decline in girls' math performance and math background from elementary school to high school. Sherman found that perception of math as a male domain in eighth grade had a negative impact on math performance in eleventh grade for girls. Interestingly, girls' attitudes toward success in math improves slightly from eighth to eleventh grade, as do student reports of mothers' and fathers' attitudes toward the student as a learner of math. However, girls' perceptions of teachers' attitudes toward the child as a learner of mathematics decline, as do girls' perceptions of usefulness of math and joy at problem solving. The means for all these variables increase for boys from eighth to eleventh grade.

[13]There is little research on reproduction of minority status for working-class women. However, evidence suggests that opportunities for working-class adolescent girls are far more restricted in sex-stereotyped ways than for more privileged girls (Rubin 1976: 10, 41).

[14]Note that this research was conducted in the late 1970s and 1980. Also, Thorne notes (1984: 7) that some teachers had changed the practice of lining boys and girls up separately due to Title IX.

[15]I have focused primarily on girls; however, others argue that by reproducing traditionally masculine men, socialization serves a double role in the reproduction of gender inequality. Chodorow (1978) contends that until men are socialized to mother, we will see little change. Gilligan (1982) implies that men must become more connected as women add independence to their repertoire. Sandler and Hall (1982) note that one of the most negative outcomes of sexism in higher education is the way in which men are taught to devalue women as equals.

References

Alexander, K.L. and M.A. Cook, 1982. "Curricula and Coursework: A Surprise Ending to a Familiar Story," American Sociological Review 47, 5: 626–40.

Bakan, D., 1966. The Duality of Human Existence. Chicago: Rand McNally.

Barrett, M., 1980. Women's Oppression Today: Problems in Marxist Feminist Analysis. London: Verso.

Bearison, D.J., 1979. "Sex-Linked Patterns of Socialization," Sex Roles 5, 1: 11–18.

Bem, S.L., 1981. "Gender Schema Theory: A Cognitive Account of Sex Typing," Psychological Review 88, 4: 354–64.

Bernard, J., 1975. "Adolescence and Socialization for Motherhood," pp. 227–52 in S.E. Dragastin and G.H. Elder, Jr. (eds.) Adolescence in the Life Cycle: Psychological Change and Social Context. Washington, DC: Hemisphere.

Best, R., 1983. We've All Got Scars. Bloomington: University of Indiana Press.

Block, J.H., 1979. "Another Look At Sex Differentiation in the Socialization Behaviors of Mothers and Fathers," in J.A. Sherman and F.L. Denmark (eds.) Psychology of Women: Future Directions of Research. New York: Psychological Dimensions.

Block, J.H., 1984. Sex-Role Identity and Ego Development. San Francisco: Jossey Bass.

Bluestone, B. and B. Harrison, 1982. The Deindustrialization of America: Plant Closings and Community Decline. New York: Basic Books.

Bowles, S. and H. Gintis, 1976. Schooling in Capitalist Society: Educational Reform and the Contradictions of Economic Life. New York: Basic Books.

Braito, R. and K. Klundt, 1984. "Adolescents' Views of Gender Roles and Appropriateness of Varied Family and Work Conditions." Paper presented at the Western Social Science Association Meetings, April, San Diego, CA.

Broverman, I.K., S.R. Vogel, D.M. Broverman, F.E. Clarkson, and P.S. Rosenkrantz, 1972. "Sex-Role Stereotypes: A Current Appraisal," Journal of Social Issues 28, 2: 58–78.

Bush, D.M. and R.G. Simmons, 1981. "Socialization Processes Over the Life Course," pp. 133–64 in M. Rosenberg and

R. Turner (eds.) Social Psychology: Sociological Perspectives. New York: Basic Books.

Bush, D.M., 1985. "The Impact of Changing Gender Role Expectations Upon Socialization in Adolescence: Understanding the Interaction of Gender, Age, and Cohort Effects," chapter 6 in A.C. Kerckhoff (ed.) Research in the Sociology of Education and Socialization, Vol. 5. Greenwich, CT: JAI Press.

Cahill, S.E., 1979. "Reexamining the Acquisition of Sex Roles: A Social Interactionist Approach," Sex Roles 9, 1: 1–15.

Cherlin, A. and P.B. Walters, 1981. "Trends in United States' Men's and Women's Sex Role Attitudes 1972–1978," American Sociological Review 46, 4: 453–60.

Chodorow, N., 1974. "Family Structure and Feminine Personality," pp. 43–66 in M.Z. Rosaldo and L. Lamphere (eds.) Women, Culture and Society. Stanford, CA: Stanford University Press.

Chodorow, N., 1978. The Reproduction of Mothering: Psychoanalysis and the Sociology of Gender. Berkeley: University of California Press.

Constantinople, A., 1979. "Sex-Role Acquisition: In Search of the Elephant," Sex Roles 5, 2: 121–33.

Cooley, C.H., 1908. Human Nature and the Social Order. New York: Scribner's.

Corder, J. and C.W. Stephan, 1984. "Females' Combination of Work and Family Roles: Adolescents' Aspirations," Journal of Marriage and the Family 46 (May): 391–402.

Crowne, D. and D. Marlowe, 1964. The Approval Motive. New York: Wiley.

Diamond, E. (ed.), 1975. Issues of Sex Bias and Sex Fairness in Career Interest Measurement. Department of Health, Education and Welfare, National Institute of Education. Washington, DC: Government Printing Office.

Duncan, B. and O.D. Duncan, 1978. Sex Typing and Sex Roles. New York: Academic Press.

Dusek, J.B. and G. Joseph, 1983. "The Bases of Teacher Expectancies," Journal of Educational Psychology 75, 3: 327–46.

Dweck, C.S., W. Davidson, S. Nelson and B. Bary, 1978. "Sex Differences in Learned Helplessness II," Developmental Psychology 14, 3: 268–76.

Eccles, J.S. and L.W. Hoffman, 1984. "Sex Roles, Socialization and Occupational Behavior," in H.W. Stevenson and A.E. Siegal (eds.) Research in Child Development and Social Policy, Vol. 1. Chicago: University of Chicago Press.

Ehrenreich, B., 1983. Hearts of Men: American Dreams and the Flight from Commitment. New York: Anchor-Doubleday.

Eisenstein, Z.R., 1979. Capitalist Patriarchy and the Case for Socialist Feminism. New York: Monthly Review Press.

England, P., 1981. "Assessing Trends in Occupational Sex Segregation, 1900–1976," pp. 273–96 in I. Berg (ed.) Sociological Perspectives on Labor Markets. New York: Academic Press.

England, P., 1984. "Wage Appreciation and Depreciation: Test of Neoclassical Economic Explanations of Occupational Sex Segregation," Social Forces 62, 3: 726–49.

Epstein, J.L. and N. Karweit (eds.), 1983. Friends in School: Patterns of Selection and Influence in Secondary Schools. New York: Academic Press.

Erikson, E.H., 1950. Childhood and Society. New York: Norton.

Frieze, I.H., B.E. Whitley, Jr., B.H. Hanusa and M.C. McHugh, 1982. "Assessing the Theoretical Models for Sex Differences in Causal Attributes for Success and Failure," Sex Roles 8, 4: 333–43.

Freud, S., 1966. Complete Introductory Lectures on Psychoanalysis. New York: Norton.

Gerson, K., 1985. Hard Choices: How Women Decide About Work, Career, and Motherhood. Berkeley: University of California Press.

Gilligan, C., 1982. In a Different Voice: Psychological Theory and Women's Development. Cambridge: Harvard University Press.

Gitelson, I.B., A.C. Petersen and M.H. Tobin-Richards, 1982. "Adolescents' Expectancies of Success, Self-Evaluations, and Attributions about Performance on Spatial and Verbal Tasks," Sex Roles 8, 4: 411–19.

Glenn, E.N. and R.L. Feldberg, 1984. "Clerical Work: The Female Occupation," pp. 316–36 in J. Freeman (ed.) Women: A Feminist Perspective, 3rd ed. Palo Alto,CA: Mayfield.

Hall, R.M. and B.R. Sandler, 1982. The Classroom Climate: A Chilly One for Women? Washington, DC: The Association of American Colleges.

Hartman, H., 1979. "Capitalism, Patriarchy, and Job Segregation by Sex," pp. 206–47 in Z. Eisenstein (ed.) Capitalist Patriarchy and the Case for Socialist Feminism. New York: Monthly Revised Press.

Herzog, A.R., J.G. Bachman and L.D. Johnston, 1983. "Paid Work, Childcare, and Housework: A National Survey of High School Seniors' Preference for Sharing Responsibilities Between Husband and Wife," Sex Roles 9, 1: 109–35.

Hill, J.P. and M.E. Lynch, 1983. "The Intensification of Gender-Related Role Expectations During Early Adolescence," chapter 10 in J. Brooks-Gunn and A. Petersen (eds.) Girls at Puberty: Biological and Psychosocial Perspectives. New York: Plenum.

Horner, M., 1972. "Toward an Understanding of Achievement-Related Conflicts in Women," Journal of Social Issues 28, 2: 157–75.

Huber, J. and G. Spitze, 1983. Sex Stratification: Children, Housework, and Jobs. New York: Academic Press.

Huston-Stein, A. and A. Higgins-Trenk, 1978. "Development of Females from Childhood Through Adulthood: Career and Feminine Orientations," pp. 237–96 in P.B. Baltes (ed.) Life-Span Developmental Psychology, Vol. 1: Development and Behavior. New York: Academic Press.

Ihinger-Tallman, M., 1982. "Family Interaction, Gender, and Status Attainment Value," Sex Roles 8, 5: 543–56.

Kanter, R.M., 1977. Women and Men of the Corporation. New York: Basic Books.

Kanter, R.M., 1983. The Change-Masters. New York: Simon and Schuster.

Katz, P.A., 1979. "The Development of Female Identity," Sex Roles 5, 2: 155–78.

Kaufman, D.R. and B.L. Richardson, 1982. Achievement and Women: Challenging the Assumptions. New York: Free Press.

Kiesler, S., L. Sproull and J.S. Eccles, 1983. "Second Class Citizens," Psychology Today 17, 3 (March): 40–49.

Lever, J., 1978. "Sex Differences in the Complexity of Children's Play," American Sociological Review 43, 4: 471–82.

Lorber, J.; R.L. Coser, A.S. Rossi, and N. Chodorow, 1981. "On The Reproduction of Mothering: A Methodological Debate," Signs: Journal of Women in Culture and Society 6, 3: 482–514.

Lueptow, L.B, 1980. "Social Change and Sex Role Change in Adolescent Orientations Toward Life, Work, and Achievement: 1964–1975," Social Psychology Quarterly 43, 1: 48–59.

Lueptow, L.B., 1981. "Sex-Typing and Change in the Occupational Choices of High School Seniors: 1964–1975," Sociology of Education 54 (January): 16–24.

Maccoby, E.E. and C.N. Jacklin, 1974. The Psychology of Sex Differences. Stanford, CA: Stanford University Press.

MacCorquodale, P., 1984. "The Effect of the Familial Division of Labor on Sex Role Attitudes." Paper presented at the Western Social Science Association Meetings, San Diego, CA, April.

Macke, A.S. and W.R. Morgan, 1978. "Maternal Employment, Race and Work Orientation of High School Girls," Social Forces 57: 187–204.

Marini, M.M., 1978. "Sex Differences in the Determination of Adolescent Aspirations: A Review of Research," Sex Roles 4: 723–53.

Mason, K.O., J.A. Czajka and S. Arber, 1976. "Change in U.S. Women's Sex Role Attitudes," American Sociological Review 41, 4: 573–96.

McHugh, M.C., I.H. Frieze, and B.H. Hanusa, 1982. "Attributes and Sex Differences in Achievement: Problems and New Perspectives," Sex Roles 8, 4: 467–79.

Miller, J. and H. Garrison, 1982. "Sex Roles: The Division of Labor at Home and in the Marketplace," pp. 237–62 in R. Turner and J. Short (eds.) Annual Review of Sociology 1982, Vol. 8. Palo Alto, CA: Annual Reviews.

Miller, J. C. Schooler, M.L. Kohn, and K.A. Miller, 1979. "Women and Work: The Psychological Effects of Occupational Conditions," American Journal of Sociology 85, 1: 46–94.

Millsap, M.A., 1983. "Sex Equity in Education," pp. 91–119 in I. Tinker (ed.) Women in Washington. Beverly Hills: Sage.

Parker, B., 1984. "Nonsexist Curriculum Development: Theory into Practice." Women's Studies Program, University of Colorado, Boulder.

Parsons, J.E., T.F. Adler, and C.M. Kaczala, 1982a. "Socialization of Achievement Attitudes and Beliefs: Parental Influences," Child Development 53: 310–21.

Parsons, J.E., C.M. Kaczala, and J. Meece, 1982b. "Socialization of Achievement Attitudes and Beliefs: Classroom Influences," Child Development 53: 322–39.

Parsons, J.E., J.L. Meece, T.F. Adler, and C.M. Kaczala, 1982c. "Sex Differences in Learned Helplessness," Sex Roles 8, 4: 421-32.

Parsons, T. and R.F. Bales, 1955. Family, Socialization, and Interaction Process. Glencoe, IL: Free Press.

Persell, C., 1977. Education and Inequality: The Roots and Results of Stratification in America's Schools. New York: Free Press.

Perun, P.J. and D. Bielby, 1981. "Towards a Model of Female Occupational Behavior: A Human Development Approach," Psychology of Women Quarterly 6: 234-52.

Pescosolido, B. and E.A. Grauerholtz, 1985. "Linking Macro and Micro Socialization Processes: Structural Shifts in Gender Images in Children's Literature, 1938-1983." Paper presented at the Midwest Sociological Society Meetings, April 11, St. Louis, MS.

Piaget, J., 1928. The Child's Conception of the World. London: Routledge Kegan Paul.

Plumb, P. and G. Cowan, 1984. "A Developmental Study of De-Stereotyping and Androgynous Activity Preferences of Tomboys, Non-Tomboys, and Males," Sex Roles 10, 9/10: 703-12.

Pogrebin, L.C., 1983. Family Politics: Love and Power on an Intimate Frontier. New York: McGraw-Hill.

Reitzes, D.C. and E. Mutran, 1980. "Significant Others and Self-Conceptions: Factors Influencing Educational Expectations and Academic Performance," Sociology of Education 53 (January): 21-32.

Rexroat, C. and C. Shehan, 1984. "Expected Versus Actual Workroles of Women," American Sociological Review 41, 3: 349-58.

Rosaldo, M.Z., 1974. "Women, Culture, and Society: A Theoretical Overview," pp. 17-42 in M.Z. Rosaldo and L. Lamphere (eds.) Women, Culture and Society. Stanford, CA: Stanford University Press.

Rosen, B. and C.S. Aneshensel, 1978. "Sex Differences in the Educational-Occupational Expectation Process," Social Forces 37, 1: 164-86.

Rosenbaum, J.E., 1976. Making Inequality: The Hidden Curriculum of High School Tracking. New York: Wiley.

Rosenfeld, R., 1980. "Race and Sex Differences in Career Dynamics," American Sociological Review 45: 583-609.

Rossi, A.S., 1980. "Life-Span Theories and Women's Lives," Signs 6: 4–32.

Rothman, S.M., 1979. Women's Proper Place. A History of Changing Ideals and Practices, 1870 to the Present. New York: Basic Books.

Rubin, G., 1975. "The Traffic in Women: Notes in the 'Political Economy' of Sex," in R. Reiler (ed.) Toward an Anthropology of Women. New York: Monthly Review Press.

Rubin, L., 1976. Worlds of Pain. New York: Harper and Row.

Ruble, T.L., 1983. "Sex Stereotypes: Issues of Change in the 1970s," Sex Roles 9, 3: 397–402.

Ryan, W., 1976. Blaming the Victim, 2nd ed. New York: Random House.

Ryan, W., 1982. Equality. New York: Vintage.

Saario, T.C., N. Jacklin, and C.K. Tittle, 1973. "Sex Role Stereotyping in the Public Schools," Harvard Educational Review 43, 3: 386–404.

Sadker, M.P. and D.M. Sadker, 1980. "Sexism in Teacher Education Texts," Harvard Educational Review 50, 1: 36–46.

Sadker, M.P. and D.M. Sadker, 1982. Sex Equity Handbook for Schools. New York: Longman.

Sadker, M.P. and D.M. Sadker, 1985. "Sexism in the Schoolroom of the 80's," Psychology Today 19, 3 (March): 54–57.

Saltiel, J., 1985. "A Note on Models and Definers as Sources of Influence on the Status Attainment Process: Male-Female Differences," Social Forces 63, 4: 1069–75.

Sargent, A., 1983. The Androgynous Manager: Blending Male and Female Styles for Today's Corporation. New York: American Management Association.

Sargent, L. (ed.), 1981. Women and Revolution: A Discussion of the Unhappy Marriage of Marxism and Feminism. Boston: South End Press.

Schulenberg, J., F.W. Vondracek and A.C. Crouter, 1984. "The Influence of the Family on Vocational Development," Journal of Marriage and Family 46, 1: 129–43.

Schur, E., 1984. Labeling Women Deviant: Gender, Stigma, and Social Control. New York: Random House.

Serbin, L.A., K.D. O'Leary, R.N. Kent, and I.J. Tolnick, 1973. "A Comparison of Teacher Response to Preacademic and Problem Behavior of Boys and Girls," Child Development 44, 4 (December): 776–804.

Sewell, W.H., R.M. Hauser, and W.C. Wolf, 1980. "Sex, Schooling, and Occupational Status," American Journal of Sociology 86, 3: 551–83.

Sherman, J., 1980. "Mathematics, Spatial Visualization and Related Factors: Changes in Girls and Boys, Grades 8–11," Journal of Educational Psychology 72, 4: 476–582.

Siltanen, J. and M. Stanworth (eds.), 1984. Women and the Public Sphere: A Critique of Sociology and Politics. New York: St. Martins Press.

Simmons, R.G., D.A. Blyth, E. Van Cleave, and D.M. Bush, 1979. "Entry into Early Adolescence: The Impact of Puberty, School Structure, and Early Dating on Self-Esteem," American Sociological Review 44, 6: 948–67.

Simmons, R.G. and F. Rosenberg, 1975. "Sex, Sex-Roles, and Self-Image," Journal of Youth and Adolescence 4: 229–58.

Speizer, J., 1981. "Role Models, Mentors, and Sponsors: The Elusive Concepts," Signs 5: 692–712.

Stallard, K., B. Ehrenreich, and H. Sklar, 1983. Poverty in the American Dream: Women and Children First. New York: Institute for New Communications.

Stericker, A.B. and L.A. Kurdek, 1983. "Dimensions and Correlates of Third Through Eighth Graders' Sex Role Self-Concept," Sex Roles 8, 8: 915–29.

Stipek, D.J., 1984. "Sex Differences in Children's Attributions for Success and Failure on Math and Spelling Tests," Sex Roles 11, 11/12: 969–81.

Tavris, C. and C. Offir, 1977. The Longest War: Sex Differences in Perspective. New York: Harcourt, Brace, Jovanovich.

Thorne, B., 1984. "Girls and Boys Together—But Mostly Apart: Gender Arrangements in Elementary Schools," in W.W. Hartup and Z. Rubin (eds.) Relationships and Development. Hillsdale, NJ: Lawrence Erlbaum.

Thornton, A.F. and D. Freeman, 1979. "Changes in the Sex-Role Attitudes of Women, 1962–1977, Evidence From a Panel Study," American Sociological Review 44: 831–42.

Thornton, A.F., D.F. Alwin, and D. Camburn, 1983. "Causes and Consequences of Sex Role Attitudes and Attitude Change," American Sociological Review 48, 3: 211–27.

U.S. Department of Commerce, Bureau of the Census, 1983. Statistical Abstract of the US 1983. Washington, DC: Government Printing Office.

Weber, M., 1947. Theory of Social and Economic Organization. Glencoe, IL: Free Press.

Weitzman, L., 1979. Sex- Role Socialization: A Focus on Women. Palo Alto, CA: Mayfield.

Weitzman, L., 1984. "Sex-Role Socialization: A Focus on Women," pp. 157–237 in J. Freeman (ed.) Women: A Feminist Perspective, 3rd ed. Palo Alto: Mayfield.

Weitzman, L., D. Eifler, E. Hokada, and C. Ross, 1972. "Sex Role Socialization in Picture Books for Children," American Journal of Sociology 77: 1125–50.

White, L.K. and D.B. Brinkerhoff, 1981. "The Sexual Division of Labor: Evidence from Childhood," Social Forces 60, 1: 170–81.

Wright, E.O., 1979. Class Structure and Income Determination. New York: Academic Press.

Zaretsky, E., 1976. Capitalism, the Family, and Personal Life. New York: Harper and Row.

CHAPTER 11

THE CAREERS OF WOMEN IN ACADEMIA

Robert T. Blackburn
Betty J. Holbert

When one compares the inroads made by women into various male-dominated professions, their progress in the professoriate may appear to be the success story of the past twenty years. On a number of dimensions—salary (especially at the entry level), percentage of the total academic work force, percent receiving Ph.D.s, and number of administrators—women have made, and are continuing to make, appreciable gains in academia. At the same time, their recent success may well portend future complications. One hears male department chairs saying that now that they have added a second female to accompany the token, affirmative action commitments have been met, and a return to "business as usual" is in order.

In addition, even the accomplishments just mentioned must be judged against additional criteria. There are other rewards in the academic career besides dollars and titles. Status—position vis-à-vis peers as determined by institutional affiliation, standing in the chosen scholarly discipline, and access to resources beyond those normally supplied by the individual's college or university—carries a higher value than does salary. Here the record of female success is less glittering. It is less certain that academic women will in the future acquire a status comparable to men's.

To assess the current state of female academics, judge the progress they have made, and estimate future trends, we will start with a human capital perspective. In a labor-intensive enterprise such as higher education, human resources are the most valuable commodity. The value of faculty as assets is unquestionable. What is less certain is the commitment of colleges and universities to the full utilization of all human resources, regardless of gender (Blackburn and Baldwin 1983).

While institutions are concerned with the broader use of human resources, faculties are made up of individuals who, in turn, bring with them certain productive skills, talents, and knowledge. This is generally defined as human capital (Thurow 1970). Human capital theory has been used as a partial explanation for occupational segregation. According to this perspective, existing gender differences in occupational rewards (e.g., salary, position) can be explained by differences in the skills, qualifications, and attitudes that men and women bring to the job market (Marrett 1985). Finkelstein (1984) embraces this explanation when arguing that in higher education, female faculty frequently differ from male faculty in both training and educational background. Unfortunately, he pays little attention to the methodological shortcomings of the studies he uses to support this thesis (Abel 1986). Evidence from other studies clearly negates the validity of the human capital perspective as a justification for the discrepant rewards of academic men and women. In her study of reward dualism in higher education, Fox (1981b) found that salary returns for women's and men's characteristics are different not only in payment level but also in structure of payment. These differences by sex are especially striking for achievements (experience, rank, and education). She concludes that women cannot expect to receive as great a payment as men for their education and rank attainment. The point is not that women's achievements are not rewarded, but that they are rewarded at a lower level than men's. These results are in agreement with the findings of Bayer and Astin's (1975) study. Analyzing data from a national survey of faculty, they found much higher correlations between publications and salary levels for men than for women. Further, even after controlling for both quality and quantity of publications, Cole (1979) found that women lag in academic rank. The statement by Lilli Hornig, executive director of the Higher Education Research Service, that "women are not promoted, paid or recognized for their accomplishments in the same fashion as men" (cited in Bruer 1984) is therefore based on solid evidence invalidating the human capital explanations. In addition, because of the minority status of women faculty in a male-dominated culture, there are performance pressures generated by the "token" status of females (Kanter 1977).

DEMOGRAPHICS

Many changes have taken place during the two decades since Bernard's (1964) early work on academic women. Demographic data document the production of Ph.D.s, the number of women in the professoriate, their salaries, employment locations, disciplines, and ranks. Salary, rank, and prestige of the employing college or university are status indicators. So is discipline, even if to a lesser degree.

Number of Ph.D.s

The production of Ph.D.s in American universities expanded at an enormous rate during the 1960s, more than doubling in a single decade. By 1970 over 32,000 Ph.D.s were awarded each year (Plisko 1983: 116). At that time just over 14% went to women, the highest percentage by far since 1964. Since 1970, the annual Ph.D. output has remained remarkably constant after its accelerated growth during the prior decade. The number has not fallen below 32,000, nor has it reached 35,000. There has been, however, a significant gender shift. The percent of women has steadily increased so that in 1980–81 (most recent figures) women earned 31% of the degrees, more than twice as many as they did 10 years earlier. While this figure is still well under 50 percent, such a gain appears to indicate a genuine accomplishment. An optimistic evaluation of this trend is dampened, however, by two considerations: (1) that women are being awarded degrees in the most overcrowded and least remunerative areas (English, foreign languages, education, and the most overcrowded social sciences), and (2) that they are entering academia at one of the worst times in terms of job opportunity and security (Fox 1984).

Number of Women Faculty

Turning to the data on academic positions, women's gains are observable, but not at a rate equivalent to the rate of increase of earned doctorates. In 1965 women were 18.2 percent of the full-time faculty (and 25.0 percent of the part-time staff) in institutions of higher education; in 1982–83 they were 27.0 percent of the full-time faculty (and 35.4 percent of the part-time staff) (National Center for Education Statistics 1983). What we have seen is that while women more than doubled their numbers in earning the required degree during the 1970s, they are concentrated in fields with limited opportunity, and their representation on the faculties of U.S. colleges and universities increased by less than 50 percent.

Where Female Academics Are Employed

As for place of work, women have made gains. One no longer finds the most highly rated doctoral departments without a single woman in a tenured position, as Rossi (1970) did in sociology departments two decades ago. Still, as one goes up the pecking order of the Carnegie (1976) classification of colleges and universities, the proportion of women decreases dramatically. The information from national statistics on the proportion of women in higher education hides the fact that only a small percentage are at the elite universities and a large percentage hold positions on community college faculties.

Graham (1978: 768) found that "the proportion of women on arts and science faculties at Harvard is 3 percent; at Yale, 1.6 percent; at Princeton, 1 percent; at Stanford, 5 percent; at Berkeley, 5.6 percent; at Chicago, 5 percent; and at Columbia, 5 percent." In his analysis of university hiring patterns, Szafran (1984: 119), using the Carnegie national survey of faculty, also found that the higher the national rating of the department, the fewer the number of women being hired. The status of academic women, then, as judged by place of work, has been minimally enhanced. As will be seen below, this failure to acquire many positions in the top-ranking colleges and universities has more than status consequences. Where one is employed affects future career development as well, especially in terms of access to resources.

Type of Job

As reported above, the number of women who are in part-time positions has nearly doubled. They are now over a third of all part-time faculty. Some women may wish less than full-time work for various reasons such as other commitments or the desire or need to be with children. However, this popular explanation of the concentration of women in part-time jobs is not likely to apply to academic women. Astin (1969), Zuckerman (1971), and Ferber and Kordick (1978) have documented that sex differences in career continuity of doctorates, academics, and professionals are very small. Given the high economic and personal costs of lengthy and highly competitive training, and the degree of commitment required for success, a part-time academic job offers a poor return for the investments made. Therefore it is more likely that for the majority of these women involvement in part-time jobs is more a function of available opportunities than personal preference.

The overrepresentation of women in these positions has serious implications because part-time faculty are second-class citizens, persons without a vote, without health care, with no retirement program and related fringe benefits. Most often they are also cheap labor and receive an inequitable fraction of what the full-time staff are paid (that is, if they work half-time they are frequently paid less than 50 percent of the full-time salary). Rarely do part-timers have access to even the very basic resources needed to develop a productive career—money for supplies, assistants, even travel to professional meetings. They are highly unlikely to have close working relationships with their full-time colleagues and hence will have diminished access to a mentor. Most important of all, part-time positions carry little job security. They are year-to-year appointments with no assurance of reappointment, even if a good project is launched. Part-timers are academic nomads. They frequently move from job to job, location to location, dissipating their time, energy, and professional dignity in the process (Fox 1984; Wilke 1979).

Salaries

The evidence on differential salary status of men and women is more complicated. To begin with, it is indisputable that women earn less. There is less agreement, however, on how much less and on whether or not the difference in pay is "justifiable." Most agree a number of factors enter into the determination of a faculty member's salary—e.g., rank, years of service, scholarly productivity, teaching effectiveness, and service. These need to be taken into account when examining salary differences.[1] But the weight each factor should receive is not universally agreed upon. Because in academia the evaluative criteria are not clear-cut, salary differentials are often explained away by introducing varying criteria and specifications (Fox 1984).

In contrast to others, Barbezat's (1985) study includes productivity measures and is based on a national sample.[2] She used the extensive data banks collected from two national studies of faculty, the 1968 American Council on Education/Carnegie Council and the 1977 Ladd and Lipset surveys. The first was done before the visible advent of affirmative action and resultant increase in the percent of women on faculties. The decade later survey was able to measure some of the consequences of affirmative action. Barbezat's economic analysis first determined the variables that best predict a male's salary—published articles and books, highest degree, academic field, years of experience, place of work. Then those same variables were weighted identically for females. That is, the actual salary for a woman with the same attributes as a man was compared to the male's salary. She found a salary difference against women of between 11.5 and 17.5 percent in 1968. The corresponding figures in 1977 were 5.5 and 11.5 percent.

In academe, then, as well as in other occupations, women earn less for the same performance. The discrepancy in academia, however, is much lower than that for the total working population (Time 1984). Barbezat's study suggests that the salary gap may be narrowing in colleges and universities. The good news of these demographics is the improvement that was made over the ten-year period. However, reports for 1982–83 show a 19 percent salary difference between male and female faculty matched by the relevant characteristics (Chronicle 1984a). This represents a reversal in the trend toward equity.

Academic Discipline

When it comes to academic discipline, women are still more prevalent in the lower-paying fields—English, Romance Languages, Nursing, Social Work, Education—the areas in which they have been historically visible (Fox 1984). It is true that the percent of women earning Ph.D.s in such disciplines as physics and mathematics is increasing,[3] but the numbers are small. The lower-paying disciplines—the humanities, for example—are also the ones with less available external resources. This means that competitions for grants and fellowships will be more intense, and the odds of those new to the occupation—women in this case—acquiring the resources needed to launch a career are likely to be low. This lack of financial support may partially explain why the time between the B.A. and Ph.D. is longer for women than for men in the humanities (but not in the natural sciences). Since women are disproportionately clustered in disciplines that pay less, have fewer job openings, and have less support available for professional development, a cautionary view of their future opportunities in academe is in order.

Academic Rank

Last, women continue to lag in rank. They still constitute a higher percent of the instructors and assistant professors than men do and, consequently, a lower fraction of the associate and full professor ranks. Evidence is lacking to sort out the reasons. One explanation is that women have not been in the system as long and hence will be found in larger numbers at the entry positions. Although time differential in the system is a genuine factor, it might not fully account for the unequal distribution within ranks. It may be that women keep getting added to the system but do not "succeed," that is, fail to get promoted and/or receive tenure. The revolving-door phenomenon clearly exists in higher education, but the extent to which it operates is simply not known.[4] In the only reported study on the issue, Blackburn and Wylie (1985) have found no difference between men and women in the tenure achievement rate. Their study, however, covered only a selected number of private liberal arts colleges and a limited time period (1979–1983), so their findings cannot be generalized.

CRITERIA FOR CAREER SUCCESS

Successful parity for women in the academic profession implies more than equity in numerical representation and salaries. Women must acquire equal reputational status through their achievements in the traditional academic tasks of teaching, research, and service.

Teaching

Teaching is the primary activity for faculty in all institutions, occupying 90 percent of a community college faculty member's time, two-thirds to three-quarters in liberal arts colleges and regional universities, and still more than 50 percent at research universities (Ladd and Lipset 1975). Despite the importance of the pedagogical role and the time given to it, an outstanding teacher does not acquire national visibility or a job offer from a first-rate institution on the basis of classroom performance. There are several reasons for this. First, a reputation for outstanding teaching rarely extends beyond the local institution (Lewis 1975). Second, the products of teaching are difficult to measure (Tuckman 1976), and standards for effective teaching vary between colleges and even departments (Wilson 1979). Lacking universal currency, teaching is a poor contributor to professional status (Fox 1985b). Moreover, a commitment to teaching is likely to impede the achievement of status since it will divert time and energy from tasks that are more highly valued.

Research

A national reputation can be acquired only through scholarly contributions to one's discipline. Published research brings visibility in the community of professional peers. The emergence of national demand for research in the early 1950s and its active promotion in the 1960s pushed research productivity to the center of the academic reward structure. Also, a far greater agreement about standards of excellence in research than in teaching makes it easier for researchers to strive for national reputations (Wilson 1979). Research findings are communicated through publications, and accordingly the most valued indicator of productivity in academia is number of publications (Katz 1973; Tuckman 1976; Tuckman and Hagemann 1976).

Because publication is a central criterion in the reward system of higher education, the investigation of gender differences in publication output is crucial for the assessment of sex discrimination in academia. While some studies find no gender differences in faculty publications (Simon et al. 1969; Holbert 1985), most report males outproducing females (Converse and Converse 1971; Astin 1978, 1981; Bayer 1973; Clemente 1973; Guyer and Fidell 1973; Centra 1974; Fulton 1975; Kirshstein 1976; Cole 1979; Helmreich et al. 1980). Some of the differences, however, may be a consequence of the sampling employed. For example, respondents in several of these studies represented faculty across institutional types and/or disciplinary combinations. In other studies only selected disciplines were sampled—sociologists (Clemente 1973), psychologists (Guyer and Fidell 1973; Helmreich et al. 1980; Over 1982), scientists (Cole 1979), or political scientists (Converse and Converse 1971). Studying productivity in the humanities, Centra (1974) controlled for discipline and found smaller, but still significant, differences in favor of males.

Some investigators who found large gender productivity differences caution that when the effects of some variables (such as the institution from which the Ph.D. was obtained, current place of work, and field) are removed or statistically controlled, publication differences became negligible (Clemente 1973; Guyer and Fidell 1973; Helmreich et al. 1980; Blackburn et al. 1978; Wanner et al. 1981; Over 1982). In other words, women's lower productivity is, in part, a function of their institutional and discipline location. Women tend to be located in les prestigious schools with fewer resources for research (and usually higher demands for teaching).

Also, because they are overrepresented in fields such as humanities, where the mode of publication is books rather than short articles, their aggregate output is artificially depressed (Wanner et al 1981).

When gender differences are not found to be significant, the power of the common predictor variables is greater for men than for women. For example, Holbert (1985), in her study of humanities professors at regional colleges and universities, found that for male tenured faculty, the best predictors of recent (three year prior to interview) publications were rate of publication at tenure review time and interest in research; recent publications were also correlated with rank. The factors were the same for women and men, but the accuracy of predicting high producers was twice as good for males as it was for females. Guyer and Fidell (1973) report a similar result, one which has led Reskin (1978: 1237) to conclude that "the greater indeterminacy of the female's productivity mirrors the higher unpredictability of their careers."

Service

Professional service and service to the university and community are the third component of academic performance. While activities such as refereeing papers for national journals, reviewing grant proposals, and holding office in national associations are highly correlated with publication productivity and are in fact a recognition of it (Fox 1985b), service to the university is seen in a different light. Committee work, although often unequally distributed, is often perceived as a routine, part of the faculty job requirements and undeserving of special rewards (Thorpe 1983). Further removed from what is valued in academia is the component of public service, since "merely being involved in public service is not a sufficient indicator of effectiveness" (Centra 1980: 135). This in spite of some evidence that universities expect public involvement by their faculties to strengthen their institutional credibility (Berte and Casella 1979; Costello 1979).

On the whole, service therefore is either valued as an indicator of scholarly success or not valued at all. To the extent that tenured women faculty are a small minority, demands to have a woman representative in all department and university committees mean that their committee load is likely to surpass that of their male colleagues. Given the dominant achievement criteria in academia, involvement in many committees represents a sterile diversion of time and effort.

In sum, research and publications are the activities most valued in academia and most conducive to rewards in terms of salary, promotion, and access to the more prestigious universities. Given the historical underrepresentation of women professors in higher education and the contemporary dominance of men in top ranks, women faculty have to prove themselves in an environment with rewards and resources controlled by men. Women do not have equal access to the "ways and means" for research productivity—collegial networks, funding opportunities, research assistants, and collaborative arrangements (Fox 1985b).

CONTEXTUAL REALITIES

Turning from the strict research literature to a more descriptive analysis of what women in the profession are probably facing can better illustrate the hazards and obstacles of female academics. In what reads like a set of Catch-22 scenarios, each of the following issues illustrates circumstances that might be experienced as gender-specific obstacles that women have to overcome.

Age

Two strong predictors of a high publication rate are early age in obtaining the Ph.D. and early age at time of first publication (Raymond 1967; Clemente 1973). Data gathered by Centra (1974) for 1950, 1960, and 1968 show that contrary to popular belief there is little difference in the mean age at which males and females earn their doctoral degrees. On the average, women are 36 and men 34 years old at the receipt of the doctorate. Although age at doctorate varies by field, only in the social sciences is the gender difference (women=35, men=31) larger than the overall two years. Examination of the age distribution reveals, however, an interesting pattern. In all fields a higher proportion of women than men got their degrees at age 25 or younger (although the size of this group is very small), yet, on the other hand, women are also overrepresented among the older groups (37–42 and over 43). So, at least for these cohorts, this pattern suggests that more women than men do their doctoral work either before or after raising a family. Given the association between early age at obtaining the doctorate and rate of publications, the older group (aged 37 or older), encompassing almost half of all Ph.D. female graduates (43 percent of the women versus 18 percent of the men), start their academic career with a clear disadvantage. This gender difference in age at graduation might also help to explain why there are smaller proportions of women than men among the prolific writers (Astin 1978; Bayer 1973; Cole and Zuckerman 1984; Ladd and Lipset 1976).

Furthermore, the persistence of gender division of labor even among professional couples (Radloff 1975; Savvy 1981) means that the group of women graduating at younger ages face obstacles to production that are gender specific. For those who raise a family the burden of child care is likely to fall more heavily on women than on their husbands. As we mentioned previously, academic women are unlikely to take time off to raise a family, and therefore they have to perform under conditions of competing demands. Astin's (1978) finding that married women publish more than single women is interpreted as a function of the greater access to collegial networks for those with academic husbands. Other studies have found, however, that women with children publish less than childless women (Cole 1979; Hargens et al. 1978). While Holbert (1985) found no difference in male/female publication rate by number of children, the important unexplored issue is the relationship between productivity and parenthood by career stage, that is, the timing of the events.

Graduate Experiences

In addition, important graduate program experiences are likely to be inferior for women. If women receive financial support, they are more often seen as the graduate assistant who stuffs newsletters into envelopes and answers the phone than they are as research assistants working with faculty on funded projects. Even in those instances when they escape the secretarial role, women are more likely to receive teaching rather than research assistantships, although the benefits of the latter in terms of publications and sponsorship are much greater. The evidence on the second-class citizenship of female Ph.D. students is quite extensive: faculty-student interaction is lower (Association of American Colleges 1982); encouragement of exchange of ideas weaker (Thorne 1979; Sternglanz and Lyberger-Ficek 1977; Speizer 1982); active faculty involvement in career direction less frequent (Holmstrom and Holmstrom 1974; Kjerulff and Blood 1973). Fox (1984) aptly describes the manifold consequences of these circumstances:

To understand the implications of this pattern, one must appreciate the pivotal consequences of faculty alliances in graduate education. For their favored students faculty members provide the research training and experience necessary for professional and intellectual development. They nominate preferred students for fellowships and awards and take stands for them in the perennial disputes surrounding qualifying examinations and degree requirements. They furnish professional visibility by introducing their protégés at meetings and conferences and by coauthoring papers and articles with them. Faculty selectively provide students the opportunity to pose important questions, solve problems, and set professional goals. Ultimately, faculty members help their favored students locate good jobs and place them on the road of career mobility. (Fox 1984: 246)

Institutional Expectations and Demands

Let us suppose that women wish to achieve equal status and are willing to play the game by the rules men have put in place (Menges and Exum 1983). What are typical institutional expectations and demands placed upon a woman faculty member solely because she is the minority person; and how do they affect the chances of her meeting the requirements for promotion and tenure?

Not atypically, the new female faculty member is requested to develop that course the department has been criticized for not offering—women in literature, women in history, or the sociology of women. Naturally, the new course will be an elective, not a required one, so enrollments might be a problem. Low enrollments can be interpreted as teaching failure. The rigor of a course that does not include the typical classical works might be questioned as falling short of departmental standards. (For a dramatic account of these and other similar situations, see Davidson's 1983 report of what happened to Vilma Hernandez.)

In addition to the Catch-22 situation that puts her pedagogical skills in question, affirmative action and the committee system can jeopardize her chances for success. Since every departmental and university committee is supposed to have a woman on it, and tenure track women are still a minority, they are likely to be overloaded with committee work. Time needed for scholarship and publications, the activity the department values, is consumed in nonrewarded activities. If she fails her tenure review, she may be criticized for her lack of judgment in "choosing" to waste her precious time in committee work—a typical "blame the victim" strategy.

Affirmative Action pressures on institutions of higher education result in the recruitment of more women students. Typically the token woman is assigned the responsibility of advising these women, so that she quickly has more than the average number of advisees. Even the women students who are not formally assigned to her turn to this female assistant professor when they have special problems. Again, the time she needs for what counts is lost. And again, if she fails the promotion review, she is likely to be blamed for carrying a burden that was imposed on her. Her commitment to students will be interpreted as an indicator of a misconception of what the role of a professor should be.

Furthermore, if she is in a doctorate-granting institution, women students will turn to her for chairing dissertations, or at least being on their dissertation committees. Dissertation guidance takes a tremendous number of hours. There is little a department chair or colleagues can do to protect her from this disproportionate burden, for no one wants to deny a student access to the faculty chair of her/his choice. Still, she will be blamed for being unable to avoid such demands. In conclusion, regardless of institutional constraints, she will be indicted for not having had the time to publish enough.

Mentor/Sponsorship Opportunities

Another Catch-22 is the female assistant professor's need for a sponsor in order to gain entry into the inner circle of resources. A sponsor can provide visibility in the professional networks—co-authoring a paper, arranging for her to be the presenter at a conference.

In addition, if one is not in the network, it is difficult to know in advance where research funding will become available. Without external dollars, one cannot hire research assistants. Without grants, one cannot buy out of some of the normal teaching responsibilities. And without these resources, completed research and published articles and books will be fewer. With below-average number of publications, it is more difficult to compete successfully for grants. Now we have come full circle.

Even the ablest women are treated as outsiders. In his story of how he discovered the structure of DNA and won the Nobel Prize, Watson never recognized Rosiland Franklin for having contributed the critical piece of evidence. He also described her as an uppish lab assistant to a male biologist when she was, in fact, in charge of her own project on DNA research (Sayre 1975: 19–20). Barbara McClintock was viewed as a troublemaker at the University of Missouri and was driven out by the dean only to be wooed back when it was learned that she had been nominated for membership in the National Academy of Sciences (Keller 1983: 85–86). (She did not return and never did secure a regular academic post.) Most recently, the fight of the famous social scientist Theda Skocpol with Harvard University on the issue of tenure exemplifies the persistence of such attitudes. Rossiter reports numerous incidents of the unequal treatment of women scientists. Among others, she quotes Nobel Prize winner Robert Millikan responding to an inquiry from the president of Duke University on how to build an outstanding physics department. Millikan writes:

> Also, in the internal workings of a department of physics at a great university I would expect the most brilliant and able young men to be drawn into the graduate department by the character of the men [sic] on the staff, rather than by the character of the women. (Rossiter 1982: 192–93)

Millikan goes on to say that if you have many undergraduate women, it might be all right to have a woman on the faculty to do some teaching, but not research.

Cole's (1979) claim that science is fair both in gender as well as in performance judgment is questionable. First of all, to believe that universal scientific criteria are universally applied is simply naive. Science is no less free from personal politics than is the Vatican. Second, even if and when finished work is judged without regard to gender of the author, women will not succeed at the same rate as men since the needed organizational resources are not equally available to them. As Fox (1985b) has demonstrated, the context of the work environment is inequitable. Even within the same type of institution (major research university, minor university, liberal arts college), women can have patterns of "heavier teaching loads, less access released time, fewer claims on in-house grants, limited opportunities for collaboration, and fewer administrative favors for travel funds and the like" (Fox 1985b: 271).

IMPLICATIONS

Kanter (1977) suggests that unless there is an increase in the numbers of minority members in certain powerful positions, there will be no change in the constraints imposed upon them. Since female faculty are in the minority, they seem to have two choices for survival: either they successfully imitate male models or based on exceptional achievements they might be permitted to chart their own career.

While the evidence is not direct, it seems that the women's movement, affirmative action, Title IX, ERA, and the related social and legal activity of the 1970s were the levers on the system that account for a large portion of the advancements women have made in the academic profession. However, the levers have not produced a complete leveling. As recently as February 1985, court action was needed to raise women's salary $500 to begin to erase pay inequities at the University of New Hampshire. Even with that increase, an admitted $1300 discrepancy remains (Chronicle 1984b). Ahern and Scott (1981), Astin and Snyder (1982), Levine (1979), and the National Research Council (1983) believe that relatively minor changes have resulted from affirmative action. However, Hyer (1985) presents case histories of three institutions which had successful affirmative action programs. In each case the president had a strong commitment to affirmative action goals, and his beliefs were supported with visible actions.

At the same time, the best colleges and universities are characterized by strong and powerful faculties. At leading institutions faculty have considerable say when it comes to who their colleagues are and will be. They set the standards for a new member; they search for that individual; and while they can only recommend to the administration which individual to hire (and cannot, themselves, actually offer a contract), the institution is unlikely to question their selection. A dean of a faculty does not have the power of a business executive when it comes to personnel. Saying we are an equal opportunity employer does not ipso facto trickle down to where the actual hiring and promoting take place.

In this instance the virtues of collegial governance might perpetuate the dominance of the majority group (men). A long record of accomplishment by a homogenous, male group is difficult to reform from within. Until such a time as there is a gender balance of composition and power, externally enforced change is most likely necessary. Even following the traditional search and review procedures, administrators can and must intervene. The able academic vice-president, provost, or dean can and must be ever vigilant and exercise the power of her or his office. It is important that organized action take place, that the president and the board monitor progress as well as demand it, and that the successes and failures be regularly and publicly displayed.

What is at stake, of course, is more than meeting affirmative action goals. When vital and creative people are kept out of the profession simply because of their gender, everyone suffers. Students are cheated by being denied superior teachers. Faculty are cheated by not having the most stimulating colleagues. The nation is cheated for it is not getting the best problem solvers it could have. The world is being cheated for critical new knowledge is not being generated at the rate or level that it could be. And, of course, when an individual is denied the opportunity for self-development simply because of her gender, she is being most severely cheated.

These, of course, are self-evident truths, ones faculties do not debate. Maybe they are not raised to consciousness as often and as forcefully as they need to be. If academic leaders wish to make their college or university the very best that it can be—and that is the principal goal of those in charge of our institutions—then they will be vigorously working to achieve full status and first-class citizenship for women in academe.

Notes

[1]Pay also differs across disciplines, institutional type, and reputation, by section of the country, and by gender mix in a unit (Fox 1981a, 1985a). Unionized institutions and colleges in a statewide system frequently have fixed pay schedules based on rank, degree, amount of schooling, and years of service. When there is no merit principle, salary differences by gender are small. Each of these factors makes across-the-board comparisons difficult.

[2]Bayer and Astin (1975) used a national data base, but over only a four year interval, 1968–1972.

[3]The large percent gain is deceptive since the numeric base was very low.

[4]Productivity is usually measured as number of scholarly articles or books published in the last three years. Sometimes citation counts or grants obtained are used as indicators.

References

Abel, E.K., 1976. "Review of American Academic Profession: A Synthesis of Social Scientific Inquiry since World War II by M.J. Finkelstein," Contemporary Sociology 15, 1: 127–29.

Ahern, N.C. and E.L. Scott, 1981. Career Outcomes of a Matched Sample of Men and Women Ph.D.'s: An Analytical Report. Washington, DC: National Academy Press.

Association of American Colleges, Project on the Status and Education of Women, 1982. "The Classroom Climate: A Chilly One for Women?" Washington, DC: Association of American Colleges.

Astin, H.S., 1969. The Woman Doctorate in America. New York: Russell Sage.

Astin, H.S., 1978. "Factors Affecting Women's Scholarly Productivity," pp. 133–57 in H.S. Astin and K.W.Z. Hirsch (eds.) The Higher Education of Women: Essays in Honor of Rosemary Park. New York: Praeger.

Astin, H.S., 1981. "Academic Scholarship and its Rewards," in M.L. Maehr and M.W. Steinkamp (eds.) Women in Science. Greenwich, CT: JAI Press.

Astin, H.S. and M.B. Snyder, 1982. "Affirmative Action 1972–82: A Decade of Response," Change 14: 26–31.

Barbezat, B.A., 1985. "Topics in Academic Labor Markets." Ph.D. Dissertation, University of Michigan.

Bayer, A.E., 1973. Teaching Faculty in Academe: 1972–1973. Washington, DC: American Council on Education.

Bayer, A.E. and H.S. Astin, 1975. "Sex Differentials in the Academic Reward System," Science 188: 796–802.

Bernard, J., 1964. Academic Women. University Park, PA: Pennsylvania State University Press.

Berte, N.R. and D.A. Casella, 1979. "Two Way Bridge Building at Birmingham-Southern," New Directions for Higher Education 27: 31–41.

Blackburn, R.T., C.E. Behymer and D.E. Hall, 1978. "Research Note: Correlates of Faculty Productivity," Sociology of Education 51: 132–41.

Blackburn, R.T. and R.G. Baldwin, 1983. "Faculty as Human Resources: Reality and Potential," in R.G. Baldwin and R.T. Blackburn (eds.) College Faculty: Versatile Human Resources in a Period of Constraint. San Francisco, CA: Jossey-Bass.

Blackburn, R.T. and N. Wylie, 1985. "Current Appointments and Tenure: Their Impact on New Faculty Careers." Paper presented at the Annual Meeting of the Association for the Study of Higher Education, Chicago, Illinois.

Bruer, J., 1984. "Women in Science: Toward Equitable Participation," Science, Technology, and Human Values 9: 3-7.

Carnegie Council, 1976. A Classification of Institutions of Higher Education. Berkeley, CA: Carnegie Council on Policy Studies in Higher Education.

Centra, J., 1974. Women, Men and the Doctorate. Princeton, NJ: Educational Testing Service.

Centra, J.A., 1980. Determining Faculty Effectiveness. San Francisco, CA: Jossey-Bass.

Chronicle of Higher Education, 1984a. (January 18): 20.

Chronicle of Higher Education, 1984b. (October 17): 4.

Clemente, F., 1973. "Early Career Determinants of Research Productivity," American Journal of Sociology 79: 409-19.

Cole, J., 1979. Fair Science. New York, NY: Free Press.

Cole, J.R. and H. Zuckerman, 1984. "The Productivity Puzzle: Persistence and Change in Patterns of Publication Among Men and Women Scientists," in M.W. Steinkamp and M. Maehr (eds.) Advances in Motivation and Achievement, Vol. 2. Greenwich, CT: JAI Press.

Converse, P. and J. Converse, 1971. "The Status of Women as Students and Professionals in Political Science," Political Science 4: 328-48.

Costello, T.W., 1979. "Service and Balance in the Comprehensive College and University," New Directions for Higher Education 27: 43-45.

Davidson, M., 1983. "Affirmative Action's Second Generation: In the Matter of Vilma Hernandez," Change (November/December): 42-46.

Ferber, M.A. and B. Kordick, 1978. "Sex Differences in Earnings of Ph.D.'s," Industrial and Labor Relations Review 21 (January): 227-38.

Finkelstein, M.J., 1984. "The Status of Academic Women: An Assessment of Five Competing Explanations," Review of Higher Education 7: 223–46.

Fox, M.F., 1981a. "Sex Segregation and Salary Structure in Academia," Work and Occupations 8: 39–60.

Fox, M.F., 1981b. "Sex, Salary, and Achievement: Reward-Dualism in Academia," Sociology of Education 54: 71–84.

Fox, M.F., 1984. "Women and Higher Education: Sex Differentials in the Status of Students and Scholars," in J. Freeman (ed.) Women: A Feminist Perspective. Palo Alto, CA: Mayfield.

Fox, M.F., 1985a. "Location, Sex-Typing, and Salary Among Academics," Work and Occupation 12: 186–205.

Fox, M.F., 1985b. "Publication Performance and Reward in Science and Scholarship," in J. Smart (ed.) Higher Education: Handbook of Theory and Research. New York: NY: Agathon Press.

Fulton, O., 1975. "Rewards and Fairness: Academic Women in the United States," in M. Trow (ed.) Teachers and Students. New York, NY: McGraw-Hill.

Gilligan, C., 1982. In a Different Voice: Psychological Theory and Women's Developmental Psychology. Cambridge, MA: Harvard University Press.

Graham, P.A., 1978. "Expansion and Exclusion: A History of Women in American Higher Education," Signs 3: 759–73.

Guyer, L. and L. Fidell, 1973. "Publications of Men and Women Psychologists," American Psychologist: 157–60.

Hargens, L., J. McCann and B. Reskin, 1978. "Productivity and Reproductivity: Fertility and Professional Achievement Among Research Scientists," Social Forces 57: 154–63.

Helmreich, R., J. Spence, W. Beane, G. Lucker and K. Matthews, 1980. "Making it in Academic Psychology: Demographic and Personality Correlates of Attainment," Journal of Personality and Social Psychology 39: 896–908.

Holbert, B.J., 1985. "Differences in Scholarly Productivity for Faculty Employed in Comprehensive Colleges and Universities." Ph.D. dissertation, University of Michigan.

Holmstrom, E. and R. Holmstrom, 1974. "The Plight of the Woman Doctoral Student," American Educational Research Journal 11: 1–17.

Horner, M.S., 1972. "Toward an Understanding of Achievement-Related Conflicts in Women," Journal of Social Issues 28: 157–76.

Hornig, L., 1979. Climbing the Academic Ladder: Doctoral Women Scientists in Academe. Washington, DC: National Academy of Sciences.

Hyer, P.B., 1985. "Affirmative Action for Women Faculty," Journal of Higher Education 56: 282–99.

Johnson, G.E. and F.P. Stafford, 1974. "The Earnings and Promotion of Women Faculty," American Economic Review 64: 888–903.

Johnson, G.E. and F.P. Stafford, 1977. "The Earnings and Promotion of Women Faculty: Reply," American Economic Review 67: 214–17.

Johnson, G.E. and F.P. Stafford, 1979. "Pecuniary Rewards to Men and Women Faculty," in D.L. Lewis and W.E. Becker (eds.) Academic Rewards in Higher Education. Cambridge, MA: Ballinger.

Kanter, R.M., 1977. "Some Effects of Proportions on Group Life: Skewed Sex Ratios and Responses to Token Women," American Journal of Sociology 82: 965–90.

Katz, D., 1973. "Faculty Salaries, Promotion, and Productivity at a Large University," American Economic Review 63: 469–77.

Keller, E.F., 1983. A Feeling for the Organism: The Life and Work of Barbara McClintock. New York: W.H. Freeman.

Kirshstein, R., 1976. "Sex Differences in the Academic Work Structure." Ph.D. dissertation, University of Massachusetts.

Kjerulff, K.H. and M.R. Blood, 1973. "A Comparison of Communications Patterns in Male and Female Graduate Students," Journal of Higher Education 44: 623–32.

Ladd, E.C. and S.M. Lipset, 1975. "How Professors Spend their Time," Chronicle of Higher Education (October 14): 2.

Ladd, E.C. and S.M. Lipset, 1976. "Sex Differences in Academe," Chronicle of Higher Education (May 10): 18.

Ladd, E.C. and S.M. Lipset, 1977. "Survey of 4,400 Faculty Members in 161 Colleges and Universities," Chronicle of Higher Education (November 21): 12, and (November 28): 2.

Lewis, L., 1975. Scaling the Ivory Tower: Merit and its Limits in Academic Careers. Baltimore: John Hopkins University Press.

Levine, D.O., 1979. The Condition of Women in Higher Education: A Decade of Progress, an Uncertain Future. ERIC Document ED 184 447.

Marrett, C.B., 1985. "Occupational Inequalities," Science 228: 484–85.

Menges, R.J. and W.H. Exum, 1983. "Barriers to the Progress of Women and Minority Faculty," Journal of Higher Education 54: 123-44.

National Research Council, 1983. Climbing the Ladder: An Update on the Status of Doctoral Women Scientists and Engineers. Washington, DC: National Academy Press.

Over, R., 1982. "Does Research Productivity Decline with Age?" Higher Education 11: 511-20.

Plisko, V.W., 1983. The Condition of Education. Washington, DC: National Center for Education Statistics.

Radloff, L., 1975. "Sex Differences in Depression: The Effects of Occupation and Marital Status," Sex Roles 1: 249-65.

Raymond, J.C., 1967. "Publications, Production of Knowledge, and Career Patterns of American Economists." Ph.D. dissertation, University of Virginia.

Rees, A., 1973. The Economics of Work and Pay. New York: Harper and Row.

Reskin, R., 1978. "Scientific Productivity, Sex, and Location in the Institution of Science," American Journal of Sociology 83: 1235-43.

Rossi, A.S., 1970. "Status of Women in Graduate Departments of Sociology: 1968-69," American Sociologist 5: 1-12.

Rossiter, M.W., 1982. Women Scientists in America: Struggles and Strategies to 1940. Baltimore: The Johns Hopkins University Press.

Sassen, G., 1980. "Success Anxiety in Women: A Constructivist Interpretation of its Source and its Significance," Harvard Educational Review 50: 13-24.

Savvy, 1981. The Savvy Survey of Executive Behavior. New York: Savvy.

Sayre, A., 1975. Rosiland Franklin and DNA. New York: Norton.

Simon, R., S. Clark and K. Galway, 1969. "The Woman Ph.D.: A Recent Profile," Social Problems 15: 221-36.

Speizer, J., 1982. "Students Should be Seen and Heard," pp. 401-04 in P. Perun (ed.) The Undergraduate Woman. Lexington, MA: Lexington.

Sternglanz, S.H. and S. Lyberger-Ficek, 1977. "Sex Differences in Student-Teacher Interactions in the College Classroom," Sex Roles 3: 345-52.

Szafran, R.F., 1984. Universities and Women Faculty: Why Some Organizations Discriminate More than Others. New York: Praeger.

Thorne, B., 1979. "Claiming Verbal Space: Women's Speech and Language in the College Classroom." Paper presented at the Research Conference on Educational Environments and the Undergraduate Woman. Wellesley College, Wellesley, Mass.

Thorpe, P., 1983. "Modes of Volunteerism in University Life," Exchange Networks. Washington, DC: The National Center for Citizen Involvement, p. 5.

Thurow, L., 1970. Investment in Human Capital. Belmont, CA: Wadsworth.

Time Magazine, 1984. November 12.

Tuckman, H.P., 1976. Publication, Teaching, and Academic Reward Structure. Lexington, MA: Lexington.

Tuckman, H.P. and R.P. Hagemann, 1976. "An Analysis of the Reward Structure in Two Disciplines," Journal of Higher Education 47: 447–64.

Wanner, R., L. Lewis and D. Gregorio, 1981. "Research Productivity in Academia: A Comparative Study of the Sciences and Humanities," Sociology of Education 54: 238–53.

Wilke, A., 1979. The Hidden Professoriate: Credentialism, Professionalism, and the Tenure Crisis. Westport, CT: Greenwood.

Wilson, L., 1979. American Academics: Then and Now. New York. NY: Oxford University Press.

Zuckerman, H., 1970. "Stratification in American Science," in E.O. Laumann (ed.) Social Stratification: Research and Theory for the 1970s. New York, NY: Bobbs-Merrill.

PART V

SOCIAL RIGHTS: HEALTH

CHAPTER 12

GOOD WOMEN AFTER ALL: CULTURAL DEFINITIONS AND SOCIAL CONTROL

Sue Fisher

There is a children's fairy tale in which a wicked queen asks a magic mirror each day to tell her who is the fairest woman in all the land. Each day the mirror assures her that she is the fairest. Although in everyday life individual women do not have magic mirrors, their definition of themselves is, at least partially, rooted in a cultural context. There are many cultural mirrors with ideological connections among them, and it is in this context that patients confronting a hysterectomy negotiate a sense of themselves as women. To do so they must resolve a conflict that revolves around conventional definitions of womanhood. There are norms which prescribe the proper roles for women as wives and mothers (Ehrenreich and English 1979; Chodorow 1978). To fulfill these roles women need their sexual and reproductive functions. Is a woman "good" only if she can reproduce? Not necessarily. If faced with a hysterectomy women <u>can</u> produce an alternative sense of self. However, being a "good" woman, even if no longer reproductive, is the opposite side of a coin which declares women "good" <u>only</u> if they reproduce. In both cases a woman's self definition is severely limited, revolving around her capacity to reproduce. Furthermore, her self-definition evolves in a cultural context which not only limits a woman's options but vests others with the power to define these options.

To see how women confronted by a hysterectomy constructed a sense of themselves, I interviewed a small group of women who had a common medical problem—an abnormal Pap smear.[1] I found that women whose reproductive capacity was left intact reported that a hysterectomy would have had severe identity consequences, while those whose childbearing capacity was terminated claimed that their identities had not been affected. Each group of women displayed their knowledge of a normative system that linked reproduction and identity, were aware of how reproductive norms were filtered through the context of their daily lives, and reflected the dominant medical attitude that after childbearing the uterus served no viable function.[2] These findings sparked my curiosity. If women are socialized to see themselves primarily in domestic roles and if these roles are supported by a cultural hegemony—an ideology that legitimates the existing social order—then why did the accounts of the women who received hysterectomies not reflect this dominant societal view and what roles did doctors play in shaping their perspectives?

INTERACTIONAL CONTEXT

In this chapter I simultaneously examine the relationship between norms as features of the common culture and norms as everyday interactional accomplishments. Social action and meaning are basic sociological concepts. Through time questions repeatedly have been asked about how individuals come to behave appropriately, and explanations have been generated which link norms or rules for behavior with action. Parsons (1951) accounted for this phenomenon by positing that individuals internalized a shared set of norms. For Durkheim (1938) it was a collective consciousness that was shared in an external and constraining social world.

These theorists lead us to believe that norms govern action— a position that has a long history of revisions and criticisms (see, for example, Gurwitsch 1964; Winch 1958; Wittgenstein 1953, among others). In this tradition Garfinkel and Cicourel have redefined and extended the concept of normative action. Garfinkel (1967) contends that individuals actively construct their behavior. Rather than being "judgmental dopes" who internalize a shared set of norms into their cognitive systems, individuals are "secret apprentices" ferreting from their daily interactions the information needed to act appropriately. While Garfinkel alludes to the context of action, he does not specify the relationship between norms and actual situations in the construction of behavior. Mehan and Wood (1975) call this neglect of the social situation in which behavior is constructed a "constitutive bias." Cicourel (1973) asks how individuals decide which norms are operating or relevant for the negotiation of social situations and concludes that general rules or policies (norms) must be interpreted within emergent, constructed action scenes. Meaning is constructed in this process of interpretation.

By posing cultural definitions of women in a reflexive relationship with the work women did to construct a sense of themselves, I was able to shed light on how the women in this study negotiated a sense of themselves—a negotiation that took place against a background of cultural definitions about women and their proper place in society. I analyzed the text of interviews conducted with twenty-one women referred to one of two outpatient clinics in the department of reproductive medicine in a large West coast teaching hospital.[3] The faculty clinic resembled a private practice in organization and was staffed by professors of reproductive oncology (cancer). The community clinic was organized much as are clinics for the indigent everywhere. Its patients were largely poor, minority women. In the faculty clinic during the research period no patients with abnormal Pap smears underwent hysterectomy. During this same period women were treated with hysterectomies in the community clinic.[4] Despite this difference, each woman's narrative had a similar quality. It was as if women who had either lost their ability to reproduce or were threatened with that loss faced themselves in a cultural mirror and asked: Mirror, mirror on the wall, if I can no longer reproduce can I be a woman after all?

There is some evidence to suggest that people when asked many not provide the "real" reasons for their behavior; there is, however, another well-established tradition which uses accounts as tools for understanding how individuals construct their social worlds (Scott and Lyman 1968; Weber 1947; Mills 1940). This work suggests that accounts and the motives they present are social. Women's narratives provide the data to explore how accounts and motives are also political: They are embedded in and are an embodiment of a capitalist economic system, a patriarchal culture and a male-dominated medical establishment.

THE MEDICAL CONTEXT

Patients did not negotiate a sense of themselves in a vacuum. Rather their negotiations took place in a particular setting—a medical setting. For the women that I interviewed, it was in this setting that they confronted their normal, taken-for-granted sense of self. They had an abnormal Pap smear and might need a hysterectomy. The possibility that they could lose their reproductive capacity created the opportunity for them to gaze into the mirror and to sort out their sense of themselves in its reflection. For the women who had hysterectomies, it was the doctor who held the cultural mirror and illuminated the cultural assumptions reflected in it. Whether doctors illuminated these assumptions or patients faced with a threat to their taken-for-granted sense of self questioned them, one thing is clear: Neither doctors nor patients generate image wholly of their own making. As cultural members many doctors share a world view which defines women—a view often shared by women. But for the women who received hysterectomies an additional set of assumptions seemed to be involved.

The dominant medical attitude supports the view that if the uterus is not being used for its intended purpose, reproduction, it might as well come out. If women reject marriage or motherhood, or if they have all of the children they want or need, then not only are their uteri unnecessary, but they are potentially disease producing as well. And furthermore, from the dominant medical perspectives these women are not diminished—physically, emotionally, or socially—by the loss of their reproductive capacity. Women are described as just as good, if not better, after their uteri have been removed (Fisher 1983; Scully 1980).

These positions are clearly stated in medical sources and have been widely referred to in nonmedical sources as well (see Fisher 1983; Scully 1980; Schiefelbein 1980; Larned 1977; Caress 1977). The ability to define reflects the institutional authority of the medical role. The institution of medicine vests its dominant actors, doctors, with the power to legitimate and the authority to reinterpret the dominant ideology about women.

The literature of medical sociology demonstrates that the practice of medicine is not, as Parsons (1951) claimed, ideologically neutral. The social context, which includes "...the world view of health professionals, the hierarchy of occupational power, and the dynamics of the world outside the walls of the treatment setting" (Krause 1977), affects not only the doctor-patient relationship but also patients' views of themselves and their lives. While illness may be physiological, the sick role (Parsons 1951), ideas about illness (Freidson 1970), and responses to symptoms (Mechanic 1968) are social. If while providing health care doctors can legitimate illness and either reinforce the dominant ideology or create alternative definitions, and if this power is not equally shared by women, then the practice of medicine is also political. If, as Zola (1972) points out, medicine is an institution of social control, then doctors are the protagonists—the agents of social control.

By reembedding the practice of medicine in its social context, connections between the institution of medicine and the capitalist economy, of which it is a part, become more evident. While capitalism and profits in medicine are not the only source of the problems which plague women's health care, as can be seen in the lack of gender-neutral medicine in socialist societies, the "big business" approach to health care intersects with patriarchal values to place women in double jeopardy. Doctors are cultural members and as such share the dominant cultural view of women. They are also largely men trained as surgeons and primarily in fee-for-service practices. It should come as no surprise, then, that as the birth rate falls there is a concomitant rise in Caesarean section and hysterectomy rates or that these practices are supported by the dominant ideology.

Connections between the male-dominated economic system and the institution of medicine are evident in other ways as well. As Navarro (1976) points out, the medical hierarchy, shaped like a pyramid with a relatively small group of predominantly higher class, white (male) physicians at the top, mirrors the class structure of society. Just as access to professional hierarchies is tied to location in the system of social stratification, so too is access to health care. Despite a rhetoric broadcasting equality, we have a dual health care system—one for the indigent and one for those able to pay. And despite repeated calls for reform, the medical establishment (the pharmaceutical, insurance, and medical suply industries as well as hospitals, nursing homes, physicians, and newer corporate medical conglomerates) repeatedly has demonstrated an amazing resistance to change (Waitzkin 1983). In the name of free enterprise quality health care as a human right is continually sacrificed in the interest of profit. And we remain the only Western industrialized nation without some system of national health insurance (Bodenheimer et al. 1974).

The doctor/patient relationship is no more immune to the contradictions of a male-dominated capitalist economy than is the medical establishment. For example, Waitzkin (1983), in examining discourse between doctors and patients, found that symptoms are differentially legitimated for men and women and that the differences are related to their real or perceived labor force participation. When talking with a male patient, symptoms were legitimated and illness was defined in accordance with the patient's ability to perform his role as a worker. However, for women symptoms and the legitimation of illness were defined in accordance with the patient's ability to perform her domestic role.

While Waitzkin related the implications of his findings to the practice of medicine in a capitalist society, he did not draw out the implications for women. Ehrenreich and English (1979) do. After examining the advice "experts" have given women over a period of 150 years, they argue that although the advice has not been particularly scientific, it has been remarkably consistent: The advice of the experts has consistently echoed the dictates of the economy and supported male domination.

THE CULTURAL CONTEXT

While for some history supports an analysis that links a capitalist economic system with the roles women are needed to play in production and/or reproduction, for others capitalism may be a necessary but not a sufficient explanation. For example, Brown (1981) argues that along with the shifts from home to industrial production and from competitive to monopoly capitalism, came a shift from private to public patriarchy. As she defines these terms:

> The private patriarchy includes the individual relations between men and women found in the traditional family, in which the individual husband has control over the individual wife, her daily reproductive labor and the product of her labor, the children. But patriarchy is not just a family system. It is a social system which includes and defines family relations. It is in the social system that we find the public aspects of patriarchy: the control of society—of the economy, polity, religion, etc.—by men collectively, who use that control to uphold the rights and privileges of the collective male sex as well as individual men. (Brown 1981: 240)

In a similar vein, Fee (1983) suggests that the social control associated with medical domination is a kind of "extended patriarchy." In Brown's terms medical relationships like family relationships (the authority of doctors like the authority of husband/fathers) are shaped in the context of a patriarchal social system—a system that simultaneously supports the rights and privileges of men as a group as well as individual men. Using somewhat different language, Fee argues that medical domination functions to reinforce male domination, a domination all too visible through history.

It was medicine in the nineteenth century that declared middle- and upper-class women too weak to think and reproduce at the same time, while lower-class women were seen as animal-like in their ability to work and reproduce. For women of the higher classes the uterus was at war with the brain for a limited supply of energy; education, it was claimed, would interfere with the development of woman's reproductive system and, hence, her ability to bear children. From puberty on, elite women were described as emotionally high strung and sickly. The cure, rest and isolation, led to a life of invalidism (Ehrenreich and English 1979; Ruzek 1978; Barker-Benfield 1976). For women of the lower classes there was no rest. And always there was the ever-present physician to "help" women over the rough spots. Once hospitals were developed and medical education associated with them, poorer women became teaching material in exchange for medical "help." Women of the upper classes were helped in a different way. As the birth rate continued to fall among the upper classes, it was physicians who led the fight against abortion and birth control. It was physicians' efforts that resulted in the Federal Comstock Law which prohibited sending "obscene" material through the mail. With physicians' "help" all women were denied access to abortion and to contraception. And their "help" didn't stop there (Luker 1984; Mohr 1978; Gordon 1974).

Menstruation became a medical problem to be "treated" with a rest cure, and pregnancy and childbirth were diseases. All three required the care of physicians. Menopause, too, was a disease—a disease which signaled the symbolic end of a woman's meaningful life—while masturbation was an evil to be rooted out surgically by removing the clitoris and/or the clitoral hood. But by far the most popular medical procedure of the nineteenth century was the removal of the ovaries. Touted as a cure-all, it was prescribed for many supposed ailments including controlling women's behavior. It was believed that by removing a woman's ovaries she was made more tractable and womanlike (Ehrenreich and English 1979; Ruzek 1978; Barker-Benfield 1976).

It is argued that while the male medical establishment legitimated and enriched itself as it diseased women's bodies, there were additional motivations. Barker-Benfield (1976) points out that the interest of doctors and those of the male dominated society were in accord. Both wanted to control women by controlling their reproductive capacity (cf. Ruzek 1978). And Daly suggests why. Men responded to the first wave of feminism with a violent, "medical enforcement of the sexual caste system" (Daly 1978: 227).

Is history repeating itself? Has the contemporary women's movement challenged men's hegemony in the public sphere? If so, why? Haven't women always worked? As more women emerge from the private sphere of home and family, are they just more visible? Or is the threat to be found in women's demand for equality—not men's work and women's work, but the best person for the job and equal pay for equal work? Is there a parallel between the Comstock Law of the nineteenth century and the movement in the twentieth century by the New Right for a constitutional amendment to ban abortions? Is there an attempt to reinforce the sexual caste system?

If, as Fee (1983) suggests, medical domination is a kind of "extended patriarchy" then the "help" of the medical profession in the nineteenth and twentieth centuries can be understood as a way for the profession to maintain itself while sustaining a male dominated society. This understanding is supported by Daly, who argues that the dominant, who she refers to as "Mind Managers," oppress women to maintain the patriarchal patterning of society. She claims that:

> Mind Managers are able to penetrate their victims' minds/ imaginations only by seeing to it that their deceptive myths are acted out over and over again in performances that draw participants into emotional complicity. Such re-enactments train both victims and victimizers to perform uncritically their preordained roles. (Daly 1978: 109)

Daly goes on to point out that gynecological practices of the nineteenth and twentieth centuries are only one example of the enactment of "deceptive myths." She outlines several others: Indian suttee (or the burning of widows with their dead husbands), Chinese footbinding, African genital mutilation, and European witch burning. And in each case women are drawn into complicity, believing that to do otherwise would proclaim them unnatural women. From this perspective the perpetuation of patriarchal notions about women and their proper place in society can be understood as strategies for explaining, justifying, legitimating, and enforcing prevailing conditions.

THE MANAGED MIND

Fourteen of the women I interviewed received treatments other than a hysterectomy—treatments that preserved their reproductive capacities. I asked these women how they thought they would have felt if their treatment had been a hysterectomy. Their answers speak eloquently, displaying in the process a cultural hegemony which legitimates women's domestic roles (wife and mother). Several of the women described themselves as less whole in either a biological or physiological sense. One woman said, "I don't think I would feel like a woman, you know, I'd feel hollow inside." Later she said:

> I don't know, I think it would have decreased everything,...that's why I really didn't want to do it [have a hysterectomy] and plus I really would, to me I wouldn't feel like a woman, I don't think.

Two other women expanded on this theme. One of them responded by saying:

> Uhm, I'm not sure, but I've heard a lot of very negative things about a hysterectomy. Uhm, I have a friend who's gone through a hysterectomy and she is still—something's off, and she feels it, and she's been to see a psychiatrist who basically said she seems to be fine. Uh, I think there's something that happens to the body when a part of the organ, and especially a vital part like that for a woman, is taken out, and I think it just messes up the balance, and I don't think it's something that psychologically can be fixed.

She continued:

> Uh, that's where life starts. I mean, that's where the whole thing is for women. That's what defines a woman and makes her a woman, and when you take that away something else has got to be affected in the body.

The other said:

Well, just the fear of not being a total woman anymore—I've heard a few, quite a few people tell me this who have had hysterectomies. I've talked to a few girls who had abnormal Pap smears and this has led into this, you know, having to have hysterectomy, and they said that they really went through a psychological thing at the time, but then it passes.

She continued by explaining what the basis of the psychological trauma was for women, and in so doing expressed her own concerns. She explained:

Uhm, I guess once your uterus is gone, then you feel you're not really what you're here on earth for—to have children. Maybe that's—you know, you're not a whole person anymore.

For these patients womanhood was defined by their capacity to bear children. Their responses displayed how totally their definition of themselves as women was identified with their ability to reproduce. From feeling hollow inside or upsetting some delicate balance (a balance that could no be redressed psychologically), to not feeling like a woman, these patients claimed that having children was what women were on earth for; what made them women. For other women the response was somewhat less global. They claimed that having a hysterectomy affected their sexuality or their sex appeal. One woman said:

Well, listening to what you hear in the streets, I think I would have felt less sexy. I would still feel that the way I am now when it comes to having sex, you know, kinda—I think there would be mental block there the first time just to see what it was like.

Another said:

There are some who say that if, if it [the uterus] is removed, then they don't feel the same effect—how do you say? I don't know...that they no longer wish to be with their husband. I don't believe so, but who knows? I'm not in their place, right? But I don't believe so. It is a matter of reasoning.

Another said:

I don't have any idea why, something to do with attracting the opposite sex. I don't know, I really don't know. I really don't understand a lot about that anyway.

And still another:

Because, like, well, okay, if I'd had my ovaries left...my female hormones would be my own. Then it wouldn't have affected me that much. But the whole idea of sexiness has to do with your ability to bear children. Somehow, I don't know, I know it's an instinct which is hard to define, but I know that if I couldn't get pregnant and a part of it [sex] for me, uh, excitement of the whole thing would be gone.

Earlier in the interview the patient compared how she felt after treatment with how she thought she would have felt if the treatment had been a hysterectomy.

Uh, if I felt like—if I had a hysterectomy, it would have sort of changed my sex, uh, my idea of my own sex appeal. But, like, a conization,[5] it really didn't tamper with my body at all, and I'm just the same.

These responses were characterized by less certainty. The women spoke about sexual difficulties, from a mental block the first time, to a lack of sexual appetite or a loss of sex appeal. Yet there was also a hint of control. Sexuality was something over which at least one woman did not feel totally powerless. For her, sexual response was a "matter of reason." The woman who spoke most clearly, who did not allude to what she had heard on the street or from other women, said that her sexuality was linked to her ability to conceive. That was where the excitement was for her. To have lost that ability would have changed her conception of herself as a woman—changed her sex—as well as confidence in her sex appeal. The next two patients most specifically linked their identities to the context of their daily lives. The first woman said:

If I'd had a hysterectomy, it's very hard for me to say, because a lot of people feel very offended. It's like, if I was going to have a hysterectomy right now what would it do to me? Right now, being alone, it probably wouldn't do too much to me, but it was the idea. If I had somebody else that

I had to say, "Gee, are you gonna accept me this way, or not?" I might feel differently. You know, if I had an—if you don't....This person that I have met, that I really like, is a doctor. He happens to be a doctor and his idea—that we've talked about it. I explained to him about having, you know, the test run, the freezing,[6] everything. And I only know him for a very short time, and now he's out to sea, and he'll be gone for eight months. And, uh, he made a couple of comments just off the top of [his] head that really hit hard. "If you were having a hysterectomy," he said, "I wouldn't be with you now."

At this point she trailed off. I prompted, "Because?" and she continued:

Because he wants somebody that can raise children whether it's me or somebody else. He has a very strong feeling to this now.

The next woman said:

Hmm, it would just make me regret even more having the abortion. But seeing how I couldn't do nothing about it, I don't think that personally I would let it worry me sick.

These women linked their feelings about themselves to events in their lives. For one woman the threat of a hysterectomy called up a recent abortion. While she claimed that she could not do anything about the regret she felt and would not let it worry her sick, I wondered whether she perceived her abnormal Pap smear and the threat of a hysterectomy it brought with it as a kind of retribution for prior misconduct—unmarried sexual intercourse, allowing herself to conceive, or choosing abortion. For the other woman comments made by a man she was interested in were named as the reason for her concern. Comments she said "really hit hard." She was divorced, had a young child, and wanted to remarry. She claimed that the man she was interested in told her that if she could no longer reproduce he would not stay in the relationship. Perhaps because she already had a child the loss of her reproductive capacity did not seem to threaten her as much as not being "chosen" again did. Her ability to bear and rear children was an asset that made her good marriage material at least with her current relationship—an asset that she did not want to lose.

There is an extensive literature that argues that women see themselves primarily as wives and mothers. Most recently Nancy Chodorow's (1978) psychoanalytically based analysis argues that the social relations of women's mothering reproduces in their daughters an ability to nurture and a desire to mother and produces in their sons a rejection of all that is feminine in themselves and in society. Furthermore, because mothers identify with daughters more than with sons, and because daughters are able to reciprocate this identification and sons are not, female children as they mature retain relatively permeable "ego boundaries." Women's sense of self is not as distinct from other peoples as is men's. They tend more than men to fashion their identities by reference to others and to maintain an ability to empathize.

Throughout the history of Western thought women's identities have been linked primarily with their domestic roles (Barker-Benfield 1976; Bullough 1974). This linkage generates a "sex-negative" attitude which permeates our history and is reflected today in women's roles and in their views of themselves (Bullough and Bullough 1977). Historically, marriage and childbearing have legitimated sex while emphasizing the "proper" role for women as subordinate to men. These works are social histories; however, their findings are supported by sociologists as well.

There are several seminal studies which argue that marriage and motherhood are the self defining characteristics of women's lives. During adolescence young women learn to conform. They learn that competition and aggression are not for them. Such unfeminine behavior could threaten the potential to achieve their desired goals (Komarovsky 1953). Once they have married and had children there is pressure to expand no further (Oakley 1980; Chodorow 1978; Lopata 1971; Rossi 1964). Those who have the greatest difficulty relinquishing the motherhood role are women who have most fully followed these role prescriptions. For them the "empty nest" of their middle years generates an identity crisis (Bart 1970). A crisis exacerbated in a society which places so much emphasis on youth and physical beauty (Lakoff and Scherr 1984; Orbach 1982; Chernin 1981; Sontag 1972).

While there is ample evidence that the traditional roles of wife and mother have been diminishing in Western industrial societies in recent decades, there is no evidence that they have disappeared. Women can choose not to parent. They are not just passive victims of societal mandates. Yet, as Chodorow (1978) argued, so long as women are the primary caretakers of children, the desire to mother will be reproduced in female offspring generation after generation. And by all accounts women are still the primary caretakers of most children. The strength of the motherhood role is dramatically expressed by the women who actively seek technological intervention—fertility testing, hormone therapy, artificial insemination, and in vitro fertilization—as well as by the women who offer themselves as surrogate mothers (Corea 1985; Arditti et al. 1984). Certainly, the accounts of the women threatened by the loss of their reproductive capacity suggest that despite the Women's Movement and women's increasing labor force participation, the motherhood role remains quite salient. The accounts display how these women constructed a sense of self around their ability to reproduce. And there is every reason to believe that the accounts provided are not idiosyncratic. Since reproductive capacity seems so important to woman's sense of self, how then can we understand the accounts of the women who received hysterectomies and lost the capacity to reproduce?

THE REFLECTED IMAGE

Seven of the women I interviewed had hysterectomies. I told these women that I would like to understand what, if anything, their hysterectomy meant to their sense of themselves and asked them what they might say in a private conversation to another woman about to go through the same procedure. In response six of the women reported that the hysterectomy had produced no changes in their lives or in their sense of themselves as women, and one told a different story. Although most of the women's reports affirmed that a hysterectomy was of little consequence to their sense of themselves, embedded in their accounts was evidence of the norms that link women's identities with their capacity to reproduce. Two women provided the same kind of global accounts that several of the women who had not received hysterectomies had spoken about. The first woman said:

> Well, I don't know, because everybody's different. If she [the hypothetical woman facing a treatment like hers] didn't want kids and if she was just scared about the operation, I'd tell her my experience, you know, nothing hurt. But, I mean, not everybody's the same.... And, uh, I believe that since I didn't want any more kids, I didn't have the feeling of being inadequate and less [of] a woman.

I asked whether she thought she would have felt differently if she had not already had children, and she responded:

> Oh, yeah...I mean, that's like never, never can have any. It's the final—uhm, I'd have felt terrible.... Never, to want something and just never able to have one. I'd feel like...I'd feel bad. Adopting wouldn't do it.

The second woman said:

> Well, in all of this the sexual relations have a great deal to do with this, right?... Well, my husband and I have not had relations in more than three years, because of his condition...I feel, well, it might be that the only thing I want to reach in life is that I be in condition to help my family. At this age one doesn't matter, not now. One's family is the important thing, the children, the husband, the house, because like in my problem...in my state, well, I have to do things that I did to see how the household goes, administer it, how the children are getting along, how everything goes. So that's what is the most important. I'm no longer important.

The first woman made a very clear distinction between being afraid of the operation and of its potential consequences. The operation, she claimed, did not hurt, and she had been very afraid that it would. She could reassure another woman about the operation itself. But, while she felt just the same about herself after the surgery, she could not assure another woman of the same outcome, and for her the critical distinction was whether or not the woman wanted children. This woman had all of the children she wanted; but when she imagined herself wanting a child or more children, she thought the operation would have made her feel "terrible." And adopting would not have helped. It is in this connection that the strength of the cultural hegemony about women is displayed in an account that ostensibly denies this notion. A similar connection is found in the second woman's account.

While the second woman claimed that the hysterectomy had no direct impact on her life, she simultaneously displayed her knowledge and acceptance of women's traditional roles. She acknowledged the importance of sex and in so doing implicitly restated the fear so prevalent in the Mexican-American community—fear that a hysterectomy would interfere with her ability to perform sexually. For her this is not a problem because her husband has been too ill for the past three years to claim his sexual prerogative. While she no longer saw herself in terms of her sexuality or her ability to reproduce, her commitment to traditional roles is all too evident. She told me quite clearly that as a person she was no longer important; it was as a mother, wife, and housewife that she was of value. For three other women the response was much less global. One woman focused almost exclusively on her sexuality; the others talked about being able to control conception. The first woman said:

> No, I feel the same.... I would tell her [a hypothetical patient with the same medical problem] not to worry, because, I mean, I hadn't been through it before and for that reason I felt frightened. But since I've been through it, I know now that it would be good for her [in her best interest].... No, I am not afraid [of feeling older]. On the contrary, I am grateful that I won't be having more children, we really can't afford it.

The next woman said:

> Everything is the same as before.... I hear them [her women friends] saying that a woman who doesn't have her uterus is hollow, that she's this or that or the other thing.... So I said to myself, how can they believe that [sex] isn't or it is going to be the same. It is something quite apart from the uterus.... I tell my friends from here one is better off. It's true.

And the other woman said:

> No more periods each month, that's one thing.... No birth control pills.... Uhm, I would say that I feel the very same as I did before I went into the hospital.

While each of these women proclaimed that they felt the same as before their surgery, they also displayed a knowledge of the importance of reproduction and sexuality to a woman's self concept. The first two women picked up themes that have already been discussed. In the first account the woman claimed that she could reassure another woman about the operation <u>and</u> about the consequences. Since she was relieved not to be able to have any more children, she seemed to assume that other women would be too. Somehow her sense of self appeared to be protected. It was not that she did not want any more children or that she had chosen to end her reproductive capacity. She could not afford any more children and was convinced that her hysterectomy was medically necessary.

The second woman was one of the youngest women in the sample to be treated with a hysterectomy. And although she had heard the women's lore about hysterectomy and sexual responsiveness, she refused to believe it, claiming that sexuality was "quite apart from the uterus." Perhaps her ability to redefine her sexuality was tied to the context of her life. Although she had been married and had children, she was now divorced and sexually active.

The last woman spoke about her relief that menstruation and birth control were no longer any concern for her. Again the context of her life may provide some clues as to how she was able to construct an alternative sense of self. First, perhaps she stood in a different position in regard to her sexuality and capacity to reproduce than did the other women who received hysterectomies. A clue for this interpretation resides in her mention of birth control. None of the other women who were treated with a hysterectomy mentioned feeling relieved that they would no longer have to control their ability to conceive. Second, while she was now divorced and sexually active, she had been married and had had three children. Perhaps, unlike the women discussed earlier who were threatened with but did not receive hysterectomies, she had had all of the children she wanted and no longer linked her sexuality with her ability to reproduce.

Each of the patients discussed thus far, while acknowledging traditional norms about women and their proper roles, constructed an alternative definition of herself. One woman was unable to do this. She said:

> The story is over for us [referring to their sex life].... I feel unserviceable, useless, useless,... Before the operation I didn't feel that I was aging. Because I had, well, all—all my uterus and my ovaries.... Now I feel older.... I feel sad.

The woman who spoke to me this way was a 63-year-old Mexican-American woman who over the course of her marriage had given birth to many children, thirteen of whom were still living. She certainly had fulfilled the expectations associated with being a woman. She had been married to the same man for many years, and they had borne and raised a large family together. At least in traditional terms, she was a success as a wife and mother. Why then did she report that after her hysterectomy she felt older and sad? Why did she tell me that her sex life had ended with the hysterectomy? These questions raise another one of broader scope. How can we make sense of the reports of the women who retained and those who lost their capacity to reproduce?

LIFE AS A LOOKING GLASS

At first glance it seems paradoxical that the women who did not have hysterectomies reported that their sense of themselves would have been severely damaged had they undergone that surgery. And only one of the women who had that surgery described any changes in her feelings about herself. The other women who received hysterectomies all confirmed that their sense of themselves had not been damaged. Yet, the paradox is not so paradoxical after listening to the women's accounts. Each account displayed how a woman threatened with a hysterectomy negotiated a sense of herself against a background of the dominant cultural values about women. Perhaps the women who retained their reproductive capacity were better able to see and report on these cultural norms because their reproductive ability was still intact. Perhaps most of the women who received hysterectomies were able to distance themselves from this norm and in so doing come to see themselves in different ways. Perhaps the woman who described herself as "unserviceable and useless" after a hysterectomy was unable to distance herself. For her the norms which so strongly link women's identities to their ability to reproduce remained all too salient.

A process of negotiation similar to the one that I am suggesting has been reported on in another study. Shumsky and Mehan (1974) described the structure of accounts and showed how individuals engaged in comparisons and justifications to produce descriptions. Comparisons occurred in both concrete and hypothetical situations and provided a way of comparing self, situation, or object with a real or hypothetical other. The women who received hysterectomies drew real comparisons. They compared how they felt pre- and post-surgery. Justifications occurred only in describing hypothetical situations and provided the grounds upon which the description rested. The women who were threatened with, but did not receive, hysterectomies described hypothetical situations and justified how they thought they would have felt.

The women who retained their reproductive capacity referenced a whole set of norms as grounds, or justifications, for their answers. They used a model which prospectively matched the anticipated situation (a hysterectomy) with the appropriate norms in a context that was hypothetical, not real. They could· project themselves into a future (hypothetical) state, compare themselves with an idealized woman, and generate a list of the cultural standards we all know and take for granted. The women who lost their capacity to reproduce took a different stance in regard to these norms. They did not prospectively match an anticipated future even with a set of norms that are known and taken for granted. They retrospectively described a real event. Their identity had been called into question. If they accepted the prevailing norms, they might come to see themselves as no longer "good" women. Their other option was to generate a way of seeing themselves which acknowledged these norms while also providing an alternative, emergent justification allowing them to see themselves more positively. All but one of the women who had a hysterectomy did just this. The one who did not found herself to be not a good woman after all.

Accepting that a process such as this one may have been going on provides insight into how women could construct emergent definitions of themselves. But it in no way tells the whole story. In important ways the life contexts of these two groups of women were very different.· If they filtered their definition of themselves through a lens which put into focus where they stood in regard to the dominant cultural norms, two very different pictures would be projected. On the average the women who did not receive hysterectomies were younger. Their average age was 27.6 years. Eight of these fourteen women were Caucasian, seven had no children, and four had only one child. Of these eleven women (seven with no children and four with one child), none was married at the time of the interview. They were either single, divorced, or widowed; and eight of them had either aborted previous pregnancies or given a child up for adoption.

By contrast, the women who lost their capacity to reproduce were older. Their average age was 39.3 years. Five of the seven women were Mexican-American, and all of them were poor. None of these women was childless. The average number of children among them was 5.4 (compared with an average of 1.7 children in the other group). Three of the women were married, and each of them had several children (5, 4, and 13 respectively), while four of them were divorced with children (6, 6, 3, and 1 respectively). None of the married women, but three of the four divorced women, reported having had abortions, and all of the divorced women claimed to have completed their families.

Looked at against the background of these life conditions, we can speculate about how the accounts of both groups of women tell a slightly different story. The women who had hysterectomies were older and, whether married or divorced, could see themselves as having satisfied the cultural dictate to be fruitful and multiple. By age alone most were past their reproductive prime of life and had more than average-size families. Even the woman with only one child reported that she had finished her family. For some the ability to see a hysterectomy positively may have been related to their earlier abortions. Abortions are not pleasant. If they had been used to limit family size, it would be easy to see how a hysterectomy and the permanent protection from conception it provided could be interpreted positively. For married women with large families sex must have often meant babies, and, given their poverty, babies could easily mean hardship. Similarly, in our society menstruation could be seen as unpleasant (Clay 1977; Weideger 1977). We learn to view the menses negatively. We learn that it is a "curse" we bear monthly. Given the conditions of these women's lives, it is no wonder that most of them could be aware of the norms about womanhood while defining themselves differently.

By contrast the women who retained their capacity to reproduce were younger. By age alone they were still in their reproductive prime of life. Most of these women were unmarried and had small families if they had children at all. Their inability to see a hysterectomy positively may have been colored by their prior reproductive histories, which were characterized by abortions. Perhaps women who have had an abortion or put a child up for adoption may have performance anxiety about their future ability to conceive. Unlike the women who received hysterectomies, these women may not have felt satisfied. They neither had all the children that they wanted nor had they fulfilled societal expectations about marriage and motherhood. It is likely that they wanted to marry, or marry again, and to have or to increase their families. In this context they could easily have seen their ability to reproduce as a highly marketable quality and to imagine that without it they might gaze into the cultural mirror, ask the magic question, and find that they were not marriageable—not good women after all.

The accounts of these women demonstrated their knowledge of a normative system that linked reproduction to identity while at the same time illustrating how these norms were filtered through the context of their daily lives, but the whole story is not yet told. Each of these women had an abnormal Pap smear, each was referred to a medical setting for diagnosis and treatment, and for each the potential, or real, loss of reproductive capacity set the stage for their negotiations. For the women who were treated with a hysterectomy,[7] medical practitioners played a pivotal role. It was they who held the cultural mirror into which the patients gazed.

THROUGH THE MEDICAL LOOKING GLASS

Medical encounters are interactions between individuals, but the interactants—doctors and patients—are not equal. Doctors have medical knowledge and technical skills that patients lack. On the basis of their knowledge and skill alone they are often in control. That is not to say that individual women or groups of women are just passive victims. But, rather, to suggest that since women live in the same social world as doctors and frequently share a reciprocal view of the appropriate roles for doctors and patients, medical control is usually not challenged. Given that doctors are the "experts" with the rationale of science to support them, it should not be too surprising that most patients accept a medical definition of reality. When, as in the cases where hysterectomies were performed, doctors are Caucasian and most of their patients are not, when doctors are of a higher class and their patients of a lower social class, and when doctors are men and their patients are women, this imbalance is heightened. Each of these relationships of subordination and domination by race, class, and gender recapitulates and reinforces each other, and in the process lends strength to the medical definition of reality. In this context it becomes especially important to understand how doctors view hysterectomies and their potential impact on women's lives.

In the medical literature there seems to be general agreement that the uterus is not required for life and not necessary for health—an agreement that is supported in the rising hysterectomy rates. "Hysterectomy is the most commonly performed major operation for women of reproductive age in the United States" (Dicker et al. 1982: 323). Eight hundred thousand are performed each year (Thompson and Birch 1981). It has been estimated that by the late 1970s a woman's lifetime chance of having a hysterectomy by the age of 70 was 62 percent (Richards 1978). Sloan claims that "after some magic age [35?], which depends somewhat on the age of the viewer, the function of pregnancy is over and menstrual periods are almost over so that much has been written by [medical] authorities who urge elective removal of the uterus as a standard gynecological procedure" (Sloan 1978: 599). He goes on to ask his readers, other obstetrician gynecologists, why the removal of a woman's uterus is considered in the patient's best interest. There is, after all, no equivalent prophylactic removal of men's prostate glands.

This move toward elective surgery for women is consistent with a view that not only sees a woman's uterus as a useless organ once reproduction is over but as a potentially disease-producing one (U.S. House of Representatives 1977; Larned 1977). Caress (1977) quotes Dr. R.C. Wright writing in a 1969 issue of Obstetrics and Gynecology, "The uterus has but one function. After the last planned pregnancy it becomes a useless symptom-producing, potentially cancer-bearing organ and therefore should be removed." This attitude has also been consistently supported in a text popular since 1941—Novak's Textbook of Gynecology (Jones and Jones 1981). By the 1981 edition even the terminology had changed from "elective hysterectomy" to "hysterectomy" for "benign disease." Menstruation and a perceived need for sterilization are the "benign diseases" for which this text recommends hysterectomy.

Sloan (1978) questions why women over 35 are assumed to be willing to part with menstruation and procreation and why the myth that sex is better without the uterus is perpetuated. His response is culture. He claims that we live in a culture which separates mind and body. As cultural members doctors are able to remove a uterus that is not diseased and to believe that there will be no psychological stress for the patient—a belief supported by the "sleeper effect." The long-term psychological consequences of hysterectomy are often not seen immediately. They do not usually appear for twelve months to two years postoperatively (Wales 1980).

The sleeper effect has also been well documented. Richards (1978) used a questionnaire with women who had recently undergone a hysterectomy. Ninety and nine-tenths percent of the women reported being happy with the surgery. Yet many other studies have found posthysterectomy depression in as many as 70 percent of the patients. Hysterectomy patients have been found to be subject to at least double the number of postoperative psychiatric hospital admissions as patients who have had any other surgery (Richards 1978; Sloan 1978). And these negative attitudes have been found to be somewhat more common among black and Hispanic women (Wales 1980). Psychiatrists agree that a hysterectomy is often a blow to a woman's identity.

Larned (1977) reports Dr. Peter Barglow's findings:

The hysterectomy is clearly and immediately visualized as an irreversible drastic procedure which removes an organ with high value in the ego's image of the body, as well, as with considerable conscious value in the woman's sense of self and identity. Surely, the loss of an organ whose presence was reaffirmed monthly cannot be so easily denied. (Larned 1977: 206)

If the physicians who recommend hysterectomies are not the same specialists who usually see women troubled by these procedures, and if these doctors believe, as the medical literature encourages them to, that there are no adverse psychological consequences after a hysterectomy, then it is easy to understand why they recommended them to women who had completed their families and who were no longer in their reproductive prime of life. And given what has been said so far, it is no wonder that patients agreed to the surgery and reported, when interviewed, that they had suffered no severe identity consequences. In this context it is also easier to sort out why the menopausal women in Bart's (1970, 1971) study, by contrast, reported severe identity consequences. It appears that different cultural attitudes are called into play when women have hysterectomies and when they are menopausal.

While there may be additional differences among these groups of women,[8] there does not seem to be any cultural attitude which will allow menopausal women to construct a sense of themselves as good women although no longer reproductive. This negative view is observable in medical texts and medical interactions as well as in the larger society (Bart 1970, 1971).

Doctors, as cultural members, are likely to share the view that menopause is a negative life event; consequently, they would be unable to tell women that postmenopause they will be as good, if not better, than before. If Dr. Reuben (1969) is to be believed, menopause represents the end of a woman's sexuality as well as her reproductivity. But again, these belief systems do not tell the whole story. When placed in a more political context, the decision to recommend a hysterectomy and its acceptance by this group of patients takes on additional significance.

In two separate articles in the New England Journal of Medicine, anesthesiologist John Bunker discusses the relationship between the opportunity for profit and the performance of surgery (cf. Scully 1980; Larned 1977). He states that in the United States there are twice as many surgeons in proportion to the population as there are in England and Wales. There are also twice the number of surgeries (Bunker 1970) and more than twice the number of hysterectomies (Bunker 1976). Since in Great Britain medicine is socialized, no one profits from the performance of unnecessary surgery. A logical extension of this argument is to claim that if physicians in the United States did not have a vested interest in performing these procedures, we would not see so many performed. In fact, when profit is controlled we do see a decrease in the number of hysterectomies. Scully (1980), reporting from an article in the New York Times Magazine, states that in a prepaid health plan where doctors are salaried and no profit is entailed, the number of hysterectomies is four times lower than in a fee-for-service plan where profit is possible—a finding that has been confirmed by others.

Profit is not the only consideration. The British health care system is organized so that the specialist is a consultant who only sees cases referred from primary physicians after a determination has been made that the expertise of the specialist is needed (Bunker 1970; see also Larned 1977). In the United States where women are free to choose their doctors, women who are not sick often go to a surgical specialist—their obstetrician gynecologist—for their routine reproductive-related care. This places the American specialist in an advantageous position to recommend surgery when such surgery is not mandated on medical grounds. In medical school, if not before, these future doctors learn both the commonly held assumptions about women and reproduction and a "sales pitch" for hysterectomies (Fisher 1983; Scully 1980). And during their residency programs they have amply opportunity to practice their sales pitch in the outpatient clinics that are the primary source of health care for poor women.

In this context a dual health care system takes on new meaning. Poor, often minority, women with few if any other options become the teaching "material" on which residents practice their salesmanship as well as their surgical skills. The facts now can be reinterpreted. All of the patients who received hysterectomies were poor women treated by residents in an outpatient clinic of a teaching hospital, and five out of seven of them were Mexican-American women—just the women most likely to experience the sleeper effect (Wales 1980). The residents in obstetrics/gynecology in this setting, like those in all such settings, had learned a set of beliefs which made these particular women good candidates by age and reproductive status for hysterectomies. They had learned a sales pitch, and even their most current gynecological text counseled that if they explained the "fact" patients could be made to understand and brought into agreement— or, as Mary Daly (1978) argues, complicity.

If I were to argue that social control was manifested only in doctors' abilities to convince women to have hysterectomies—to convince them that even without the capacity to reproduce they would still be good women—I would be sidestepping a major issue. Left undiscussed would be how the medical profession functions to sustain itself, while helping to maintain a male-dominated society. Doctors, like patients, in this study, demonstrated their knowledge of a normative system that linked women's identities with their ability to reproduce. They also illustrated how these norms were filtered through the context of the medical world—a world which gave doctors the power to reinterpret the dominant ideology about women in ways that were consistent with their interests.

Yet, as I pointed out earlier, this power to define is not wholly of doctors' own making.' As cultural members they share a world view which defines women. These cultural definitions and their reenactment in medical settings are consistent with the roles women are needed to play in production and/or reproduction. It makes little difference if women are encouraged to see themselves as good if no longer reproductive, or good only if they reproduce. In both cases women's self-definition is severely limited by a patriarchal ideology which legitimates the social order and women's place in it.

But as Brown pointed out, more is at risk here than the roles women are allowed to play. Cultural definitions such as these reserve the control of society for men collectively and, in so doing,

protect the privileges of men as a group as well as of individual
men. Medical domination then is just one among many forms of
domination—domination expressed in every aspect of women's lives.
Normalcy, as Daly (1978) suggested, is so elusive that it needs
constant reinforcement. For her, as for me, such reinforcement
does not suggest a conspiracy. Physicians, spokespersons for the
New Right, and other patriarchs do not sit down together and plan
how they will reward complicity and punish or recapture defectors.
Rather, most of us through our socialization—our enculturation—are
drawn into complicity performing our parts in this drama
uncritically.

Notes

[1]Pap smears are preventative health measures. They are
recommended for most women once a year as a screen for cervical
cancer. The results traditionally come in five classes—class 1 is
normal and class 5 is most abnormal and may be indicative of
invasive disease. Classes 2, 3, and 4 represent a gray area
between normal and invasive. They often indicate displasia—
abnormal changes in the cells that are believed to be precursors to
cervical cancer but are not yet cancerous. None of the women in
this study had invasive disease. And none of the women who had
hysterectomies had their ovaries removed.

[2]No women in this study chose not to have children or were
feminists, but I suspect that either the active decision to be childless
or a strong feminist awareness would affect women's reported
identity consequences.

[3]An examination of the relationships among patients' class
and ethnicity and the organization and staffing of the medical
setting in which they received care, while critical to an
understanding of the negotiation of treatment decisions, is not the
topic of this chapter.

[4]Since I was interested in both how decisions were reached
and in how such decisions affected women's sense of themselves, I
followed patients from first referral through the diagnostic-
treatment process, interviewing them after recovery. The
interviews were taped and transcribed for later analysis. I was the
interpreter in all of the doctor/patient interactions; however, after
recovery all of the Spanish-speaking women were interviewed by a
native Spanish-speaker with me in attendance. The native speaker

also transcribed all of the Spanish portions of the audio tapes.

[5]A cone biopsy is a surgical procedure in which a thin cone-shaped slice is cored out of the endocervical canal. If the upper limits of this sample are free of abnormal cells, this diagnostic procedure preserves reproduction and is regarded as therapeutically effective.

[6]Freezing or cryosurgery is an office procedure in which the transformation zone of the cervix is frozen, abnormal cells are killed and sloughed off. This procedure preserves reproduction and has been found to be therapeutically effective when the entire area of abnormal cells can be visualized.

[7]While seven hysterectomies were performed in this sample of patients, none of the hysterectomies was medically necessary. Yet most of the women, when interviewed after their surgery, reported that their treatments had been medically necessary. Although there might be other reasons to account for this finding, the doctor's role in selling the hysterectomy cannot be overlooked (see Fisher 1983 for a fuller discussion of the selling of hysterectomies).

[8]Bart's patients were preselected for identity consequences, i.e., they were institutionalized for depression. The patients in this study were not preselected in the same way; they were part of a medical, not a psychological, population. While Bart's findings as a whole cannot be said to describe the entire population, the negative attitude about menopause in cultural lore is more generalizable.

References

Arditti, R., R.D. Klein and S. Minden, 1984. Test-Tube Women: What Future in Motherhood. Boston, MA: Pandora Press/ Routledge and Kegan Paul.

Barker-Benfield, G.J., 1976. The Horrors of the Half-Known Life. New York: Harper.

Bart, P.B., 1970. "Portnoy's Mother's Complaint," Transaction (November-December): 69–74.

Brat, P.B., 1971. "Depression in Middle-Aged Women," in V. Gorneck and B.K. Moran (eds.) Women in Sexist Society. New York: Basic Books.

Bodenheimer, T., S. Cummings, and E. Harding, 1974. "Capitalizing on Illness: The Health Insurance Industry," International Journal of Health Services 4 (April): 583–98.

Brown, C., 1981. "Mothers, Fathers and Children: From Private to Public Patriarchy," pp. 239–68 in L. Sargent (ed.) Women and Revolution. Boston, MA: South End Press.

Bullough, V., 1974. The Subordinate Sex: A History of Attitudes Toward Women. Baltimore, MD: Penguin.

Bullough, V. and B. Bullough, 1977. Sin, Sickness and Sanity: A History of Sexual Attitudes. New York: Meridian.

Bunker, J.M.D., 1970. "Surgical Manpower: A Comparison of Operations and Surgeons in the United States and in England and Wales," New England Journal of Medicine 282, 3 (January 15): 135–44.

Bunker, J.M.D., 1976. "Elective Hysterectomy: Pro and Con," New England Journal of Medicine 295, 5 (July 29): 264.

Caress, B., 1977. "Womb-boom," Health/Pac Bulletin (July/August.

Chernin, K., 1981. The Obsession: Reflections on the Tyranny of Slenderness. New York: Harper and Row.

Chodorow, N., 1978. The Reproduction of Mothering: Psychoanalysis and the Sociology of Gender. Berkeley, CA: The University of California Press.

Cicourel, A.V., 1973. Cognitive Sociology: Language and Meaning in Social Interaction. London: McMillan.

Clay, U.S., 1977. Women: Menopause and Middle Age. Pittsburgh, PA: Know Inc.

Corea, G., 1985. The Mother Machine. New York: Harper and Row.

Daly, M., 1978. Gynecology. Boston: Beacon Press.

Dicker, R.C., M.J. Scally, J.R. Greenspan, P.M. Layde, J.M. Oryhmaze, and J.C. Smith, 1982. "Hysterectomy Among Women of Reproductive Age," Journal of the American Medical Association 248, 3 (July 16): 323–27.

Durkheim, E., 1938. The Rules of Sociological Method. Chicago: University of Chicago Press.

Ehrenreich, B. and D. English, 1979. For Her Own Good. Garden City, NY: Anchor Press/Doubleday.

Fee, E., 1983. "Preface," pp. 7–12 in E. Fee (ed.) Women and Health: The Politics of Sex in Medicine. Farmingdale, NY: Baywood Publishing Co.

Fisher, S., 1983. "Doctor Talk/Patient Talk: How Treatment Decisions are Negotiated in Doctor-Patient Communication," pp. 135–58 in S. Fisher and A. Todd (eds.) The Social Organization of Doctor-Patient Communication. Washington, DC: The Center for Applied Linguistics.

Freidson, E., 1970. Profession of Medicine. New York: Dodd, Mead.

Garfinkel, H., 1967. Studies in Ethnomethodology. New Jersey: Prentice-Hall.

Gordon, L., 1974. Woman's Body, Woman's Right: A Social History of Birth Control in America. New York: Penguin.

Gurwitsch, A., 1964. The Field of Consciousness. Pittsburgh, PA: Duquesne University Press.

Jones, H. and G.S. Jones, 1981. Novak's Textbook on Gynecology, 10th ed. Baltimore, MD: Williams and Wilkins.

Komarovsky, M., 1953. Women in the Modern World. Boston: Little Brown.

Krause, E.A., 1977. Power and Illness. New York: Elsevier.

Lakoff, R. and R. Scherr, 1984. Face Value: The Politics of Beauty. Boston: Routledge and Kegan Paul.

Larned, D., 1977. "The Epidemic in Unnecessary Hysterectomy," in Claudia Dreifus (ed.) Seizing Our Bodies: The Politics of Women's Health. New York: Vintage.

Lopata, H., 1971. Occupation: Housewife. New York: Oxford University Press.

Luker, K., 1984. Abortion and the Politics of Motherhood. Berkeley: University of California Press.

Mechanic, D., 1968. Medical Sociology. New York: Free Press.

Mehan, H. and H. Wood, 1975. The Reality of Ethnomethodology. New York: John Wiley.

Mills, C.W., 1940. "Situated Action and Vocabularies of Motives," American Sociological Review 5 (December): 904–13.

Mohr, J.C., 1978. Abortion in America: The Origins and Evolution of National Policy. New York: Oxford University Press.

Navarro, V., 1976. Medicine Under Capitalism. New York: Prodist.

Oakley, A., 1980. Women Confined: Toward a Sociology of Childbirth. New York: Schocken.

Orbach, S., 1982. Fat is a Feminist Issue II. New York: Berkeley.

Parsons, T., 1951. The Social System. New York: Free Press.

Reuben, D.R., 1969. Everything You Always Wanted to Know About Sex* but Were Afraid to Ask. New York: McKay.

Richards, B.C., 1978. "Hysterectomy: From Women to Women," American Journal of Obstetrics and Gynecology 131, 4 (July 15): 446–52.

Rossi, A.S., 1964. "Equality Between the Sexes: An Immodest Proposal," Daedalus (Spring): 607–52.

Ruzek, S.B., 1978. The Women's Health Movement. New York: Praeger.

Schiefelbein, S., 1980. "The Female Patient: Heeded? Hustled? Healed?" Saturday Review 29 (March): 12–16.

Scott, M. and S. Lyman, 1968. "Accounts," American Sociological Review 33 (December): 46–62.

Scully, D., 1980. Men Who Control Women's Health. Boston, MA: Houghton Mifflin.

Shumsky, M. and H. Mehan, 1974. "The Comparability Practice in Two Evaluative Contexts." Paper presented at VII World Conference of Sociology, Toronto, August 18–23.

Sloan, D., M.D., 1978. "The Emotional and Psychosexual Aspects of Hysterectomy," American Journal of Obstetrics and Gynecology 131, 6 (July 15): 598–605.

Sontag, S., 1972. "The Double Standard of Aging," Saturday Review of the Society (September 23).

Thompson, J.D., M.D., and H.W. Birch, M.D., 1981. "Indications for Hysterectomy," Clinical Obstetrics and Gynecology 24, 4 (December): 1245–58.

U.S. Congress, House, 1977. Important Cost and Quality Issues of Health Care. Hearings Before the Subcommittee on Oversight and Investigations of the Committee of Interstate and Foreign Commerce, 95th Cong., 1st sess.

Waitzkin, H., 1983. The Second Sickness: Contradictions of Capitalist Health Care. New York: The Free Press.

Wales, E., 1980. "Sexual Rehabilitation After Gynecologic Surgery," The Female Patient 5 (July): 61–66.

Weber, M., 1947. The Theory of Social and Economic Organization. New York: Free Press.

Weideger, P., 1977. Menstruation and Menopause. New York: Dell.

Winch, P., 1958. The Idea of Social Science and Its Relation to Philosophy. London: Routledge and Kegan Paul.

Wittgenstein, L., 1953. Philosophical Investigations. London: Basil Blackwell and Mott.

Zola, I.K., 1972. "Medicine as an Institution of Social Control," Sociology Review 20: 487.

CHAPTER 13

CUSTOM-FITTED STRAIGHTJACKETS: PERSPECTIVES ON WOMEN'S MENTAL HEALTH

Esther D. Rothblum
Violet Franks

> The media was saying it was easy to be
> Just like the women on the ads on TV.
>
> The Ovarian Sisters
> (Tasmania, Australia)

Given the salience of gender differences in our society, it is not surprising that mental illness rates differ for women and men. This chapter will illustrate the similarity between feminine sex role stereotypes and psychiatric disorders in which women predominate. Abnormal or deviant behavior has been attributed to a variety of causes in the past, ranging from demonic possession to genetic factors, faulty childrearing, socialization, and institutional structures. Yet psychological distress must be interpreted or labeled deviant by professionals in order to constitute mental illness (Schur 1984). Psychiatric classification of abnormality can serve as a vehicle of social control. We will discuss the degree to which such labeling may be influenced by sexism in the current diagnostic system. The remainder of the chapter will attempt to demonstrate the relationships between women's traditional roles in society and mental illness. In this manner we view women's roles—and the suffering they may engender—as "custom-fitted."

Joffe (1982) has coined the phrase "the cause of the causes" to describe the underlying commonalities of several seemingly unrelated phenomena. In our previous collaboration (Franks and Rothblum 1983) we asked chapter authors to describe individual diagnostic categories (such as depression, agoraphobia, and sexual dysfunction) in which women predominate and to focus on the relationship between the particular diagnostic category and women's socialization. Here we are doing the reverse. Our emphasis is on elucidating various societal institutions (such as marital status, motherhood, and employment) and relating these to women's mental health in general. Thus we are stressing the cause of the causes.

SEX ROLE STEREOTYPES AND PSYCHIATRIC DISORDERS: WOMEN HURT THEMSELVES, MEN HURT OTHERS

Both women and men hold strong beliefs about what is appropriate female or male behavior and consider male attributes more socially desirable (Rosenkrantz 1968). These beliefs, or sex role stereotypes, are widely held by members of our society. In their now classic study, Broverman, Broverman, Clarkson, Rosenkrantz, and Vogel (1970) demonstrated that mental health professionals are not immune from such stereotyping in their conceptions of what are appropriate characteristics for healthy women and men. Table 1 lists the items which clinical psychologists, social workers, and psychiatrists rated as typical for "mature, healthy, socially competent" women versus men. Mental health professionals categorized the typical healthy woman as gentle, quiet, and tactful, with a strong need for security and sensitivity for the feelings of others. Healthy males were described as aggressive, dominant, adventurous, and competitive. Furthermore, there were more than twice as many adjectives used to describe men as there were about women. When asked to rate a mentally healthy adult, mental health professionals used corresponding attributes to those of the healthy male, which were significantly different from the attributes of the healthy female. Thus, in the eyes of clinicians, the terms "healthy woman" and "healthy adult" were virtually mutually exclusive.

It does not require much professional training to realize that there are vast differences between the way women and men express psychological distress. It is almost as rare to find men who seek therapy in order to lose weight as it is to find women referred for therapy for explosive rage. Today's private practitioner virtually expects to treat women who are depressed, agoraphobic, unassertive, or anxious about their weight, and men who are alcoholics or who have stress-related disorders due to pressure in the workplace.[1] Clinicians who work with individuals who are institutionalized in psychiatric hospitals will find a preponderance of men who are diagnosed as drug abusers or antisocial and women who are classified as displaying "borderline personality disorders."

Table 1

Clinicians' Judgments of Psychological Health for Women and Men
(From Broverman et al. 1970)

Female-Valued Items	Male-Valued Items
Very talkative	Very aggressive
Very tactful	Very independent
Very gentle	Not at all emotional
Very aware of feelings of others	Almost always hides emotions
Very religious	Very objective
Very interested in own appearance	Not at all easily influenced
Very neat in habits	Very dominant
Very quiet	Likes math and science very much
Very strong need for security	Not at all excitable in a minor crisis
Enjoys art and literature very much	Very active
Easily expresses tender feelings	Very competitive
	Very logical
	Very worldly
	Very skilled in business
	Very direct
	Knows the way of the world
	Feelings not easily hurt
	Very adventurous
	Can make decisions easily
	Never cries
	Almost always acts as a leader
	Very self-confident
	Not at all uncomfortable about being aggressive
	Very ambitious
	Easily able to separate feelings from ideas
	Not at all dependent
	Never conceited about appearance

The Third Edition of the Diagnostic and Statistical Manual of Mental Disorders (DSM III 1980) presents the gender ratio of all psychiatric disorders for which this information is available. Table 2 displays these disorders grouped by prevalent gender (excluding disorders for which there is either no gender difference or no available information on gender differences). It is evident from this table that women predominate in passive, "acting in" disorders such as depression, anxiety, and sexual dysfunction; men prevail in "acting out" disorders such as antisocial behavior, fire-setting, gambling, and explosive rage. Basically, women hurt themselves; men hurt others.

It is also clear that current categories of psychiatric disorders, when grouped by prevalent gender, correspond closely to the Broverman et al. (1970) sex role stereotypes. "Female

Table 2

DSM-III* Categories of Psychological Distress in which
Women and Men Predominate (From Fodor and Rothblum 1984)

Women Predominate	Men Predominate
Axis I Disorders: Clinical Diagnoses	
Depression	Alcoholism
Agoraphobia	Drug Abuse
Sexual dysfunction	Antisocial behavior
Simple phobias	Paraphilias
Anxiety states	Transsexualism
Somatization disorder	Factitious disorder
Multiple personality	Pathologic gambling
Psychogenic pain disorder	Pyromania
	Intermittent explosive disorder
Axis II Disorders: Personality Disorders	
Histrionic personality disorder	Paranoid personality disorder
Borderline personality disorder	Antisocial personality disorder
Dependent personality disorder	Compulsive personality disorder

*The Diagnostic and Statistical Manual of Mental Disorders (Third Edition; APA 1980) provides diagnostic criteria for each disorder that specify duration, symptomatology, and level of impairment.

disorders" could be characterized by the stereotypes passive, submissive, home oriented, dependent, and not at all self-confident. The stereotypes aggressive, blunt, rough, and loud could describe the "male disorders." If members of society, including clinicians, accept the Broverman et al. stereotypes as healthy, then the DSM III disorders constitute extreme versions of these stereotypes for women and men. Thus dependent women are healthy; extremely dependent women are depressed. Independent men are healthy; overly independent men are antisocial. When individuals behave too much like the exaggerated appropriate stereotype for their gender, they meet criteria for psychiatric disorders. In this regard women and men who are most like the ideal for their gender are in fact mentally ill. Gender-specific DSM III disorders present virtual caricatures of sex role stereotypes.

Connections between psychiatric disorders and stereotypes are not discussed in DSM III. One example of such a connection will be presented. Agoraphobia is the Greek term for "fear of the market place." In its extreme form agoraphobia encompasses a fear of leaving the house that can last for an individual's lifetime (Brehony 1983). Not surprisingly, the overwhelming majority of agoraphobics are women. Fodor (1974) has described agoraphobia as the logical extension of the feminine sex role stereotype of passivity and fearfulness. Given women's socialization for dependency and domesticity, Brehony (1983) asks: Why are not all women agoraphobic?

Just as agoraphobics represents the extreme feminine sex role stereotype, rapists portray the sex role stereotype that is most extremely masculine. Men are both socialized to be tough and aggressive and excused for violent behavior. Resick (1983) has described legal and moral tolerance for violence against women from biblical times to the present. Research shows that 40 percent of college males indicated they would rape if there was assurance of no punishment (Malamuth 1982). In her influential book on rape, Brownmiller (1975) has stated that all men are potential rapists. Pithers (1982) has defined rape as the extreme version of the masculine sex role stereotype of aggression.

Thus we socialize girls to fear going out alone at night and boys to take the "aggressive" role during sex. At the extremes of these roles there are men who rape and agoraphobic women who are afraid to leave their homes (and this does not deny the reality of rape within the home setting). It is ludicrous to suggest that rapists and agoraphobics are merely diagnosed as such by clinicians with stereotypic assumptions about male and female behavior. Males who choose to stay at home to pursue domestic interests and females who commit sexual violence are, despite overwhelming media coverage, extremely rare.

GENDER DIFFERENCES IN PSYCHOPATHOLOGY: SEXIST CLINICIANS?

"Social groups create deviance by making the rules whose infraction constitutes deviance" (Becker 1963, in Schur 1984). Feminists (e.g., Chesler 1972; Kaplan 1983) have argued that women and men are assigned different diagnoses as a result of the sexism of clinicians. As we have seen, clinicians have stereotypic views of appropriate feminine and masculine behavior. Does this account for gender differences in prevalence rates of psychopathology? We will examine this question by focusing on Kaplan's (1983) influential article on this subject.

According to Kaplan, differences in rates of mental illness are "codified in diagnostic criteria and thus influence diagnostic and treatment patterns" (786). She concludes (791):

> adaptiveness and maladaptiveness are arbitrarily defined. In other words, not only are women being punished (by being diagnosed) for acting out of line (not acting like women) and not only are traditional roles driving women crazy, but also male-centered assumptions—the sunglasses through which we view each other—are causing clinicians to see normal females as abnormal.

Kaplan acknowledges the importance of prior socialization in the etiology of psychiatric disorders in which women predominate. However, her primary focus is on the influence of sexist diagnostic criteria on clinicians' judgments.

Although the DSM III diagnostic categories on which there is information about sex ratios reveals a virtual caricature of sex role stereotypes, the <u>diagnostic criteria</u> for Axis I categories of DSM III are generally free of sex role bias. For example, symptoms of major depression include poor appetite or weight loss, insomnia or increased sleep, psychomotor agitation or retardation, loss of interest in usual activities, loss of energy or fatigue, feelings of worthlessness, diminished concentration, and suicidal ideation. None of these symptoms corresponds to the feminine sex role stereotype cited by Broverman et al. (1970). A possible exception is "worthlessness," which could relate to but is not synonymous with the stereotypic feminine sex role characteristic "not at all self-confident." In this regard, DSM III is considerably <u>less</u> apt to stereotype than are other symptom checklists of depression that include symptoms such as crying, dependence, self-devaluation, and indecisiveness (Rothblum 1983), and that consequently do correspond with some of the Broverman et al. stereotypic sex role characteristics for women.

Kaplan reviews four theories about sex differences in psychopathology. The first is that "women are not sicker, they are just more willing to express symptomatology" (786). Although Kaplan states that there is little research that investigates this theory, it is our contention that the research which exists does not support this theory. Women do have higher rates of self-disclosure about personal topics than do men (Jourard and Lasakow 1958; Snoek and Rothblum 1979). Yet epidemiologic studies find women to exceed men in rates of depression, whether the survey interviewed individuals about themselves (c.f. Weissman and Klerman 1977, for a review) or whether one family member was interviewed about the rest of the family (Siassi et al. 1974). This finding weakens the argument that it is women's greater self-disclosure about emotional problems that results in higher rates of depression, since the symptoms of depression are discernible by other family members as well (although one cannot rule out the notion that family members know about these women's depression through self-disclosure rather than observation).

The second theory that Kaplan reviews relates psychopathology to women's disadvantaged status in society. The third theory is based on research by Gove (Gove 1979; Gove and Tudor 1973) which suggests that married women are at increased risk for mental illness. We will discuss in later sections how women's roles in society are related to "passive" psychiatric disorders, particularly roles reflecting housework and childcare. It is obvious that socialization for women and men to assume their roles in society takes place before the onset of symptoms of psychopathology. DSM III diagnostic criteria for Axis I disorders do not incorporate characteristics inherent in certain societal roles. Thus, once again, DSM III is value-free in this regard.

The fourth theory that Kaplan describes regarding sex differences in psychopathology suggests that women's identities are more greatly influenced by their interpersonal relationships and that consequently women are more dependent on others than are men. This theory is supported by research; a number of studies have demonstrated that women are more adversely affected than are men by the lack of a social network or an intimate relationship (Brown et al. 1975; Weissman et al. 1971; Pearlin and Johnson 1977). Once again, we argue that the relationships reflect societal socialization and are unrelated to the specific diagnostic criteria on Axis I of DSM III.

Kaplan concludes that "most sex role related theories about women's higher treatment rates await further empirical validation" (788). It is our opinion that empirical evidence exists for all theories reviewed by Kaplan except for the first one, which is perhaps most closely related to her thesis that it is the manner in which diagnostic information is obtained (i.e., via self-report) that inflates the prevalence of psychopathology in women.

In conclusion, we are not denying that a diagnostic system such as DSM III is developed in a sociocultural context nor that it attributes blame on the afflicted for the causes of their disorder (c.f. Rothblum et al. in press, for a discussion of sociopolitical factors in DSM III). Nor would we argue that mental health professionals are free of societal values; the study by Broverman et al. (1970) is a convincing demonstration of the fact that mental health professionals have viewed positive mental health and female gender as mutually exclusive. The notion that sexism begins at the point of diagnosis is wishful thinking. This denies the importance of early socialization for women to become passive and helpless as well as the existence of discrimination against women in society. It is our opinion that prevention of women's mental health problems should focus on eliminating sexism in society rather than on "purifying" DSM III.

The next sections will focus on women's traditional and nontraditional roles in society. We will examine how rates of psychopathology for women correspond to their societal roles.

WOMEN'S MARITAL STATUS AND MENTAL HEALTH: SWALLOWING THE LIE

Mary Daly (1984) uses the word "reversal" to refer to a warped indoctrination or interpretation of facts. To use her examples, Coca-Cola as "the real thing" (despite contrary evidence on the list of ingredients) and nuclear submarines as "instruments of peace" are evidence of "compulsory/compulsive lie-swallowing." Such reversals are numerous in mental health research and policy, where, despite years of research evidence to the contrary, false beliefs and implementations persist.

Table 3 illustrates our view of the contradiction between stereotypes or widespread beliefs about women's marital status and the general research evidence. Each category of marital status will be discussed separately.[2]

Never Married Women

The majority of young women expect to marry; only 5–6 percent express a plan to remain single (Donelson 1977). The stigma of singleness includes such societal fears as loneliness, isolation, sexual and interpersonal unattractiveness, sexual frustration, and lesbianism. Donelson (1977) remarks that our society is considerably more "antisingle" than it is "pro-marriage." According to her (233):

Table 3

Correspondence Between women's Marital Status, Societal Beliefs
About the Desirability of the Marital Status, and Mental Health
Research on women of the Marital Status

Marital Status	Societal Stereotype	Mental Health Research
Never-Married	Negative	Positive
Married	Positive	Negative
Divorced	Negative	Negative
Widowed	Neutral	Negative
Lesbian	Extremely Negative	Positive

The pressures toward marriage and away from singleness are so pervasive and intense in contemporary society that many people have not in fact freely chosen the marriage they have or intend. There has been an idolatry of marriage as the only way to find peace and fulfillment: 'And they live happily ever after...' The external pressures from other people are often strongly internalized, so that many young women and men feel an unexamined compulsion to get married. They assume that marriage is desirable for themselves without considering that assumption, or they have difficulty admitting even to themselves that they have some reservations about marriage.

Women who never marry are referred to as "old maids" or "spinsters." In contrast, single men are called "swinging bachelors" and expected to lead sexually exciting and emotionally satisfying lives.

Donelson (1977) has elaborated on the process by which women "become" single. Often there is not so much an active decision as a gradual drifting into a comfortable lifestyle. Even older women may no totally eliminate the possibility of marriage, despite relative comfort in their current life. Single women have economic independence, higher education, and greater psychological autonomy than do married women (Donelson 1977). Yet, ironically, parents and friends alike urge marriage for reasons of "security" and love.

Despite tremendous societal pressure to be married, mental health statistics reveal that never married women are psychologically "healthier" than married men, married women, and never married men (U.S. Department of Health, Education, and

Welfare 1970, in Donelson 1977). Never married men are the most distressed category of the above groups, proving them to be anything but "swinging." Never married women are also protected, relative to married women, from the chances of developing clinical depression (Gove 1972; Radloff 1975; Radloff and Rae 1979) or agoraphobia (fear of being in public places)(Roberts 1964; Brehony 1983).

Married Women

Although the average age of marriage for women in the U.S. is now 22.3 and increasing (Hacker 1983), the majority of women will be married at some point in their lives. A woman's wedding is given more attention than most other events in her life, and few other events are as expected. Although married women report feeling happy with life (Donelson 1977), women's marriage is a risk factor for increased rates of mental illness.[3] Married women are more likely than single women to experience nervousness, insomnia, and inertia (U.S. Department of Health, Education, and Welfare 1970; in Donelson 1977), as well as depression and agoraphobia, as mentioned earlier. Married women comprise such a large proportion of agoraphobics that Roberts (1964) has termed agoraphobia a condition of "housebound housewives."

Two theories have been presented to account for married women's increased psychological distress. First, married women (but women in no other marital status category) may be housewives. Being a housewife has become a low-status role (Gove 1972). The role requires no formalized training, no "entrance exam," and no standards. Status is determined by the husband's occupation, not the housewife's expertise or efficiency. Many domestic tasks are highly repetitive, boring, and stressful. Society views the role of "just a housewife" as occupying few skills. In fact, the term "housewife" encompasses many roles, including those of cook, maid, babysitter, teacher, social hostess, secretary, and receptionist, to name a few. In her satirical article entitled "Why I Need a Wife," Judy Syfers (1973: 612) writes:

> I want a wife who will take care of my physical needs. I want a wife who will keep my house clean. A wife who will pick up after my children, a wife who will pick up after me. I want a wife who will keep my clothes clean, ironed, mended, replaced when need be, and who will see to it that my

personal things are kept in their proper place so that I can find what I need the minute I need it. I want a wife who cooks the meals, a wife who is a good cook. I want a wife who will plan the menus, do the necessary grocery shopping, prepare the meals, serve them pleasantly, and then do the cleaning up while I do my studying. I want a wife who will care for me when I am sick and sympathize with my pain and loss of time from school. I want a wife to go along when our family takes a vacation so that someone can continue to care for me and my children when I need a rest and a change of scene.

Just as married women acquire many of the above roles on their wedding day, married men acquire someone to take domestic and supportive roles off their shoulders. Not surprisingly, mental illness rates for married men are lower than for never married men.

A second theory emphasizes the increasing numbers of married women who are not housewives but employed outside the home. According to this theory, married women are expected to be "superwomen," performing a nine-to-five job in the worksetting followed by a five-to-nine job taking care of housework and childcare. Radloff (1975) has demonstrated that employed married women perform nearly as much domestic work as homemakers do. Employed married men, on the other hand, perform only a fraction of such work. Even female managers and executives are not immune from housework and children. A survey conducted by Savvy (1981), the magazine for women in business, indicated that women perform most household duties themselves, regardless of their income.

Just as management of the home and family cannot always be relegated to evenings and weekends, professional women cannot easily keep their schedules to an eight-hour day. How do married women with a career cope with overload? Poloma (1972) surveyed married couples in which the wife was involved in medicine, law, or college teaching. Women in her sample typically used one of four methods to cope with stress: (1) they highlighted the benefits and downplayed the costs of their lifestyles; (2) they decided which role had precedence in case of conflicts (in almost every case this resulted in ranking family over career); (3) they compartmentalized by keeping both roles separate (although husbands often brought work home or discussed the family at work); or (4) they compromised, by adjusting their careers to meet the demands of their family. Little wonder that married women excel in nervousness, depression, and inertia.

Divorced Women

Despite socialization to become married and "live happily ever after," the proportion of women who are divorced, separated, or widowed is substantial. The divorce rate is approximately 50 percent of all marriages. Although the chance of divorce is equal for women and men, the chance of remarriage is much lower for women, particularly for women who are older or for those who have children. In fact, most divorced women will obtain custody of their children and will experience a marked financial loss; divorced men will experience a significant financial gain (Weitzman 1985). Solomon and Rothblum have summarized remarriage rates as follows (1985: 316–17):

> Given the social stigma, it is not surprising that "single-again" women are considered to occupy a temporary role "between men" and are expected to remarry. Yet the probability that women will remarry is less than that for men. About 13% of eligible men remarry each year compared with 4% of eligible women. The peak age of remarriage for women is 20–24 years; for men it is 25–29 years (Bloom, Asher, and White, 1978). For women, rates of remarriage are highest for young women without children (Hetherington et al., 1979).... Remarriages also tend to show greater age discrepancies between partners. Bloom et al. indicate that while brides are ten or more years younger than grooms in less than two percent of first marriages, in remarriages, 27% of brides are ten or more years younger than their grooms. Thus, the woman over 30, especially if she has children, has a greatly decreased chance of ever remarrying, especially if she has a low income. In contrast to pressures on women to remarry, there is some evidence that remaining single has interpersonal advantages for women. Women who left their spouses and who did not become reinvolved reported better social adjustment than those who did resume relationships with men (Rounsaville, Prusoff, and Weissman, 1980).

In a two-year longitudinal study of divorced couples, Hetherington et al. (1979) compared the effects of divorce on women and men. For women, divorce implied loss of primary identity and status through marriage (in contrast to the findings of Rounsaville et al. above), lowered social activity, diminished contact with former friends, continuing attachment to former spouses, and tremendous financial pressures. These experiences were less evident for men, who were more likely to feel a lack of structure or rootlessness, but were more often involved with former friends and often engaged in heightened social activities at bars and parties. Divorced women may also be blamed for the dissolution of their marriage (Brandwein et al. 1974). Women who were married for a long period may be unprepared for the interpersonal and financial autonomy required of "single-again" status. Despite the prevalence of divorce and even multiple divorce, societal views of divorces are still negative. As Epstein states (in Rohrbaugh 1979: 198):

Divorce, it is almost universally agreed, is a civilized institution...and as such nearly everyone now tolerates, even approves of, divorce. Except, that is, for themselves. Divorce generally seems as admirable, an altogether logical solution—for others.

Mental health statistics indicate that divorce and separation place both women and men at risk for psychological distress. Depression rates are highest for separated and divorced women, followed by rates of depression for single, widowed, and divorced men (Hirschfeld and Cross 1981). Women are more likely to become depressed as the result of a marriage terminating than are men (Brisco and Smith 1973). Divorced women have higher rates of suicide than women in general (Bloom et al. 1978). Worell and Garrett-Fulks (1983) have remarked that society has legally permitted divorce but there are few strategies provided for adjustment after divorce except remarriage. They describe four roles that are inherent in female (but not male) socialization that provide single-again women poor coping strategies: (1) economic dependency; (2) subordination to male power; (3) reliance on a husband for a social identity; and (4) "investment in the superwife/supermom roles."

Widows

Even women who remain with their spouse are four times as likely to outlive him than to predecease him (Worell and Garrett-Fulks 1983) and thus to end up unmarried. Women not only live longer than men but also tend to marry men who are older. Society has clearer guidelines for the role of widow (Brandwein et al. 1974), and widows, unlike divorced women, cannot be held accountable for the termination of their marriage. Thus societal views of the role of widowhood could be regarded as neutral rather than negative.

Like divorced women, widows experience great distress following the termination of their marriage and adapting to their new role. Social isolation and loneliness, intense mourning, and disorganization mark the first year of widowhood (Worell and Garrett-Fulks 1983; Hyde and Rosenberg 1980). Widows are at increased risk for depression and suicide (Rothblum 1983). Among nonwhite females the highest category of completed suicides is among widows (Bloom et al. 1978). Although widowhood is also a stressor for men, far fewer men than women become widowed.

Lesbians

There is no question that, even today, the social stigma of lesbianism is so great that most lesbians fear the consequences of openly acknowledging their sexual orientation to parents, employers, and friends. Lesbians in the military are considered a "security risk," and lesbian teachers and parents are accused of "causing" homosexuality in children (despite the fact that most homosexuals had heterosexual parents and teachers). Stereotypes about lesbians encompass their appearance, gender identity, sexual behavior, and attitudes about men. The majority of Americans consider homosexuality, lesbianism included, obscene, vulgar, and "harmful to American life" (Hyde and Rosenberg 1980).

The stigma of lesbianism runs counter to thirty years of research indicating that lesbians experience positive adjustment and mental health. In 1953 Kinsey's surveys identified that 11–20 percent of females had some homosexual experience, and that 1–3 percent were exclusively homosexual. Ten percent of the women who responded to the Hite Report survey (1976) were lesbians. In 1958 Hooker demonstrated that mental health professionals could not differentiate between the Rorschach responses of male homosexuals who were not in therapy and heterosexual controls. In

1971 Thompson, McCandless, and Strickland matched male and female homosexuals and heterosexuals on age, gender, and education and presented them with several personality measures. There was no significant difference between homosexuals and heterosexuals of either gender on personal adjustment, self-confidence, and self-evaluation. In fact, there was a tendency for male homosexuals to be less defensive than male heterosexuals, and lesbians to be more self-confident than female heterosexuals. Hyde and Rosenberg (1980) have reviewed more recent research comparing lesbians and heterosexual women. Except for lesbians' higher self-esteem, there are no consistent differences in mental health. Given the extremely homophobic societal views during the past decades, it is amazing that lesbians have coped so well.

Despite the prevalence and adjustment of lesbians, mental health professionals have mirrored society's perspective in their understanding and treatment of lesbians in therapy. The psychodynamic perspective in lesbianism as reflecting narcissism due to inadequate sexual development in childhood has had a major influence. Behavior therapists attempted to eliminate homosexual behavior with aversive techniques, such as pairing electric shock or nausea-inducing drugs with pictures of homosexual behavior. Even when such therapy was "successful," it is doubtful that changes were long-lasting or that individuals were able to engage in heterosexual relationships.

In 1973, as the result of pressure by gay and feminist activists, the American Psychiatric Association voted (an interesting method given the existing research evidence) to eliminate homosexuality as a "sexual deviation" under the category "sociopathy" or crimes against society. The substituted category "ego-dystonic homosexuality" reflects the continuing split in this professional organization regarding attitudes about homosexuality. Despite continuing research demonstrating lesbians' (and gay men's) comparable functioning with heterosexual women, bias and homophobia among mental health professionals persist.

Conclusion

In sum, there is almost total incongruence between societal stereotypes about various forms of marital status for women and research on mental health. Being married is the only desirable state for women, according to society. Widows have neutral status, divorced and never married women are viewed as needing to remarry, and lesbians are regarded most negatively. Yet women who are never married fare best on mental health indices. Lesbians are equal in mental health to comparable samples of heterosexual women. Married and formerly married women are highest on psychological distress.

WOMEN AND CHILDREN: SLAVES TO THE NUCLEAR FAMILY

The word "family" in Latin originally referred to the number of slaves possessed by one man. In the 1980s we are again faced with a "profamily" movement that is attempting to "strengthen the American family" (Family Protection Act 1980). Proposed legislation has included antiabortion, anticontraception measures for adolescent females, and the repeal of laws concerning spouse and child abuse (Family Protection Act 1980).

A central and pervasive focus of this movement (and similar movements throughout history) is women's "instincts" to bear and raise children. Russo has described this focus as the "motherhood mandate." She states (1981: 275):

> Put simply, the mandate of motherhood in its traditional form requires that a woman have at least two children (historically as many as possible, and preferably sons), and raise them "well." She can, however, become educated, work, and be active in public life, as long as she first fulfills this obligation. The kicker in this scheme is the definition of "well." A "good" mother must be physically present to serve her infant's every need. As the child enters school, a mother may pursue other activities—but only those permitting her to be instantly available should her child need her.

Mothers are quickly held responsible for negative attributes of their children. Psychotherapy, particularly Freudian therapy, relates even adult psychopathology to faulty mothering.

On the other hand, Germaine Greer has elaborated on the "anti-child" nature of present-day society (1984: 2):

> the modern Western infant is wanted by fewer people than any infants in our long history, not only by fewer parents but by smaller groups of people. Historically, babies have been welcome additions to society; their parents derived prestige

and pleasure and pride from their proximity and suffered little or no deterioration in the quality of their lives, which could even have been positively enhanced by their arrival. Parents, themselves still relatively junior in the social hierarchy, had not to cudgel their brains to decide if they were ready for the experience, for they were surrounded by people who watched their reproductive career with passionate interest, who would guide them through the fears and anguish of childbirth and take on a measure of responsibility for child rearing. Historically, human societies have been pro-child; modern society is unique in that it is profoundly hostile to children.

Although Greer's historical analysis omits such obviously "antichild" practices as infanticide, abandonment of children, selling of children into bondage, and child religious sacrifices, she argues that few societies have been as global in their disdain of children. Thus women with children are in the unenviable position of being "mandated" to raise children by a society that is hostile to children.

Regarding the effects of children on mothers' mental health, Shapiro et al. (1979) indicate that no other factor relates as heavily to conflict on women as young children in the home. Research by Brown and Harris (1978) demonstrated that the presence of three or more children under age 14 in the home was one of four major risk factors for depression in women. Among unmarried individuals, raising children is viewed as a major life strain (Pearlin and Johnson 1977). Finally, the presence of preschool children is related to marital stress (Orden and Bradburn 1968). It is not surprising that women's psychological distress is least prevalent when children have grown and left the home (Radloff 1980). An insidious societal reversal is the belief (and propagation by the media) of "the empty nest syndrome" and its relation to isolation and loneliness in women. In fact, a "full nest" is a far greater risk for women's distress.

EMPLOYED WOMEN: COMPETING WITH STEREOTYPES

Workforce participation of women has increased dramatically in the past decades. Fewer than one-third of all women were employed in 1947, whereas almost half of all women were in the labor force by 1978 (Russo 1981). This increase is primarily the result of married women entering the workforce.

We have described how employed married women continue to take major responsibility for housework and childcare. Furthermore, the role of employed women is inconsistent with feminine sex role stereotypes, particularly for women in nontraditional occupations (Schein 1973; Powell and Butterfield 1979; Massengill and DiMarco 1979). When female and male managers in a business setting perform assertively, research indicates that women are rated more negatively (Wiley and Eskilson 1982).

It would appear that employed women, particularly those who are married, would suffer distress from the stress of "out-of-role" behavior. However, the reverse is the case. Full-time employed women score higher on satisfaction (Hall and Gordon 1972) than either part-time employed women or housewives. Among depressed women recovery is faster for employed women than for housewives (Mostow and Newberry 1975). Brown and Harris (1978) found employment to have a protective effect for women even when they had other risk factors (such as young children in the home) for depression. It should be noted, however, that most research has focused on women who are in more traditional jobs. Preliminary research on women physicians indicates that they have high rates of depression, particularly those who have experienced prejudice in training or employment (Welner et al. 1979). There is little research on the mental health of women engaged in other nontraditional occupations.

WOMEN, RACE, AND CLASS

The majority of research on women's mental health has focused on white, middle-class women. Yet a variety of social forces operate for nonwhite women, particularly on black women. Black women are more likely to be employed out of economic necessity and to be heads of households. Nevertheless, black women earn lower incomes than white women, who earn lower incomes than white and black men (Hyde 1985). Black professional women are more likely than their white female colleagues to be unmarried or married to men lower in professional status (Hyde 1985). Black women who identify with the black movement as well as the feminist or lesbian community may have difficulty coordinating the two. Finally, black women live in a society where white standards of physical appearance and family constellations may lead to lower self-esteem. Thus black women face a number of "Catch-22" situations.

Poverty is an increasing phenomenon for women, who tend to work in low-paying "women's occupations" (e.g., waitresses, babysitters, hospital attendants) and to earn less than men do even when holding similar jobs. Perlman (1976) has listed four labor market factors as influencing women's inadequate income: (1) a low frequency of labor market participation; (2) high frequency of part-time and sporadic jobs; (3) concentration in low-paying jobs; and (4) lower pay than men receive who hold the same jobs. This is particularly grave when women are heads of households and when they are supporting children.

As Gladwin (1967: 1) has stated, poverty means "being poor, being despised, being incompetent, being powerless." It is not surprising that poverty, which affects women in general and women who are members of minority groups in particular, is related to increased rates of mental illness. The poor are more likely to have high rates of alcoholism and depression (Goodman 1983) and to receive more custodial care in psychiatric hospitals rather than individual psychotherapy (Hollingshead and Redlich 1958). Furthermore, individuals with severe psychopathology may begin to "drift" into the lowest socioeconomic classes because of inability to maintain employment (Rushing 1971). Research on the influence of race and class issues on mental health is most inadequate and work is urgently needed in this area.

PROGRAMMATIC IMPLICATIONS: "IT IS HARD TO FIGHT AN ENEMY WHO HAS OUTPOSTS IN YOUR HEAD"

The previous sections illustrate that the oppression of women by the mental health field is covert. Although "scientific evidence" is held in high esteem, research that gainsays widely held beliefs is easily ignored, or its implications are trivialized. Thus we are guilty of omission when we (for example) provide empathy and reassurance to female clients who seek therapy because they are unmarried or childless rather than pointing out the difficult aspects of the married-with-children status with its negative mental health implications. Marriage is a desirable state—for men. As professionals our training has indoctrinated us to hold models of "man" equally valid for both genders. In the years since the Broverman et al. (1970) study, texts on women in therapy report sexism on the part of psychotherapists toward female clients (Howell and Bayes 1981; Rawlings and Carter 1977). As Fodor and Rothblum have stated (1984: 87):

Themes involving sexism in the Report of the Task Force on Sex Bias and Sex-Role Stereotyping in Psychotherapeutic Practice conducted in 1974 (Brodsky and Holroyd, 1981) include the following: (a) the therapist fostering the traditional sex role, by advocating marriage, housework, or childrearing for women, and deferring to the husband's needs in therapy; (b) devaluation of women via sexist jokes, demeaning comments, or inaccurate labels to describe women; (c) sexist use of psychodynamic concepts, such as "penis envy," "vaginal orgasm," or "castrating female"; and (d) responding to women as sex objects or seducing female clients.

Given that women are often in better psychological health when their roles are held in poor esteem by society (e.g., lesbians, child-free, never married), and given that mental health professionals are often trained to mirror the assumptions and biases of society at large, what are some implications for changing the "Catch-22's" of women in psychological distress?

First, we recommend deemphasizing individual therapy as a solution for women's problems. Given the universality of women's socialization, costly hours of one-to-one contact with therapists will not begin to decrease women's suffering. An emphasis on primary prevention in the community is indicated (see Albee 1982 for a review of this area). Shifting the cause of mental health problems from individual deficiencies or socialization to structural conditions such as race, ethnicity, poverty, and occupational discrimination changes the "blame" from individual to societal forces. We are also aware of pressures to maintain the status quo. Psychologists, social workers, and psychiatrists trained as therapists have higher prestige and income than community organizations or social activists. Application rates to medical schools and clinical psychology programs exceed those to public health programs. Yet there are increased benefits to society when funding is allocated to community programs as opposed to waiting until psychological distress is evident before intervening. A second recommendation is allocation of resources for issues specifically related to preventing mental illness in women.

Next, we urge mental health professionals to play a pivotal role in educating professional colleagues, clients, schools, and community organizations about societal issues confronting women's mental health. We urge feminists, conscious of reversals, to educate co-workers, therapists, and friends about the inequities around them. We acknowledge society's disapproval of women who are risk-takers, especially when such acts disturb the comfort of routine. We applaud the "in-sights" of women who have the ability to perceive discrimination in a society that has socialized them to fit in.

It is not our purpose in this chapter to argue that women should avoid intimate personal relationships, parenthood, or nontraditional employment because of the potential mental health risks associated with these roles. As we have seen, it is the dual burden of housework and employment that is a risk factor for women who are married, the experience of prejudice that correlates with depression among women physicians, etc. We recognize that women are creating new roles in their relationships and their places of work. In this way the antecedents of psychological distress can be minimized.

Finally, we acknowledge that societal changes of the magnitude we are recommending are slow. Possibly, only a societal revolution can effect such large-scale change. One hopes the decades to come will continue to challenge and broaden our knowledge of women's mental health disorders and how to prevent them.

Notes

[1] Although 70 percent of women with school-age children are currently in the labor force (Bureau of Labor Statistics 1985), there is evidence that women are not as vulnerable to stress-related disorders as are men.

[2] Most of the mental health research concerning marital status has focused on white, middle-class individuals and used traditional categories of marital status (that is, individuals are either never married, currently married, or no longer married). Thus we do not examine the effects of ethnicity and class on marital status and mental health.

[3] In addition to married women, there are now nearly two million couples living together who are not married (Hacker 1983). Although there is little research investigating mental health rates of such couples, women in such relationships may share some of the difficulties of married women in terms of dual responsibility for domestic tasks and employment.

References

Albee, G., 1982. "Preventing Psychopathology and Promoting Human Potential," American Psychologist 37: 1043–50.

Bloom, B.L., S.J. Asher and S.W. White, 1978. "Marital Disruption as a Stressor: A Review and Analysis," Psychological Bulletin 85: 867–94.

Brandwein, R.A., C.A. Brown and E.M. Fox, 1974. "Women and Children Last: The Social Situation of Divorced Mothers and Their Families," Journal of Marriage and the Family 36: 498–514.

Brehony, K.A., 1983. "Women and Agoraphobia: A Case for the Etiological Significance of the Feminine Sex-Role Stereotype," in V. Franks and E.D. Rothblum (eds.) The Stereotyping of Women: Its Effects on Mental Health. New York: Springer.

Brisco, C.W. and J.B. Smith, 1973. "Depression and Marital Turmoil," Archives of General Psychiatry 39: 811–17.

Brodsky, A. and J. Holroyd, 1981. "Report of the Task Force on Sex Bias and Sex Role Stereotyping in Psychotherapeutic Practice," in E. Howell and M. Bayes (eds.) Women and Mental Health. New York: Basic Books.

Broverman, I.H., D.M. Broverman, F.E. Clarkson, P.S. Rosenkrantz and S.R. Vogel, 1970. "Sex Role Stereotypes and Clinical Judgments of Mental Health," Journal of Consulting and Clinical Psychology 34: 1–7.

Brown, G.W., M.N. Bhrolchain and T. Harris, 1975. "Social Class and Psychiatric Disturbance Among Women in an Urban Population," Sociology 9: 225–54.

Brown, G.W. and T.O. Harris, 1978. Social Origins of Depression. London: Tavistock.

Brownmiller, S., 1975. Against Our Will: Men, Women and Rape. New York: Simon and Schuster.

Chesler, P., 1972. Women and Madness. New York: Avon.

Cox, S., 1981. Female Psychology: The Emerging Self. New York: St. Martin's Press.

Daly, M., 1984. Pure Lust. London: The Women's Press.

Donelson, E., 1977. "Becoming a Single Woman," in E. Donelson and J.E. Gullahorn (eds.) Women: A Psychological Perspective. New York: John Wiley.

Diagnostic and Statistical Manual of Mental Disorders (3rd ed.), 1980. Washington, DC: APA.

Family Protection Act, 1980. (S.1808, H.R. 6028), "Section-by-section Summary and Constitutional Analysis." Washington, DC: Library of Congress.

Fodor, I. and E.D. Rothblum, 1984. "Strategies for Dealing with Sex Role Stereotypes," in C.M. Brody (ed.) Women Working With Women: New Theory and Process of Feminist Therapy. New York: Springer.

Fodor, I.G., 1974. "The Phobic Syndrome in Women: Implications for Treatment," in V. Franks and V. Burtle (eds) Women and Therapy. New York: Brunner/Mazel.

Franks, V. and E.D. Rothblum, 1983. The Stereotyping of Women: Its Effects on Mental Health. New York: Springer.

Gladwin, T., 1967. Poverty U.S.A. Boston: Little, Brown.

Goodman, A.G. et al., 1983. "The Relationship Between Socioeconomic Class and Prevalence of Schizophrenia, Alcoholism, and Affective Disorders Treated by Inpatient Care in a Suburban Area," American Journal of Psychiatry 140: 166–70.

Gove, W.R., 1972. "The Relationship Between Sex Roles, Marital Status and Mental Illness," Social Forces 51: 34–44.

Gove, W.R., 1979. "Sex Differences in the Epidemiology of Mental Disorder: Evidence and Explanations," in E.S. Gomberg and V. Franks (eds.) Gender and Disordered Behavior: Sex Differences in Psychopathology. New York: Brunner/Mazel.

Gove, W.R. and J. Tudor, 1973. "Adult Sex Roles and Mental Illness," American Journal of Sociology 73: 812–35.

Greer, G., 1984. Sex and Destiny: The Politics of Human Fertility. New York: Harper and Row.

Hacker, A., 1983. A Statistical Profile of the American People. New York: Viking Press.

Hall, D.T. and F.E. Gordon, 1972. "Career Choices of Married Women: Effects on Conflict Role Behavior and Satisfaction," Journal of Applied Psychology 58: 42–48.

Hetherington, E.M., M. Cox and R. Cox, 1979. "Stress and Coping in Divorce: A Focus on Women," in J.E. Gullahorn (ed.) Psychology and Women: In Transition. New York: John Wiley.

Hirschfeld, R.M.A. and C.K. Cross, 1981. "Psychosocial Risk Factors for Depression," in D.A. Regier and G. Allen (eds.) Risk Factor Research in the Major Mental Disorders. National Institute of Mental Health. DHHS Pub. No. (ADM)

81–1068. Washington, DC: Supt. of Docs., U.S. Government Printing Office.

Hite, S., 1976. The Hite Report. New York: Macmillan.

Hollinghead, A.R. and S.C. Redlich, 1958. Social Class and Mental Illness: A Community Study. New York: Wiley.

Hooker, E., 1957. "The Adjustment of the Male Overt Homosexual," Journal of Projective Techniques 1: 18–31.

Howell, E. and M. Bayes (eds.), 1981. Women and Mental Health. New York: Basic Books.

Hyde, J.S., 1985. Half the Human Experience: The Psychology of women, 3rd ed. Lexington, MA: D.C. Heath.

Hyde, J.S. and B.G. Rosenberg, 1980. Half the Human Experience: The Psychology of Women, 2nd ed. Lexington, MA: D.C. Heath.

Joffe, J., 1982. "Approaches to Prevention of Adverse Developmental Consequences of Genetic and Prenatal Factors," in L.A. Bond and J.M. Joffe (eds.) Facilitating Infant and Early Childhood Development. Hanover, NH: University Press of New England.

Jourard, S.M. and P. Lasakow, 1958. "Some Factors in Self-Disclosure," Journal of Abnormal and Social Psychology 56: 91–98.

Kaplan, M., 1983. "A Women's View of DSM-III," American Psychologist 38: 786–92.

Kinsey, A.C., W.B. Pomeroy, C.E. Martin and P.H. Gebhard, 1953. Sexual Behavior in the Human Female. Philadelphia: W.B. Saunders.

Malamuth, N.M., 1982. "Rapists and Normal Men," Treatment for Sexual Aggressiveness News 5.

Massengill, D. and N. DiMarco, 1979. "Sex-Role Stereotypes and Requisite Management Characteristics: A Current Replication," Sex Roles 5: 561–70.

Mostow, E. and P. Newberry, 1975. "Work Role and Depression in Women: A Comparison of Workers and Housewives in Treatment," American Journal of Orthopsychiatry 45: 538–48.

Orden, S.R. and N.M. Bradburn, 1968. "Working Wives and Marriage Happiness," American Journal of Sociology 74: 392–407.

Pearlin, L.J. and J.S. Johnson, 1977. "Marital Status, Life-Strains and Depression," American Sociological Review 42: 704–15.

Perlman, R., 1976. The Economics of Poverty. New York: McGraw-Hill.

Pithers, W., 1982. Personal communication.

Pitts, F.N., B. Schuller, C.L. Rich and A.F. Pitts, 1979. "Suicide Among U.S. Women Physicians 1967–1972," American Journal of Psychiatry 136: 694–96.

Poloma, M.M., 1972. "Role Conflict and the Married Professional Woman," in C. Safilios-Rothschild (ed.) Toward a Sociology of Women. Lexington, MA: Xerox.

Powell, G.N. and D.A. Butterfield, 1979. "The 'Good Manager': Masculine or Androgynous?" Management Journal 22: 395–403.

Radloff, L., 1975. "Sex Differences in Depression: The Effects of Occupation and Marital Status," Sex Roles 1: 249–65.

Radloff, L.S., 1980. "Depression and the Empty Nest," Sex Roles 6: 776–81.

Radloff, L.S. and D.S. Rae, 1979. "Susceptibility and Precipitating Factors in Depression: Sex Differences and Similarities," Journal of Abnormal Psychology 88: 174–81.

Rawlings, E.I. and D.K. Carter, 1979. "Divorced Women," The Counseling Psychologist 8: 27–28.

Resick, P.A., 1983. "Sex Role Stereotypes and Violence Against Women," in V. Franks and E.D. Rothblum (eds.) The Stereotyping of Women: Its Effects on Mental Health. New York: Springer.

Roberts, A.H., 1964. "Housebound Housewives—A Follow-Up of Phobic Anxiety States," British Journal of Psychiatry 110: 191–97.

Rohrbaugh, J.B., 1979. Women: Psychology's Puzzle. New York: Basic Books.

Rosenkrantz, P., S. Vogel, H. Bee, I. Broverman and D.M. Broverman, 1968. "Sex Role Stereotypes and Self-Concepts in College Students," Journal of Consulting and Clinical Psychology 32: 287–95.

Rothblum, E.D., 1983. "Sex-Role Stereotypes and Depression in Women," in V. Franks and E.D. Rothblum (eds.) The Stereotyping of Women: Its Effects on Mental Health. New York: Springer.

Rothblum, E.D., L.J. Solomon and G. Albee, in press. "A Socio-Political Perspective of DSM III," in T. Millon and G. Klerman (eds.) Contemporary Issues in Psychology. New York: Guilford.

Rounsaville, B.J., B.A. Prusoff and M.M. Weissman, 1980. "The Course of Marital Disputes in Depressed Women. A 48-Month Follow-Up Study," Comprehensive Psychiatry 21: 111–18.

Rushing, W.A., 1971. "Individual Resources, Societal Reaction and Hospital Commitment," The American Journal of Sociology 77 (November): 511–26.

Russo, N.F., 1981. "Overview: Sex Roles, Fertility and the Motherhood Mandate," in S. Cox (ed.) Female Psychology: The Emerging Self. New York: St. Martin's Press.

Savvy, 1981. The Savvy Survey of Executive Behavior. New York: Savvy.

Schein, V.E., 1973. "The Relationship Between Sex Role Stereotypes and Requisite Management Characteristics," Journal of Applied Psychology 57: 95–100.

Schur, E.M., 1983. Labeling Women Deviant. New York: Random House.

Shapiro, D.A., G. Perry and C. Brewin, 1979. "Stress, Coping and Psychotherapy: The Foundations of a Clinical Approach," in T. Cox and C. Mackay (eds.) Psychophysiological Response to Occupational Stress. New York: International Publishing.

Siassi, I., G. Crocetti and H.R. Spiro, 1974. "Loneliness and Dissatisfaction in a Blue Collar Population," Archives of General Psychiatry 30: 261–65.

Solomon, L.J. and E.D. Rothblum, 1985. "Skills Training for the Special Problems Experienced by Women," in L. L'Abate and M.P. Milan (Eds.) Handbook of Social Skills Training and Research. New York: Wiley.

Syfers, J., 1973. "Why I Want A Wife," in A. Levine and A. Rapone (eds.) Radical Feminism. New York: Quadrangle.

Thompson, N.L., B.R. McCandless and B.R. Strickland, 1971. "Personal Adjustment of Male and Female Homosexuals and Heterosexuals," Journal of Abnormal Psychology 78: 237–40.

Weissman, M.M. and G.L. Klerman, 1977. "Sex Differences and the Epidemiology of Depression," Archives of General Psychiatry 34: 98–111.

Weissman, M.M., E.S. Paykel, R. Siegel and G.L. Klerman, 1971. "The Social Role Performance of Depressed Women: Comparisons with a Normal Group," American Journal of Orthopsychiatry 41: 390–405.

Weitzman, L., 1985. The Divorce Revolution. New York: The Free Press.

Welner, A., S. Martin, W. Wochnick, M.A. Davis, R. Fishman and P.J. Clayton, 1979. "Psychiatric Disorders Among Professional Women," Archives of General Psychiatry 36: 169–72.

Wiley, M.G. and A. Eskilson, 1982. "Coping in the Corporation: Sex Role Constraints," Journal of Applied Social Psychology 12: 1–11.

Worell, J. and N. Garrett-Fulks, 1983. "The Resocialization of Single-Again Women," in V. Franks and E.D. Rothblum (eds.) The Stereotyping of Women: Its Effects on Mental Health. New York: Springer.

PART VI

POLITICAL AND LEGAL RIGHTS

CHAPTER 14

POLITICAL RIGHTS

Marian Lief Palley

BACKGROUND

The Orthodox Hebrew morning prayer includes the words "I thank thee, O Lord, that thou hast not created me a woman." Also, traditionally women have been virtually excluded from the religious rituals of Judaism. Christianity did not improve the role of women in religion and ritual. Thus in the First Letter of Paul to Timothy it is written:

> I permit no women to teach or to have authority over men; she is to keep silent. For Adam was created first, then Eve; and Adam was not deceived, but the woman was deceived and became a transgressor. yet women will be saved through bearing children, if she continues in faith and love and holiness, with modesty. (Oxford Annotated Bible 1965)

The inferior position of women in relation to men was perpetuated by both Catholics and Protestants. Women were not allowed to be Catholic priests, and the Protestant Reformation did not improve substantially the lot of women. Martin Luther, for example, was very clear in his belief that women's place was in the home caring for their families (Ruether 1974).

The onset of the Industrial Revolution in many ways fostered an entrenchment of a subordinate position for women (Palley 1974). Industrialization led to a separation of home and employment. Prior to the Industrial Revolution many crafts were produced and distributed in the home, and thus women could work with men while they cared for their families. The movement of paid work out of the home in response to efforts to centralize the production and distribution of goods in shops led to an environment in which married women tended to remain at home to care for the needs of their families. Men left their homes to produce and distribute goods and services. In an economic system rooted in the marketplace, women were excluded as producers and sellers of goods and services. Thus, in an industrial society they became totally economically dependent on their husbands since they were barred from the market place. Women assumed a role not too different from that of children who are totally dependent on their parents. Henrick Ibsen in his play <u>A Doll's House</u> addresses this relationship when he has Nora's husband say to her, "Try to calm down, and recover your balance, my scared little song bird. You may rest secure. I have broad wings to shield you" (Ibsen 1906). In the United States the traditional role of women was not dissimilar from the role of women in other Western societies. Women in frontier communities often had to care for their farms as well as their families when their husbands were away; but when the men returned, women reverted back to their primary roles as wives and mothers.

Women who did not have fathers or husbands to support them were often required to work. The daughters and wives of more affluent families stayed at home. Some of these women were educated—though rarely at a level equivalent to that of men. In fact, it was these women who became involved in the Abolitionist Movement and who provided the intellectual, spiritual, and organizational momentum for the Women's Movement in the nineteenth century, which evolved into the suffrage movement of the twentieth century.

In 1777 Abigail Adams, in a letter to her husband John, wrote:

In the new code of laws...I desire you would remember the ladies and be more generous and favorable to them than your ancestors.... If particular care and attention is not paid to the ladies, we are determined to foment a rebellion.... (Flexner 1974)

Though the founding fathers did no heed her plea, rebellion was not forthcoming. In fact, it was not until after the Civil War that any sort of women's movement began to take form. In part this early social movement developed in response to the enactment of the

Fifteenth Amendment, which provided black men with the right to vote but which did not extend voting rights to women. The constitutional grant of women's suffrage finally was provided by the Nineteenth Amendment many years later in 1920.

The role expectation patterns for women that excluded them from participation in the political process and maintained a separate place for women outside of the economic marketplace, or in marginal positions in the economic system, generally was accepted by women as well as men. Abigail Adams's prediction of rebellion was not realistic. In fact, changes in role expectation patterns that have evolved have done so very gradually. In terms of contemporary issues and politics, traditional sex role expectations can be seen as one factor that has continued to hamper the effectiveness of the women's movement. Thus, when issues are defined in terms of role change rather than in terms of role equity, the political support for issues is lessened. Role equity issues, such as equal credit opportunity and pension rights, have been much easier to "sell" to the American public and to lawmakers.

> Role equity issues are those policies which extend rights now enjoyed by other groups (men, other minorities) to women and which appear to be relatively delineated or narrow in their implications, permitting policy makers to seek advantage with feminist groups and voters with little cost or controversy. In contrast, role change issues appear to produce change in the dependent female role of wife, mother, and homemaker, holding out the potential of greater sexual freedom and independence in a variety of contexts. The latter issues are fraught with greater political pitfalls, including perceived threats to existing values, in turn creating visible and often powerful opposition. (Gelb and Palley 1982)

It is increasingly difficult to separate economic problems from political problems, and thus the political from the economic barriers that hinder women. There is clearly a relationship between the two spheres. In large measure the political solutions sought by the women's movement have been to issues of economic inequality and perceived injustice. When political solutions have been sought for issues that have been defined by their detractors in noneconomic terms, the women's movement has been less successful. For example, free choice regarding abortion and the Equal Rights

Amendment (ERA) have been defined in role change and not in role
equity terms; as predicted, the women's movement has been
stymied in its efforts to achieve these goals.

Religious tradition, economic developments, and perceptions
of appropriate role behavior have all affected the maintenance of
both implicit and explicit barriers that curtail full political and
economic opportunities for women. However, it would be a mistake
to suggest that the contemporary women's movement has not been
successful over the past 15 years in influencing both the American
public and political decision makers to foster substantial changes in
the law to improve the economic and political position of American
women. In the pages that follow the role of the contemporary
women's movement will be considered and then the political
responses to contemporary problems that affect women will be
discussed.

THE ROLE OF THE WOMEN'S MOVEMENT

During the 50 years that followed the passage of the
Nineteenth Amendment there was a hiatus in organized feminist
activities. The contemporary women's movement is a product of
the 1960s and 1970s. Though this is the case, it would be a
mistake to discount activities in behalf of women that occurred
during the entire five-decade period. Numerous attempts were
made to have an Equal Rights Amendment introduced onto the floor
of the Congress; and finally, in 1963, Congress passed the Equal
Pay Act. Also, during this 50-year period women began to move
out into the workforce in greater numbers, and educational
opportunities for women were expanded response to needs for their
labor during World War II.

Nonetheless, it has been in the past two decades that
political, social, and economic barriers that have hindered the
advancement of women have begun to fall with some deliberate
speed. Women as a group traditionally received "second class"
status in the political, economic, and social realms. With the advent
of the contemporary women's movement in 1966—marked by the
formation of the National Organization for Women (NOW)—women
systematically and deliberately demanded change in their roles in
society. This occurred as expectations expanded in response to
improved educational opportunities and technological advances that
transformed the role of women as mothers and housekeepers, and
as women moved in greater numbers into the paid workforce. In

fact, from 1950 to 1970 female labor force participation nearly doubled, and that growth still continues in the 1980s.

Since the end of World War II educated women have reached adulthood encountering the most contradictions in their lives. They have had achievement-oriented values that were often contradicted by expectations associated with the "traditional" female role. These were the kind of women described by Betty Friedan in her book The Feminine Mystique. Moreover, these were the women who became the leaders of the women's movement in the 1970s and 1980s. It is worth noting that working-class, especially black women, have had to deal with traditional female roles demands and occupational demands for as long as we have had information. However, the occupational component of the lives of these women was not achievement driven in the manner that this new cohort of working women has been oriented. Instead, they had to be concerned with survival under adverse circumstances.

The term "the women's movement" is a shorthand phrase used to describe the wide range of groups and individuals who support the goals of equal rights for women. In fact, the women's movement should be understood as two separate though related phenomenon: the women's moment as a set of interest groups that are involved in lobbying activities, and the women's movement as a social movement. The interest groups that are associated with the women's movement, with one or two exceptions, are not mass membership groups. Rather they are leadership groups. The interest groups in the women's movement all fit into a fivefold classification scheme. Most of these groups are single issue groups, specialized litigation or research organizations, or electoral campaign organizations. There is one major mass membership group, NOW, with about 250,000 members. Finally, traditional women's groups (such as The League of Women Voters and Business and Professional Women) increasingly have become interest group partners in the women's movement. Given this leadership phenomenon, it should not be too surprising that the issues addressed by the women's movement groups tend to be separated from each other as lobbying efforts. Thus the ongoing campaigns to protect abortion rights are organizationally discrete from the efforts to improve women's pension rights. In fact, different but very specialized groups take the leadership positions on the separate issues addressed by the movement. By virtue of separating the issues, it becomes possible to build coalitions with a wide array of groups on different issues. Although the Catholic church, for example, is opposed to abortion rights, it is supportive on issues such as rights for pregnant women.

The women's movement as a social movement draws on a much broader, undifferentiated citizenry. Men and women who support equal opportunities for women and who are sympathetic to the other more specific goals of the women's movement—such as free choice regarding abortion, the Equal Rights Amendment, comparable worth, public support for day care facilities, and the various titles of the Economic Equity Act—are part of this broader societal support base.

To the extent that demands made by the interest group actors in the women's movement to eliminate discrimination based on sex are becoming institutionalized, they have been successful in expanding opportunities and improving conditions for women. Nonetheless, legislation, administrative guidelines, and judicial decisions have not eliminated all discrimination; but the extent of discrimination has been reduced in areas as disparate as free choice regarding abortion, sex discrimination in education, equal credit opportunity, pregnancy discrimination, pension rights, and employment. More women hold elective office today and are succeeding in the professions and business than at any other time in our nation's history. Although more women have received advanced degrees in medicine, law, and other fields, and professional opportunities have opened for them, not all positions are as readily accessible to women as they are to men. There were, for example, more women in President Ronald Reagan's cabinet during his first term of office than there were women commentators on the network television news shows (Goodman 1984). Also, many of the prestigious law firms do not have women partners, and the corporations listed among the Fortune 500 have few women directors.

Where the women's movement interest groups have been successful in their efforts to influence the political decision makers— most successfully in role equity cases—it has been due to their knowledge, understanding, and successful utilization of the political process. Women lobbyists have been consummate political game players. E.E. Schattschneider, in his book The Semisovereign People (1956), discussed the existence of a "mobilization of bias" in American politics that limits access to power for newcomers to the political process. This "mobilization of bias" is a set of predominant values, beliefs, rituals, and institutional procedures that operate to benefit some groups and at the expense of other groups. Those people who defend the status quo occupy key positions of power and thus are in a position to secure their own interests. Inasmuch as the women's movement is rooted in the middle and upper-middle classes of society, the interest group participants have understood how the political process operates and have been able to gain access to the political decision makers (Gelb and Palley 1982).

There are four basic rules that must be used by newcomers to the political process if they are going to be successful in achieving their political goals:

1) To be effective in American politics, groups must be perceived as legitimate.
2) In order to appear legitimate, groups will find it necessary to focus on incremental issues. In this regard role equity issues are less threatening than role change issues.
3) In order to appear legitimate, groups will stress the provision of information and concentrate on mobilizing their allies. They will seek to avoid confrontation that comes from the use of protest tactics. They will form policy networks, and they will be willing to define success in terms of "increments."
4) Like other conventional interest groups, emergent groups will engage in a struggle over the definition of the situation. This struggle will almost always involve the manipulation of symbols favorable to one's cause. At times, these symbols will be employed to socialize conflict. At other times, symbols will be used to privatize conflict (for example, by defining the issue as one involving just role *equity*). (Gelb and Palley 1982)

The women in the movement groups reflect society's "mobilization of bias," and thus they have not been excluded from the political process. Many know and use the "rules of the game" with great skill. For example, when the Regulation was being written to implement the Equal Credit Opportunity Act, the Center for Women's Policy Studies was hired by the Federal Reserve Board to serve as a consulting body for the Federal Task Force on Credit. Whenever issues of concern for the women's movement are being considered by the Congress, or regulations are being formulated by the Federal bureaucracy, representatives of the organized women's movement are called in and ongoing contacts are maintained. Moreover, extensive networks have been built by the women's leadership with members of Congress and their staffs and with appropriate members of bureaucratic agencies.

When it has been necessary to show broad-based support for an issue, it has been possible to generate enthusiasm from among a vast array of state and locally based chapters of national organizations. Letter writing campaigns have been organized, and other indications of voter support developed. The former certainly has been the tactic used by the women's movement in its endeavors to retain freedom of choice regarding abortion. More significant perhaps is that when "quiet campaigns" are deemed more appropriate, mass constituency involvement can be minimized. In 1972 the women's movement kept a very low profile when Title IX of The Education Amendment was being considered by Congress. This was a deliberate tactic so as not to call too much attention to the provision of Title IX that required that there be no discrimination against women in education, including athletics. This latter point became a point of contention as soon as the implications of the law were clear. It was not until 1984 that the "bite" of this Amendment was blunted.

Several sets of events have transpired in the past five years that have led to some refocusing of issues by the leadership of the women's movement. First, the Reagan administration assault on social welfare programs had had a disproportionate impact on women, especially on low-income working women and their children. The administration has attacked affirmative action, abortion rights, and equal educational opportunity. Moreover, the Equal Rights Amendment failed to be ratified by the necessary number of states. Finally, there has been an increasing awareness that poverty is not distributed equally between the sexes. There is a greater likelihood of being at risk of poverty if one is a woman. Cutbacks in programs have led to an entrenchment of the "feminization of poverty."

In 1984 the National-House Democratic Caucus issued its report, Renewing America's Promise. The reported noted that:

> In 1960 23.3 million American women were workers; in June 1982, 47.7 million women—43% of the entire work force— were job holders.

> The jobs women held were largely at the lowest end of the pay scale; in 1981, eight out of ten clerical workers were women; more than six out of ten sales people were women and seven out of ten teachers were women; moreover, only

14% of lawyers, 14% of doctors, and 4% of engineers were women.

Eight out of ten women wage earners work in just 25 of the 420 types of jobs available in America.

One family in three headed by women lives in poverty.

More than one out of every two black American households headed by women live below the poverty line.

For every dollar men earned in 1982, women earned 62 cents. Even though the percentage of women holding managers' jobs doubled between 1960 and 1980—to over 28%—their salaries slipped in relation to men's to 55%, instead of 58%. In our schools, where 82% of the elementary teachers are women, those women earned in 1981 only 82% of the average salary paid to their male colleagues.

Tree-trimmers in Denver earn more than emergency-room nurses. In New York City, many secretaries receive less compensation than parking-lot attendants. In 1982, only one woman worker in ten received more than $20,000 in pay.

Women with college degrees and full-time jobs bring home less income, on average, than men who never finished high school. In 1981, almost two decades after passage of the Equal Pay Act, the average woman computer operator earned $355 a week, while her male counterpart got $488. A female engineer was paid $371 a week; a male, $547. A 25-year-old female college graduate can count on earning $474,000 in her lifetime; a male can expect $1,165,000.

Poverty is a reality for 17.5 percent of all women over 65. Of America's elderly poor, 72 percent are women—2.8 million in all—and 90 percent of them live solely on their Social Security checks.

In many cases, women's retirement benefits do not fairly reflect the contributions they made—to the Social Security system or to family income. Women with jobs, for instance, often have no pension plans or do not qualify for existing plans because family responsibilities keep them from building up the required seniority at work. Homemakers, of course, have no access to private pension plans. And those who receive Social Security or civil service retirement benefits are often not equitably recompensed for the work they did before they married, for working as homemakers—especially if they divorced before ten years of marriage—or for being the lower-paid of two wage-earners. (House Democratic Caucus 1984)

Given these conditions, it is clear that there is still much to be done to improve conditions for women in American society. Incursions have been made on abortion rights and equal education opportunity. Abortion rights is a role change issue and, therefore, has been a very difficult area for women's groups to contain. Equal educational opportunity is a role equity issue. However, inasmuch as Title IX of the Education Act of 1972—the law that bars sex discrimination in education—controls school athletics, it is sometimes interpreted as role change.

In the pages that follow several selected issues will be considered to help illustrate the opposition that the women's movement has had to confront in trying to maintain the gains made in behalf of women's rights. Also, some of the ongoing barriers that make it difficult to improve conditions for women will be discussed.

RECENT POLITICS AND THE WOMEN'S MOVEMENT
Education

In 1984 the Supreme Court handed down its decision in Grove City v. Bell (U.S. 104, S.C. 1211), which provided a narrow interpretation of the federal law barring sex discrimination in education. The case concerned the scope of Title IX and the question as to whether or not an entire educational institution or simply a specific program that is receiving federal money should be bound not to discriminate on the basis of sex. The Nixon, Ford, and Carter administrations supported a broad interpretation of the law. The Reagan administration has supported a narrow "program specific" approach to bias. The Supreme Court, in a 6–3 decision, held that the government does not have broad, institutionwide authority to enforce Title IX whenever educational institutions receive federal money. This decision was seen as limiting the scope of the legislation that prevents discrimination against the aged, the handicapped, and racial and ethnic minorities too.

Legislation was introduced into Congress that would have specifically enacted a broader interpretation into law. The proposed legislation, The Civil Rights Act of 1984, was endorsed and supported by a broad-based coalition of women's groups, civil rights groups, groups representing the aged and the handicapped, and labor union organizations.

Groups representing these constituency interests all worked in tandem under the aegis of the Leadership Conference on Civil Rights and the National Coalition of Women and Girls in Education. Almost immediately after the Supreme Court handed down its decision, about 40 groups met to consider the situation and to draw up a strategy. A decision was made to look beyond Title IX and its impact on women and to consider the effects of the Court's decision on the other groups that were going to be affected by the Grove City decision. The goal of the coalition was to have Congress enact legislation that would restore the law to its pre-Grove City status. It was decided to press their congressional supporters to put the proposed legislation on a "fast track." A subcommittee of the steering committee of the coalition drafted a bill within one week of the coalition's inception. Members of Congress were lobbied aggressively. Grass-roots lobbying was pursued actively in efforts to gain congressional cosponsorship for the bill. In the Senate there were 63 cosponsors and in the House there were 25. Relations with the press were limited because the coalition members did not want to provide their opposition with time to develop a counterstrategy. The Reagan administration lobbied actively against the bill. Part of this opposition was premised on opposition to the activist role of government in enforcing civil rights and affirmative action laws and regulations. Dissent in the administration was also based on the belief that the federal government's role in social welfare program areas should be reduced. There also seems to be some evidence to support the view that the administration is not too concerned about improving conditions for women. Congressional opposition to the proposed legislation was spearheaded by Senator Orin Hatch (R., Utah). Despite the significant range of support for the passage of a law that would ensure the broader interpretation of the law, the proposed legislation was not approved by Congress, a result acclaimed by the administration.

Abortion Rights

During the 1984 presidential election campaign, President Reagan reiterated his opposition to the Supreme Court's 1973 decision in Roe v. Wade (410 U.S. 113) which guaranteed women the right to have an abortion to terminate a pregnancy. In fact, Mr. Reagan reiterated his support during this campaign for a constitutional amendment that would forbid abortions to be performed.

Since 1973 and the Supreme Court's prochoice decision there have been numerous attempts made to restrict abortion rights. Congress has restricted the use of Medicaid funds to pay for abortions for medically needy women. Also, federal funds cannot be used to pay for abortions for residents of the District of Columbia and Peace Corps volunteers. Moreover, congressional attacks on abortion rights have been made on Title X of the Public Health Service Act of 1970. Title X forbids spending any money authorized by law where abortion is utilized as a means of family planning. It has been the contention of antiabortion forces, including members of Congress and members of antiabortion groups, that family planning groups such as Planned Parenthood counsel abortion as a family planning mechanism. Also, the Reagan administration has blocked foreign aid that is channeled to organizations that provide for abortion-related services. This policy applies to governments, United Nations agencies and private funded organizations (Congressional Quarterly Weekly Report 1984).

Prochoice groups, especially the National Abortion Rights Action League (NARAL) and Planned Parenthood, have been in the forefront of the movement to maintain freedom of choice. They have held back some of the onslaught of the Right to Life Movement, but they have experienced very strong and well organized opposition in the national, state, and local arenas. In the past few years the prochoice groups have moved to mobilize support at the grass-roots level in response to the prolifers' activities that have involved efforts to generate support for a constitutional amendment that would ban all abortions and have targeted candidates for public office who do not take antiabortion positions. Both the National Abortion Rights Action League and Planned Parenthood have experienced increases in their membership and in financial contributions. Also, NARAL-PAC and Planned Parenthood PAC have expanded their campaign activities (Newsweek 1985). Since the mid-1970s prochoice activists have had to maintain constant vigilance as a very well organized Right to Life movement has worked to chip away at the choice protections afforded women by the Supreme Court in its decision in Roe v. Wade.

Economic Equity Act

As noted above, Reagan administration policies have had a disproportionately negative economic impact on women, and thus the women's movement recently has focused more of its attentions onto economic issues. More specifically, the movement has turned its attentions to the passage of several of the titles of the Economic Equity Act (EEA). The EEA is a multititled act that includes provisions for pension equity, unisex insurance, equal apportionment of economic responsibility between divorced parents, and more extensive day care coverage for children of working parents. Also, the issue of equal pay for work of comparable worth, referred to as pay equity, is in the forefront of concerns of the women's movement at this time. This issue has been addressed primarily at the level of state and local government as opposed to the national decision-making arena.

The 98th Congress enacted a national pension protection law. Several groups were particularly active in the campaign to enact this law. In particular, the Women's Equity Action League (WEAL), the Pension Rights Project to the Pension Rights Center, and the American Association of University Women (AAUW) were involved from the very start of the activities to have a law passed by Congress that would extend additional pension protections to women. Other groups joined in their efforts. Toward the end of 1982, after the failure to ratify the ERA, the Republican Party in the Congress, in particular Senator Robert Dole (R., Ka.), decided to provide a leadership role in the efforts to enact a pension equity law. Public opinion polls showed that there was a good deal of support for a law that would provide more equitable pension conditions for women, and there was little vocal opposition to such a law in either house of Congress (Gelb and Palley 1986). Thus, in 1984 the Retirement Equity Act was enacted. This law:

(1) Lowers from 25 to 21 the age at which employers must enroll most workers in pension plans;
(2) Lowers from 22 to 18 the age at which employees begin to earn credits toward vesting;
(3) Prevents counting a one-year maternity or paternity leave as a break in service and permits workers to stay away from their jobs for five years without sacrificing pension credits;

(4) Prevents employees from waiving coverage for survivors without written consent of their spouses;

(5) Gives state courts the authority to treat pensions as joint property in divorce cases;

(6) Grants death benefits to the spouse of a worker who is fully vested even if the worker dies before the company's early retirement age. (Vise 1984)

This legislation is incremental, not vast and sweeping. It does not take into account the fact that many people are not participants in any pension plans at all. Thus service workers, who are often women, are usually uncovered by any pension plan. On a broader scale this legislation does not address issues relating to vesting, portability, or integration of pension benefits.

Also considered during the 98th Congress was the Nondiscrimination in Insurance Act (Unisex Insurance). The proposed legislation would have prohibited discrimination in both the establishment of fees and benefits on the basis of sex, race, color, or national origin. Whereas the question of pension reform did not generate too much opposition in the affected industry or in the Congress, the issue of unisex insurance coverage did generate significant opposition by the insurance companies, and ultimately in Congress. Some observers have suggested that since costs incurred by changes in the pension laws could be passed on to the pensioner, opposition by pension funds was minimal (Reuss and Forman 1984). On the other hand, the insurance industry envisions high changeover costs if they have to implement unisex insurance coverage. The insurance industry mounted a million dollar campaign to defeat unisex insurance legislation. They were opposed to incursions by the federal government that would regulate their industry and they were trying to forestall the changeover costs that would occur should a unisex system be mandated by law. Congress responded to the industry pressures, and no new legislation was enacted. Groups within the women's movement have focused their attention since 1984 on trying to get the insurance companies to break ranks. Also, they have sought to bring changes in state laws (Gelb and Palley 1986).

Pay Equity

The other economic issue that is receiving particular attention by the women's movement is the issue of equal pay for jobs of comparable worth (pay equity). This is a particularly significant issue since women tend to hold jobs different from those favored by men. The pay scales are significantly lower in female-dominated positions than in male-dominated jobs. In fact, it is estimated that the more a job category is dominated by women, the less it pays, with the average compensation going down approximately $54 per year for each additional percentage point of women employed in the category (Mann 1983). There are several reasons for the wage gap. However, a 1981 National Academy of Sciences Report noted that one-half of the wage gap could not be explained by anything but sex discrimination. In fact, women have lower earnings than men of equal educational background at every educational level. Even the federal government, our nation's largest employer, is guilty of wage discrimination. As recently as 1981 in the federal service, animal health technicians—94 percent male—earned an average yearly salary of $19,340 while nursing assistant—67 percent female—earned an average of $13,890 a year (Mayer 1984).

Women workers perform many of the most important jobs in society. They predominate as teachers for our children, providers of health care in hospitals and nursing homes, and they are the "backbone" of the financial and business office world. Women earn on average just a little more than three-fifths of what men earn. This is the situation despite enforcement of The Equal Pay Act and Title VII of the Civil Rights Act of 1964. The rhetoric of equal opportunity and affirmative action has not led to a situation in which women and men have come close to achieving equality in the types of jobs that they hold. Women tend to be segregated in a small number of occupations.

The U.S. Department of Labor divides job types into 12 major occupations which are subdivided into 427 detailed occupations. Fifty-two percent of all employed women work in 2 of the 12 major occupations—clerical and service, other than household. Fifty percent of women work in just twenty occupations. In 1982 half of all employed women worked in occupations that were 75 percent female, and 22 percent of employed women worked in jobs that were 85 percent female. Also, 80 percent of clericals were women, 97 percent of private household workers were women, and 59 percent of nonhousehold service workers were women. Though more women have been entering traditionally male professional, technical, and blue-collar jobs, the overall degree of job segregation has not changed. For every woman entering a traditional male field, there are more women entering traditionally female fields.

Moreover, even as women enter new occupational fields, they remain segregated in a small number of jobs within those groupings (The Wage Gap 1983).

It is significant to note that despite the economic inequity, Congress has not been willing to seriously consider pay equity legislation. The rhetoric of the free market as well as issues of cost, intrusive government regulation, and a likely redistribution of economic resources from men to women has led to strong opposition to legislation not only in Congress but in the business community and within the Reagan administration. In fact, in 1985 Administration spokesmen even began to question the need to maintain the affirmative action guidelines that have assisted some women to enter into male- dominated job categories.

Also, despite the fact that the issue of comparable worth has been endorsed by a coalition of women's groups including the National Commission on Pay Equity, which itself represents about 150 groups, as well as unions, such as the American Federation of State and Municipal Employees (AFSME), there is an ambivalent feeling about the likelihood of achieving national legislation. However, there is a shared view that this is an issue that can be used to "scare" decision makers and thus be used as a "tactical wedge" to achieve other goals of the women's movement (Gelb and Palley 1986). For the most part there has been state and local litigation spurred on by the 1983 federal court decision in the State of Washington v. Gunther (452 US161) which found the state guilty of discrimination against 15,000 employees. The unions, in particular AFSME, have been most involved in this litigation.

Day Care

There are several other issue areas of central concern to women in which there has been little positive movement by government decision makers. In particular, there is no comprehensive day care policy in the United States. This poses a problem for many women. Even if there is another household earner, women often must work to maintain their families' basic living standards. From 1974 to 1984 the two-paycheck family increased by 25 percent. By middecade three of every five married couple families included at least two wage earners (The Wage Gap 1983). By 1984, 48 percent of all children under the age of six had working mothers, and almost one-half of all married women with children under the age of one were members of the paid workforce (US Congress 1985).

Many of the women in the paid labor force are not "comfortable." Many are finding it very difficult to balance family and workforce roles and to provide basic needs—food, clothing, and shelter—to their families. Put in somewhat different terms, many women confront difficult decisions regarding their multiple roles. If auxiliary services such as child care are not provided, they often cannot fulfill these roles properly. The implications of this condition can be very serious, indeed devastating to the fabric of the family and to the development and maturation of children. It creates a catch 22 situation for women in the workforce be they single mothers, married mothers, or women without children who are contemplating family formation. It is an issue of critical significance to nonworking women too. There is a cadre of women who do not participate in the paid workforce because they cannot obtain adequate affordable child care. As a result, some of these women become dependent on public assistance to maintain their families; others of these women live in families that can barely make ends meet; and still other women, who have husbands who can support their families adequately, become dissatisfied and often depressed with their lives. However, the supply of affordable child care lags far behind the need in the United States. As many as 6 to 7 million children under age 13 (including preschoolers) have no care while their parents work (U.S. Congress 1985).

Private child care provision is often expensive if it is available and in many areas it is insufficient and of dubious quality (Adams and Winston 1980). To date, the federal government has confined its efforts to the provision of child care for the poor. In fiscal year 1985 it provided limited funding under the rubric of the Social Services Block Grant. (Of course, the funds provided to the states by this grant can be used for a variety of other services as well as child care.) In addition, Head Start provides for some limited child care services for the poor. The Dependent Care Tax Credit helps families that can find child care in that it provides some limited tax credits. Of course, a credit is not refundable, and therefore low-income people who do not owe any taxes do not benefit from this scheme.

Moves to provide broad-based child care services have been stymied. The Comprehensive Child Development Act of 1971, which called upon the government to assure "every child a fair and full opportunity to reach his full potential," passed Congress only to be vetoed by President Nixon. In his veto message the president explained that he objected to the program on the grounds that it undermined the American family (Adams and Winston 1980). This notion is dated at best and was perhaps never intended to be taken seriously. In fact, President Nixon supported child care legislation for welfare clients on the grounds that it supported family cohesion. More recent efforts to develop a comprehensive child care program have not been successful.

Child care is a women's issue that has not been addressed by the women's movement, though the groups in the movement have supported, albeit quietly, the efforts of others. There are several reasons for their nonaction. Child care has been defined as an interest area for a small group of working women for a short period of time. It has not been defined as an issue of central importance to most women. It has not been seen as a core component of a program that will assist women in achieving equality in the workplace (Kamerman 1985).

CONCLUSIONS

There have been several factors that have been working to mitigate against the success of the women's movement during the past half-decade. First, attitudes and beliefs rooted in history and religious belief have been very hard to change. Thus it has been difficult to alter the traditional role expectations that most women and men adhere to regarding the appropriate behaviors for women. Though there has been the development of a network of interest groups and a mass movement supportive of improving conditions for women, progress has been slow, albeit steady. The successes of the women's movement have been greatest when issues relating to role equity have been addressed while issues relating to role change have triggered much greater opposition. One need only look at the campaigns to prevent freedom of choice to understand this phenomenon.

The conservative counterrevolution that swept Ronald Reagan into the White House in 1980 and then again in 1984 has served to chill the advancements of women's rights. Also, the failure to ratify the Equal Rights Amendment, and the increasing awareness that the risk of being poor is far' greater for women than for men—a factor reinforced by the program cutbacks of the Reagan administration—has led to some defeatism among women activists as well as some sense of enhanced vigor for other women in the women's groups that are collectively referred to as the women's movement.

References

Adams, C.T. and K.T. Winston, 1980. Mothers at Work: Public Policies in the United States, Sweden and China. New York: Longman.

Congressional Quarterly Weekly Report, 1984. (September 1): 2146.

Flexner, E., 1974. Century of Struggle. New York: Atheneum.

Gelb, J. and M.L. Palley, 1982. Women and Public Policies. Princeton, NJ: Princeton University Press.

Gelb, J. and M.L. Palley, 1986. Women and Public Policies, 2nd edition. Princeton, NJ: Princeton University Press.

Goodman, E., 1984. "Campaigns have Feel of Ball Games," The News Journal Papers (October 23): D3.

Ibsen, H., 1906. A Doll's House. Translated by W. Archer. New York: Charles Scribner's Sons.

Kamerman, S., 1985. "Child Care Services: Issue for Gender Equity and Women's Solidarity," Child Welfare 64 (May-June): 260.

Mann, J., 1983. "Equal Pay," The Washington Post (September 21).

Mayer, C.E., 1984. "The Same Pay for Different Jobs," The Washington Post Weekly Edition (August 6): 9.

National-House Democratic Caucus (The), 1984. Renewing America's Promise. Washington, DC: The National-House Democratic Caucus.

Palley, M.L., 1974. "Women and the Study of Public Policy," Policy Studies Journal 4 (Spring): 289–91.

The Oxford Annotated Bible with the Apocrypha, Revised Standard Edition, 1965. New York: Oxford University Press.

Ruether, R.R. (ed.), 1974. Religion and Sexism. New York: Simon and Schuster.

U.S. Congress, Congressional Budget Office, 1985. Reducing Poverty Among Children (May).

Vise, D.A., 19??. "The Next Pension Bill Could Cost Companies Money," The Washington Post National Weekly Edition (November 19): 22.

CHAPTER 15

UNEQUAL PROTECTION UNDER THE LAW: WOMEN AND THE CRIMINAL JUSTICE SYSTEM

Rosemary C. Sarri

> No State shall make or enforce any law which shall abridge the privileges or immunities of citizens of the United States; nor shall any State deprive any persons of life, liberty or property, without due process of law; nor deny to any person within its jurisdiction the equal protection of the laws.
>
> U.S. Constitution, 14th Amendment, 1868

Inequities faced by the majority of women in the United States are magnified many times in the lives of female offenders and victims in this society. Although crime committed by women, or that which affects women, now receives greater attention from judicial officials, correctional personnel, as well as the media and public, that attention is not directed toward reducing the inequities experienced by women but rather toward subjecting larger and larger numbers of women to coercive control and incarceration. The criminal justice system for women has been referred to as the "dark side of the feminist movement," an apt description for an area so seldom receiving positive consideration.

Despite the interest in sex role differences in recent decades, one of the areas in which gender differences are most pronounced, but largely ignored, is that of crime. Neither female criminality nor female offenders attracted the attention of policy makers, correctional administrators, or even criminologists, until the late 1970s. Female crime was viewed as a minor concern by law enforcement officials when compared with male crime. In 1983, 8,851,823 males were arrested, compared to 1,705,486 females, a ratio of nearly six to one (United States Department of Justice, 1984). A similar pattern was observed among juveniles, although the ratio of four to one was lower (987,435 juvenile males and 265,793 juvenile females).

Despite the marked sex differences in criminal behavior, it should not be assumed that female offenders have been dealt with justly, benignly, or humanely by society and its agents. Anyone familiar with the plight of the female offender quickly observes this lack of attention has not operated to her advantage. Moreover, the situation has deteriorated in the 1980s when the incarceration of women offenders has increased more rapidly than either the frequency or seriousness of their criminal behavior. Several court decisions have documented the unequal treatment of women in correctional programs (for example, <u>Bounds v. Smith</u> 430 US 817, 1977).

It is perhaps no coincidence that the 1980s have produced rapid increases in the number of female single parents accompanied by high poverty rates for these women and their children; increasing criminal justice processing of women, especially for property crimes; and rapidly escalating incarceration of women whose offenses previously would have resulted in probation supervision. Women are being subjected to more coercive social control at the same time that social welfare supports for them are being reduced or terminated. Stallard and associates (1983) conclude that the increase in property offense behavior by women is attributable to their increased poverty and family responsibility. There appears to be a deliberate attempt to blame the victim for her plight in order to force her back to traditional female roles.[1]

Most of the criminology literature treats offenders and victims as distinctly different groups. However, in the instance of the female offender who is typically poor, nonwhite, alone, and a single parent, she is often victimized by society. She is expected to work and earn an adequate income for herself and her children, to provide a safe home, and to perform her parental role fully and properly—within the legal and normative structures of society. When she is unable to do so and resorts to crime—usually theft— she is punished for her misdeeds but is given little or no assistance in meeting her family obligations (e.g. witness the recent incarceration of women for AFDC violations). There are serious social structural constraints that place her in repeated Catch-22 situations as she tries to resolve problems causes by the lack of resources. Testing this proposition would require extended analysis, but this chapter attempts to provide support for its validity by examining women and the criminal justice system—historically and contemporaneously. In accord with the other chapters in this volume, this discussion focuses on the adult woman offender, but occasional reference will be made to female juvenile offenders and/or victims where that is particularly useful in the analysis of this critical social issue of the 1980s.

HISTORICAL PERSPECTIVES ON FEMALE CRIME

In the midst of growing interest in the female offender it is easy to forget that she is not a new phenomenon. One hundred years ago Lambert Quetelet, the Belgian statistician, noted that females accounted for about 25 percent of all arrests—not very different from 1985, although the percentage has declined in the United States to 16.6 percent (Hindelang 1977; U.S. Department of Justice 1984).

Theories of female crime can profitably be examined from a historical perspective because of the marked changes which have paralleled the development of more general knowledge of female behavior and of women's roles in society. The many theories of female crime can be ordered into two major categories: (1) Behavioral—those that address the phenomena behaviorally, attempting to explain whether female crime differs significantly from male crime in its causality, type, or frequency; and (2) Societal control—those that consider whether official control of women versus men differs significantly in the various stages of processing from police arrest through court action and correctional programs. Students of the behavioral perspective have been interested in determining whether male and female crime is similar or different in terms of frequency and type of deviance and in investigating causal models that explain male and female criminal behavior. These authors give little attention to how the crime is responded to by control agencies. In contrast, those interested in control theories emphasize equity and inequity in intervention and processing. Where they exhibit interest in the behavior itself, they have studied women's changing social roles and responsibilities rather than the criminality per se. Some observe that women, as compared with men, are treated unequally—sometimes more benignly and in other instances more punitively, but always differently. Those who argue that intervention is essentially equal between men and women usually conclude that its results from the rational operation of a bureaucratic system and from due process protection.

This paradigm is useful in highlighting the Catch-22 phenomenon. For example, if a theory asserts that male/female crime is equal in all instances, then it would follow that societal control should be egalitarian. When that does not occur, we have the classic Catch-22. For example, males and females might be equally involved in prostitution, but only women might be prosecuted and punished. Figure 1 presents this paradigm diagrammatically. Because most studies concur that adult females commit crime far less frequently and less seriously than do males, most research has focused on equity in formal social control. The point of interest is to verify whether the responses of the criminal justice system correspond to the behavioral differences of individuals. In the case of juveniles there is more similarity among males and females, especially with regard to status offenses (truancy, running away, incorrigibility, etc.), use of drugs and alcohol, and petty theft. In this instance the focus for investigation is to determine whether the control responses are similar for male and female delinquents. For example, there are few sex differences in the incidence and frequency of running away from home, but females are far more likely to be arrested and incarcerated than are males (cell 2). In the case of larceny, however, the behavior is relatively similar among males and females (especially juveniles), and there is greater equity in social control processing (cell 1).

Cell 3, spouse homicide, is an example of another Catch-22 situation emerging from equal responses to different behavior. Most women who kill their husbands or partners do so after extended periods of battering and abuse. However, the courts have been reluctant to consider the homicide as justifiable self-defense, and most of these women have received "equal" treatment that might be assigned for any first- or second-degree murder. Cell 4 represents instances where the incidence of female crime is below that of males, but where females who commit such acts are punished more severely than are males. Sexual abuse, especially of children, is an exemplar of this type. Thus we see that there are substantial differences in the assumptions which are made to justify different treatment, and also that there are situations in which de facto differences are ignored. In our review of the major theories of female crime, we will try to identify where issues of equality or inequality are addressed explicitly or implicitly.

Historically, assumptions about gender roles have obscured the study of facts concerning women's involvement in crime. The earliest theories of crime contended that female offenders were evil, immoral, or possessed of demons; but with a few noteworthy exceptions they were viewed as a minor problem because of their small numbers (Rasche 1974; Erikson 1966). In the latter half of the nineteenth century there was a search for constitutional or physiological causes, represented in the work of Lombroso and his peers (Lombroso and Ferrero 1916). They argued that female criminality was unnatural—the result of inherent tendencies which

Figure 1

Behavior and Control--Equality and Inequality

BEHAVIOR

		Equal	Unequal
SOCIAL	Equal	1 Larceny	3 Spouse homicide
CONTROL	Unequal	2 Running away	4 Sexual abuse

deserved punishment because such women violated their womanhood. Female offenders were said to be more wicked and perverse than their male counterparts because crime was considered to be consistent with male tendencies, but it was an aberration of nature for women. Both Freud and Lombroso emphasized that the intellectual inferiority of women made them susceptible to crime. Others emphasized genetic factors, asserting that criminality was inherited, but they too emphasized behavior that involved interpersonal relationships, particularly sexual behavior (Fernald 1920; Healy and Bonner 1926). Obsession with sexuality and mental stability remains a dominant element in theories of female criminality in contrast to those of male behavior which was perceived as more utilitarian or more in accord with the aggressive nature of the male (Wilson and Herrnstein 1985).

In the early twentieth century the Gluecks (1934) viewed female crime in terms of the interaction of constitutional and environmental factors. They did their studies almost exclusively in female correctional institutions, and their work set the stage for gender-based services that emphasized the training of women in traditional social roles. Later, Pollak's work (1950) had a significant impact on subsequent research, especially on adult female offenders. He argued that there were no real male/female differences in criminality, but that what differentiated them was the inherent deceitfulness of the female. Like Freud, he also emphasized sexual factors as paramount, for he saw criminal women as trying to extend their sexual role so that they would achieve greater power in nontraditional areas.

The emphasis on sexuality as central in female crime grew rapidly and furthered the notion that female and male crime were both different and unequal (Konopka 1966; Vedder and Sommerville 1970; Sarri 1976). Sutherland and Cressey's (1966) theory of differential association was concerned almost exclusively with male crime, which they saw as arising from peer associations and influence. Their theory was paralleled by authors such as Morris (1964), Cowie, Cowie, and Slater (1968), and Konopka (1966, 1976) who argued that adolescent female crime was the result of ineffective family socialization. The latter authors paid little attention to empirical data about the actual criminal behavior patterns of women, because theft, fraud, and substance abuse-related offenses were largely ignored. Not surprisingly, theories about sexuality and ineffective family socialization had little to say about behavior linked to poverty, race, and occupational discrimination. These authors argued that lack of parental supervision was a far more important factor in female delinquency than in male delinquency. All strongly asserted that there were significant male/female differences in criminal behavior and implied that treatment and control should also be differentiated. Heavy emphasis was placed on psychiatric intervention rather than traditional correctional programs. In the instance of female juveniles, control over sexuality was the most central concern, but there was little interest in parallel control over the more frequent male sexual behavior. Juvenile women were institutionalized for long periods of time for sexual promiscuity or even for appearances of sexuality, as was mandated in the State v. Matiello case in Connecticut (4 Conn. Cir 55, 225 A. 2d 507, 1966).

The period of the 1960s and 1970s was one in which far greater emphasis was placed on theories of formal social control of crime and on the operation of the criminal justice system. Studies of the processing of women and men through the criminal justice system led to emphasis on differentiation, discrimination, and disparity in the treatment of female and male offenders (Rafter and Stanko 1982). Initially more attention was directed toward prisons rather than courts and probation agencies, influencing the behavior which was studied and the conclusions reached. In the case of females, studies of female institutionalization dominated and produced information which ultimately influenced policymakers to modify the discriminatory institutionalization of females for status offenses (Schlossman and Wallach 1978; Chesney-Lind 1977, 1978). They documented that females were far more likely to be handled punitively by the courts and institutionalized for long periods of time than were males. Passage of the federal Delinquency Prevention and Control Act in 1974 led to the emptying of many state training schools for females in the late 1970s when status offenders were no longer to be held in closed institutions (Krisberg and Schwartz 1983).

This same period produced several studies of adult and juvenile inmate social systems (Tittle 1972; Heffernan 1972; Giallombardo 1966, 1974; Ward and Kassebaum 1965; Propper 1981). Although they did not directly address the question of equal and unequal treatment of females, they were influenced by earlier male prison studies. Where they attempted to distinguish male/ female differences, they came up with mixed results, although they did observe some consistent differences in the structure of the inmate social systems.

In the mid-1970s attention was directed toward studies of adult court processing and sentencing of females and males. Issues of discrimination and disparity became more central, as the work of Simon (1975, 1979), Bernstein (1979), Nagel and Hagen (1983), and Figueira-McDonough (1985) illustrate. Research results provided little clear evidence of discrimination because under some conditions women were treated more benignly and in others more punitively. However, their work clearly indicates that there are complex interactions to be addressed before any clear propositions can be tested.

The criminology literature of the seventies and eighties, which addressed the influence of the women's movement on female crime, suggested a relationship between changed sex roles and crime (Adler and Simon 1979; Steffensmeier et al. 1978, 1981; Anderson 1983; McCord and Otten 1983). This question has been studied from a number of perspectives and in a variety of ways. Two variant theories predominated in this literature: "discriminatory control" and "equal opportunity." The latter suggests that with greater equality females are more likely to engage in criminal behavior because they have the opportunity to do so. The former argument is that women receive biased treatment from social control agencies in arrest, detention, and disposition, as for example, when in the processing of prostitution or family violence the woman is charged with offending against her attacker. Figueira-McDonough (1984) tested the equal opportunity theory and found weak and contradictory links between various dimensions of feminist orientation and delinquency. She concluded that the influence was complex, tenuous, and not supportive of the "equal opportunity" thesis.

Noting that the gender gap in crime is as great as ever, despite sex role changes, Wilson and Herrnstein (1985) speculate that sex differences in aggressive and other primary drives that flow into fundamental definitions of sex roles provide the basic explanation. They conclude that the emphasis on interpersonal, moral, and sexual behavior was more characteristic of female offenders, whereas male crime was viewed as provoked by utilitarian motives and as a result of social structural factors such as social class, access to legitimate opportunities, and differential association—and last but not least, caused by constitutional factors. These authors thus return to the dominant theories of the early part of the century, although they argue that contemporary research supports their conclusions. However, there is sharp disagreement today about the validity of assertions that constitutional factors are predominant (Rutter and Gillis 1983).

Last, an alternate view of gender and crime can be found in radical social theory, which asserts that what counts as crime is established by powerful persons in society (Quinney 1970; Smart 1976; Cloward and Piven 1979; Schwendinger and Schwendinger 1985). In other words, crime is that which is labeled as such by formal agents. Thus abortion now is a crime in some jurisdictions but not in others—as is rape in marriage, substance abuse, or prostitution. Moreover, labeling theorists incorporate control perspectives in that they argue that the poor, minorities, and females are likely to be processed for behavior that would not lead to processing when committed by majority males.

Feminist theories of crime and gender view criminal behavior of women more broadly than do traditional criminologists. Heidensohn (1968) was the first criminologist to voice the need for theory which took the female sex role into consideration, and in doing so she facilitated the radical revision of theory of female crime. Her particular contribution was to draw attention to the effects of women's everyday experience on their criminality, and in doing so she triggered the political consciousness of other women researchers.[2]

As Goffman (1970: 11) observed, "Society establishes the means of categorizing persons and the complement of attributes felt to be ordinary and natural for members of each of these categories." With few exceptions, gender and sex differences are important because female offenders are responded to in terms of their traditional social roles. A female is to be a good mother, homemaker, and marital partner. She is to be moral, deferential, feminine. And when she deviates from these roles, her behavior may well be defined as criminal, or in other contexts as mentally ill. Many social scientists have perpetuated this myth in their formulation of theory. For example, Albert Cohen's (1955) highly influential theory of role frustration explains male delinquency in terms of social rather than biological or psychological factors; but in the instance of females, he shifts his explanation almost wholly to the individual level:

> ...the female's situation in society, the admiration, respect, and property she commands, depend to a much greater degree on the kinds of relationship she establishes with members of the opposite sex.... The most conspicuous difference [between male and female delinquency] is that male delinquency...is versatile, whereas female delinquency is relatively specialized. It consists overwhelmingly of sexual delinquency. (Cohen 1955: 141, 144)

In contrast to this wholly sexist perspective, Smart (1976) and Naffin (1981) argue that social control agents today more readily define deviant behavior by women as violent and masculine because of majority male hostility toward the women's movement and the numerous societal changes associated with it. Poor women have been especially victimized, so it is little wonder, Smart (1976) and Giordano et al. (1981) note, that these women do not identify with the women's movement and remain traditional in their orientation. These women may often be forced to crime because of their economic marginality and single parenthood rather than any notions of new or equal opportunity with males. This pattern did not change with the growth of the women's movement, which largely affected middle-class women. It is possible that many poor women who are forced to be independent would prefer traditional sex role differentiation which they perceive to offer them some protection in child rearing and employment.

WHO ARE THE FEMALE OFFENDERS?

Because of the great variation in local, state, and federal statutes, the definition of female crime and the female offender differs substantially by jurisdiction, particularly at the juvenile level and for minor crimes in which women are more likely to predominate. Moreover, the amount of crime will vary depending upon whether one measures crime according to the official reports of law enforcement agencies or according to the reports of victims or offenders. Official crime reports include only persons arrested, regardless of subsequent outcomes. They reflect the administration of criminal law, not the actual differences in criminal behavior (Hindelang 1979). On the other hand, self-report surveys of offenders indicate that the vast majority of persons over fifteen years of age have committed one or more misdemeanors or felonies, but the prevalence, frequency, and seriousness of all self-reported and official crime is far less for females than for males (U.S. Dept. of Justice 1983; Feyerhelm 1981; Elliott and Ageton 1980; Hindelang 1979). These studies also document the high levels of crime for which there is no apprehension, and also the fact that racial differences in criminal behavior are far less pronounced than in official reports.

Information from various sources (U.S. Department of Justice 1985a) provides the following profile of the adult female offender:

1) Young—two-thirds of those apprehended and processed are under thirty years of age.
2) Minority status—Nearly 25 percent of arrestees are from minority groups, but they compose nearly two-thirds of those incarcerated.
3) Undereducated—Offenders are educationally disadvantaged—half not having completed high school and with lower than expected educational performance scores.
4) Single mothers—The majority are single, separated, widowed, or divorced, but most are mothers.
5) Poor—The majority have sporadic work histories in low-income service industries.
6) Social service clients—Over half of the incarcerated have been recipients of public welfare, and many have had extended psychiatric and/or substance abuse treatment.

Arrest data from official reports in Table 1 indicate that both in 1974 and in 1983, female crime was much less than male crime, with the differences most pronounced for the most serious violent crimes.[3] Although arrests for both males and females increased substantially, their comparative position remained essentially

Table 1

Arrest Patterns in the United States, 1974 and 1983

| | 1974 | | | 1983 | | |
| | | Females | | | Females | |
	Total Arrests	% Total Arrests	% Under 18	Total Arrests	% Total Arrests	% Under 18
Property[a]						
Females	139,169	22.5	41.7	384,906	22.5	34.5
Males	497,676			1,322,508		
Index[b]						
Females	159,011	19.4	40.3	432,809	20.1	32.9
Males	660,351			1,718,311		
Violent Crime[c]						
Females	19,720	10.9	22.1	47,903	10.8	16.8
Males	161,803			395,783		
Total						
Females	540,987	16.9	31.6	1,705,486	16.6	21.4
Males	2,655,339			8,581,823		

Source: Crime in the United States, 1974 and 1983. Uniform Crime Reports. Washington, DC: Federal Bureau of Investigation, 1975 and 1984, pp. 184–86 (1974) and pp. 179–87 (1984).

a. Includes burglary, auto theft, larceny, theft, and arson.

b. Includes criminal homicide, rape, robbery, aggravated assault, burglary, larceny and auto theft.

c. Includes criminal homicide, rape, robbery, aggravated assault.

unchanged. Overall, female arrest rates declined only from 16.9 percent to 16.6 percent. Younger women under eighteen show the greatest decline in all categories, probably a reflection of their declining numbers relative to the total (U.S. Department of Justice 1984). Only in the instance of fraud (40%), forgery (33%), and larceny (29.5%) do females approach males in frequency of arrests by crime category. Most of these offenses are relatively petty, although the offender may have a record of frequent and chronic criminal behavior. The relationship among poverty, unemployment, minority status, single parenthood, and crime is unmistakable for the majority (Figueira-McDonough et al. 1981).

Steffensmeier's (1981) longitudinal analysis of female criminal behavior supports the patterns observable in the official crime reports. Females made few gains in traditional "male" crimes; rather, the increases were in larceny and forgery/fraud, in which females had traditionally been heavily represented. He also notes that reporting patterns need careful examination because they vary over time, by geographical area, and by organizational attributes of processing agencies. Women are viewed less paternalistically today and therefore may not be dismissed from official processing as readily as they were in the past (Steffensmeier 1981). Thus changes in formal social controls may have produced these results rather than individual behavior changes of female offenders. Comparisons over time by Burke and Sarri (1982) indicated that in the thirty-year interval from 1950 to 1982 the percentage of females arrested for violent crime remained essentially 10 percent, while property arrests increased from 11 to 22 percent and were responsible for most of the overall increase in female arrests.

Wilson and Herrnstein (1985) report that their analysis of 44 available official and self-report studies convinces them that there has not been a convergence of female/crime ratios, and that the area of notable increase in female crimes is that of petty property crime. Using National Crime Survey data between 1973 and 1980, Lynes (1983) concludes that male and female crime are converging, but that the female increase is not due to changes in the types or in the overall incidence of female crime. Rather, it is the seriousness within category that has changed. He also finds that labor force participation is associated with increases in seriousness. Black males and females are converging more than white males and females. These results, however, are somewhat contradictory because black labor force participation declined relative to white in this time period when white females entered the labor force in such large numbers. He does observe that crime seriousness increases with economic stress for both males and females; this period in the mid- and late 1970s was one of great economic stress for blacks because of economic recession and unemployment.

Lynes tests the propositions of both Adler and Simon and concludes that neither can be fully supported because Simon suggested no increase in seriousness, while Adler suggested that increased labor force participation would increase the incidence and intensity of female crime. Since most women entered the low-wage secondary labor force, Adler's hypothesis about the impact of the women's movement was problematic from the beginning.

Is female crime becoming more serious, as some argue? Obviously, this is an important question, given the fact that incarceration has increased substantially. If female crime is more serious, then the drastic action is perhaps justifiable, but if it is not, we have evidence of a Catch-22: regardless of what she does, a female offender will be subjected to more control. During the past two decades there has been an almost continuous debate as to whether the incidence and seriousness of female crime is increasing. The general evidence is inconclusive with mixed results among researchers. Some studies show little change in seriousness, others have observed a decline in seriousness, and still others find increases. Clearly, the location and time of the surveys, as well as the sampling procedures, are so variable as to make cross-study comparison meaningless. There is no disagreement, however, that female offenders are economically disadvantaged, of minority status, and disproportionately single parents.

WOMEN AS VICTIMS

There is a close linkage for women between being a victim of crime and being an offender. All too often through a process of "blaming the victim," women are transformed into offenders, as in sexual assault, spouse battering, prostitution, and sexual harassment (Rafter and Stanko 1982; Anderson 1983). Crime is supposedly a violation against society as well as against an individual, but the criminal justice system minimizes the harm of the above behaviors except when they are committed by women; then the penalty may often be more severe than for males. When women are victims, male law enforcement officials are likely to take these crimes less seriously because they arise out of the social relations of domination. Women are viewed as being at least partially responsible for the crimes because, it is said, "if they behaved as proper women and mothers," such events would not occur. Only in the instance of sexual assault has there been some change in recent years, as a result of concerted action by women's organizations.

The National Crime Survey reports that women are less likely to be victimized by crime than are men. However, this annual national survey excludes the critical issues of sexual violence against women in the home, including spouse battering, marriage rape, and sexual abuse. Thus it is debatable that women in fact are less victimized, given the prevalence of domestic violence (Dobash and Dobash 1977; Finkelhor et al. 1983). The lack of annual systematic information about all types of sexual violence is another indicator of the relative political powerlessness of women. Until that is remedied, we will not have accurate statistics on the gender of crime victims.

Sexual violence in the family is private and invisible behavior, perhaps more so today than earlier because of the decline in the extended family. Additionally, as men have lost autonomy in the workplace because of bureaucratization, the home has been enshrined as each man's castle and fortress against external intrusion. But this gain for men is a loss for women since it renders them invisible and unable to object to family abuse or neglect.[4]

The most profound outcome of protracted family violence occurs when a woman kills her spouse or partner after an extended period of abuse. In such instances the woman has seldom been successful with self-defense pleas because she cannot establish that she had a genuine and reasonable belief that she was in imminent danger of death or serious injury or that she used only a reasonable degree of force to protect herself. The dependency status of women is reflected in the laws governing domestic violence and sexual assault in the home. They have resulted in legal practices that deny women recourse to the law (Creach 1982). For example, laws that relate to domestic assault, reflecting the Common Law, have denied women the defenses available to men. A man traditionally had the right to beat his wife, but she had no corresponding rights.[5] Court rulings have now modified this principle, but there are still few states that prohibit rape in marriage. It is unclear what the outcome would be if a woman being raped by her husband took a weapon and killed him during the act.

Those opposed to the self-defense plea by a woman who kills her husband suggest that she was free to leave the relationship at any time. Findings from research on the battered wife syndrome usually present a picture of attacks over a number of years, but women do not leave the relationship because of children, lack of resources, or demoralization and depression from the extended abuse. It is also possible that women who were themselves reared in a family where there was violence are desensitized to violence until a crisis occurs (Hilberman 1980). Creach (1982) concludes that traditional self-defense theory is inadequate for many battered wife cases where the woman kills her husband after extended battering. He further suggests that criminal law can assimilate partial determinism into existing imperfect self-defense doctrine, mitigating the crime.

Schneider (1980) argues that the law of self-defense is flawed because the sexual stereotypes of women and male orientation built into the law prevent judicial officials from appreciating the circumstances of battered women's acts of self-defense. She further argues for a more individualized approach that permits the trier to consider the facts of the particular circumstances and perceptions under which a woman kills her batterer. These observations about female homicide in instances of spouse battering indicate that reducing or stopping violence toward women is an essential first step but that it is linked to the overall liberation of women from oppressive social and economic relations in the home, community, and workplace.

When one considers sexual assault and rape more generally—outside the home as well as within—it becomes clear that this behavior represents to women one of the most profound forms of victimization. It highlights the powerlessness and isolation of women. For example, rape is defined as sexual penetration by a man of a woman without her consent, but all too often judges and prosecutors are unwilling to acknowledge her lack of consent. The very crime which women are supposed to have the power to prevent turns out to be the one which they often have the least power to prevent—another Catch-22. The requirement for medico-legal corroboration of the elements of force, lack of consent, and carnal knowledge means that the former rather than the latter elements may determine the outcome for a woman. Frequently the treatment of rape victims by law enforcement and medical staff further reinforces the notion that this is an act which could have been prevented with more diligence on the part of the woman or persons close to her, in the case of a juvenile.

Anderson (1983) has suggested that to understand sexual assault fully theoretical explanations in four areas need to be studied and ordered. These include psychological, subculture of violence, sex role learning, and political-economic status theories. Psychological theories focus on the individual characteristics, on psychopathology, and the distorted psychosexual development of males. With the assumption that only abnormal men rape, there is an implicit race and class bias and also an underemphasis on the environment as a causal factor. This is further exacerbated by the fact that disproportionately those apprehended and convicted are poor and of minority status. In contrast, the subculture of violence theories emphasize the importance of the environment, but they are even more biased in their emphasis on black and working-class men. Little or no attention is directed toward sexual assault by the dominant middle-class males. Sex role learning theories direct attention to the dominant culture and its emphasis on masculinity as a learned pattern of aggression and domination. This perspective incorporates sexual assault among acquaintances as well as strangers since it is asserted that men learn to force women to have sex against their will (Brownmiller 1975). The political economy perspective asserts that women were defined historically as the chattel of men; thus they became sexual objects like other pieces of property. The widespread use of women in advertising and pornographic literature as sexual objects and the increasing sanction of violence against women reflects their economic and political powerlessness in patriarchical societies. Thus in order to intervene to alleviate the victimization of women who are sexually assaulted, one must change major social institutions because they are the result of long-standing gender relations and the societal status of women.

Overall, black women and women between the ages of 16 and 24 are the most likely victims of crime, especially violent crime. To some extent the conditions of poverty and single parenthood under which many of these women live place them at high risk for victimization (just as they placed them at risk for being offenders because of their economic marginality). Following the reductions in social welfare programs in 1981–82, many female single parents were victimized in a variety of ways because of their loss of welfare benefits. They were forced to live in substandard housing, in dangerous neighborhoods, and in conditions where they experienced frequent crises—such as running out of money and food, being burglarized, having their utilities turned off, becoming seriously ill, and being forced to crime in order to support their children (Sarri et al. 1984; Belle 1982).

The media suggest that elderly persons are the most frequent victims of crime, but that is not the case. Single-parent women and children are far more frequently victimized, and their plight receives little attention (Bowker 1981). The National Crime Survey indicates that poor single women are the most likely to be raped and assaulted (U.S. Dept. of Justice 1983). The rate is three times as high for the poorest women as compared with middle-income women.

LAW AND CRIMINAL JUSTICE SYSTEM PROCESSING
Law and the Ideology of Social Control

It is argued by Scutt (1981) and Edwards (1984) that criminal law preserves the dependency and subordinate status of women although there may not have been a conscious and deliberate attempt to do so. Some laws ignore basic inequalities between the sexes (physical strength in instances of spouse battering) whereas others assert inequality where none exists (e.g., the female's superiority at child rearing). These laws are based on English Common Law and on tradition which denied civil liberties and due process to women, assuming that women were incapable of acting independently of their husbands or fathers. The growth of capitalist economies in the eighteenth century increased crime opportunities, and not surprisingly, criminal law emerged as the agent of social control. In her criticism of the liberalism of this period, Windschuttle (1981) notes that women's roles were those of moral and spiritual guardian of the family and society, whereas those of men related to public life and the economy. In accord with the dominant ideology, the woman who violated her role in the family threatened the social order in three ways: by her specific act, from the impact of her act on society's moral order, and through her children who were likely to follow her behavior. None of these prescriptions applied to men—thus the double standard emerged. Even today, however, any examination of law in Western society reveals sexism in both the law and legal practice.[6]

The latter problem is further exacerbated by the fact that at most levels of the criminal justice system, the agents of social control are overwhelmingly male and white, which has especially negative consequences for black female offenders, as Iglehart (1977) has shown. Figueira-McDonough et al. (1981) also observed black women property offenders were more likely than white females to be incarcerated rather than placed on probation. While incarcerated black women made up nearly 75 percent of the prison population, once again they were subjected to the control of majority males who provided little or no program that would aid their movement out of poverty. Not surprisingly, the vicious circle was not interrupted—poverty, crime, prison, and return to impoverished conditions.

The nature of law and its relation to social structure are the subject of much debate, but most often that debate centers on class, race, or ethnicity, not on sex or concepts of law and patriarchy. The latter would focus attention on the family and the economic, sexual, and reproductive relations between the sexes in a household unit. Criminal laws may make specific reference to a female defendant as wife, mother, single parent along with the functional rights and obligations of these roles—thus providing a rationale for the organization of sexual differences in criminal justice processing. Sex-gender divisions that are the basis of disparate treatment of males and females in the family and the accommodation of both in their social roles are notable features in both law and legal practice (Schur 1983). For example, laws defining infanticide, rape in marriage, prostitution often make explicit reference to one sex rather than both with no objective basis for this inequality. Edwards (1984) alludes to this situation in her observation that many jurisdictions now acknowledge that women are capable of committing an indecent assault on a male, whereas previously they were deemed physically incapable of doing so. However, many courts have long been willing to assert that women engaged in "contributory negligence" in rape cases because that belief agreed with traditional notions about female responsibility for male sexual behavior.

The statutory treatment of prostitution and promiscuity clearly illustrates unequal protection under the law. For both of these behaviors it is still almost exclusively women who are prosecuted. Discrimination arises because some laws define prostitution as a sex-specific law to the activities of females and do not penalize males either as customers or actors. And new laws may not correct the situation. New York enacted a law stating that "patronizing a prostitute" was a violation with a maximum sentence of imprisonment for 15 days (Dorsen 1972). However, the penalty for the prostitute was far more severe—a maximum sentence of three months, an obvious double standard. In an interesting historical analysis of prostitution, Hewitt and Mickish (1983) observed that between 1900 and 1920 nearly equal numbers of males and females were arrested, tried, and convicted for prostitution in Muncie, Indiana. Then in the 1920s the laws and practices were changed, illustrating the fact that deviance occurs in the context of social institutions that have the power to label some persons as deviant and others not so. Efforts by some judges to correct the imbalance in the prosecution of women only for prostitution often resulted in their reassignment to other types of cases by their fellow judges (De Crow 1974).

Laws governing differential sentencing of men and women have been responded to inconsistently by the courts, and therefore legislation such as the Equal Rights Amendment is essential, argues Temin (1973). She further observes that historically, the indeterminate sentence provision was used more widely for females than males—resulting in longer periods of incarceration for women. It was argued that women had a greater need for rehabilitation and individualized treatment than did men. Not only had the woman broken the law, but she had betrayed her normative responsibility to uphold the law; therefore, she was doubly criminal and needed more thoroughgoing rehabilitation. As recently as the late 1970s states such as Massachusetts, New Jersey, Iowa, and Pennsylvania had laws that permitted confinement of a woman for up to five years for a misdemeanor while the maximum for men was one year.

The concept of "individualized justice" appears to govern the sentencing of females far more than males because of the ideology of sentencing officials, the structure of the sentencing process, and the viability of certain forms of sentence for the females, considering the gender conceptions of her role (Edwards 1984). For example, women who are mothers with minor children may be placed on probation with certain specifications regarding parental responsibility, but such sentencing would not take place for men. Some male judges are reluctant to believe that women are capable of criminal behavior but prefer instead to believe that they are ill (Crites 1978). Only in the instance of violation of traditional sex roles are they held culpable. Their views are reinforced by laws which may make specific reference to the functional obligations of females as wife, mother, or single parent.

Juvenile delinquency laws have been particularly notorious in their discrimination against females in terms of specific status offenses for which only females were charged, or variable age limits for females as compared with males (Chesney-Lind 1977). Most of the latter are now unconstitutional, but many states have not changed their statutes accordingly. Thus there is no automatic enforcement of equity. Passage of the federal Juvenile Justice and Delinquency Prevention Act in 1974 (PL-93–415) resulted in removal of status offenders from many secure institutions. Females benefited disproportionately from their removal from training schools, but that act did not mean that this at-risk population would be normalized and allowed to grow up without court surveillance. Since 1978 they have appeared in increasing numbers in private institutions and in mental health facilities (Schwartz et al. 1983; Sarri 1983). The fate of these young women today may now be even worse, for their access to due process protection is now more tenuous than ever. In addition, those juveniles who remained in the justice system had longer periods of stay than their male counterparts even though they have far less serious criminal records (Michigan Department of Social Services 1986).

Court Processing

Gender patterns in court processing vary substantially between males and females. Researchers who report preferential treatment of women submit evidence that women are less likely to be detained prior to trial, convicted, or if convicted, sentenced to incarceration. Several empirical studies support the hypothesis of preferential treatment, beginning with the national study by Nagel and Weitzman (1971) of 11,258 criminal cases in 1962. They concluded that there was preferential treatment and that the courts displayed paternalistic attitudes toward women. This study is dated and does not reflect current attitudes and practices; moreover, the study failed to control for prior criminal record, and minor misdemeanants were excluded. Subsequent studies in California and Alabama produced contrasting results, but there is still a strongly held myth of preferential treatment (Crites 1978).

In a case record study of theft, forgery, fraud, and drug violations (offenses more common for female offenders), Krutschnitt (1981) observed that overall, females appeared to have a slight advantage in terms of sentence leniency, but she was unable to control fully for variations in offense, offense history, and processing experience. She did observe sex and race-linked discrepancies in that nonwhite males and older females were significantly more likely to receive harsher sanctions regardless of their offense. In a similar study in the same state, Minnesota, Sarri (1986) observed that controlling for offense, women, especially mothers, were more likely to receive probation sentences, but the length of sentence was far longer.

In the processing of larceny, drug, and sex crimes in Washington, D.C., Figueira-McDonough (1985) observed marked male/female differences, but few differences in the treatment of person or serious property crime. Men and women were treated similarly in crimes in which males predominated, but where females predominated there were large differences in plea bargaining, rates of guilty pleas, and sentence bargaining. Women were less able to bargain effectively, were less often represented by counsel, and were more willing to plead guilty to the original charge. Seriousness of offense and prior record were weaker predictors of sentences for females than for males. In fact, controlling for prior record, race, and residence, women were nearly as likely to receive sentences of similar severity for larceny and sex crimes as for violent offenses.

Butler and Lambert (1983) observed that the treatment of males and females varied markedly in the two midwestern cities in which they studied court processing. Seriousness of the offense, past record, race, and type of pleas were better predictors of males' outcomes than of females. They concluded that incapacitation models were better predictors for males, whereas treatment rehabilitation models more often influenced judicial decision making for females. These findings further corroborate the proposition that the female offender is deemed in need of treatment because of her deviance, regardless of the nature of the offense.

Bernstein et al. (1979) found no gender differences in court outcomes as far as dismissals were concerned, but they concluded that overall, men received harsher sentences. They did observe that being married and having children was less likely to result in incarceration for both males and females, not just females, as earlier studies had observed. However, these investigators excluded sexual and moral offenses in which women might be expected to be more represented.

Daly (1981) argues that consideration of gender, class, and race variables and their interactions is essential if one is to understand the confused state of beliefs which are maintained by court actors and their practices toward female defendants. She points to the need for careful study of within-group as well as between-group differences. She also suggests that feminist theory of patriarchy can be usefully applied in examining court adjudications. Court agencies expect women to perform family labor, and as a corollary, they expect that men will be the primary breadwinners. This leads them to assume that the heterosexual marriage is a stable primary group and should be reinforced by the court, despite the considerable evidence to the contrary in rates of divorce and family violence.

In order to reduce sentence discrepancies, several states have introduced statutory sentencing guidelines. For example, in Minnesota, prior to the implementation of guidelines, women were convicted of less serious crimes than men but had nearly as high rates of incarceration (Sarri 1986). Moreover, when they were put on probation or in prison, their sentences were longer for similar types of crime. The guidelines took into consideration the frequency and seriousness of the offense as well as prior record, but the former received the greatest weight in the index. Following implementation, the guidelines resulted in reduced incarceration of property and less serious offenders, and thereby reduced incarceration of women because of their less serious criminal behavior. However, as Knapp (1982) points out, prosecutors and legislators can often act to reinstate previous more punitive practices. Knapp's (1983) evaluation of the Minnesota sentencing guidelines' impact indicates that substantial reduction in the prison commitments for women was achieved after they were implemented. However, two years later prosecutors obtained discretionary authority, and with judges' acquiescence, the number of females sentenced to prison increased disproportionately. There had been such a substantial drop in the women's prison population, notes Knapp (1983), that it might have been closed—so such an event had to be prevented in one way or another. The lowest severity property crimes had the largest rates of increases in incarceration; thus females with property offenses were disproportionately impacted when prosecutors dismissed fewer cases in order to build higher criminal history scores and thereby required incarceration.

Women in Custody

Despite the discrimination and inequities that exist among police, judges, and prosecutors, the most serious problems for female offenders exist in residential facilities: jails, reformatories, lockups, and prisons. In mid-1984 the adult prison population totalled 463,866, of which 20,853 (4.5%) were female. During the 1980s there has been a 135 percent increase in the incarceration of women, with the annual percentage change exceeding that of males, although the total number of males remains vastly greater (U.S. Department of Justice, BJS 1984). In addition, the average sentence lengths were increased. The United States has the second or third highest rate of incarceration among Western countries. Moreover, the rate of incarceration varies sharply among the states and is not related to crime per se, but rather to poverty, percent minority population, education, and the availability of prison beds (Nagel 1977; Mullen 1981; Downs 1977). The probability of going to prison also varies with the state of residence, because 40 percent of all female prisoners are in California, Texas, Florida, Ohio, and New York. What explains this remarkable increase in female incarceration between 1975 and 1985 when the crime rate for serious crime was not increasing proportionately, as Table 1 indicates? Among the three factors often cited are: (1) demographic—the large increase in the size of the at-risk cohort between the ages of 15 and 25 years in the 1970s; but that had already begun to decline in the 1980s, and the incarceration rate still increased. (2) The impact of two economic recessions was greatest for the poor and minority working-class women, placing them at greater risk for economic crime. They were incarcerated far more rapidly for such crimes than were their white sisters, who were more likely to receive probation for the same crime. (3) The building of new facilities also supported attitudes among judicial officials which permitted more incarceration (Nagel, 1977; Mullen 1980; Figueira- McDonough 1982). Judges became aware of the existence of new facilities and incarcerated female offenders who otherwise would have been placed on probation. Last, the length of sentences also increased significantly in the 1980s.

The incarceration of adult women in separate prison facilities developed in the midnineteenth century; for adolescent females the use of separate facilities is of more recent origin, dating from the early 1900s. Prisons were purportedly established to provide female inmates with treatment and education in accord with ideologies about female traditional social roles. Male reformists believed that women needed sexual morality and sobriety if they were to "resume their predestined roles as homemakers, mothers, and wives." There was no recognition that the majority were single parents and the sole supporters of their families. Prisons were located in isolated and inaccessible rural areas, and the public knew little about the persons or events inside, in contrast to the voluminous popular and scientific literature about male prisons.

Prisons for women in 1985 in most states have changed relatively little since the beginning of the century in terms of their location and the types of programs which they provide for offenders. Far less than half of women inmates are enrolled in educational programs, although most are educationally disadvantaged; there are few nontraditional jobs in the limited prison industries which exist. Most spend their days in idleness subjected to monotonous control and discipline. Programs for economic rehabilitation and legal services are far fewer than in male programs (Chapman 1980). Those who do assert independence and motivation to change are punished—often with long periods of solitary confinement. "Doing your time and playing it cool" remains the best way to get along with staff and other women, although such behavior is antithetical to normative demands which women face after discharge.

Characteristics of women in prison have changed relatively little in recent years, although today more are parents and the percentage of nonwhites is now well over 50 percent. The mean age of female adult inmates is 29 and that of juveniles 15.7 years (U.S. Dept. of Justice, BJS 1983). More than 90 percent of adult inmates have borne children, but the mean number of 1.7 children is nearly identical to current national fertility levels. The vast majority are in prison for property crimes: larceny, forgery, fraud, and drug abuse. Although the average female adult sentence is five years, the median length of stay in 1983 was 16 months (U.S. Department of Justice, BJS 1983).[7]

Several recent complaints on behalf of female offenders have successfully charged the prison administrators with unequal protection under the law because they lacked equal and appropriate programming for women in prison (e.g., Glover v. Johnson E.D. Michigan Court Action No. 77-71229, Oct. 25, 1979, and Bounds v. Smith, 430 U.S. 817, 1977). Typically, the only programs available were those linked to a limited range of sex-segregated occupations, many of which are closed to persons who have been convicted of a felony. The majority of women had no access to appropriate educational or vocational programs. Unfortunately, although the federal courts concurred with the charge of unequal protection, their decisions have had little impact because of prison overcrowding, the dominance and resistance of male administrators, the punitive attitudes of legislators and court officials, and the fact that many social action organizations have ignored the plight of these offenders.

Since society has so often used incarceration of women to reinforce traditional female roles, it is incongruous that with few exceptions there are no provisions for children to visit overnight in most facilities or to stay with their mothers when they are very young. Moreover, incarcerated women are given no legal or social assistance to maintain their maternal and parental responsibilities. A recent Michigan proposal would terminate maternal guardianship of female felons without assurance of adequate due process. Glick and Neto (1977) observed that minimal health care is lacking or wholly inadequate, but in California 50 percent of the women inmates regularly received tranquilizers administered by nonmedical personnel. Medicating juvenile and adult women accords with the illness ideology, but it is used largely for social control purposes. Three out of four incarcerated women have problems of substance abuse even when that is not the basis of their commitment (Goetting and Howsen 1983). Women offenders are more likely than male offenders to be addicted to heroin, amphetamines, and barbiturates; but the vast majority of women have no access to drug treatment, and only one in three reported ever having been in a drug treatment program prior to or during incarceration (Goetting and Howsen 1983). Comprehensive substance abuse treatment is wholly lacking in prisons despite the seriousness of this problem.

The juvenile justice system incarcerates young women at far higher rates than the adult system and retains them as long on the average, so the concepts of "lesser penetration," "shorter stay," and more access to normalized programming do not apply here either. Once again, minority youth are more likely to be incarcerated regardless of offense.

THE LIABILITY OF BEING FEMALE, POOR, BLACK, SINGLE, AND YOUNG

Criminal offenders and victims in the United States are disproportionately poor, black, single, and young (U.S. Department of Justice 1985b). Being female is also a profound liability, because regardless of their behavior, females are at greater risk for being victimized in ways that also increase the likelihood that they will become offenders in a system that persists in using double standards. These women are constantly in double jeopardy; thus their loser status is reinforced. Although minority women have long been in the labor force, that position is now jeopardized by the persistently high unemployment rates, the lack of union protection of their jobs and benefits, and the hostility of the federal government toward affirmative action. Moreover, women have increasingly lost eligibility for welfare benefits and are socially denigrated when they attempt to establish their rights to these entitlements (Murray 1984; Gilder 1981) Instead, the society seems quite willing to permit them to drift into crime in order to survive; then they end up in correctional facilities where the cost of their care exceeds any welfare benefit that they might have received by several hundred percent. Moreover, their children will be placed in foster care, which is both damaging and costly for them and for society. This is nearly the ultimate Catch-22.

CONCLUSION

The criminal justice system in the United States today victimizes women whether they break the law, are processed by the justice system, or are victims of the law. The women's liberation movement has had almost no impact on this system—in fact, the number of women incarcerated today would suggest that their plight might be negatively correlated with the benefits received by middle-class women from the women's movement. Nowhere are women more in need of effective political and economic power. It is uncertain whether recognition of the myriad problems confronting this system and the women and men in it will produce ad hoc responses or a sound reassessment and establishment of more gender-sensitive comprehensive social policies. Progressive change toward more humane and just intervention is long overdue. Equal protection under the law was never more relevant than it is today for female offenders and victims. To enact "equal protection under the law" for female offenders and victims, after over a century of delay, is obviously a matter of great urgency for progress towards a just society.

Notes

[1]Welfare reform proposals by the Reagan administration in 1986 are likely to exacerbate the problems and suffering of this population between 1987 and 1991 as welfare entitlement and benefits are further reduced or eliminated. Explicit statements are made that federal welfare policies have caused welfare dependency, single-parent female-headed families, and sexual irresponsibility by females.

[2]More recently, the works of Rafter and Stanko 1982, Edwards 1984, and Mukherjee and Scutt 1981 are in the same tradition.

[3]Mukherjee (1981) argues that the only valid way to compare over time is by cross-sex percentages or with data standardized to sex-specific rates per 100,000 population. Some authors argue that female crime is increasing more rapidly than male and will soon overtake it. However, in their analysis they compare within-group differences over time. Such a procedure is invalid for comparison, given the tremendous female/male differences.

[4]Displaced homemakers are another illustration of this invisibility and lack of power of women, as is the lack of enforcement of child support following divorce or separation when the mother is given custody of the children.

[5]An extreme example of this inequality is reported by De Crow (1974) about a Texas law which provided that the killing of a wife by her husband, when he discovered her in an act of adultery, need not be unlawful.

[6]Summaries of the International Human Rights proposals for women (Fraser 1985) indicate just how prevalent this sexism is throughout the world. For example, in Korea in 1985 a woman may not own property in her own name, regardless of her age, marital status, or occupation. If she has no husband or father, then her brother, uncle, or other male relative will hold title to the land.

[7]The actual length of time in prison is always less than the sentence, on the average, because of provisions for reducing one's sentence time by good behavior or because of parole board or court actions as in the case of overcrowded prison conditions. The latter has led to a "revolving door" criticism in some states.

References

Adler, F. and R. Simon, 1979. The Criminality of Deviant Women. Boston, MA: Houghton, Mifflin.

Anderson, M.L., 1983. Thinking About Women: Sociological and Feminist Perspectives. New York: Macmillan.

Belle, D. (ed.), 1982. Lives in Stress. Beverly Hills, CA : Sage.

Bernstein, I.N., J. Cardascia and C.E. Ross, 1979. "Defendant's Sex and Criminal Court Decision," pp. 329–54 in R. Alvarez and K.G. Lutterman (eds.) Discrimination in Organizations. San Francisco: Jossey-Bass.

Bowker, L., 1981. Women and Crime in America. New York: Macmillan.

Brownmiller, S., 1975. Again Our Will. New York: Simon and Schuster.

Burke, C. and R. Sarri, 1980. "The Female Offender: Review of Research and Theory," pp. 1–20 in J. Figueira-McDonough, R. Sarri and A. Iglehart (eds.) Women in Prison in Michigan 1968–1978: A Study of Commitment Patterns. Ann Arbor, MI: University of Michigan, Institute for Social Research.

Butler, A. and S. Lambert, 1983. "Examining Sentencing Models for Two Midwestern Courts: Gender Differences." Paper presented at the Annual Meeting of the American Criminology Association, Denver, Colorado.

Chapman, J., 1980. Economic Realities and the Female Offender. Lexington, MA: Lexington.

Chesney-Lind, M., 1977. "Judicial Paternalism and the Female Offender," Crime and Delinquency 23 (April): 121–30.

Chesney-Lind, M., 1978. "Young Women in the Arms of the Law," in L. Bowker (ed.) Women, Crime, and the Criminal Justice System. Lexington, MA: Lexington.

Cloward, R. and F. Piven, 1979. "Hidden Protest: The Channeling of Female Innovation and Resistance," Signs 4, 4: 651–69.

Cohen, A., 1955. Delinquent Boys. Glencoe, IL: The Free Press.

Cowie, J., V. Cowie and E. Slater, 1968. Delinquency in Girls. New York: Humanities Press.

Creach, D., 1982. "Partially Determined-Imperfect Self-Defense: The Battered Wife Kills and Tells Why," Stanford Law Review 34: 615–38.

Crites, L., 1978. "Women in Criminal Court," in W. Hepperle and L. Cutes (eds.) Women in the Courts. Williamsburg, VA: Center for State Courts.

Daly, K., 1981. "Gender Differences in Criminal Court Outcomes: Towards a Theoretical Formulation Linking Class and Gender Relations." Paper delivered at the American Criminology Society Annual Meeting, Washington, D.C., November.

De Crow, K., 1974. Sexist Justice—How Legal Sexism Affects You. New York: Random House.

Dobash, R.E. and R. Dobash, 1977. "Love, Honor and Obey: Institutional Ideologies and the Struggle for Battered Women," Contemporary Crises 1: 403–15.

Dorsen, N., 1972. "Women, the Criminal Code, and the Correctional System," in New York State Commission on Human Rights (ed.) Women's Role in Contemporary Society. New York: Avon.

Downs, G., 1977. Bureaucracy, Innovation and Social Policy. Lexington, MA: Lexington.

Edwards, A.S.M., 1984. Women on Trial. Manchester: Manchester University Press.

Elliott, D. and S. Ageton, 1980. "Reconciling Differences in Estimates of Delinquency," American Sociological Review 45: 95–110.

Erikson, K., 1966. Wayward Puritans. New York: Wiley.

Fernald, M., M.H. Hayes and A. Dawley, 1920. A Study of Women Delinquents in New York State. 1968 edition. Montclair, NJ: Patterson Smith.

Feyerhelm, W., 1981. "Gender Differences in Delinquency," in L. Bowker (ed.) Women and Crime in America. New York: Macmillan.

Figueira-McDonough, J., 1982. "Gender Differences in Informal Processing: A Look at Charge Bargaining and Sentence Reduction in Washington, D.C.," Journal of Research on Crime and Delinquency 22, 2: 101–33.

Figueira-McDonough, J., 1984. "Feminism and Delinquency," British Journal of Criminology 24, 4: 325–42.

Figueira-McDonough, J., R. Sarri and A. Iglehart, 1981. Women in Prison in Michigan 1968–1978: A Study of Commitment Patterns. Ann Arbor, MI: University of Michigan, Institute for Social Research.

Finkelhor, D., R. Gelles, G. Hotaling and M. Straus, 1983. The Dark Side of Families: Current Family Violence Research. Beverly Hills, CA: Sage.

Fraser, A., 1985. The State of the World's Women: 1985. Minneapolis, MN: University of Minnesota, Hubert Humphrey Institute of Public Affairs. Reprinted from the United Nations Publication, July.

Giallombardo, R., 1974. The Society of Impressed Girls. New York: Wiley.

Giordano, R., S. Kerbel and S. Dudley, 1981. "The Economics of Female Criminality," in L. Bowker (ed.) Women and Crime in America. New York: Macmillan.

Glick, R. and L. Neto, 1977. National Study of Women's Correctional Programs. Washington, DC: United States Government Printing Office.

Glueck, E. and S.D. Glueck, 1934. Five Hundred Delinquent Girls. New York: Alfred Knopf.

Goetting, A. and R. Howsen, 1983. "Women in Prison: A Profile." Unpublished paper. Bowling Green, KY: Western Kentucky University.

Goffman, E., 1970. Stigma. Harmondsworth, England: Penguin II.

Healy, W. and A. Bonner, 1926. Delinquents and Criminals: Their Making and Unmaking: Studies in Two American Cities. New York: Macmillan.

Heffernan, E., 1972. Making It In prison: The Square, the Cool and the Life. New York: Wiley.

Heidensohn, F., 1968. "The Deviance of Women: A Critique and an Inquiry," British Journal of Sociology 19, 1: 170.

Hewitt, J.D. and J.E. Mickish, 1983. "The Legal Control of Female Sexual Behavior During the Progressive Era: A Local History." Paper presented at the Annual Meeting of the

American Criminology Society, Denver, Colorado, November.

Hilberman, E., 1980. "Overview: The Wife-Beater's Wife Reconsidered," American Journal of Psychiatry 137, 11: 1336–47.

Hindelang, M., 1979. "Sex Differences in Criminal Activity," Social Problems 27: 143–56.

Iglehart, A., 1977. "Differences in Black and White Female Criminality." Unpublished paper. Ann Arbor, MI: University of Michigan School of Social Work.

Knapp, K., 1982. "Impact of the Minnesota Sentencing Guidelines in Sentencing Practices," Hamline Law Review 5, 2: 237–56.

Konopka, G., 1966. The Adolescent Girl in Conflict. Englewood Cliffs, NJ: Prentice Hall.

Krisberg, B. and I. Schwartz, 1983. "Rethinking Juvenile Justice," Crime and Delinquency 29, 3: 333–65.

Konopka, G., 1975. Young Girls: A Portrait of Adolescence. Englewood Cliffs, NJ: Prentice Hall.

Krutschnitt, C., 1981. "A Nature-Nurture Controversy: Attempting to Understand the Relationship Between Sex and Severity of Disposition." Minneapolis, MN: University of Minnesota, Department of Sociology.

Lombroso, C. and W. Ferrero, 1916. The Female Offender. New York: Appleton.

Lynes, M., 1983. "The Seriousness of Female Crime and Female Labor Force Participation: An Examination of the National Crime Survey." Ph.D. dissertation, University of Michigan.

McCord, J. and L. Otten, 1983. "A Consideration of Sex Roles and Motivations for Crime," Criminal Justice and Behavior 10: 3–12.

Michigan Department of Social Services, 1986. The Residential Centers, 1985 Annual Report. Lansing, MI: Michigan Department of Social Services, January.

Morris, R., 1964. "Female Delinquency and Relational Problems," Social Forces (October): 82–89.

Mukherjee, S.K. and J. Scutt (eds.), 1981. Women and Crime. Sydney: Allen and Unwin.

Mullen, J., 1981. American Prison and Jails. Washington, DC: U.S. Department of Justice, National Institute of Justice.

Naffin, N., 1981. "Theorizing About Female Crime," pp. 70–91 in S.K. Mukherjee and J. Scutt (eds.) Women and Crime. Sydney: Allen and Unwin.

Nagel, I. and J. Hagen, 1983. "Gender and Crime: Offense Patterns and Criminal Court Sanctions," pp. 91–144 in M. Tonry and N. Morris (eds.) Crime and Justice, Vol. 4. Chicago: University of Chicago Press.

Nagel, S. and L. Weitzman, 1971. "Women as Litigants," Hastings Law Journal 23: 171–98.

Nagel, W., 1977. "On Behalf of a Moratorium on Prison Construction," Crime and Delinquency 23, 2: 154–72.

Pollak, O., 1950. The Criminality of Women. Philadelphia, PA: University of Pennsylvania Press.

Propper, A., 1981. Prison Homosexuality. Lexington: Lexington, MA.

Rafter, N. and E. Stanko, 1982. Judge, Lawyer, Victim, Thief: Women, Gender Roles and Criminal Justice. Boston, MA: Northeastern University Press.

Rasche, C.F., 1974. "The Female Offender as an Object of Criminological Research," Criminal Justice and Behavior I: 301–02.

Rutter, M. and H. Gillis, 1983. Juvenile Delinquency: Theories and Perspectives. New York: Penguin.

Sarri, R., 1983. "Gender Issues in Juvenile Justice," Crime and Delinquency 29, 3: 381–98.

Sarri, R., 1986. "Gender and Race Differences in Criminal Justice Processing," International Women's Studies Forum (forthcoming).

Sarri, R., N. Beisel, J. Boulet, S. Churchill, S. Lambert, A. Ray, C. Russell and J. Weber, 1984. The Impact of Federal Policy Change on AFDC Recipients and their Children. Ann Arbor, MI: University of Michigan, Institute for Social Research, Center for Political Studies.

Schlossman, S. and S. Wallach, 1978. "The Crime of Precocious Sexuality: Female Delinquency in the Progressive Era," Harvard Educational Review 48 (February): 65–94.

Schneider, E.L., 1980. "Equal Rights to Trial for Women: Sex Bias in the Law of Self-Defense," Harvard Civil Rights-Civil Liberties Law Review 15: 623–47.

Schur, E., 1983. Labelling Women Deviant: Gender, Stigma and Social Control. Philadelphia, PA: Temple University Press.

Schwartz, I., J. Jackson-Beeck and R. Anderson, 1984. "The 'Hidden' System of Juvenile Control," Crime and Delinquency 30, 3: 371–85.

Schwendinger, H. and J. Schwendinger, 1985. Adolescent Subcultures and Delinquency. New York: Praeger.

Scutt, J., 1981. "Sexism in Criminal Law," pp. 1–21 in S.K. Mukherjee and J. Scutt (eds.) Women and Crime. Sydney: Allen and Unwin.

Simon, R., 1975. Women and Crime. Lexington, MA: Lexington.

Smart, C., 1976. Women, Crime and Criminology. London: Routledge and Kegan Paul.

Stallard, K., B. Ehrenreich and K. Sklar, 1983. Poverty in the American Dream: Women and Children First. Boston, MA: South End Press.

Steffensmeier, D., 1978. "Crime and the Contemporary Woman: An Analysis of Changing Levels of Female Property Crime, 1960–1975," Social Forces 57, 2: 566–84.

Steffensmeier, D., 1980. "Assessing the Impact of the Women's Movement on Sex-Based Differences in the Handling of Adult Criminal Defendants," Crime and Delinquency 26, 3 (July): 333–43.

Sutherland, E. and D. Cressey, 1966. Principles of Criminology. 6th edition. Philadelphia, PA: Lippincott.

Temin, C., 1973. "Discriminatory Sentencing of Women Offenders," American Criminal Law Review 2 (Winter): 358–72.

Tittle, C.R., 1972. Society of Subordinates: Inmate Organization in a Narcotics Hospital. Bloomington, IN: Indiana University Press.

United States Department of Justice, 1983. Sourcebook of Criminal Justice Statistics. Washington, DC: United States Government Printing Office.

United States Department of Justice, 1985a. Prisoners in 1981, 1982, 1983, 1984. Washington, DC: United States Department of Justice, Bureau of Justice Statistics.

United States Department of Justice, 1985b. Prison Admissions and Releases 1982. Washington, DC: United States Government Printing Office.

United States Department of Justice, Bureau of the Census, 1926. Prisoners in State and Federal Institutions. Washington, DC: United States Government Printing Office.

United States Department of Justice, Federal Bureau of Investigation, 1981 and 1984. Uniform Crime Reports. Washington, DC: United States Government Printing Office.

Vedder, C. and D. Sommerville, 1970. The Delinquent Girl. Springfield, IL: Thomas.

Ward, D. and G. Kassebaum, 1965. Women's Prison. Chicago, IL: Aldine.

Wilson, J. and R. Herrnstein, 1985. Crime and Human Nature. New York: Simon and Schuster.

Windschuttle, E., 1981. "Women, Crime and Punishment," pp. 31–50 in S.K. Mukherjee and J. Scutt (eds.) Women and Crime. Sydney: Allen and Unwin.

PART VII

CONCLUSIONS

CHAPTER 16

OVERCOMING THE OBSTACLES TO EQUAL RIGHTS

Rosemary C. Sarri
Josefina Figueira-McDonough

PERSPECTIVES ON GENDER EQUALIZATION

Although there is universal agreement on the existence of gender stratification in U.S. society, there is some disagreement about the desirability of gender equalization of rights, especially among the dominant groups who benefit significantly from this stratification. This book has examined the contemporary status of women with respect to personal rights—of reproduction, of occupational choice and caregiving—economic rights in the workplace, and for welfare benefits, social rights in health and education, and last, political and legal rights. In all of these sectors the evidence is substantial that women are denied full and equal rights as individuals in a democratic society, regardless of the effort which they put forth.

Let us consider some of the arguments which are frequently raised in opposition to the full extension of equal rights to women. Many defenders of traditional gender organization base their position on beliefs of a preordained natural order. Intervention to alter such order, they argue, provokes social disequilibrium. They buttress such an argument by relating a myriad of contemporary social problems (juvenile delinquency, teen pregnancy, domestic abuse, divorce, welfare depedency, substance abuse, and unemployment, etc.) to the alteration of traditional gender roles. The defense of the assignment of women to a restricted and subordinate sphere is accompanied by statements about their moral superiority, their special vocation of motherhood, and their unique role in maintaining the social order. Even some who would classify themselves as liberals or centrists (e.g., Governor Charles Robb,

1986, Senator Daniel Moynihan, 1986) raise questions about the desirability of gender equality when they suggest that one of the most serious problems confronting American society is the increasing numbers of female-headed households. They attribute the problems of these families to their structure rather than to their overwhelming lack of resources. Theirs is a victim-blaming analysis because the deficiencies are correctable by appropriate social policies for children's allowances, child care, health care, and comparable worth in wages, as most European societies long ago acknowledged.

The denial of female access to specific roles is argued by some as necessary for maintenance of the social order. This argument is particularly evident among those who oppose the ordination of women as ministers in various religious denominations. They cite biblical text to support their assertion despite evidence to the contrary presented by distinguished theologians—female and male—and despite the more active participation of women in many religious sects.

Biological, biblical, and selective historical evidence is brought together to support gender inequality (Gilder 1973; Goldberg 1974; Illich 1982). The same traditional arguments that have often been utilized in the past to justify the position of "inferior" groups are invoked: predestination, greater happiness and protection, and separate but equal.

Most contemporary opinion surveys show that the majority of United States residents no longer subscribe to gender inequality. Certainly, the expanding literature on women's role in society is unequivocal in its call for equalization. There is also agreement that the roots of discrimination can be traced largely to cultural assignments and role prescriptions that produced a pervasive male-dominated hierarchy (Anderson 1983; Lerner 1986). In order to neutralize gender as a criterion of access to opportunity and distribution of social status—the ultimate goal of the women's movement—most concur that strategies are necessary that will enable women to obtain and control needed resources. However, it is this last goal which is being opposed stringently by the present federal administration when it argues against the need for affirmative action, comparable worth, child care, and similar policies to provide increased access to resources to women and other minorities.

In contrast to those who oppose equality are the women's groups who have an active interest in the attainment of equality in all spheres of life. At least three clearly identifiable perspectives exist among these groups: the radical, socialist, and liberal. Radical groups contend that the only way to overcome the historical constant of patriarchal dominance is the creation of a separate women's order (Eisenstein 1979; Daly 1978; Bunch 1975). They further argue that because men's dominance is so pervasive and controls women's lives in global ways, their ties to men must be severed if they are to develop their own resources and power. This position is often derogatorily referred to as the lesbian movement, but that characterization is a gross oversimplification of a movement that emphasizes a separatist strategy for the formation of interest groups. Separatism has been used by ethnic (e.g., black power) and religious minorities (e.g., Catholics in Northern Ireland) as a strategy to build their power base. It is also worth noting that the women's suffrage movement in the nineteenth century was considered to be radical by many in various walks of life. The resolutions adopted at the 1848 Seneca Falls, New York, Convention shocked the nation because they included a call for equal rights in marriage, education, employment as well as political life, because, they asserted, "woman is man's equal, was intended to be so by the Creator, and the highest good of the race demands that she should be recognized as such" (Griffith 1984).

Socialist feminists propose a less drastic solution since they perceive more narrowly the source of women's subordination. The emergence of the capitalist organization of production is viewed as having contributed to the economic status of dependence of all workers but most dramatically of women who were to a large extent denied any economic status. Since power is defined in a capitalist society by access to economic resources, only a socialist order can redress unequal power for all workers, including women (Hartman 1976; Jaggar and Struhl 1978; Firestone 1970; Mitchell 1971; Zaretsky 1976). Just as radical feminists are dismissed, socialists are often dismissed as communists not truly concerned with women's status but with serving party interests. Evidence of gender inequalities in communist countries are noted as invalidating the socialist argument, even when these countries do not fit the socialist model proposed.

Finally, liberal feminists take a "working within the system" approach and place primary emphasis on legislative, judicial, and normative changes to create gender equality. It is this group that has gained ascendancy in the women's movement in recent years. It should be acknowledged, however, that both its ideology and strategies have been and continue to be affected by the impulses of the other more radical groups.

Liberal feminists' legitimization and support within the United States are a function of their acceptance of "mainstream" political ideologies. The principal women's organizations all basically share this characteristic, although each may have a particular focus to its activity. Included would be organizations such as the Women's Equity Action League, the National Organization of Women, the League of Women Voters, the Women's Divisions of the Democratic and Republican Parties, the Coalition of Women and the Budget, the Congressional Caucus for Women's Issues, and the National Women's Political Caucus, as well as the state women's commissions in the majority of the fifty states. In fact, there are more than a hundred such groups in the United States in the 1980s (Coalition on Women and the Budget 1984). In various ways these organizations seek to achieve equal treatment under the law, protection from discrimination on the basis of sex, physical self-determination, and political and economic power for women as a class (Eastwood 1979).

The movement for women's equality has not always been as strong as it is today. Following passage of the women's suffrage amendment in 1920, a period of inactivity set in. As one observer notes, "Winning the vote was accepted as an end in itself, which it was not. Having won political power, women have never used it. Therein lies our failure" (O'Donnell 1970). During the 1920s Freeman (1979) notes that feminism "died"; and by the time the grandchildren of the suffragists voted, the word "feminist" had a negative connotation. Even during the 1940s and World War II when women entered the labor force in large numbers to replace men who were in the armed services, feminism was still not in vogue. Finally, in the 1960s the Commission on the Status of Women appointed by President Kennedy documented the unequal status of women. Not long after that NOW was born, and the women's movement was rekindled. It gathered momentum in conjunction with the Civil Rights' Movement, but it had its own perspective and far more comprehensive goals than the earlier movement. Obviously, since the 1960s there have been ups and downs, but the movement remains vital and strong. With the opposition of the Reagan administration to equal rights and affirmative action, liberal feminists walk a narrow path between reform and accommodation since they have to work within existing institutions. Nonetheless, women's groups of all types have emerged throughout the United States and have been involved in a variety of equalization activities from consciousness-raising to political and economic action. They have been particularly successful at the state level in legislative change and to a lesser degree in the economic sphere. Events such as the Windom Eight Bank Strike and the Stevens Textile strike were important in effecting economic change for blue- and white-collar women, whereas professional women probably benefited more from affirmative action programs. However, the evidence is substantial that national legislation is essential if full female equality is to be achieved.

The second area on which women's groups are rightly focusing their attention is on the implementation of gender-egalitarian legislation. The recent efforts to assure the enforcement of child support by the noncustodial parent, to implement comparable worth in wage determination, to reinforce efforts toward affirmative action, and actions to ease women's access to credit are all examples of activity now underway at both the federal and state levels.

Last, there has been considerable effort to utilize the courts to ensure equal protection under the law in numerous areas. Judicial decisions have often been the initial area in which systematic efforts for change were undertaken, followed sometime later by legislative action when there was sufficient precedent. For example, in the instance of abortion, the decision of the U.S. Supreme Court provided the basic protection for women's rights to privacy. At the time, legislatures all over the country responded variably to special interest group's pressure for punitive actions against women who exercised their right to privacy with respect to abortion.

These three types of activity are of considerable relevance to the topic of this book because most of the specific problems analyzed emerge from the absence of a context of gender equality that can only be created through policy and the lack of specific prescriptions and proscriptions for behavior as is specified, for example, in the implementation of affirmative action regulations. Another important factor leading those problems are the institutional mechanisms utilized in the differential social control of men and women. These mechanisms are reinforced through the organizational "treatment" of women by a variety of organizations and are subject to change as values and policy goals of the society shift.

On the one hand, consideration of policy issues in gender justice raises the question of equal versus compensatory treatment since women were long denied access to many statuses and rights.

As a result, it is often concluded that women are less capable, less motivated, less experienced, and so forth than are men. However, when women have equal access to education and experience, there are few performance and tenure differences between men and women. The question, therefore, is not only equality of opportunity or treatment but equality of circumstances if the competition for resources is to be considered fair. On the other hand, analysis of reinforcers of negative status for women demands a reevaluation of the basis for deviant classifications. Each of these issues is addressed in the subsequent sections of this chapter.

EQUITY OR EQUALITY: THE PROCESSUAL AND THE COMPENSATORY ARGUMENTS

John Stuart Mills wrote that "the great error of reformers...[is]...to nibble at the consequences of unjust power instead of redressing the injustice itself" (1848: 5, chap. 2, sec. 9). In a more contemporary comment Cohen (1981: 14) complained that "social democrats are sensitive to the effects of exploitation on people, but not to the fact of exploitation itself...they want to succor the exploited while minimizing confrontation with those who exploit them." The implication of these comments is twofold: (1) That injustice is almost wholly social in character (e.g., man-made), and that it can therefore be undone by man (Titmus 1958: 3), and (2) that the redress will require a change in the social order.

As argued in the introductory chapter, social changes are threatening to those comfortable within the ongoing social order. Historians describe the resistance of artisans to mechanization, of landed aristocracy to trade, of planation owners to free labor, of industrialists to organized labor. At each juncture in the process of social change, the social evils of disorganization are assumed to demonstrate the path of self-destruction that the innovations are leading to. Simultaneously, when the change objective gains legitimization, alternative paths avoiding structural reordering are proposed to achieve the change goal (Flora and Heidenheimer 1981). For example, in the labor struggle in the United States industrial welfare was presented as an alternative to unions, and unions were accepted as preferable to an institutionalized labor party.

Assuming that equal gender access to rights has gained national legitimacy, it is important to consider the alternatives offered to pursue such a goal and their rationalization and potential for goal achievement. The two alternatives we will consider here are the implementation of processual or passive rights versus compensatory or active rights.

How Liberal Is the Liberal State?

The recent book by Kirp, Yudof, and Franks (1986) on gender justice represents a classic example of the process posture. The authors claim that there are only two alternatives to promote equality: to treat everyone equally or to ensure that everyone lives equally. The first alternative is equated with the principles of liberty and freedom in a democratic society, the second with a planned, totalitarian society oblivious to the rights of individuals.

Kirp and associates go on to argue that the equal treatment of everyone will not ensure individual outcomes because it guarantees equal rights and therefore free choice. Thus they conclude that the issues of gender injustice have less to do with the different statuses of men and women than with how these statuses come about. It follows that the concern of a liberal government is with rectification of biased legal processes, not with the achievement of an egalitarian society.

The projection of the liberal-individualist ideology in this position is clear. The government role in equalizing gender inequalities should be reduced to guarantees of equal treatment, the differential outcomes of equal treatment depend on the free choices of men and women. This argument accords with that of Garfinkel (1985) and others who argue for parent responsibility and minimal parental benefits because women and men freely choose to have children. From this perspective the paradigm of sexual oppression, whether focused on the system of production or reproduction, is seen as a feminist ploy to absolve women from responsibility for their present position in society.

The principle of equal treatment and individual freedom precludes state intervention to correct individual choices and guarantees an equalitarian society. In fact, such interventions (protection) can be construed as an interference in individuals' autonomy and therefore a limitation of the groups' freedom, making them in fact dependent on the government. From this point of view the formal policy toward gender justice should include only reforms geared to the expansion of women's liberties. Once those are achieved it is up to women to improve their status in society. Little or no consideration is given to compensation for past discrimination or neglect. Because this position has gained predominance with the Reagan administration and is the official rationale for the dismantling of egalitarian policies (including Affirmative Action) inherited from the 1960s, it deserves to be analyzed in detail.

The liberal principles under which social control has been established in the United States call for guarantees of personal freedoms and minimal state intervention in individual's decision making. On the other hand, such a system was expected to guarantee a correspondence between individual pursuit of self interest and the collective interest. Like many other supporters of the system, Kirp and associates claim that the success of the nation is proof that there is a correspondence between both types of interests and that liberal principles are successful. This position is open to at least three criticisms: (1) to explain the "success" of the United States as a direct function of the free market economy reflects a reductionist view of the many factors that contributed to the development of this nation, (2) to claim that this country stands as an example of nonstate interference contradicts historical evidence, and (3) to infer equality from liberty ignores the contradictory pulls of these social goals and their impact in shaping modern democracies.

The economic and social success of this nation owes as much to historical and resource circumstances as it does to the economic system adopted (Potter 1954). Furthermore, the belief that the government has maintained a passive role not interfering with the forces of the market, except to guarantee personal rights, is not supported by the facts.

An assessment of the integrity of the liberal model as operationalized in the United States is needed. What is the evidence that the government has maintained a passive role, not interfering with the forces of the market, except to guarantee personal rights? Titmus argues that from the onset, claims of government neutrality in liberal governments are hard, if not impossible, to prove. Interventions to correct the market and incentives for certain industries date from long before the 1930s. There were numerous examples of government intervention throughout the period of industrialization in the nineteenth century (e.g., railroads, utilities). The Depression, representing a dramatic collapse of the market, gave rise and legitimation to a vast system of intervention from tax exemptions (what Titmus calls fiscal welfare) to occupational welfare (social security, unemployment benefits, etc.), to industrial and agricultural subsidies, to public works, and to public welfare (Bell 1983). All those policies are clearly a departure from the passive role of the government and the acceptance of an active role in the formation, administration and distribution of public wealth.

According to Flora and Alber (1981), the increased activism of the state emerged as a result of the tension between the egalitarian promises of democracy and the unequal distributions resulting from free competition. To depict the United States government as the liberal ' prototype distorts history and misrepresents contemporary realities. For example, Thurow (1984) explains that the interdependence of contemporary markets makes subsidies to farmers legitimate since controls over the value of the dollar, food prices, and exports contribute to their lack of profitability in spite of production efficiency. Services to the nation also elicit from the government compensatory programs, as is the case with veterans. What is of interest is that women as a group are seldom the beneficiaries of these types of benefits. The frequent use of the liberal ideal to justify lack of action in favor of minority groups (poor, black, women) suggests an intentional exclusion of certain citizens from protection that the government extends to others.

The responses to increasing contradictions between the citizenry's demands to share in the social benefits of the nation and a competitive market that produces progressively greater inequalities do not necessarily lead to one of the solutions proposed by Kirp and associates—either a socialist state with no individual freedom or a free state with no concern for egalitarian outcomes.[1] There is a third alternative—a modified market system permitting the coexistence of social justice and freedom (Marshall 1965).

Supporters of passive rights share the assumption that people need to be assured freedom of choice in order to pursue their best interests. This presupposes on the one hand a rather simple society where the consequences of alternative choices of action are easily assessed (Thurow 1980). The problem is one of providing equal access to available opportunities. This approach is also ahistorical in that it does not take into consideration past events which affect current reforms as well as past experience with inequality that has de facto restricted access. Weitzman's (1985) analysis of no-fault divorce is a case in point. To treat equally the partners, not taking into consideration the past missed opportunities of the wife due to her specific contributions to the family unit, is equivalent to failing to recognize the opportunities missed by a soldier while fighting for his/her country. Clearly, compensation has been more readily legitimized in the second than the first case. The criteria for compensation is the recognition that an individual has foregone certain opportunities because of service to the nation. It is therefore puzzling that killing the enemies of the country entitles veterans to compensation, but raising the children of America entitles women to nothing.

Lack of Compensation as Negation of Equality

The issue of active rights and compensation has also arisen because minorities have experienced discrimination and lack of equal opportunity over extended periods of time. Affirmative action was expressly established to be more than a policy of antidiscrimination. An organization is obliged to take definitive action in a specified period of time to secure employees who represent various minority groups—usually in numbers which reflect their presence or availability in the population. Thus the U.S. Supreme Court has permitted police and fire departments to "pass over" white males on registries to select women, blacks, and minority ethnics in proportion to their representation in the population of the community. Not surprisingly, there has been criticism and opposition by white males to such action.

Clearly the state not only guarantees positive rights but also protects against deprivation or encroachment, in other words, negative rights. Goodin (1985: 25) argues that it is often difficult to distinguish between the two. Omissions are analytically indistinguishable from actions because not to act is in itself an action (Davis 1980). For example, the act of withholding a benefit is an act as much as is that of providing one. Correspondingly, when there is a positive obligation to provide someone with a benefit, there is a duty not to withhold it. Thus the old saying by Balzac that everyone in Paris had the right to sleep under the bridges of the Seine could be expanded to the right of everyone to sleep in a decent home. In fact, many U.S. cities passed ordinances in the 1980s to provide a "right to shelter." In the instance of Food Stamps and other welfare benefits, social workers are expected to see that eligible persons are not denied benefits because of their lack of knowledge or access. However, in the mid-1980s the decline in Food Stamp distribution is attributed largely to the lack of outreach by agencies (Center on Budget and Policy Priorities 1986). Requirements that information be made available in various languages is another acknowledgment of a positive right to benefits.

If it can be shown that acts and omissions—negative and positive duties—are morally equivalent, both have to be treated equally. Because our society is based on a strong commitment to the first principle of not harming individuals, then it follows that active rights have to be strengthened as well. The absence of active rights with regard to women's special circumstances is, to a large extent, due to their ambiguous status as individuals.

Part of the problem is that individualism is an ideal as unreal as we have shown liberalism to be. A common expression to communicate the rights to personal privacy is to refer to one's home as his own castle. Since home is often not only a place but the residence of a family, whose rights are protected in the castle when the family members are at odds with each other? Evidence of the reluctance of present policies to enter the castle indicates that children and women, even when abused, are not entitled to the same rights as the lord of the castle. Many of the existing policies supposedly aimed at the protection of individual rights are in fact geared to the protection of the male head of the family. The absence of social policy for child care, comparable worth, and caregiving for the elderly is based on the idealization of a family structure which is statistically on its way to extinction. Nonetheless, social planning is still undertaken with the assumption that women are full time housewives supported by their husbands. The numbers of women in the labor force, the incidence of divorce and of single motherhood appear not to have changed these assumptions. The reality, however, is that women are faced with the demands of providing economically for themselves and their dependents and with the ultimate responsibility to nurture any family member. The woman is asked to adapt within a structure that is oblivious to her new reality. Schools proceed in scheduling their day conferences and half-days according to their staff convenience, day care demands are dismissed as un-American, work schedules and women's choice of flexible schedules are taken as evidence of their marginal commitment to work.

Overcoming gender inequality requires fundamental as well as incremental changes in perceptions and policy. The contemporary debate over family policy is an excellent example of the changes that are required. We have chosen to examine this issue in greater detail because of its importance and because it provides an opportunity to highlight several issues discussed above.

The Case of the Family and Ubiquitous Family Policy

There has been an almost uninterrupted public discussion about the family and the state since the mid-1970s—with particular reference to changing female roles and the growth in the number of single-parent female-headed households. That this issue is thought to be important by many is reflected in the numbers of books on this topic since 1980—Moroney (1980); Gilder (1981); Elsthain (1982); Murray (1984); McAdoo and Parham (1985); Moynihan (1985); Hewlett (1986)—to mention only a few that present contrasting perspectives. A second illustration of the importance of "the family crisis" is the appointment of two, not just one, special committees for the study of family policy by the United States Congress. The House of Representatives appointed in 1984 a Select Committee on Children, Youth and Families chaired by Representative George Miller, and in 1986 the Senate appointed a Special Committee on Families, Youth and Children with Senator Daniel Moynihan as chair. Senator Moynihan, as evidenced by the several books and papers which he has authored on the topic, has had a long interest in the family and in the negative consequences for society of the lack of comprehensive family policy.

What do these various efforts have in common? Several authors (Moynihan 1986; Murray 1984; Gilder 1981) emphasize the need for comprehensive family policy. Implicit in their recommendations is the long-term goal to return to the traditional male-headed family in which women are housewives and caregivers first and foremost. They tend to view the female-headed family as pathological, particularly if the woman is poor and has minor children. For example, Moynihan, in his Congressional statement requesting the establishment of the Committee, argues strongly for a new approach; but in his assessment of the problems he says, "The link between poverty and the rise in female-headed families is documented by estimates of the Congressional Research Service. If the proportion of children in female-headed households had not increased over the past 25 years, there could have been 3 million fewer children in poverty in 1983" (Moynihan 1986).

These criticisms of contemporary families and women focus their attention primarily on family structure, namely, the increasing numbers of female-headed families. The resource circumstances of the family are hardly noted as causal factors, for if there were adequate wages for women workers, child and health care, and some flexibility in work schedules, present problems need not arise (Kamerman 1985). They also fail to note the fact that the median income of these families is less than 50 percent of male-headed single-parent families despite the woman's working full time (U.S. Bureau of the Census 1985).

The critics of female-headed households also appear woefully ignorant of history and anthropology, for this and many other societies have had large proportions of female-headed families when men were gone for years at a time, to war, to trade, to explore, and so forth. Joanna Stratton's report (1981) of pioneer women in Kansas poignantly reveals, through the dairies and letters of women, how much of the time they were alone rearing and supporting their families. Immigrant families in the past and present have often had extended periods in which mothers were left alone to rear children. Similar reports are heard today from many countries of the developing world where women and children are left alone to fend for themselves. These observers also fail to note that there have been numerous matrilocal or matrilineal societies that have been very functional. Instead, there appears to be an implicit value preference for the traditional nuclear family in which the woman is a housewife at home. However, such structures are no longer socially normative nor are they economically feasible given the wage levels and cost of living in the U.S.

Economist Sylvia Hewlett (1986) observes that family supports are essential for all women workers and especially female-headed families because males do not assume responsibility for time-consuming caregiving and household maintenance. She points out that the U.S. is alone among 117 countries in not providing maternity leave, child care and allowances, and job protection to women having children. As a result, she argues, women earn less than men and never catch up throughout their work career. She further argues for career ladders tailored to women's needs, not those of men or industry. She notes, "Liberals press for rigorous enforcement of anti-discrimination legislation while conservatives tend to say that women 'choose' to have families and 'choose' to limit their careers, low female wages are a result of individual choice and should not be interfered with by government (77).... For women the wage gap sets up an infuriating Catch-22 situation. They do housework because they earn less, and they earn less because they do housework" (Hewlett 1986: 90). However, when conservatives also push for required Workfare for all poor women who apply for AFDC, they make no provisions for children or child care. In fact, federal allocations have been sharply reduced for these programs under Titles XX and IVA of the Social Security Act, and even more draconian changes are proposed in the 1987 budget (Center on Budget Priorities 1986).

The demographic changes which have occurred in the family and in women's participation in the labor force are such that reestablishment of the traditional nuclear family is impossible. In 1985, 70 percent of all women with children between six and eighteen were in the labor force, and 48 percent of women with infants were working (U.S. Bureau of Labor Statistics 1985). These percentages compare favorably with information on labor force participation in Sweden, but there single parents are provided with substantial support by the noncustodial parent and by the state. As a result, women, and especially children, are not denigrated or placed in jeopardy for survival because of single parenthood (Hultaker 1984; Myrdal 1968). Moynihan's forward to Myrdal's presentation of Swedish family policy in 1968 provides an interesting contrast to his recent position statements. Then he said,

> ...the welfare state in Sweden, with its incomparable array of public services, combined with a passionate concern for individual liberty and personality, is one of the rare achievements of human history. In a very considerable measure it derives from, consists of, the principles and programs that evolved under the rubric of a population and family policy, and in that measure the policy must also be judged an extraordinary success. (p. ix)

Comparable worth is also an essential policy for women who can be expected to head families, as well as other women, given the need to rectify the unfair wage gap which developed because of their occupational segregation and the need to have a modified career ladder if they were to fulfill their societal responsibility of childbearing. Hewlett (1986) further points out that women in Sweden and Germany have higher per capita incomes than in the U.S. and in addition have social benefits which equalize their resource status with males who head families. Thus, if U.S. women are to improve their social and economic position, special treatment in the workplace is essential.

The debate over the family and family policy today appears, first and foremost, to be a debate about the desirability of the changing female roles—as if historical change could be reversed! Moreover, women who are caught in the various Catch-22 situations are declared deviant and subjected to further deprivation and social control. The chapters by Zinn and Fox in this volume highlight some of the dynamics of this process.

TOWARD JUST TREATMENT: REEVALUATION OF DEVIANCE AND RESPONSIBILITY CRITERIA

Reactions to deviance are usually based on consideration of two factors: (1) how damaging are the consequences of deviance for self, others, or society, and (2) how responsible is the person for his/her deviant behavior (Hart 1968; Rawls 1971; Feinberg 1970). Value considerations enter into the evaluation of damage and responsibility because they cannot be considered independently of the sociocultural setting within which responses to deviance emerge. In the seventeenth-century European states heresy was considered highly damaging. Often persons identified as heretics, who by today's standards might have been considered seriously mentally ill, were held fully accountable for their actions. The degree to which heresy was seen to be a threat to society was directly related to the supremacy of the church and the concepts of responsibility to the knowledge (or lack thereof) of behavior determinants.

Modernization has affected these two factors in ways that increasingly excuse individuals from responsibility and expand the areas of deviance. It is a commonly supported observation that as societies become more complex, they require increased regulation for concerted action. This becomes specially evident in mass societies that are not only complex but highly participative (Marshall 1965; Kornhauser 1959). The more regulated a society (formally and informally), the greater the probability of deviance because with more rules there are greater chances of breaking any one of those rules. It has been argued, for example, that the number of children considered retarded increased drastically following the implementation of policies which required high school education. Today, as standards move toward the "normalization" of expectation for a college education, a new brand of deviants "learning disabled" students has emerged.

The implications of this perspective for a mass society are twofold. On the one hand it establishes a democratic expectation for full and equal participation; on the other hand, in fulfilling this expectation it tolerates little deviance. With respect to the definitions and treatment of deviance, we are interested in the functional validity of the rules and standards that have been established. Dexter (1984), in his essay on stupidity, raises this issue. He argues that while education and training are functional for society, the requirement of credentials is not. For example, the task descriptions of many jobs do not justify their requirement of a high school diploma. He concludes that credentials requirements serve another purpose—a criteria for exclusion. In a society that expects all able-bodied, able-minded citizens to work but does not ensure full employment, the creation of "objective" criteria of exclusion hides the incongruency of the system.

From this perspective it is possible that many of the standards that emerge in mass societies might in fact function as justifications for the failure of those societies to fulfill the promise of mass participation. For example, concern is expressed about the value of education and the importance of higher levels of achievement on standardized tests to indicate that all our children are being well educated. But, when children cannot perform at that level, there is a tendency to dismiss them as unable to learn—particularly if they are from poor and minority backgrounds. There is relatively little concern among policy makers about the very high minority school drop-out rate in urban centers and rural areas. Fewer than 30 percent of youth who enter high school actually complete the twelfth grade in many urban communities, and among many of those who do complete, high levels of functional illiteracy are reported (Detroit Free Press 1986). This exclusion from education later becomes the justification for exclusion from employment. These cumulative processes reproduce themselves creating a marginalized sector of the population which does not share in the American way of life.

Developments in the social sciences have greatly contributed to a restricted view of moral responsibility. The more we learn about the determinants of behavior, the less we are willing to accept a model of unrestricted free choice. This is evident in the legal processing of convicted offenders. Circumstantial, social, and psychological dimensions are increasingly taken into consideration in evaluating the extent of responsibility of offenders. For example, in instances of homicide, defendants have been exonerated as mentally incompetent.

The increased sophistication and legitimization of the social sciences coupled with more uniform definitions of normative performance in a variety of areas of human activity (family, school, job, recreation, housing, health, appearance, diet, child socialization, etc.) have given rise to a society oriented to "therapy" (Rieff 1968).

Treatment professions and organizations have proliferated with the mandate of "rehabilitating" deviants. The assumption made is, of course, that the therapists know what causes the deviant behavior and can intervene to alter the behavioral determinants. Correspondingly the client is perceived to have limited responsibility or ability to determine appropriate treatment for herself/himself. Little or no interest is expressed in determining objectively whether the deviant behavior is problematic for the individual or society. Professionals and authorities assume, with little or no review, that the social control goals of the agency serve the self-interest of the client. Obviously, such is not the case in many instances, as is frequently illustrated in closed institutional programs for the mentally handicapped criminal or for the mentally ill.

Deviants who cause serious damage to others and society, and for whom no valid excuses of responsibility are found, are condemned and dealt with by the criminal system. The distinction between various types of deviance, degrees of responsibility, and appropriate response is often not that clear-cut. Evaluations of degree of damage and responsibility tend to be consensual at the extremes but much more controversial and problematic in between, where most cases of deviance fall. Studies of seriousness evaluation of acts such as assaultive behavior, reckless driving, heroin trafficking, robbery, murder, and embezzlement have shown remarkable consensus (Rossi et al. 1974). On the other hand, there is much less agreement about social damage in the use of marijuana, prostitution, abortion, trespassing, etc. Also, in terms of responsibility, the extremes—the assessment of full responsibility based on evidence of intentionality, planning, and knowledge of outcome versus nonresponsibility based on demonstrated insanity or immaturity—are the least controversial. Determination of partial and reduced responsibility is a more complex task requiring a process of assignment of weights to various factors. On these noted judges often disagree.

It stands to reason that both the criteria and treatment of deviants in the areas of less consensus are more susceptible to the processes of influence discussed in the introductory chapter. The definition and treatment of gender-specific female deviance is more likely to emerge as forms of gender control in these areas. A review of the chapters in this book shows that they are precisely addressing issues of the legitimacy of deviant definitions and assessments of responsibility. An important outcome of such analyses is that they provide a framework to evaluate the appropriateness of the treatment women are subjected to and serve as a basis for rectification action.

In Table 1 we exemplify the interaction of deviance and responsibility in determining societal responses to deviance. In each cell examples from issues dealt with in the book are given.

Punishment is the appropriate response to responsible individuals who cause serious damage to others and society (cell 1). Treatment is designed for individuals who function abnormally due to some sort of diminished capacity (cell 2). Protection is extended to individuals who cannot assume responsibility for themselves (cell 4), and the sphere of legitimate behavior pursued by responsible citizens corresponds to the activation of their rights (cell 3).

The discussions in this book examine how social responses to women can be justified in terms of degree of deviance and responsibility. For example, Sarri argues that the degree of deviance (in terms of social damage) common among women offenders does not justify the punishment they receive. She further gives evidence that such punishment is less related to criteria of social damage than to the purpose of discouraging women from certain activities incongruous with traditional gender roles. For example, women are punished as seriously and sometimes harassed even more for prostitution than for theft, fraud, or forgery.

The status of "sick" describes both deviance from health and nonresponsibility. However, the clinical approach relates sickness to individual deficiency and such a diagnosis carries with it some type of stigma. The consequences for the patient of the diagnosis depends on the relation between the specific disability and his/her self concept. The impact of this process in the case of hysterectomy can be devastating for women who equate womanhood with motherhood. How the diagnosis is made and the intervention decided are important in restricting the definition of disability (deviance) and the sense of control of outcomes (responsibility).

The discussion on mental health also raises issues about the process of diagnosis and treatment frequent in cell 2 of Table 1. In this instance attribution of deviance and responsibility are still more problematic. For example, Rosenblum and Franks suggest that depression among housewives appears to be a normal response to a devalued role and to isolation. In this instance a clinical diagnosis locating the source of dysfunction in the individual rather than in her life circumstances might not only be ineffective but costly for the woman.

Table 1

Expected Treatments as a Function of Degree of Deviance and Responsibility

	Responsible	Not Responsible
Deviant Behavior	1 Punishment (female offenders)	2 Treatment (physical and mental health)
Non-Deviant Behavior	3 Rights (abortion)	4 Protection (wife battering)

Somewhere in between cells 1 and 2 falls the case of welfare. Zinn's discussion of the attribution of "dependence" to welfare mothers shows how their lack of economic self-sufficiency is perceived as deviance. On the other hand, restrictions imposed on welfare recipients have been demonstrated to be punitive in character (Street et al. 1979; Feagin 1975). The rationale for such restrictions is unambiguously based on the assumption that the poor are to a large extent responsible for their failure to achieve economic self-sufficiency. Little serious attention is given to the health status of these families, to the failure of men to provide child support, or to the lack of pay equity in the wages earned by women.

In all three instances (female crime, health, and welfare) both the degree of deviance and the locus of responsibility are in question. We assert that both need to be revised and the responses to deviance adjusted accordingly. For example, if most of the crimes women get involved in are nonserious, then according to the criteria of social damage their punishment should be light. Inclusion of extraneous criteria, not related to damage and responsibility, has to be opposed as a restriction on women's rights. To the extent that women's mental health symptoms can be traced to unhealthy situations, the treatment effort should be targeted at changing the situations rather than at correcting the individual. In this case the diagnosis is of crucial importance since acceptance of traditional institutions might desensitize professionals to their negative aspects. For example, the "battered wife syndrome" needs to be understood in relation to the roles and options for the women in violent relationships, not merely as a characteristic of the individual women without reference to that relationship.

Last, investigations into the feminization of poverty have traced its origins to the breakdown of the nuclear family with its system of specialized parental responsibility for dependent children. It would therefore appear appropriate to move welfare to cell 4. Mothers left with the double responsibility of nurturing and providing for their children can hardly be defined as deviant nor can their plight be assumed to be exclusively their responsibility. They can more appropriately be described as victims of social change who need protection in order to fulfill an important social function (childrearing) under precarious conditions.

Although cells 3 and 4 describe nondeviant situations, they are nonetheless relevant to the discussion on control of women. This is so in part because the dimensions of deviance and responsibility are continuous rather than dichotomous. The frail boundaries between deviance and nondeviance can be exemplified by the case of abortion. At the present time abortion is legal and the choice rests with the pregnant woman. Therefore abortion stands as an instance of women's reproduction rights. Present efforts to reverse the Roe decision indicate the vulnerability of this right. The success of the prolife movement would mean that abortion would move into cell 1, and those involved in it responsibly would be subjected to punishment. Such a change would automatically increase the area of deviance and restrict the area of personal rights for women.

Cell 4 is of special interest in instances of ambiguous responsibility. Wife battering can serve as an example of how responsibility ambiguity might work. In this case women are the victims of a deviant act; they do not commit the act. Carlson argues convincingly that their victimization is a function of their inability to protect themselves (dependence). This puts these women clearly in cell 4 and therefore entitled to protection. However, the overwhelming evidence is that such protection has not been available. Probing for the reasons for this failure, we find that it is mostly based on resistance to defining the abuser's behavior as deviant. The abuser's behavior tends to be assigned either to cells 3 or 4 rather than 1 or 2. As a consequence no action is taken against the abusing male, and the woman cannot seek help because of the further threat that action might provoke. The tendency to blame the victim also plays a role in ignoring or excusing the abuser, thereby moving him from cell 1 into cell 2. Studies on the social response to prostitution and rape show similar processes of ambiguity in the ascription of deviance and responsibility (McIntosh 1978; Brownmiller 1975; Clark and Lewis 1977). Reluctance in defining male behavior as deviant results in shifting the responsibility of the behavior to women. In more general terms there is some evidence that when a member of a dominant group commits a deviant act against a member of a weaker group there will be a tendency to excuse the deviance by attributing at least some of the responsibility for the act to the victim.

Evaluation of women's issues as suggested in this discussion are extremely important since redefinitions of deviance and responsibility have a direct impact on women's rights. Furthermore, a continuous evaluation of the functional validity of criteria of "normalcy" in the various spheres of social activity is a must. Such criteria can often be used as strategies for exclusion of women from full participation in a society unwilling or unable to extend to them the opportunities that should characterize a mass society.

WHERE DO WE GO FROM HERE?

Ours has been an effort to analyze the consequences for women of the formal and informal systems of deviance control in our society and how these affect their personal, social, economic, political, and legal rights. Substantial progress was affected in gender equalization of these rights in the 1960s and 1970s, but full equality is still an unrealized goal. In fact, the lack of progress and the stagnation of the 1980s place a sense of urgency on the need for further change.

The various chapters in this book have shown that women's positions reflect interactions among limited opportunities, social constraints, and their self-concepts. Choices between work, family, community, and self are determined by perceived opportunities, incentives, and constraints. Being a woman today clearly highlights the many daily dilemmas that such choices produce. What then can be done to ease some of the conflict and difficulties which arise as one attempts to make choices or is forced to do so? Clearly, professionals in human service organizations can reach out and provide more effective assistance and advocacy than they have up to now. Moreover, they can act to ensure that problems which women face in their various roles are not exacerbated through the intervention of these organizations in their social control functions. For example, decriminalization of prostitution and drug abuse, use of support groups for health and mental health, opening of "real" opportunities for education and work, etc.

Changes in policies and norms about who is responsible for and how children will be raised are urgently needed for the benefit of children as well as women. Moreover, changes which require greater paternal involvement in daily family life and responsibility can benefit men as well. The current strategy of blaming and victimizing women will not solve the current problems of poverty, family dissolution, and so forth. In fact, we argue that this should be a matter of top national priority since present systems of misplaced deviance and control of women are directly affecting one-fourth of the children in America. The combination of attributed responsibilities and reduced opportunities that created the feminization of poverty also jeopardize the future of nearly 30 percent of the children of this nation raised in poverty.

Last, our analysis suggests that there are some specific areas where policy change is called for, primarily at the federal governmental level, but these also have their comparable demands on the state and local government and on the private sector. First, pay equity for jobs of comparable worth is a policy long overdue and one where delay in its implementation is unjustified. The actions taken in the states of Minnesota and Washington indicate the feasibility of orderly change to an economic structure where women would be reimbursed on the basis of the skill, knowledge, and competence required to perform their jobs. In their employment women must receive benefits in the form of health care, maternal and parental leaves, educational leave, vacations, and other entitlements commonly accepted in male employment. Ultimately, the implementation of benefits for all workers will probably require that these be socialized if equity is to be fully achieved. Many Western countries have long demonstrated that socialized health and welfare benefits have positive rather than negative outcomes for the society as a whole.

Second, working mothers and children have a right to publicly funded and provided childcare and preschool education. The models for such systems have long been available and are clearly affordable. Relying on the private sector to provide adequate childcare and preschool education is not advisable if our concern is the well-being of all children. The changes in federal social legislation since 1980 demonstrate unequivocally that those who suffered most from the cutbacks in federal programs were the poor, minorities, the disadvantaged, and handicapped. The private sectors—voluntary or corporate—have been unable to assume responsibility for the provision of services to this high-risk population. It is a responsibility that must be shared by the entire society. The implementation of publicly funded and provided childcare can reduce or eliminate many of the Catch-22 situations that have inevitably negative consequences for women.

Third, employment policies that provide for job sharing and flexible hours have been shown to be possible and even advantageous by many companies. Their implementation would remove many of the criticisms commonly leveled against female workers because of their dual responsibilities to work and family.

Last, for the benefit of society at large, as well as women, there is a need for the passage of legislation which would assess the impact of law, industrial development, and other planned change on the family. We have enacted legislation which requires assessment of the impact of law, industrialization, and so forth on the environment (i.e., requirement of environmental impact approval before action can be taken). Certainly it is no less important to consider the impact of social change and planning on the family. Such legislation is operative in Sweden and in states in Australia and was even proposed in the United States in the early 1970s. Its passage in the 1980s is overdue. Family policy advocates now decry the state of the family, but they have not proposed legislation that would go beyond the bandaid approach to fixing the current situation (e.g., reduce teenage pregnancy).

Our analysis suggests that there is a deep tendency in U.S. society to blame the individual—in the instance that we have examined, women—for the problems which we confront. Instead, it may be possible to work toward an alternate society, namely, one in which social structures and systems are created to provide for the optimal well-being and development of all its citizens. To the extent that this society is committed to individualism, both as a value and as an effective means to productivity, the fulfillment of its potential depends on the extension of full citizenship to women.

Notes

[1]Let us assume we have three cities: a closed city, a selective city, and an open city. The closed city does not permit the entrance of outsiders, and the selective city might accept only blue-eyed persons. In either instance it is clear that there is no free access to the city. If the open city is characterized by permitting entrance to any outsider, does this mean that it is assuring equal opportunity? Not necessarily. Outsiders might live at different distances and have varying means of transportation, so that their chances of entering the city, even assuming equal desire to do so, will vary greatly. The alternative is not necessarily to force everyone to enter the city and encroach on individual freedom. But if transportation is provided as a function of distance, truly equal opportunity has been created without restricting individual choice.

References

Anderson, M.L., 1983. Thinking About Women: Sociological and Feminist Perspectives. New York: Macmillan.

Bell, W., 1983. Contemporary Social Welfare. New York: Macmillan.

Brownmiller, S., 1975. Against Our Will. New York: Simon and Schuster.

Bunch, C., 1975. "Lesbians in Revolt," pp. 29–38 in N. Myron and C. Bunch (eds.) Lesbianism and the Women's Movement. Oakland, CA: Diana Press.

Center on Budget and Policy Priorities, 1986. "Budget Would Make Large Cuts in Low Income Programs." Washington, DC.

Clark, L. and D. Lewis, 1977. Rape: The Price of Coercive Sexuality. Toronto, Ont.: Women's Press.

Coalition on Women and the Budget, 1984. Inequality of Sacrifice: The Impact of the Reagan Budget on Women. Washington, DC.

Cohen, G.A., 1981. "Freedom, Justice and Capitalism," New Left Review 126: 3–16.

Daly, M., 1978. Gyn/Ecology. Boston, MA: Beacon.

Davis, N., 1980. "The Priority of Avoiding Harm," pp. 172–214 in B. Steinbock (ed.) Killing and Letting Die. Englewood Cliffs, NJ: Prentice Hall.

Detroit Free Press, 1986. Editorial. March 13, p. 8.

Dexter, L., 1964. "On the Politics and Sociology of Stupidity in our Society," in H. Becker (ed.) Perspectives on Deviance: The Other Side. New York: Free Press.

Eastwood, M., 1979. "Feminism and the Law," pp. 385–404 in J. Freeman (ed.) Women: A Feminist Perspective. Palo Alto, CA: Mayfield.

Eisenstein, Z. (ed.), 1979. Socialist Feminism and the Case for Capitalist Patriarchy. New York: Monthly Review Press.

Elsthain, J.B., 1982. "Feminist Discourse and its Discontents," Signs 7: 603–21.

Feagin, J., 1975. Subordinating the Poor. Englewood Cliffs, NJ: Prentice Hall.

Feinberg, J., 1970. Doing and Deserving: Essays on the Theory of Responsibility. Princeton, NJ: Princeton University Press.

Firestone, S., 1970. The Dialectic of Sex: The Case for Feminist Revolution. New York: William Morrow.

Flora, P. and J. Alber, 1981. "Modernization, Democratization and the Development of Welfare States in Western Europe," in P. Flora and A. Heidenheimer (eds.) The Development of Welfare States in Europe and America. New Brunswick, NJ: Transaction.

Flora, P. and A.J. Heidenheimer, 1981. "The Historical Core and Changing Boundaries of the Welfare State," in P. Flora and A. Heidenheimer (eds.) The Development of Welfare States in Europe and America. New Brunswick, NJ: Transaction.

Freeman, J., 1979. Women: A Feminist Perspective. Palo Alto, CA: Mayfield.

Garfinkel, I., 1985. "Child Support Assurance: A New Tool for Achieving Social Security." Mimeograph. Madison, WI: University of Wisconsin, Institute for Research on Poverty.

Gerson, K., 1985. Hard Choices: How Women Decide About Work Career and Motherhood. Berkeley, CA: University of California Press.

Gilder, G., 1973. Sexual Suicide. New York: Quadrangle.

Gilder, G., 1981. Wealth and Poverty. New York: Basic Books.

Goldberg, S., 1974. The Inevitability of Patriarchy. New York: William Morrow.

Goodin, R.E., 1985. Protecting the Vulnerable. Chicago, IL: The University of Chicago Press.

Griffith, E., 1984. In Her Own Right: The Life of Elizabeth Cody Stanton. New York: Oxford University Press.

Hart, H., 1968. Punishment and Responsibility: Essays in the Philosophy of Law. New York: Oxford University Press.

Hartman, H., 1976. "Capitalism, Patriarchy and Job Segregation by Sex," Signs 1, 3: 137–69.

Hewlett, S., 1986. A Lesser Life: The Myth of Women's Liberation in America. New York: William Morrow.

Hultaker, O., 1984. "Work, Economic Policies, and Welfare Consequences and Responsibilities," Proceedings of the 20th International CFR Seminar on Social Change and the Family. Melbourne, Australia: Australia Institute of Family Studies, Vol. 2, pp. 1–54.

Illich, I., 1982. Gender. New York: Pantheon.

Jaggar, A. and P.R. Struhl, 1978. Feminism Framework: Alternative Theoretical Accounts of the Relations Between Women and Men. New York: McGraw-Hill.

Kamerman, S., 1985. "Young, Poor and a Mother Alone: Problems and Possible Solutions," pp. 1–38 in H. McAdoo and T.J. Parham (eds.) Services to Young Families. Washington, DC: American Public Welfare Association.

Kirp, D., M. Yodof and M. Franks, 1986. Gender Justice. Chicago, IL: The University of Chicago Press.

Kornhauser, W., 1959. The Politics of Mass Society. Glencoe, IL: Free Press.

Lerner, G., 1986. The Creation of Patriarchy. New York: Oxford University Press.

Marshall, T.H., 1965. Class, Citizenship and Social Development. Garden City, NY: Doubleday.

McAdoo, H. and J. Parham, 1985. Services to Young Families: Program Review and Policy Recommendations. Washington, DC: American Public Welfare Association.

McIntosh, M., 1978. "Who Needs Prostitutes?" in C. Smart and B. Smart (eds.) Women, Sexuality and Social Control. London: Routledge and Kegan Paul.

Mills, J.S., 1848. Principles of Political Economy. London: Parker.

Mitchell, J., 1971. Woman's Estate. New York: Pantheon.

Moroney, R., 1980. Families, Social Services and Social Policy. Washington: U.S. Department of Health and Human Services, PHS. ADMHA.

Moynihan, D., 1985. Family and Nation. New York: Harcourt Brace.

Moynihan, D., 1986. Senate Resolution 330 Establishing a Special Committee on Families, Youth and Children. Congressional Record, 99th Cong., 3 February, Vol. 132, p. 8.

Myrdal, A., 1968. Nation and Family. 2nd Edition. New York: Harper.

Murray, C., 1984. Losing Ground. New York: Basic Books.

O'Donnell, G., 1970. Statement in Hearings of the Constitutional Amendment Subcommittee of the U.S. Congress, Senate Committee on the Judiciary on S.J. Res. 61, 91st Cong., 5th sess., May, p. 664.

Potter, D., 1954. People of Plenty: Economic Abundance and the American Character. Chicago, IL: The University of Chicago Press.

Rawls, J., 1971. A Theory of Justice. Cambridge: Belknap Press of Harvard University Press.

Rieff, D., 1968. The Triumph of the Therapeutic. New York: Harper and Row.

Robb, C., 1986. Speech at Hofstra University. Quoted in New York Times (April 20).

Rossi, P., E. White, C. Bose and R. Burk, 1974. "The Seriousness of Crimes: Normative Structures and Individual Differences," American Sociological Review 39, 2: 224–37.

Stratton, J., 1981. Pioneer Women. New York: Simon and Schuster.

Street, D., G. Martin and L. Gordon, 1979. The Welfare Industry. Beverly Hills, CA: Sage.

Thurow, L., 1980. The Zero-Sum Society. New York: Basic Books.

Thurow, L., 1984. Dangerous Currents. New York: Vintage.

Titmus, R.M., 1958. Essays on the Welfare State. London: Allen and Unwin.

U.S. Bureau of the Census, 1985. Money, Income and Poverty Status of Families in the United States: 1984. Washington: U.S. Department of Commerce.

U.S. Bureau of Labor Statistics, 1985. "Labor Force Activity of Mothers of Young Children Continues at Record Pace," NEWS. Washington, D.C., USDL85–381, September 19.

Weitzman, L., 1985. The Divorce Revolution. New York: Free Press.

Zaretsky, E., 1976. Capitalism, The Family and Personal Life. New York: Harper and Row.

Contributors

Jan Allen is assistant professor in the Department of Child and Family Studies at The University of Tennessee in Knoxville. Her doctorate is in Child Development from Purdue University. Her most recent research has focused on the social interactions of young children in day care and preschool, political socialization, and children's fears and coping strategies. Her applied interests in public policy and parent education also have focused on day care and families, children and stress, and child advocacy.

Robert Blackburn is a professor of Higher Education at the University of Michigan. He received his Ph.D. from the University of Chicago. He has also taught at San Francisco State College and Shimer College. Dr. Blackburn is a member of several professional organizations, including having served as chair of professors of higher education for the American Association of Higher Education. He has authored more than 100 publications, including Artists as Professors (with Morris Risenhoover); Black Students on White Campuses: The Impact of Increased Black Enrollments (with Peterson, Gamson, Arce, Mingle, and Davonport); and, College Faculty: Versatile Human Resources in a Period of Constraint (with Roger Baldwin).

Diane Mitsch Bush is assistant professor of sociology at Colorado State University. She received her doctorate in sociology from the University of Minnesota. Her research interests are in gender role socialization; adolescent girls and attitudes toward violence; the public/private split and the politics of gender; feminist theory and violence against women. She has published on these topics in the American Sociological Review, Social Problems, Sociology of Education, the Sociological Quarterly, Public Opinion

Quarterly, Youth and Society, as well as in feminist and social psychology anthologies.

Bonnie E. Carlson received her Ph.D. in social work and psychology from the University of Michigan. She is assistant professor, School of Social Work, Rockefeller College of Public Affairs and Policy, State University of New York at Albany. She has done research and published in the areas of family violence, dual-earner families, and child development and is currently studying children's beliefs about punishment and the impact on children of observing violence between parents.

Catherine Chilman is a professor in the School of Social Welfare, University of Wisconsin—Milwaukee. She served for many years as a policy analyst in the Department of Health, Education and Welfare in Washington. She has been involved for the past four decades in practice, policy, and research concerning family issues, both nationally and internationally. She is associate editor of the Journal of Marriage and the Family and editor of Marriage and Family Review. She has published over 60 articles on family issues, sexual behavior, and adolescent pregnancy. Her most recent book is Social and Psychological Aspects of Adolescent Sexuality and Related Human Service Programs.

Josefina Figueira-McDonough is professor of social work and urban studies at Michigan State University and faculty associate at the Center for Political Studies, Institute for Social Research, the University of Michigan. She received her doctorate in sociology and social work from the University of Michigan. The bulk of her research and publication has been in the areas of gender, deviance, and social policy. She has over 30 articles on topics of gender differences in delinquency, court processing, and correctional treatment. More recently she has been studying the interaction of gender egalitarian attitudes and differential opportunities on behavioral choices of adolescents. She is preparing a book on the latter topic. She is editor of the Journal of Education in Social Work.

Sue Fisher is assistant professor of sociology at Wesleyan University. She received her doctorate in sociology from the

University of California at San Diego. She has taught in sociology and women's studies' departments at the University of Tennessee and San Diego State University, respectively. She also had an adjunct appointment in Family Medicine at the Center for Health Sciences of the University of Tennessee. Her areas of research include: medical sociology, women's health, and sociolinguistics. Her recent research examines the micropolitics of medical communication: how physicians and women patients communicate to reach medical decisions, as well as how this communication is influenced by the institutional authority of the medical role. She has edited two volumes with Alexandra Dundas Todd: The Social Organization of Doctor-Patient Communication (1983) and Discourse and Institutional Authority (in press), and has published several articles. She is presently writing a book, In the Patient's Best Interest.

Greer Litton Fox is professor of sociology and chair of the Department of Child and Family Studies at the University of Tennessee. Previously she taught sociology at Wayne State University and was associate director of the Merrill-Palmer Institute for Family and Human Development Research. She has done extensive research on intergenerational female socialization and is presently directing a project on parent-child communication funded by the Center for Population Research of NICHD and the Office of Adolescent Pregnancy Programs of DHHS.

Mary Frank Fox is a research scientist at The University of Michigan's Institute for Social Research. Her research focuses upon stratification processes in science and academia and sex stratification in organizations and occupations. Her current work is a study of Research Productivity and the Environmental Context, funded by The National Science Foundation. SHe is author of articles in 20 different journals amd collections; coauthor of Women at Work (1984); and editor of Scholarly Writing and Publishing (1985). She is associate editor of Gender & Society and chair of the American Sociological Association's Section on Sex and Gender.

Violet Franks is Director of Psychology at the Carrier Foundation in Princeton, New Jersey. She received her doctorate in psychology in the Department of Psychiatry of the University of London. She has taught the psychology of women as well as women and psychotherapy at Rutgers University and at the Universities of Hawaii and Melbourne in Australia. She is the author of Women and Therapy and co-author of Gender and Disordered Behavior (with Edith Gomberg) and The Stereotyping of Women: Its Effects on Mental Health. She also has a private clinical practice with women.

Betty J. Holbert, M.S.N., is an assistant professor in the Department of Nursing Education, Eastern Michigan University, specializing in maternal-child health. Currently, Ms. Austin is a doctoral candidate in the Center for Study of Higher Education, the University of Michigan, completing her research on differences in scholarly productivity for male and female faculty. She is also involved in research on Developing a Mentoring Academy: A Model for Encouraging Academic Achievement.

Nancy R. Hooyman is an associate professor in the School of Social Work, University of Washington, Seattle, where she is coordinator of the Project on Aging and chairperson of the Community Organizational Services Track. She received her MSW and her Ph.D. from the University of Michigan, and an MA in Sociology from University of Pennsylvania. She has served as cochair of the Concerns of Older Women Committee for the Western Gerontological Society and is currently chair of the Council on Social Work Education Commission on Women, on the National Commission for Women's Issues for the National Association of Social Workers, and on the Older Women's Task Force for the Gerontological Society. Her recent research has focused on family caregivers of the elderly; she has conducted numerous workshops on women as caregivers and is co-authoring a book on working with family caregivers, to be published by Free Press. She was recently selected by the University of Washington for a faculty exchange to the University of Bergen, Norway, where she will lecture on and conduct research on women as caregivers to the elderly.

Marian L. Palley is professor of political science at the University of Delaware. She has served as departmental chair and as secretary of the American Political Science Association. Her areas of research are intergovernmental relations, political parties groups. Her most recent work has focused on the impact of public policies on women. Among her numerous publications are Urban American and Public Politics (Lexington, 1977), Tradition and Change in American Party Politics (Crowell, 1975), The Politics of Federal Grants (Congressional Quarterly Press, 1981), Race, Sex, and Policy Problems (Lexington, 1979), and Women and Public Policies (Princeton, 1982).

Esther D. Rothblum is an assistant professor of psychology at the University of Vermont. She received her Ph.D. from Rutgers University and completed two years of postdoctoral work at Yale University. She has written extensively on clinical therapy and has a special interest in issues of women in therapy. Her work has appeared in the Journal of Counseling Psychology, Journal of Nervous and Mental Disease, American Geriatric Society, The American Journal of Psychiatry, Journal of Organizational Behavior Management, Current Feminist Issues of Therapy, Behavior Modification and Adolescence. In 1983 she edited with Violet Franks The Stereotyping of Women: Its Effects on Mental Health. She has also written a variety of therapy handbooks.

Robyn Rowland is a senior lecturer in social psychology and women's studies at Deakin University in Melbourne, Australia. She has also taught at Exeter University in England. She is internationally known for her research into the social and psychological consequences of human artificial insemination—most recently on the consequences of in vitro fertilization procedures. She edited Women Who Do and Who Don't Join the Women's Movement (1984) and authored the women's studies interdisciplinary text Woman Herself: A Women's Studies Perspective on Self-Identity (1984). She has articles in Signs and in Test-tube Women: What Future for Motherhood? (1984), in the Women's Studies International Forum (1986), and is also a poet, having published two books of poetry.

Rosemary Ryan is a doctoral candidate in the School of Social Work at the University of Washington. Her current research examines attitudes toward family responsibility held by persons who provide case management services to frail elders. She has also done research on barriers to employment encountered by people with disabilities. She was also a Peace Corps Volunteer in Brazil.

Rosemary Sarri is a professor of social work and faculty associate in the Center for Political Studies, Institute for Social Research, the University of Michigan. Her research interests have included studies of children and youth welfare systems, deviance and criminal justice systems, women and poverty, and the effects of social policy and social administration on the delivery of human services. She has served as advisor and consultant in social welfare and social work education at national and international levels. She is the author of more than 60 books and articles on juvenile justice, female crime, women and poverty, the management of human services, school malperformance, child welfare, and social policy. Her most recent volume is The Impact of Federal Policy Change on AFDC Recipients and Their Families (1984).

Deborah Zinn received her doctorate in sociology and social work from the University of Michigan. She is a research and policy analyst for the Brotherhood of St. Laurence in Melbourne, Australia—a social research and social advocacy organization. Zinn has a broad background in social welfare. During several years of employment with the Department of Welfare in West Virginia she participated in policy development and implementation of a variety of programs ranging from the writing of Title XX policy to delivering Food Stamps and AFDC applications in rural areas during the height of the 1974–75 recession. She has done research on the impact of policy change on single-parent families, on the processing of female offenders, on the design and development of computerized information systems for a variety of human service organizations, and on corporate compensation and benefit policies. She is the author of articles in Signs, Social Work in a Turbulent World.

NOTES

NOTES

NOTES

NOTES

NOTES